Death, Art, and Memory in Medieval England

Death, Art, and Memory in Medieval England

THE COBHAM FAMILY AND THEIR MONUMENTS, 1300–1500

NIGEL SAUL

OXFORD
UNIVERSITY PRESS

OXFORD

UNIVERSITY PRESS

Great Clarendon Street, Oxford OX2 6DP

Oxford University Press is a department of the University of Oxford.
It furthers the University's objective of excellence in research, scholarship,
and education by publishing worldwide in

Oxford New York

Athens Auckland Bangkok Bogotá Buenos Aires Cape Town
Chennai Dar es Salaam Delhi Florence Hong Kong Istanbul Karachi
Kolkata Kuala Lumpur Madrid Melbourne Mexico City Mumbai Nairobi
Paris São Paulo Shanghai Singapore Taipei Tokyo Toronto Warsaw

and associated companies in Berlin Ibadan

Oxford is a registered trade mark of Oxford University Press
in the UK and certain other countries

Published in the United States
by Oxford University Press Inc., New York

© Nigel Saul 2001

British Library Cataloguing in Publication Data
Data available

Library of Congress Cataloging in Publication Data
Data available
ISBN 0-19-820746-8

1 3 5 7 9 10 8 6 4 2

Typeset by Best-set Typesetter Ltd., Hong Kong
Printed in Great Britain
on acid-free paper by
Biddles Ltd,
Guildford and King's Lynn

For Jane, Dominic, and Louise

'These monuments throw a lot of light on English society, and I always study them most carefully.'

(K. B. McFarlane, *Letters to Friends, 1940–1966*, 59)

Preface

My interest in the Cobhams and their brasses goes back a good many years. I first discovered an interest in monumental brasses as a boy. The experience of leafing through books on brasses and brass rubbing and looking at pictures of knights in armour is one that I still vividly recall. As an undergraduate at Oxford my interest in brasses grew deeper and focused more on the brasses of the Middle Ages. While doing research into the gentry as a postgraduate, I began looking into the careers of some of those commemorated by brasses. One day in the Bodleian Library I came across Robert Glover's notes from the Cobham charters in *Collectanea Topographica et Genealogica*, volume vii. I sensed the considerable importance of this material for establishing an historical context for the brasses of the Cobham family. In my leisure moments I followed up one idea suggested to me by the material. In Glover's notes there were references to a series of charters place-dated at Clyffe Pypard (Wilts.). The existence of these charters set me thinking about the brass of an unidentified knight in Clyffe Pypard church. I suspected that the memorial commemorated a junior member of the Cobham line. In 1979 I published a short article arguing this case in the *Transactions of the Monumental Brass Society*—the first piece of work which I undertook on the family. A decade or so later, when I was engaged on a biography of Richard II, I developed a particular interest in the family's most distinguished member, John, 3rd Lord Cobham, a leading figure in the troubled politics of Richard's reign. John was a soldier and a courtier. He was also a great builder; and in 1362 he founded Cobham college. John's career and achievements led me back to the brasses, in particular to his own, with its curious epitaph. I found myself asking questions—some of them obvious questions like 'Why are there so many brasses at Cobham?'—but also more complex ones lying at the intersection of material and documentary evidence. For example, what do the brasses tell us about the Cobham family? And what does our knowledge of the Cobham family tell us about the brasses? These are interesting questions in their own right. But they are also significant for our understanding of gentry culture more generally. At this stage, my thoughts were largely concerned with the Cobhams in Kent, for Kent was the family heartland. Then one day in 1995 I visited the church at Lingfield (Surrey), where the

Cobhams of Sterborough were buried. The sight of this second impressive array of Cobham tombs and brasses made me think again. I realized that there was more to a study of the Cobhams than Cobham itself; the other Cobham mausoleums needed to be taken into account. Accordingly, the idea of a much broader study was born. I found myself going in search of the Cobhams in Surrey, Wiltshire, Essex, and further afield still.

I have been engaged in the writing of this book for some four or five years. Originally, I had been inclined to think that the material could be distilled into a series of articles. But later, as the scale of the project grew, I considered a monograph more suitable. I was obviously attracted by the idea of bringing together everything that illuminated the Cobhams' commemorative tastes in two covers, but there was also the argument that a study of this kind could serve as a model for others—indeed, as a paradigm for a new approach to the subject. I am very grateful to Tony Morris, who was history editor at the Oxford University Press when I submitted the proposal, for his courage in taking the project on.

In the course of my work I have incurred a good many debts. It is a pleasure, first, to record my gratitude to the incumbents and staff of the two main churches discussed here, Cobham and Lingfield. At Cobham I am especially grateful to the Reverend Steve Davie for his kindness in allowing the Monumental Brass Society to hold a study day at the church in May 1998. On my regular visits to Cobham I have benefited more, I dare say, than he ever realized from discussion with Bill Pritchett. Bill's wide-ranging knowledge of Cobham and the Cobham family saved me from a good many errors and omissions. I am only sorry that his sudden death in March 2000 prevented him from seeing the book in print. At Lingfield I owe particular thanks to Ian Dobson and Pat Stanford-Stinson for their interest in my work and their initiative in inviting me to address a meeting of the newly formed Friends of Lingfield Church in May 1999. At both Cobham and Lingfield I have drawn constant encouragement from the obvious interest and pride which the two congregations take in their churches and the treasures they contain. I can only hope that this book contributes something to a wider appreciation of the churches' heritage.

A number of friends and colleagues have assisted on particular points. John A. Goodall FSA has aided my understanding of the Cobhams' heraldry—a valuable and significant subject in its own right. Sue Pratt has drawn my attention to the complexity of the building history of Lingfield church. Tim Boyle has helped me with the history of Hever. Nigel Ramsay, Paul Brand, Philip Morgan, Michael Jones, Robert Swanson,

Sam Barnish, and Caroline Barron have supplied me with references. I am grateful to them all.

High-quality illustrations are obviously essential to the success of a book of this kind. The illustrations of the brasses at Cobham itself are derived from the artwork for William Lack's book (with Philip Whittemore and myself), *The Monumental Brasses of St Mary Magdalene, Cobham, Kent* (1998). I am very grateful to Mr Lack for making the artwork available. The illustrations of the brasses at Lingfield and Hoo St Werburgh are from rubbings by my son Dominic and myself. I am grateful to Martin Stuchfield, the Hon. Secretary of the Monumental Brass Society, for providing scaled-down reproductions of the rubbings for the publisher. I am also grateful to Martin Stuchfield for reproductions of the brasses at Chrishall and Westminster Abbey. It is both a pleasure and an honour to be able to thank Mr A. F. Kersting for his photographs of the Cobham tombs at Lingfield. I have long been an admirer of Mr Kersting's work. I never thought the day would come when I would be able to make use of it in a book myself.

Finally, I would like to thank Sally Badham, David Carpenter, Tim Tatton-Brown, and Richard K. Morris for reading drafts of chapters and for offering comments on them. I am particularly grateful to Peter Coss for reading a draft of the entire book in typescript.

Nigel Saul

June 2000

Contents

Illustrations

Genealogies

Maps and Diagram

Abbreviated References

Full details of titles are to be found in the Bibliography.

AC	*Archaeologia Cantiana*
BL	British Library
CChR	*Calendar of Charter Rolls*
CCR	*Calendar of Close Rolls*
CFR	*Calendar of Fine Rolls*
CIPM	*Calendar of Inquisitions Post Mortem*
CKS	Centre for Kentish Studies
CPR	*Calendar of Patent Rolls*
d.	died
d.s.p.	died without issue
DNB	*Dictionary of National Biography*
EHR	*English Historical Review*
House of Commons	*History of Parliament: House of Commons* (4 vols.; Stroud, 1992)
JEH	*Journal of Ecclesiastical History*
MBS	Monumental Brass Society
PRO	Public Record Office
SAC	*Surrey Archaeological Collections*
SHC	Surrey History Centre
TMBS	*Transactions of the Monumental Brass Society*
VCH	*Victoria County History*

Brasses are generally identified by their 'M.S.' number—that is, their number in Mill Stephenson's standard *List of Monumental Brasses in the British Isles* (London, 1926, repr. Ashford, 1964). To take an example: M.S. XI at Cobham is the eleventh brass by chronological listing in Stephenson's book—the brass of Sir Nicholas Hawberk.

⇸ 1 ⇷
Introduction: Problem and Method

COBHAM is a picturesque little village set on a ridge of the North Downs near Rochester. Its single narrow street is rich in vernacular architecture. On the north side, at the western end, is the celebrated Leather Bottle, where Charles Dickens's Mr Pickwick discovered the curiously inscribed stone. A little to the east is the eighteenth-century Darnley Arms, and further on Mr Gander's shop, a fine timber-framed dwelling of the fifteenth century. A mile or so beyond the village, set deep in a wooded park is Cobham Hall, the seventeenth-century seat of the dukes of Lennox and later of the earls of Darnley. At the opposite end of the village, on rising ground, is an older set of buildings. Fronting straight onto the street is the fourteenth- and seventeenth-century Stone House, a mainly flint structure which was once a school. Further up, and set back, are the buildings of the chantry college founded in 1362 by John, Lord Cobham. Adjacent to the college, and at the highest point, is the church of St Mary Magdalene. This large, dignified building, dating mainly from the thirteenth to the fifteenth centuries, spreads long and low among the trees. Externally, it exudes aristocratic presence as it stands high above the street. Internally, it disappoints a little: the design is austere, and the nineteenth-century fittings and stained glass are unworthy. Yet to many this church is a place of pilgrimage. Visitors are drawn here from all over the world. For stretching impressively across the chancel floor is the largest and most spectacular collection of brasses in Britain.

Much has been written in celebration of the Cobham brasses. R. F. Jessup described them as the finest in Christendom, while John Newman, in the Kent 'Pevsner' maintained that nowhere was there a series to compare with it.[1] The praise is amply justified. Among the nineteen

---

[1] R. F. Jessup, *Kent*, 7th edn. (London, 1950), 130; J. Newman, *West Kent and the Weald* (Harmondsworth, 1969), 219.

or more brasses are a number of the highest quality and importance. Joan de Cobham's (c.1300–10) is one of the earliest—as well as one of the grandest—to have come down to us; while for sheer beauty and elegance that of Sir Nicholas Hawberk is probably without equal. But even more than the individual brasses, it is the series as a whole that impresses. J. G. Waller, who made a detailed study of the brasses and wrote a seminal article on them in the 1870s, claimed that the Cobham series was the most complete to have survived.[2] If Waller's claim is justified—and rival claims might be entered for the series at Cirencester and New College, Oxford—it is perhaps worth adding that the impression of completeness is one partly created by Waller himself. In the mid-nineteenth century the brasses were in an unhappy state. All of them had suffered losses, in some cases substantial, and many of the inscriptions and canopies were mutilated. A couple of restorations were carried out, the first in 1840–1 under John Gough Nichols, and the second and more substantial in 1865–6 by Waller. For the most part, Waller based his restorations on a set of sixteenth-century drawings of the brasses,[3] but where evidence was lacking he resorted to guesswork. It is fortunate in the circumstances that the restored pieces are generally recognizable by their lighter hue.

The processes of decay and restoration of the Cobham brasses have recently been charted in P. J. Whittemore's and W. Lack's portfolio volume for the Monumental Brass Society.[4] Surprisingly, this volume is the first specialist study to have been made of the Cobham brasses since Waller's. It is true that the brasses have often figured in general discussions of brasses and in volumes illustrative of the history of costume; and Joan de Cobham's (M.S. I) has recently been cited in the context of debate over the dating of the earliest brasses.[5] But relative to their fame and importance the brasses have received strangely little detailed attention. They are simultaneously the best known and the least studied of their genre.

The relative neglect of the brasses is surprising, for there are many questions about them that need answering. The first and most obvious concerns their sheer number. Why are there so many brasses at Cobham? And, more particularly, why are there so many to members of one

[2] J. G. Waller, 'The Lords of Cobham, their Monuments and the Church', AC, 11 (1877), 49–112; quotation at 52.

[3] The drawings were by William Smith, Rouge Dragon: BL, MS Lansdowne 874, fos. 60ᵛ–62ʳ.

[4] W. Lack, N. E. Saul, and P. J. Whittemore, *The Monumental Brasses in St Mary Magdalene, Cobham, Kent* (London, 1998), esp. 20–32.

[5] See below, 84–5.

family? No other lesser noble lineage appears to have been so preoccupied with the matter of its commemorative self-image.[6] A second question relates to the layout of the brasses in the church. The brasses are currently laid in two long rows in front of the altar. The arrangement seems almost too orderly—too artificial. Is the arrangement original, or is it the work of restorers? And thirdly, as Waller observed long ago, many of the inscriptions call for comment. Among their number are some of the most interesting and distinctive to have survived. What are their sources, and what do they tell us about the aspirations of the commemorated?

When Waller wrote in the 1870s, the study of brasses was already well established. The antiquarian study of the subject had begun back in the eighteenth century.[7] The most important of the early writers was Richard Gough (1735–1809), a Hertfordshire landowner and antiquary. Gough's *Sepulchral Monuments*, a comprehensive record of British monuments and brasses from the Middle Ages, was a work of unprecedented quality and scale.[8] In the process of gathering material for his study Gough not only amassed huge numbers of notes and drawings; he also assembled a large collection of brass rubbings—indeed, he seems to have been the first scholar to have used rubbings on any scale. In the next fifty years a series of writers sought to bring brasses to wider notice. In 1846 C. R. Manning compiled a substantial county-by-county list, while three years later Charles Boutell produced a high-quality monograph and, to accompany it, a beautifully illustrated volume of engravings.[9] In 1861 Herbert Haines, a chaplain and master at Gloucester Cathedral School, placed the scholarly study of brasses on an entirely new footing with his *Manual of Monumental Brasses*—a major work which not only examined brasses in their art-historical context but identified styles of engraving and speculated on workshop origin.[10] The growing popular interest in brasses led in 1887 to the establishment of the Monumental Brass

---

[6] There are many other gentry mausoleums, of course: e.g. those of the Malyns's at Chinnor, the Bovilles at Letheringham, the Russells at Strensham. But none of these is so grand or so concentrated in effect as Cobham.

[7] For a survey of the literature on brasses, see J. Bertram, 'Past Writers on Brasses', in J. Bertram (ed.), *Monumental Brasses as Art and History* (Stroud, 1996), 24–36.

[8] R. Gough, *The Sepulchral Monuments of Great Britain* (3 vols. in 5; London, 1786–99).

[9] C. R. Manning, *A List of the Monumental Brasses remaining in England* (London, 1846); C. Boutell, *Monumental Brasses and Slabs* (London, 1847); idem, *The Monumental Brasses of England: A Series of Engravings on Wood* (London, 1849).

[10] H. Haines, *A Manual of Monumental Brasses* (London, 1861, repr. Bath, 1970).

Society and, later, to the publication of a series of popular textbooks on the subject. These various turn-of-the-century works were of mixed quality. The two best were Macklin's *Monumental Brasses* and *The Brasses of England*; also valuable were the monographs by Druitt and Suffling.[11] The others were mostly mediocre. Methodologically, these volumes were all costume-driven: that is to say, their authors classified and described brasses according to the attire of the commemorated. Little or no consideration was given to other possible interpretations. The art-historical context of brasses was largely ignored, and Haines's seminal insights on styles of engraving were overlooked or forgotten. It was not until the post-Second World War period that significant new thinking was brought to the subject. In 1949 J. P. C. Kent took up Haines's suggestion of stylistic analysis.[12] In a pioneering article Kent offered a complete stylistic classification of military effigies from 1360 to 1480; and twenty years later a group of younger scholars, following his lead, extended his scheme to the remaining late medieval brasses and to the products of the local schools.[13] At the same time, a series of innovative studies were made of other aspects of the subject. John Page-Phillips devoted a major monograph to palimpsests—that is, to brasses taken up and reused—while Binski, Rogers, and Blair looked afresh at the earliest brasses, arguing a case for their origin in the early fourteenth rather than the late thirteenth century.[14] Much of this revisionist work received appropriately magisterial summation in Malcolm Norris's *Monumental Brasses. The Memorials* and *The Craft*, published in 1977 and 1978 respectively.[15]

Today, brasses are better understood than any other type of medieval or early modern funerary monument. Not only is the general history of

---

[11] H. W. Macklin, *Monumental Brasses*, 1st edn. (London, 1890; many subsequent edns.); idem, *The Brasses of England* (London, 1907); H. Druitt, *A Manual of Costume as Illustrated by Monumental Brasses* (London, 1906, repr. 1970); E. R. Suffling, *English Church Brasses from the 13th to the 17th Century* (London, 1910, repr. 1970).

[12] J. P. C. Kent, 'Monumental Brasses: A New Classification of Military Effigies, c.1360–c.1485', *Journal of the British Archaeological Association*, 3rd ser., 12 (1949), 70–97.

[13] R. Emmerson, 'Monumental Brasses: London Design, c.1420–1485', *Journal of the British Archaeological Association*, 131 (1978), 50–78; S. Badham, *Brasses from the North East: A Study of the Brasses made in Yorkshire, Lincolnshire, Durham and Northumberland* (London, 1979); idem, 'The Suffolk School of Brasses', *TMBS*, 13 pt 1 (1980), 41–67; R. Greenwood, 'Haines's Cambridge School of Brasses', ibid., 11 pt 1 (1971), 2–12.

[14] J. Page-Phillips, *Palimpsests: The Backs of Monumental Brasses* (London, 1980); J. Coales (ed.), *The Earliest English Brasses: Patronage, Style and Workshops, 1270–1350* (London, 1987).

[15] M. W. Norris, *Monumental Brasses: The Memorials* (London, 1977); idem, *Monumental Brasses: The Craft* (London, 1978). A more recent summing-up is in Bertram (ed.), *Monumental Brasses as Art and History*.

brass engraving reasonably well charted; the origins of brasses in the incised slab workshops have been proved beyond question, and the basic principles which informed the design of brasses identified and mapped out.[16] Much of the most recent scholarly work on brasses will never need to be done again. All the same, it would be wrong to suppose that the study of brasses has reached its intellectual limits. While a good many questions about brasses have been answered, there are new ones which need to be asked and new methods which it is tempting to explore. The time has come for scholarly writing on brasses to move on.

The most significant challenge currently facing students of brasses is to make the study of the subject more outward-looking. If any criticism, however mild, can be levelled at the recent revisionist work, it is that it is too inward-looking. Brasses have been looked at largely for their own sake. In too many cases, there has been a tendency for brasses to be inter-preted in isolation—in isolation from other types of monument, and in isolation from the society which produced them.[17] All too often, the assumption has been made that brass design was determined by its own internal dynamic. Largely self-referential language and structures have been employed. In the context of modern art-historical criticism these assumptions appear dated. Today, it is generally appreciated that the interpretation of any art, or art-related, form requires external factors to be taken into account.[18] Thus the character and development of brass engraving need to be reviewed in the light of the social and religious functions which funerary sculpture performed. This is a point of particu-lar importance in relation to a large family commemorative scheme like the Cobhams'. A mausoleum on the scale of Cobham can never be understood in the context of a purely formalist critique. The gradual build-up of memorials at Cobham over time was the product of a complex web of influences emanating from the commemorated. Brasses—indeed, church monuments generally—formed part of people's material culture.[19] They were conceived as serving a variety of

---

[16] The origins of brasses are discussed below, Ch. 4.

[17] A notable exception is recognition of the art historical context: see N. Rogers, 'Brasses in their Art-Historical Context', Bertram (ed.), *Monumental Brasses as Art and History* (Stroud, 1996).

[18] Eric Fernie has articulated a powerful critique of formalism in the writing of architectural history: E. C. Fernie, 'Contrasts in Methodology and Interpretation of Medieval Ecclesiastical Architecture', *Archaeological Journal*, 145 (1988), 344–64.

[19] This is a point well understood by students of early modern brasses and monuments. See e.g. N. Llewellyn, 'Honour in Life, Death and the Memory: Funeral Monuments in Early Modern England', *Transactions of the Royal Historical Society*, 6th ser., 6 (1996), 179–200; idem, *The Art of Death: Visual Culture in the English Death Ritual, c.1500–c.1800* (London, 1991).

functions. In the first place, they provided a link between the living and the dead. Brasses formed the centre-piece of the annual rituals of commemoration, and the inscriptions on them usually included an appeal for prayers. Secondly, brasses and monuments were pivotal to the rituals of bereavement and mourning which were conducted for the benefit of the living. Finally—and this is where the values of the secular world most clearly intruded—brasses were crucial to the strategies of legitimation by which families drew attention to their status and affirmed their position in the élite. Any attempt to understand an elaborate commemorative programme like that at Cobham must accordingly embrace the religious and social processes which influenced its character. Commemoration was inseparable from the wider dynamics of society.

The brasses at Cobham thus claim our attention for at least two reasons: in the first place, because of their sheer number and importance; and, secondly, because of the interpretative challenge which they pose to traditional ways of looking at the subject. But there is a further reason for studying them. The opportunity is given to consider the commemorative tastes of the different branches of a family. Partly because they were so fecund, the Cobhams established a number of junior branches. By the mid-fourteenth century there were Cobham collaterals resident at Randall and Beluncle, both near Cobham itself, at Sterborough in Lingfield (Surrey), at Clyffe Pypard (Wilts.), and Blackborough (Devon). Like the parent branch of the family, the members of these junior lines usually sought commemoration by brasses. One of the group, indeed—the Cobhams of Sterborough—created a second family mausoleum, at Lingfield. Lingfield is neither so generally known, nor so often visited, as Cobham, for the brasses there are less numerous. None the less, the total ensemble of church, brasses, and tombs is scarcely less impressive. Lingfield, like Cobham, was a church converted into a college. In 1431 the third Sir Reginald Cobham established a foundation of six chaplains, one of whom was to be master, four clerks, along with thirteen poor persons, to pray 'for the good estate of Sir Reginald and all other benefactors while living and for their souls after death'. Reginald himself was commemorated by a magnificent tomb in the centre of the chancel. The tomb of his grandfather, a knight of the Garter, stood immediately to the north, and that of his father a little further off. Early on, the masters of the college, like their counterparts at Cobham, developed a taste for commemoration by brasses: four of the masters are commemorated by brasses in the chancel. Viewed as a whole, the tombs and brasses at Ling-

field form an impressive series. Yet the character of the Lingfield mausoleum is very different from that at Cobham. The monuments to the
Cobham family were not concentrated in one area: they are scattered
between the chancel and the north chapel. Moreover, the family's commemorative style is less uniform: tomb chests jostle with floor brasses,
and large brasses with small. How are these differences to be explained?
And to what extent are the differences indicative of contrasting aspirations on the part of the two families?

The attraction of looking at the Cobhams and, in particular, at their
tombs and brasses is thus more than the opportunity it affords to
re-examine the celebrated series at Cobham itself. A considerable
number of other brasses can be looked at: those at Lingfield (Surrey),
Hever and Hoo St Werburgh (Kent), Chrishall (Essex), Clyffe Pypard
(Wilts.), and even Westminster Abbey. Lost brasses, too, can be considered—in particular, those at Nettlestead and St Mary Overy, Southwark.
What begins as a study of limited aim—examining the tombs and
brasses of one family—soon becomes something more: an examination
of the memorials of a whole clan. This broader canvass makes the study
more valuable. The Cobhams' commemorative interests can be appreciated, to an extent, for their paradigmatic quality: in other words, for the
insights which they afford into the tastes of the English nobility or
gentry more generally. But the conception of a broader study also opens
up other possibilities. Particularly attractive is the opportunity to explore
the working of intra-family relations. Because the many branches of the
Cobhams were sprung from the same stem, it is tempting to suppose that
their members all thought and acted in the same way. However, there are
indications that this was not the case. The question thus arises of how far
the themes of family solidarity and fracture were reflected in the commemorative schemes. Did the junior members of the family seek burial
alongside the senior at Cobham? Or did they seek burial in other
churches? And did the various members of the family give their business
to the same workshop or did they, rather, support different ones? In
answering these questions it will be possible to learn something of the
extent to which the cadet branches established identities of their own or
simply followed the lead of the parent line.

It is a matter of good fortune that a rich archival resource survives, to
go alongside the evidence of the brasses. By comparison with many
other gentry families, the Cobhams' affairs are well documented. The
single most important source is probably Robert Glover's collection of
transcripts from the charters and deeds at Cobham Hall, published by

J. G. Nichols in *Collectanea Topographica et Genealogica* in 1841.[20] Glover, a sixteenth-century herald with a keen interest in family charters, was an avid collector of information in the muniment rooms that he visited.[21] Although his notes on the Cobham muniments are highly abbreviated, a great deal can be learned from them about marriage alliances, intrafamily relations, the descent of lands, and so on. Glover's transcripts can be supplemented by various other sources. Among the most valuable is the Cobham cartulary, an early fourteenth-century compilation preserved in the muniment room of Hatfield House.[22] A lay cartulary is a relative rarity. While the Cobhams' is by no means among the largest of the genre, it helpfully illuminates the growth of the family estates and their division between the various branches, and it appears to have been used by Francis Boteville, alias Thynne, when he compiled his history of the Cobham and Brooke families in the sixteenth century.[23] Another major source is the collection of charters, business documents, and account rolls originally assembled by Sir Edward Dering and now in the Harley Collection in the British Library. From this much can be learned about the Cobhams' financial affairs and, more particularly, about the endowment of Cobham college and the 3rd Lord Cobham's building projects at the college and at Cooling. Thirdly, there is the complementary cache of Dering material in the Capper Brooke Collection in the Centre for Kentish Studies at Maidstone.[24] This is of particular value in providing information about land transactions and about John, Lord Cobham's dealings with the London citizenry. Finally, there are the standard printed sources for the study of the medieval gentry—the chancery enrolments, calendars of inquisitions post mortem, and so on.

Inevitably, in a study of this kind from time to time there will be technical discussion of matters relating to the style and dating of brasses. But these will be treated only as a means to an end—the interpretation of the brasses in the context of the Cobhams' social and religious preoccupations. The over-riding aim will be to explore the complex interrelation of status, religion, and commemoration. For the medieval gentry and

---

[20] J. G. Nichols, 'Memorials of the Family of Cobham', *Collectanea Topographica et Genealogica*, 7 (1841), 322–43.

[21] For a recent assessment of Glover, see N. L. Ramsay, 'Introduction', in R. Glover and T. Milles, *The Kings of England Ever Since It Was So Called*, ed. D. Parker (London, 1995), pp. ix–xviii.

[22] Hatfield House, MS 306.

[23] Thynne's account was published by Holinshed: R. Holinshed, *Chronicles of England, Scotland and Ireland* (6 vols.; 1807–8), iv, pp. 778–9.

[24] CKS, U 601 (Capper Brooke Collection). The deeds and charters were bought by Francis Capper Brooke at the second Dering sale in July 1861.

nobility, religion and social position were inseparable. A family like the Cobhams, when they commissioned their monuments or founded chantry colleges, were doing more than securing intercessory prayers; they were making statements about social position and power. Because of this, a key aim of the book will be to consider what the brasses can teach us about the process of fashioning and manipulating the family's self-image. The brasses will be our window onto the Cobhams' world— a window onto the view which they had of themselves, their place in society, and their relations with one another. If, as is commonly said, it is through their works that we know people, then it is through their commemorative works that we know the Cobhams. The Cobhams left a particularly distinctive and eye-catching set of memorials. Our task is to read them, and to interpret them, just as the historian would any other set of source material at his disposal.

The Cobhams: The Family and Their Experience

B Y the late fourteenth century the Cobhams, the lords of Cobham, were among the leading landowning families of south-eastern England. For three generations from 1313, the heads of the family were honoured with personal summonses to parliament.

For a family which rose to such enviable distinction the Cobhams' origins were strangely humble. Unlike most recruits to the peerage in the fourteenth century, they were not descended from senior royal servants or members of the judiciary, although they were to show administrative talent on the way; their roots lay in the ranks of the middling freeholders.

The founder of the family fortune was apparently one Henry de Cobham, the son of Serlo, who died around 1230. According to a history of the family written in the 1580s by Francis Botevile, Henry bought the manor of Cobham, together with lands in Shorne, from his lord, Sir William Quatremere, a knight of Henry II.[1] In 1208–9 Henry obtained from King John a charter of confirmation of his lands and rights in Kent. A couple of decades later, Henry's son and heir, John, added to the family's holdings by acquiring the nearby manors of Cooling and West Chalk. The price which he paid for Cooling was 400 marks, or roughly twenty years' purchase.

Francis Botevile's account, which is confirmed by the charter evidence from which it is partly derived,[2] raises problems. Who was Henry de

---

[1] Holinshed, *Chronicles of England, Scotland and Ireland*, iv, 778–9. Francis Botevile, *alias* Thynne, was Lancaster Herald: C. S. Perceval, 'Notes to the Pedigree of Cobham of Sterborough', *SAC*, 2 (1862), 191.

[2] Nichols, 'Memorials of the Family of Cobham', 322–43; Hatfield House, MS 306, fos. 30ᵛ, 42ʳ (cartulary of the Cobham family). The cartulary is evidently the source for Quatremere's connection with Henry II; it adds that he was of Norman origin: 'Redditus domini Johannis de Cobham del gavelland in Schornes de dono domini Regis Henrici Secundi facto domino Willelmo de Quatremere militi suo de Normand' (fo. 44ʳ).

Cobham? And where did he and his son manage to find their money? It is difficult to answer these questions with any confidence. Waller suggested that Henry had distinguished himself at the siege of Acre and that the family's later adoption of the Moor's head as an emblem was 'a memento' of his prowess.[3] However, not only is there virtually no evidence to support such an hypothesis; the family's early use of a non-armorial seal seems to argue against it.[4] It is altogether more likely that the background to Henry's rise is to be found in local conditions in Kent. Strongly suggestive of this are Henry's links with two of Kent's leading ecclesiastical landowners, Christ Church, Canterbury, and Rochester cathedral priory. Henry appears in the records of Christ Church as a significant lender. He made a number of loans to the convent from 1214 to his death, most of them small, but cumulatively substantial. He was subsequently held in high regard by the monks, who honoured him as a benefactor, and in his will he bequeathed money to them for the purchase of wine.[5] It is a reasonable inference from this evidence that Henry enjoyed a business relationship of sorts with the community. Henry's ties with the other house, St Andrew's, Rochester, are equally suggestive. From roughly the mid-1190s Henry was a regular charter witness for the priory, which lay only a few miles east of his residence.[6] Quite possibly,

[3] Waller, 'The Lords of Cobham', 53.

[4] Henry's three sons used a fleur-de-lis seal, or signet, in their partition of his lands after his death in 1231: Nichols, 'Memorials of the Family of Cobham', 321, 345. The family had adopted a properly armorial device by the third quarter of the century. The earliest certain use of this coat, *gules, on a chevron or three lions rampant*, seems to be in a charter of John 'the younger', of 1265: ibid. 339. However, the fleur-de-lis is found on the chevron as late as 1288 (ibid. 330). Contrary to what Waller said, use of the Moor's head has little bearing on the matter of the family's origins: the device is found not uncommonly as a crest in the Middle Ages: John, Lord Bourchier rests his head on a Moor's head helm on his tomb at Halstead (Essex): M. Jones, 'The Fortunes of War: The Military Career of John, second Lord Bourchier (d. 1400)', *Essex Archaeology and History*, 26 (1995), pl. 3. So do others, e.g. Sir Bernard Brocas in Westminster Abbey (M. Burrows, *The Family of Brocas of Beaurepaire*, London, 1886, 128), and John de la Pole, duke of Suffolk, 1491, at Wingfield, Suffolk (F. H. Crossley, *English Church Monuments A.D. 1150–1550*, London, 1921, 23). At Wingfield a wooden helm with the Moor's head or 'Soldan' hangs above the tomb (ibid. 159). At Bures, Essex, there was a 'Soldan' upright on the tomb of John de Vere, 8th earl of Oxford (G. Probert, 'The Riddles of Bures Unravelled', *Essex Archaeology and History*, 16, 1984–5, 60–3). Moreover, crusading in the Holy Land was more likely to impoverish a family than enrich it.

[5] J. A. Quick, 'Government and Society in Kent, 1232–1280', (Univ. of Oxford D.Phil. thesis, 1986), 57, 59. For Henry's posthumous reputation at Canterbury, see the entry in the priory's confraternity register, BL, Arundel MS 68, fo. 52[r], 10 Kalend Jan' (23 Dec.): 'Item obiit Henricus de Cobham frater et benefactor noster pro quo servicium in conventu sicut pro uno archiepiscopo nostro et expenditur in refectionem conventus 30s et 10s in usu pauperum'.

[6] *Report of Manuscripts in Various Collections*, vii (London: Historical Manuscripts Commission, 55; 1914), 25–6; *Registrum Hamonis de Hethe Diocesis Roffensis A.D. 1319–1352*, ed. C. Johnson (Canterbury and York Society; 2 vols.; 1948), i, 5; *Registrum Roffense*, ed. J. Thorpe (London, 1769), 152,

his involvement with the house reflected no more than the working of the familiar ties of neighbourhood; and it is interesting that he is never referred to in the witness lists as a steward or other officer. On the other hand, the regularity of his appearance seems to imply a closer—perhaps a business—relationship with the house. The likelihood that he had acquired a measure of administrative expertise is strengthened by what is known of his later career. By the middle of John's reign at the latest he had moved from private to public service. In 1208 he was acting as the sheriff of Kent's sergeant ('serviens'), and eight years later as sheriff or under-sheriff.[7] Early in the next reign he was regularly employed as a juror on the grand assize, itinerant justice, and justice of assize.[8] And by 1221 he was acting as sub-lieutenant of Dover Castle.[9] Very likely, the key to Henry's career lies in his range and versatility as an administrator. It is tempting to compare him with such later medieval men of affairs as Thomas Tropenell and Bartholomew Bolney. Tropenell was a lawyer and steward in Wiltshire, and Bolney a steward, justice of the peace, and general man of affairs in Sussex.[10] Both were versatile, self-made admin-istrators, who made a fair amount of money and invested it in land. For them, as perhaps too for Cobham, all-round ability held the key to advancement. The indispensability of their sort to employers both public and private is a characteristic of English history.

---

169 (bis), 258, 258–9, 282, 530, 535, 540–1, 633, 639, 647–8, 687–8. All of these charters are undated. However, in most cases a date-range is indicated by internal evidence. The appropria-tion of Aylesford church (Registrum Roffense, 152) can be dated to Richard I's reign (E. Hasted, The History and Topographical Survey of the County of Kent, 2nd edn. (12 vols.; Canterbury, 1797–1801), iv, 443). The charters of Bishop Gilbert de Glanvill can be dated to the years of his episcopacy, 1185–1214 (Registrum Roffense, pp. 258, 530, 687–8). Likewise, the charters given by or attested by Bishop Benedict, his successor, can be dated to the years of his episcopacy, from 1215 (ibid. 258–9, 540–1).

[7] Memoranda Roll for the Tenth Year of the Reign of King John (1207–8), ed. R. A. Brown (Pipe Roll Society, new series, 31; 1957), 75; Curia Regis Rolls, vii, 1213–15 (London, 1935), no. 216. He was probably the under-sheriff of Reginald de Cornhill.

[8] Curia Regis Rolls, xi, 1223–24 (London, 1955), nos. 416, 793, 959; CPR 1216–25, 208, 480, 577; 1225–32, 283, 292, 307, 355. The implication of Henry's service on the grand assize is that he was a knight. He was also a collector of the fifteenth in 1225: CPR 1216–25, 563.

[9] S. P. H. Statham, History of the Castle, Town and Port of Dover (London, 1899), 330.

[10] Tropenell was the builder of Great Chalfield manor, Wilts. Bolney is commemorated by a brass at Firle, East Sussex (C. E. D. Davidson-Houston, 'Sussex Monumental Brasses, Part II', Sussex Archaeological Collections, 77 (1936), 175–6). The similarity between these two men and the Cobhams even extends to their attitude to landholding. Tropenell and Bolney, anxious to protect their titles, each compiled a cartulary; so too, in the early fourteenth century, did the Cobhams: The Tropnell Cartulary, ed. J. S. Davies (Wiltshire Archaeological Society, Devizes 1908); Book of Bartholomew Bolney, ed. M. Clough (Sussex Record Society, 63; 1964). Cartulary-making was evidently a characteristic of men on the make.

Henry de Cobham's administrative talents were inherited by his sons. All three were regularly employed as royal office-holders in Kent. John, known as John 'the elder', who succeeded his father in Cobham, served as keeper of Rochester castle from 1236 to 1241.[11] For two years from 1241 he acted as under-sheriff of Kent; and intermittently in the 1240s and early 1250s he was appointed an itinerant justice and justice of common pleas.[12] His youngest brother Reginald was even more frequently employed. Reginald was sheriff of Kent for nearly eight years from 1249 to his death—administering the county in person for all but one year of that period.[13] He was also, like his brother, periodically a justice and commissioner, and for two years from 1255 to 1257 held the important office of castellan of Dover and warden of the Cinque Ports. William, the middle brother, served as a justice and commissioner in the 1250s.[14] All three brothers played an indispensable role in county affairs. They were characteristic of that rising ministerial class on whom an assertive monarchy depended. There were other families which did well for themselves in royal service at this time: the Nevilles are an obvious example.[15] But few seem to have risen as far and as fast as the Cobhams.

The brothers' administrative success was underpinned by their possession of landed wealth. When their father died in or around 1230,[16] his lands were divided between them according to the custom of gavelkind, or partible inheritance, which operated in Kent.[17] John succeeded to the patrimonial lands at Cobham and Randall in Shorne, while Reginald and William divided the residue between them.[18] All three added piecemeal to their holdings as their means increased. In the 1230s John 'the elder'

[11] This was an office which every generation of the Cobham family was henceforth to hold.

[12] Details of these appointments, and those of other members of the family, can be found in T. May, 'The Cobham Family in the Administration of England, 1200–1400', *AC*, 82 (1968), 1–31.

[13] For the terms of his appointment, see D. A. Carpenter, *The Reign of Henry III* (London, 1996), 175.

[14] May, 'Cobham Family in Administration', genealogy opp. 2, shows William as the youngest, but according to William Smith's pedigree, in Society of Antiquaries MS 728/3, fo. 17ᵛ, he was the second born.

[15] C. R. Young, *The Making of the Neville Family 1166–1400* (Woodbridge, 1996), 8, 20, 144.

[16] The last reference to Henry is in Jan. 1230, when he was appointed a justice of assize: *CPR 1225–32*, 355. Christ Church, Canterbury, celebrated his anniversary on 23 Dec. (BL, Arundel MS 68, fo. 52ʳ; year of death not given). It seems reasonable to suppose that he died in Dec. 1230 or, at the latest, in the same month 1231. His son John was active as head of the family by 1236: *CPR 1232–47*, 169.

[17] For gavelkind, see F. Pollock and F. W. Maitland, *History of English Law before the Time of Edward I* (2 vols.; Cambridge, 1898), ii, 271–3; F. R. H. Du Boulay, 'Gavelkind and Knight's Fee in Medieval Kent', *EHR*, 77 (1962), 504–11.

[18] Nichols, 'Memorials of the Family of Cobham', 320–1.

acquired the manors of Cooling and Chalk.[19] In 1241 he purchased the lordship of the hundred of Shamel, in which Cobham and Randall lay.[20] And in 1253 his brother Reginald acquired some lands at Southfleet, west of Cobham.[21] It is indicative of the brothers' success that they had no difficulty finding the cash they needed. All three made loans to Christ Church, Canterbury. John lent £4. 16s. 8d. to the monks in 1239, and William and Reginald £5 each in 1235 and 1239 respectively. None of them, however, lent on the scale that their father had. Over a period of fifteen years the latter had loaned over £100.[22] His administrative career brought him capital means well beyond what he had invested in land.

The Cobhams maintained their level of involvement in local administration over the next two generations. Family members were regularly appointed as commissioners, sheriffs, and justices. In the late 1250s, however, the onset of political instability presented the family with a challenge. In June 1258 Henry III was forced to accept the Provisions of Oxford, which subjected the central organs of government to conciliar supervision, while in the following year a further package of measures—the Provisions of Westminster—extended reform to the shires. John Cobham the younger's sympathies were very much with the reformers. This is apparent from his appointment as sheriff of Kent in December 1259: late 1259 was the high point of reform.[23] It is likely that his reforming sympathies were widely known. Two months previously the council had ordered that sheriffs were to be chosen at the exchequer by four local knights, who were themselves to be chosen in the county court.[24] It is a reasonable inference that John's sympathy with reform had recommended him to the Kent electors. His period in office lasted for just under two years. In July 1261 he was dismissed, along with twenty other baronial sheriffs, in a purge that restored royal control over the shires.[25] For the next couple of years, during which the king's position steadily

---

[19] Holinshed, *Chronicles of England, Scotland and Ireland*, iv, 779; see above, 11.

[20] Hatfield House, MS 306, fos. 26[r-v].   [21] Ibid. fos. 18[v]–19[r].

[22] For these loans, see Quick, 'Government and Society in Kent, 1232–1280', 57. See also, above, 12.

[23] *CPR 1258–66*, 64. The timing of the appointment leaves little doubt of his sympathy for reform. But how is that sympathy to be explained? One possibility is that he resented the dominance in Kent after 1232 of the royal household knight, Bertrand de Criel. Only when Criel vacated the shrievalty in 1248 was his uncle, Reginald, appointed (Carpenter, *Reign of Henry III*, 175).

[24] *Documents of the Baronial Movement of Reform and Rebellion 1258–1267*, ed. R. F. Treharne and I. J. Sanders (Oxford, 1973), 151, 155.

[25] J. R. Maddicott, *Simon de Montfort* (Cambridge, 1994), 212.

strengthened, there was an uneasy calm in England. In the spring of 1264, however, the long-delayed showdown came. Louis IX's arbitration award in the king's favour in January made war between the two sides inevitable. Henry and the royalists made the first move. On 5 April a royalist force seized the Montfortian-held town of Northampton.[26] De Montfort himself, who was in London, was taken by surprise. Rallying his men in the south-east, he decided to respond with an attack on Rochester, a fortress garrisoned for the king by John de Warenne. Outside the town his forces were joined by those of Gilbert de Clare, earl of Gloucester, who had come from his castle of Tonbridge. At this stage John Cobham appears to have joined in. His role in events is uncertain, but his presence on the rebel side at Rochester is attested by royal letters ordering the seizure of his lands 'because he was with the king's adversaries at the taking of Rochester'.[27] It is a reasonable assumption that he was in Earl Gilbert's retinue, for ties of locality and association would have drawn him to the earl.[28] However, it is doubtful if he was much more than an observer of events. After the lifting of the siege, Earl Gilbert accompanied Simon southwards on the campaign which was to end in the latter's victory at Lewes. John, however, almost certainly held back. No further action was taken against him by the royalists: the implication being that he gave no further offence. Like most of his fellow gentry in Kent, he probably thought it prudent to await on events.

After 1266, and the making of peace, John resumed his career as a royal servant. In 1268 he was appointed a justice of common pleas in Surrey, and from 1271 he was serving regularly on eyre circuits in the southern counties.[29] In 1273, after Edward I became king, he was appointed one of the justices of common pleas at Westminster, and three years after that he became a baron (i.e. a judge) of the exchequer.[30] From this time on, his energies were increasingly absorbed at Westminster: he was not only engaged in judicial work there during term, he was also summoned to sessions of the council. All the same, he was still appointed to commissions in the shires, in particular to commissions of oyer and

---

[26] For the military action which followed, see D. A. Carpenter, *The Battles of Lewes and Evesham* (Keele, 1987), 12–14.　　　　　　　　　　　　　　　[27] *CPR 1258–66*, 316–17.

[28] There is no evidence of a formal association between the two, but it would be optimistic to expect one given the imperfect de Clare archive.

[29] For his appointments, see May, 'The Cobham Family in Administration', 18–20.

[30] *Select Cases in the Court of King's Bench under Edward I*, i, ed. G. O. Sayles (Selden Society, 55; 1936), pp. xliii, cxxxv–cxxxvi; E. Foss, *The Judges of England* (9 vols.; London, 1848–64), iii, 77–8.

terminer.[31] In the final years of his life he was probably among the most widely employed of the king's justices.[32]

Naturally, this busy bureaucrat reaped ample reward for his work. His exchequer position carried with it a salary of 40 marks per annum.[33] On top of this he could reckon all the *douceurs*, retaining fees, and consultancies offered to him by clients in return for his services.[34] On top of these again he could number the wardships and other windfalls that came his way: notable among the latter being the grants of some of the lands of Sir Roger de Bavent and of the marriage of Thomas, son of Thomas de Stodham.[35] By the mid-1290s John was wealthy enough to be able to make some sizeable loans. In 1297 he lent the king as much as 500 marks, secured on the custody of some of the de Bavent lands.[36] In the manner of the upwardly mobile of his day, John invested a fair proportion of his wealth in land. He made a number of small acquisitions in his immediate locality in Kent.[37] But his biggest investment was the purchase of a string of manors in Wiltshire: Bincknoll, Broad Hinton, Beckhampton, and Clyffe Pypard.[38] The manors were sold to him by one Sir Michael de Columbers. The Columbers family established a network of links with the Cobhams at this time. Michael's elder brother Matthew, a former baronial sympathizer, was probably known to John through his judicial work: in the 1270s he was a justice on circuits in southern England.[39] In the early 1270s the heads of the two families arranged a series of marriage alliances: Sir John de Columbers, a member of his family's senior branch, took as his wife Alice, one of the daughters and coheiresses of Sir Stephen de Penchester of Penshurst (Kent), while Joan, the other

---

[31] May, 'Cobham Family in Administration', 18–20. A commission of *oyer et terminer* was a commission to hear and determine a particular case.

[32] He was so widely employed that by the time of his final illness he had to beg the king's leave to retire: *CPR 1292–1301*, 485–6.   [33] Foss, *Judges of England*, iii, 78.

[34] For the practice of offering fees to the king's justices, and some idea of the fortunes which the latter could accumulate, see J. R. Maddicott, *Law and Lordship: Royal Justices as Retainers in Thirteenth- and Fourteenth-Century England* (*Past and Present* Supplement, 4; 1978). The justices' avarice made them highly unpopular. A possible hint of John's unpopularity is given by the burning of his property by one Simon de Scharstede in 1293 (*CPR 1292–1301*, 108).

[35] *CPR 1292–1301*, 302, 314, 429; *Documents Illustrating the Crisis of 1297–98 in England*, ed. M. Prestwich (Camden Society, 4th series, 24; 1980), 129.

[36] *CPR 1292–1301*, 302, 314; *CCR 1296–1302*, 71.

[37] Hatfield House, MS 306, fos. 27ᵛ, 28ʳ.

[38] *CPR 1281–92*, 178. The date of his acquisition of the manors is not recorded, but it is likely to have been 1278 or early 1279: in the summer of 1279 he travelled to Wiltshire to enter into seisin of the properties: BL, Harley Roll C 28. John also took a lease on the Columbers' manor of East Tytherley (Hants.): *CCR 1307–13*, 387; *VCH Hampshire* (5 vols.; London, 1900–12), iv, 515.

[39] Foss, *Judges of England*, iii, 79–80.

daughter, was married to Sir Henry de Cobham of Randall.[40] It may have been a condition of the sale of the manors that yet another match was arranged, for Maud, the young widow of Sir Matthew de Columbers,[41] was betrothed to Sir John de Cobham's son and heir, Henry, and the former Columbers manor of Chisbury was settled on them.[42]

The acquisition of the Wiltshire properties led to a redirection westwards of the Cobhams' interests. This revealed itself in a number of ways. In the first place, the Cobhams began holding office in the western counties; from January 1304 to May 1305, for example, Sir Henry de Cobham of Cobham served as sheriff of Wiltshire.[43] Secondly, several more west-country marriage connections were forged. Sometime in the 1290s Sir Henry's younger brother John married the Devon heiress Amice Bolhay and by that means acquired an inheritance at Blackborough in the Blackdown Hills.[44] Early in the next century Sir Henry arranged a match between his son and heir, John, and Joan, the daughter of Sir John Beauchamp of Hatch (Somerset).[45] Lastly, and by way of fitting climax, in 1341 a match was arranged between John, son of John, 2nd Lord Cobham, and Margaret, daughter of Hugh Courtenay, earl of Devon.[46] This series of marriages, and in particular the last, led to a broadening of

[40] C. Moor, *Knights of Edward I* (Harleian Society, 80–4; 1929–32), i, 218, 227. The main branch of the de Columbers family held the barony of Nether Stowey (Somerset). How they were related to the brothers Matthew and Michael is not clear.

[41] Not Michael Columbers, as in May, 'Cobham Family in Administration', facing p. 2.

[42] *Feet of Fines relating to Wiltshire for the Reigns of Edward I and Edward II*, ed. R. B. Pugh (Wiltshire Record Society, i; 1939), no. 33. The marriage had been arranged by 1285, when the settlement was made. John took the opportunity to consolidate his control of the Wiltshire manors at the same time: Chisbury was settled on Maud and Henry and their heirs in return for the former's surrender of her dower rights in the other manors (*CPR 1281–92*, 178). Maud was the daughter of Sir Eudo de Morville (*VCH Hants*, iv, 515). The two wives given to Henry by May, 'Cobham Family in Administration', facing p. 2, are one and the same person.

[43] *List of Sheriffs for England and Wales* (PRO, Lists and Indexes, 9; 1898), 152.

[44] James, Amice's father, had died before 1290, and his daughter's marriage had been acquired by Queen Eleanor (*CFR 1272–1307*, 288). After the latter's death in 1290, it had been acquired by Sir Guy Ferre (ibid.). It was presumably with Guy that either John or Henry Cobham negotiated the match. Philippa de Bolhay, presumably Amice's mother, held the manor in 1303 (*Feudal Aids*, 6 vols., London, 1899–1920, i, 368).

[45] *Complete Peerage*, iii, 344. John was an executor of, and a beneficiary under, Beauchamp's will: BL, Add. Ch. 40616. For the Beauchamps of Hatch, see J. Batten, 'The Barony of Beauchamp of Somerset', *Proceedings of the Somerset Archaeological and Natural History Society*, 36 (1890), 20–60.

[46] In Glover's notes from the College of Arms, the marriage is variously dated 5 Edw. III and 6 Edw. III (i.e. 1331, 1332): Nichols, 'Memorials of the Family of Cobham', 323, 324. However, these dates are probably misreadings for 15 and 16 Edw. III (i.e. 1341, 1342). 15 Edward III is the date of a grant of herbage in Chisbury by Sir John to his son and daughter-in-law (BL, Harley Ch. 48 E 9); and the grant may have coincided with the marriage. A further point is that Sir John himself had not entered into his inheritance in 1331 or 1332, whereas he had done so ten years later.

the Cobhams' horizons. No longer were the family so exclusively identified with Kent as they had been. Their itineraries became more extensive. Members of the family made visits to, or resided in, the west country.[47] Henry, Lord Cobham, in his later years appears to have virtually abandoned Kent for Somerset; it was at Stoke-sub-Hamdon that he died and was buried.[48] The Cobhams had become a family of regional rather than purely local importance.

The westward redirection of the Cobhams' interests slowed—indeed, it was largely halted—in the time of John, the 2nd Lord. The powerful Courtenay connection was still important to the family: as late as the 1380s a Cobham was admitted to the Courtenay retinue.[49] But John, the 2nd Lord's, activities were more largely confined to Kent than his father's had been. Well before the latter's death in 1339 he had taken his place in the ranks of the Kent office-holding élite. He was a commissioner of array from 1324 and a keeper of the peace in 1329.[50] By the early 1330s he had established himself as one of the leading figures in the county. In 1334 he was appointed constable of Rochester castle, at first jointly with his father, and later in his own right. And from the early 1340s he was a justice of the peace and of oyer and terminer. Unlike his father, he was hardly ever appointed to local office outside Kent. He was never a figure of any importance in Wiltshire. The charter evidence suggests that he used the family's Wiltshire estates chiefly as endowment for his younger kin.[51]

[47] In the summer of 1279 John Cobham made the journey to Chisbury, Broad Hinton and Bincknoll to take possession of those manors ('pro seisina maneriorum de Chissebury Henton et Bencknoll'). For an account of his expenses, see BL, Harley Roll C 28. John Cobham, Henry's son and heir, issued letters of attorney at Stoke-sub-Hamdon in 1314 (Nichols, 'Memorials of the Family of Cobham', 322). Margaret de Cobham's entry into the famously aristocratic nunnery of Amesbury (Wilts.), c.1330–40, may have been aided by her family's Wiltshire connections (ibid. 336).

[48] Nichols, 'Memorials of the Family of Cobham', 322, 329. Henry, while retaining, at least nominally, the keepership of Rochester, held no office in Kent after 1327 (May, 'Cobham Family in Administration', 23). Stoke-sub-Hamdon was a manor which belonged to his son-in-law Sir John Beauchamp of Hatch. The Beauchamps themselves were buried there—in the chapel of St Nicholas, a free-standing building in the courtyard of their manor-house. In the sixteenth century Leland commented on the splendour of the Beauchamp tombs and on the fine heraldic glass in the chapel: *The Itinerary of John Leland*, ed. L. Toulmin Smith (5 vols., London, 1907–10), i, 158–9. It seems likely that there would have been a monument to Henry Cobham there. All trace of the chapel and its contents, however, is lost.

[49] This was John Cobham of Hever: *House of Commons, 1386–1421*, ii, 607. For his brass at Hever, which calls him 'John Cobham of Devonshire', see below, 213.

[50] For John's appointments, see May, 'Cobham Family in Administration', 26–7.

[51] BL, Harley Ch. 48 E 9; Nichols, 'Memorials of the Family of Cobham', 322, 333. This follows the pattern from the previous generation. In 1332 the members of the family assessed at Hinton, Bincknoll and Clyffe Pypard had been Henry's sons: *The Wiltshire Tax List of 1332*, ed. D. A. Crowley (Wiltshire Record Society, 45; 1989), 57, 73, 97.

The background to John's adult career was provided by the renewal of hostilities with Scotland and France. In 1333 Edward III had given his backing to Edward Balliol's bid for the Scottish crown, and in 1338 he launched an invasion of the Continent in support of his own claim to the crown of France. The young John Cobham, as befitted a high-ranking member of his class, was expected to assist in the business of military administration and command. Already, in the 1320s, he had served as an arrayer and keeper of the coasts in Kent. In the following decade, as the scale of hostilities increased, he was given responsibility at a national level. In the spring of 1335, in anticipation of a major expedition that Edward planned against the Scots, he was appointed admiral in the south and the west.[52] However, the signs are that he did not acquit himself with much distinction. On 16 August Edward rebuked him for his tardiness in supplying ships and threatened him with forfeiture, and in September he dismissed him from office.[53] In the 1340s, when the fighting in France intensified, his record was scarcely more distinguished. He did not take part in the Crécy expedition of 1346, and he only belatedly joined in the siege of Calais.[54] John was in danger of being outshone by his more brilliant kinsman, Reginald, Lord Cobham, of the Sterborough branch. Reginald was one of the most illustrious soldiers of his age.[55] He had first seen active service in 1334 and 1335 in Scotland, and later in the decade he led contingents in the king's major expeditions to the Low Countries. In the following decade he played a leading role in the Crécy campaign and was present at the siege of Calais, while ten years after that he accompanied the Black Prince on the *chevauchée* which culminated in the battle of Poitiers. Reginald's rapidly increasing wealth earned him a summons to parliament from 1347, while his achievements in the field brought him election to the Order of the Garter in *c.*1352. By comparison with this enviable record of achievement John, Lord Cobham, could show little. Perhaps the note of defiance struck on his epitaph at Cobham—'Ces enemis mortels fist abatre'[56]—was a conscious response to an undistinguished career.

[52] *Rotuli Scotiae*, i, ed. D. Macpherson *et al.* (London, 1814), 368.

[53] Ibid. 374; *CCR 1333–7*, 435. For discussion, see R. Nicholson, *Edward III and the Scots* (Oxford, 1965), 209.

[54] He was receiving wages at Calais by 6 Mar. 1347 (*Crecy and Calais*, ed. G. Wrottesley, London, 1898, 207). His retinue consisted of 1 knight, 30 esquires, 33 archers, and 19 Welshmen (ibid. 200). The only evidence of his activity in 1346 is his appointment as a keeper of the coasts in Kent on 10 Mar. (ibid. 75).

[55] Reginald's career is discussed at greater length, below, 124–30; full references are given there.

[56] 'Those mortal enemies he made lie low'.

The shift in the balance of fortune between the two families was reversed in the next generation. Reginald, Lord Cobham, died in 1361, leaving a son under age; while his kinsman John, the 2nd Lord Cobham, was succeeded by an heir who possessed all the vigour and ability which his father had lacked. John, 3rd Lord Cobham (c.1330/5–1408), was to be the most distinguished of the Cobham line. An active soldier and politician, he was also a man of culture and discernment much admired by his contemporaries. It was he who founded Cobham college and gave the chancel at Cobham the character of a family mausoleum.

John's adult career began in the 1350s. In April 1354, a year before his father's death, the king conferred on him the rank of knight banneret, which suggests that he had already had some military experience.[57] However, the first expedition in which he can be shown to have participated was Edward III's winter campaign in France of 1359–60. Edward's aim had been to secure French submission by taking the city of Rheims, where the French kings were crowned, but in the end the weather defeated him and he had to withdraw. The English force was a large one, and John's contingent was composed of two knights, twenty-two esquires, and twenty-eight archers.[58] John saw active service again in 1369 and 1377, on the latter occasion heading a sizeable contingent in Thomas of Woodstock's expedition at sea.[59] But from the 1360s on, following the Anglo-French reconciliation at Bretigny, his talents were more usually employed in diplomacy. In May 1363 he crossed to Calais to secure the return of the hostages for the French king's ransom after the failure of negotiations for payment.[60] Four years later, he was sent on two delicate missions to Rome to secure Urban V's agreement to

[57] *CPR 1354–8*, 27: a grant to John Cobham of 100 marks yearly to maintain him in the status of banneret, which he has just received from the king. This grant is usually taken (e.g. in *Complete Peerage*, iii, 344) to refer to John's father, the 2nd Lord. But such a reading is highly improbable. The 2nd Lord would hardly have needed a grant to augment his status when he was already in full enjoyment of the income from his estates. The grant would only have been needed if the grantee had no other source of income: which was the case with the younger Sir John; and the fact that at the beginning of the next reign he obtained an *inspeximus* (or confirmation) of the letters seems to clinch the case (*CPR 1377–81*, 103). The likelihood is that John was raised to banneret status in 1353 when he briefly appears in the wardrobe book as a banneret of the royal household (PRO, E101/392/12, fo. 40ᵛ). [58] PRO, E101/393/11, fo. 81ᵛ.

[59] For 1369, see J. Sherborne, *War, Politics and Culture in Fourteenth-Century England*, ed. A. Tuck (London, 1994), 5 n. 15, 87; for 1377, PRO E101/36/29. On the latter occasion John again served with a large retinue—110 men-at-arms and 110 archers; he was in receipt of wages from 23 Oct. 1377 to 26 Jan. 1378.

[60] For the background to this episode, see E. Perroy, *The Hundred Years War* (London, 1965), 142.

the appointment of William of Wykeham as bishop of Winchester.[61] In the 1370s and 1380s he was appointed to several more embassies. In 1375 he was a member of the delegation which negotiated a two-year truce with the French at Bruges, while in 1384 he was an envoy at the Leuling-ham conference at which a draft peace agreement was agreed with the French.

After Richard II's accession in 1377 Cobham found himself becoming more involved in domestic politics. The new king was a minor, and the day-to-day running of the country was entrusted to a series of 'continual councils'. Cobham was appointed to the first of these in July 1377.[62] Two years later, in the parliament of April 1379, when the Commons voiced concern over the misdirection of patronage, he was appointed a supervisor of the king's person in the household, and he received wages for this duty until 18 February 1380.[63] In the early to mid-1380s Richard's extravagance and repeated requests for taxation led to further parliamentary criticism. In the session of 1386 a 'continual council' was appointed for a year to implement a major programme of financial reform; and among the council's members, all of them moderate and respected men, was Lord Cobham.[64] Richard's response to the council's appointment was to leave Westminster for the midlands and consult the judges about his powers. When news of the judges' strongly royalist opinions leaked out, Richard's opponents, principally Gloucester, Arundel, and Warwick, sensed danger. Hastily summoning their retinues, they mustered at Haringey. Richard sent a group of councillors, including Cobham, to discuss possible settlement terms with them.[65] The councillors' mediatory efforts, however, were a failure, and in December hostilities broke

---

[61] *CPR 1364–7*, 407. For discussion, see J. R. L. Highfield, 'The Promotion of William of Wickham to the see of Winchester', *JEH*, 4 (1953), 37–54. The dates of Cobham's visits were 28 Oct. 1366–29 Jan. 1367 and 3 June–mid July 1367.

[62] *CPR 1377–81*, 19. For discussion, see N. B. Lewis, 'The "Continual Council" in the Early Years of Richard II', *EHR*, 41 (1926), 246–51.

[63] A. Tuck, *Richard II and the English Nobility* (London, 1973), 43–4. For a useful discussion of Cobham's role in the politics of Richard's reign generally, see C. Given-Wilson, 'Richard II and the Higher Nobility', in A. Goodman and J. L. Gillespie (eds.), *Richard II: The Art of Kingship* (Oxford, 1999), 112–13.

[64] *The Westminster Chronicle*, ed. L. C. Hector and B. F. Harvey (Oxford, 1982), 167–77. Cobham had probably been affronted by Richard's attempts to establish two of his favourites, Sir Simon Burley and Robert de Vere, in Kent. Burley had been appointed constable of Dover in 1384, and de Vere was granted Queenborough in the following year: ibid. 56; N. E. Saul, *Richard II* (New Haven and London, 1997), 163–4.

[65] Saul, *Richard II*, 210. Earlier, Cobham, with the archbishop of Canterbury and others, had been employed informally by the lords to explore talks with the king: *Knighton's Chronicle, 1337–1396*, ed. G. Martin (Oxford, 1995), 404.

out. The opposition lords, now including Derby and Nottingham, and known as the 'Appellants', mounted a brisk offensive and defeated a royalist force at Radcot Bridge. Richard had no alternative but to submit to his opponents' will. In the parliament of February 1388 a group of his leading favourites was put on trial.[66] The Appellants and their supporters were keen to despatch business quickly, but Cobham, ever the moderate, urged caution. In April, along with two other councillors, he asked the Commons to give Burley and his co-accused a second chance to reply, but his request was turned down.[67] Later in the same month he was asked by Richard to try again. He put it to the Commons, the Westminster writer reports, that Burley was sick 'and ought to be treated with more gentleness and indulgence, but this, like other arguments, found little favour with the Commons'; Burley was executed.[68]

After the ending of the crisis, and Richard's reassertion of power, Cobham was less active in politics. Although appointed to supervise the king after the Merciless parliament, it is doubtful if he ever acted in this capacity.[69] In the early 1390s he served as lieutenant in the Court of Chivalry, while the constable, the duke of Gloucester, was abroad;[70] and he also attended sessions of the council.[71] Increasingly, however, his activities became more local in nature. From 1387 he was involved with Sir Robert Knolles in the rebuilding of Rochester bridge, and in 1395 he undertook the endowment of a chantry in the bridge chapel.[72] By now he was getting old—he was probably in his sixties[73]—and, according to John Gower, the poet, had sought refuge in a Carthusian monastery. But

---

[66] Cobham may have been instrumental in apprehending one of them, the chief justice, Sir Robert Tresilian. Tresilian had sought refuge from Appellant justice in the sanctuary of Westminster and, according to the Westminster chronicler, he and Gloucester were responsible for dragging him out (*Westminster Chronicle*, 332). Precipitate action of this sort, however, seems uncharacteristic of Cobham, and it may be significant that at another point in the monk's narrative the chronicler attributes Tresilian's removal solely to Gloucester (ibid. 310).

[67] *Westminster Chronicle*, 322.   [68] Ibid. 330.

[69] Ibid. 232.   [70] *CPR 1391–6*, 17, 42, 306.

[71] He attended a number of sessions in the period covered by John Prophet's minute book, i.e. from Jan. 1392 to Feb. 1393. His attendance was most frequent in the first two months of that period. Thereafter it was rare: J. F. Baldwin, *The King's Council in England during the Middle Ages* (Oxford, 1913), Appendix II.

[72] R. Britnell, 'The New Bridge', in N. Yates and J. M. Gibson (eds.), *Traffic and Politics: The Construction and Management of Rochester Bridge, AD 43–1993* (Woodbridge, 1994), 43–59.

[73] Waller, 'The Lords of Cobham', 84, and *DNB*, 11, 156, make him a nonagenarian. Waller, whom the *DNB* followed, was misled by Glover's note to the effect that John was married in 5 Edw. III (Nichols, 'Memorials of the Family of Cobham', 323). But this note is probably an error of transcription (above, n. 46). It is more likely that John was married in 15 Edw. III (i.e. 1341). On the assumption that in that year he was aged around ten to fifteen, he would have been in his seventies in the 1390s.

in January 1398 his past returned to haunt him. In July the previous year Richard had arrested three of the former Appellants, Gloucester, Arundel, and Warwick, and charged them with treason for their 'crimes' in 1388.[74] Shortly after their condemnation, Richard moved against the secondary objects of his anger, among them Lord Cobham. Cobham was arraigned in the Shrewsbury parliament. An eye-witness account of his trial is contained in Adam of Usk's chronicle. The repartee was vigorous. To the charge of membership of the 1386 council, Cobham replied that he had served only because commanded by the king to do so. Richard retorted, 'You know very well that I gave the order unwillingly.' 'That is untrue', said Cobham.[75] Lancaster, as steward of England, condemned the latter as a traitor, but the king commuted the sentence of death to perpetual banishment on Jersey. 'Be grateful for that', said Lancaster; Cobham, however, simply expressed disdain for the earthly life.[76] Cobham languished in confinement for a little under two years. When Henry Bolingbroke seized the crown in October 1399, the forfeitures of the previous reign were reversed and Cobham was restored. In Henry's first parliament Cobham spoke forcefully against the former king's policies.[77] His last public appointment was as a trier in the parliament of 1401.[78] In his final years he probably went into retirement again. According to an account of his household expenses, he died at the Augustinian house of Maiden Bradley (Wilts.) in January 1408.[79]

[74] Arundel was executed, Warwick imprisoned on the Isle of Man, and Gloucester despatched to Calais, where he died (probably murdered).

[75] *The Chronicle of Adam Usk, 1377–1421*, ed. C. Given-Wilson (Oxford, 1997), 38.

[76] This was a very characteristic response, which matches the tone of the epitaph on his brass: see below, 98.

[77] He did so in strongly religious terms, saying that the condition of the English people had sunk lower even than that of heathens; the English, although they were Christian and should profess the truth, nevertheless, for fear of ruin, never dared speak the truth: *Chronicles of the Revolution, 1397–1400*, ed. C. Given-Wilson (Manchester, 1993). There was a powerful religious strain to Cobham's thought.

[78] *Rotuli Parliamentorum* (6 vols.; London, 1767–77), iii, 455.

[79] H. C. Maxwell Lyte, 'An Account Relating to Sir John Cobham, A.D. 1408', *Antiquaries Journal*, 2 (1922), 339–43. This account settles the doubt over John's place of interment. A puzzling reference in a sixteenth-century list of burials at Grey Friars, London, suggests that he was buried there: 'in a tomb raised up at the end of that altar by the door under the cross (transept) lies John de Cobham, Baron of the County of Kent' (J. G. Nichols, 'Register of the Sepulchral Inscriptions in the Church of the Grey Friars', *Collectanea Topographica et Genealogica*, 5, 1838, 274; see also 387). Since there is absolutely no doubt that John was buried at Cobham, it is unclear whose tomb the note refers to. One possibility is that it was that of Sir John Cobham, 'son of the Countess Marshal' (d. 1378), a collateral kinsman who was active in the military affairs of the day. This John, being childless, left his estates to the crown 'out of love and affection' for the Black Prince: *Rotuli Parliamentorum*, iii, 8–9. His connections with Kent were few—which would explain his burial in London.

An impression of Lord Cobham's personality emerges from the comments of his contemporaries. Walsingham, writing after 1400, described him as 'a very old man, straightforward and upright'.[80] To John Gower, the poet, he was 'honest, patient, upright and pious, strong through the power of virtues';[81] his piety, often the mainspring of his actions, is to be numbered among his most notable characteristics.[82] In political terms, he was very much the moderate. In the 1380s he favoured household reform because he was critical of Richard II's excesses. However, in the blood-letting of 1388 he was equally critical of his opponents' extremism. At a time of intense polarization he found a moderate position difficult to uphold. None the less, he should not be dismissed as a lightweight. On occasion, he could be firm and decisive, even harsh. In the parliament of October 1399 he spoke strongly in favour of prosecuting the fallen king's favourites.[83] He was able, experienced, and respected.[84] The range of his friendships was impressive. He was a close associate of Edward, the Black Prince, and was one of the princess of Wales's executors.[85] He was on intimate terms with William of Wykeham, the powerful bishop of Winchester.[86] During the crisis of 1388 he won the trust of men as sharply at odds as Gloucester and Burley. In 1391, before departing on crusade, Gloucester appointed him a feoffee.[87] In Kent he was a collaborator of Sir Robert Knolles in the building of Rochester bridge.[88] He enjoyed the respect of the poet Gower. He gives the impression of a man of integrity, intelligence, and sound judgement.[89]

---

[80] T. Walsingham, *Ypodigma Neustriae*, ed. H. T. Riley (Rolls series; 1876), 379.

[81] Gower's tribute comes in the *Cronica Tripertita*, ll. 213–32 (*The Complete Works of John Gower*, ed. G. C. Macaulay (4 vols.; Oxford, 1899–1902), iv, 326). The Latin reads: 'Unus erat dignus patiens, pius, atque benignus, / Providus et justus, morum virtute robustus, / Non erat obliquus, regni sed verus amicus.' [82] His piety is discussed below, 98–101.

[83] *Chronicles of the Revolution*, 204–5. Cobham's speech to his fellow peers is reported by Walsingham. There is a note of bitterness in his remarks, but also an obvious concern for justice.

[84] It is a mark of the regard for him that in the parliament of 1385 he was appointed, with Bishop Brantingham of Exeter, a supervisor of taxation, the supervisors' responsibility being to ensure that the proceeds of the lay subsidy were not misspent: *Rotuli Parliamentorum*, iii, 204.

[85] *Testamenta Vetusta*, ed. N. H. Nicolas (2 vols.; London, 1826), i, 14. For this John, see above, n. 79.

[86] The friendship had its origins in Cobham's endeavours at Rome in 1367, eventually successful, to secure Wykeham's appointment to the see of Winchester. For a letter from Wykeham to Cobham of this time, see Highfield, 'Promotion of William of Wickham', 49 (Appendix 5), reprod. as the frontispiece to G. H. Moberly, *Life of William of Wykeham* (Winchester, 1887). Wykeham and Cobham were to be colleagues on the continual council of 1386–7.

[87] *CPR 1388–92*, 482. See also, for a grant by Gloucester to Cobham, Nichols, 'Memorials of the Family of Cobham', 345. [88] See below, 235.

[89] He was also of more than conventional religious sensibility: see below, 98–101.

John, 3rd Lord Cobham, the most distinguished of his line, was also the last. Whatever judgement is passed on his political career, as a dynast he failed. His marriage to Margaret Courtenay produced no son. The couple's only child—or, at least, their only surviving child—was a daughter, Joan. While the girl was still an infant, John secured her betrothal to Sir John de la Pole of Castle Ashby (Northants.). The match was a promising one. Sir John was a wealthy man. He owned six manors in Northamptonshire and Suffolk, and another seven elsewhere.[90] His grandfather, the Hull merchant, Richard de la Pole, elder brother of the better-known William, had established the family in the 1340s, and his father, another William, had won it chivalric renown by going on crusade.[91] The prospects for the family seemed bright. But sadly the match, like that of Joan's parents, was dynastically a failure. Joan bore her husband only one son, William, who died prematurely in 1380. The heir to the combined fortunes of the two families was their daughter, another Joan.[92] This Joan was a remarkable woman who lived into her seventies. Five times married, like the Wife of Bath, she was one of the most sought-after heiresses of her time. Her life story, and that of her husbands, is inseparable from the story of the Cobham brasses.

Joan's first match had probably been arranged by her parents. The husband chosen for her was a distinguished Norfolk knight, Sir Robert Hemenhale of Polstead in Burnham Norton. Hemenhale died in September 1391 leaving as his heir a five-year-old boy William, described later as an 'idiot'.[93] His widow held Radwinter Hall (Essex) and five Suffolk

---

[90] L. H. Butler, 'Robert Braybrooke, Bishop of London (1381–1404), and his Kinsmen' (Univ. of Oxford D.Phil. thesis, 1952), 94–6.

[91] E. B. Fryde, *William de la Pole: Merchant and King's Banker* (London, 1988), 9, 211–12; A. Luttrell, 'English Levantine Crusaders, 1363–1367', *Renaissance Studies*, 2 (1988), 145; *CPR 1361–4*, 250. For full discussion of the de la Poles, see below, 199–202, 205–6.

[92] In 1396 her father settled his estates on the heirs of his body, with remainders to the collateral branches in tail male (Nichols, 'Memorials of the Family of Cobham', 350–1). For an aristocratic estate to be settled other than in tail male at this time is highly unusual (K. B. McFarlane, 'The English Nobility in the Later Middle Ages', *The Nobility of Later Medieval England*, Oxford, 1973, 268–78). The implication, which was presumably accepted by Lord Cobham, was that his inheritance would descend to his granddaughter. For further discussion, see below, 236.

[93] For Robert's inquisition, see *CIPM*, xvii, nos. 62–3. Robert had made an enfeoffment of his estates in 1389, the purpose of which was clearly to avoid a wardship (*CCR 1389–92*, 90). The ruse was uncovered after William's death in 1402 (*CIPM*, xix, nos. 154–5), and an inquiry ordered in 1406 (*CPR 1405–8*, 304). In his will Robert had requested burial in the choir of the Carmelite friary at Burnham (PRO, PROB 11/1, fo. 60ᵛ), but his wishes were overridden and he was buried in Westminster Abbey, in St John the Evangelist's chapel (B. Harvey, *Westminster Abbey and its Estates in the Middle Ages*, Oxford, 1977, 378). It is unclear what achievements or connections qualified him for this honour. The family had a strong military tradition. For evidence of their performance of miltary service, see PRO, C76/15 m. 20 (John Hemenhale, 1340); C76/38 m. 17 (Ralph Hemenhale, 1359); C61/82 m. 7 (Sir William Hemenhale, 1369). Perhaps Robert had a distinguished soldiering record, although there is no mention of him in the chronicles.

manors in dower.[94] Immediately afterwards, she married again. Her husband this time was Sir Reginald Braybrooke, a junior member of an important east-midland family distantly related to the princess of Wales. Joan had been negotiating with Sir Reginald's father, uncle, and brother for the sale of the de la Pole manors of Castle Ashby and Chadstone (Northants.) and Chesterton (Hunts.). Opportunely, when Hemenhale died, the Braybrookes won his widow's hand for Reginald, and the manors of Castle Ashby and Chadstone were settled on them and their male issue.[95]

Reginald was the longest surviving of Joan's husbands: he lived until 1405. Reginald's background lay in royal service. In the 1380s he had been taken on as an esquire of the household, perhaps as a result of his family connections, and in 1390 he was raised to the rank of knight. After his marriage, and consequent acquisition of an inheritance, however, he left the court and settled down to the life of a country gentleman.[96] He and his wife resided at Cooling: in 1396 Cobham had leased the estate to the couple, presumably after his retirement and entry into monastic surroundings.[97] Braybrooke, it seems, was readily absorbed into the ranks of Kent society.[98] In 1403 he was selected as one of the knights to represent the county at a great council, and in the following year he was elected an MP After 1399 he was regularly appointed to a range of local commissions. In 1400, 1402, and 1403 he acted as a commissioner of array, and from 1401 to his death he was a justice of the peace. After the resumption of hostilities with the French in 1403, he responded to the royal call to arms. In 1404 he served in an expedition at sea; and in the following year he accompanied Thomas of Lancaster to Flanders. On the latter occasion, during the unsuccessful attack on Sluys, he sustained a wound that was to prove fatal. Lingering for four months, he died at Middleburg on 20 September. His body, appropriately, was brought to Cobham for burial.

Joan's next husband was almost certainly found for her by the king.

---

[94] Butler, 'Robert Braybrooke, Bishop of London (1381–1404) and his Kinsmen', 94–5.

[95] *House of Commons*, ii, 349–50.

[96] However, he took part in Richard's 1394 expedition to Ireland: *CPR 1391–6*, 498.

[97] Hatfield House, Deed 78/9. In 1398 he obtained a royal grant of custody of the forfeited Cobham estates in Kent. These were to be restored in 1399 (*House of Commons*, ii, 350).

[98] Because of its proximity to London, Kent society was probably more open than society further to the north and west. An unusually large number of the county's MPs were comparative newcomers: *House of Commons*, i, 454. Braybrooke's arms appear several times in the impressive armorial of Kentish gentry society in the cloister vault of Canterbury cathedral: R. Griffin, 'The Heraldry in the Cloisters of the Cathedral Church of Christ at Canterbury', *Archaeologia*, 66 (1915–16), 465, 519, 526 (coats nos. 15, 403, 479). Two years before his death Braybrooke was admitted to the confraternity of Christ Church, Canterbury: BL, Arundel MS 68, fo. 53ᵛ.

Sir Nicholas Hawberk, a self-made man of apparently limited means, had begun his career, like Braybrooke, in the royal household. He first appears as a king's esquire around 1391, and he was knighted shortly after.[99] His origins and background are obscure. He cannot have been related to the Leicestershire gentry family of Hawberk, for his arms are different.[100] His name suggests that he was probably of German descent. His coat-of-arms has close affinities with some German blazons, and the triple mount and chapourny partition are better accommodated in the context of Rhenish than English heraldry.[101] A reasonable hypothesis may be to see him as a member of the German and Bohemian retinue that came to England in the wake of Richard II's marriage to Anne of Bohemia, the emperor's daughter.[102] If the case for his foreign origin is accepted, then he is probably to be identified with the 'Here Nikel Bergo' whom Richard retained in December 1393.[103] Whatever lands, grants, and offices he picked up in England, he owed to royal patronage. In 1396 Richard appointed him to the important offices of sheriff and constable of Flint.[104] Eight months later he was given the hand in marriage of Maud, widow of John, Lord Le Strange of Knockin (Salop)—a grant which strengthened his position in the Welsh marches.[105] In 1399,

[99] *CPR 1388–92*, 487; *1391–6*, 205. In Nov. 1390, as simply 'Nicholas Hawberk esquire' (not yet 'king's esquire'), he was pardoned at Baldwin Bereford's behest for a murder (*CPR 1388–92*, 319).

[100] The Leicestershire Hawberks bore *argent on a bend sable three knots of rings or* (J. Nichols, *The History and Antiquities of Leicestershire*, 4 vols.; London, 1795–1811, ii, pt 1, 350).

[101] I am grateful to John A. Goodall for advice on the Hawberk heraldry. The arms found on the brass today are *checky argent and gules, a chief chapourny gules and or*; Waller in his notes on Cobham described them as *checky argent and gules, a chief parted per wave, gules and or* (Church Notes, i, Society of Antiquaries MS 423). As noted by Glover, on the evidence of Hawberk's seal, they were *checky argent and gules, a chief nebulee per fess gules and or* (Nichols, 'Memorials of the Family of Cobham', 330). [102] Saul, *Richard II*, 92–3.

[103] *CPR 1391–6*, 344. This was a few months after he took part in a tournament at Smithfield: Waller, 'The Lords of Cobham', 90–1. It is true that the identification with 'Nikel Bergo' is apparently ruled out by the king's retention of 'Nicholas Hawberk, knight' ten months earlier, in February (ibid. 205). However, the difficulty is by no means as serious as it seems. In February this 'Nicholas Hawberk' had been retained at a fee of £40 per annum (ibid. 205). In January the following year, on surrender of these earlier letters, he was retained at a higher fee of 100 marks per annum (ibid. 352). Interestingly, the retention of 'Nikel Bergo' came only five weeks before this, on 18 Dec., and the fee awarded to him, as to 'Hawberk', was 100 marks. It is at least arguable that the grants refer to the same man. It may be that the two grants were enrolled in error: this was hardly unknown at the time. On the other hand, the repetition may have been deliberate. The grant to 'Bergo' laid down the condition that he perform liege homage to the king—for the obvious reason that he was an alien. This may explain why use was made of the German form of his name: to indicate why that stipulation was necessary. [104] *CPR 1396–9*, 49.

[105] H. Le Strange, *Le Strange Records: A Chronicle of the Early Le Stranges* (London, 1916), 323, 339. Richard also indicated his favour by granting him the 1,000 marks adjudged against James Clifford of Gloucestershire by the king's council: *CPR 1396–9*, 193. But whether he actually obtained this sum is questionable.

in common with many other of Richard's knights, he successfully managed the transition to Lancastrian service. The esteem in which he was held by the new king is indicated by the diplomatic tasks entrusted to him. In 1401 he accompanied Richard's widow, Isabelle, on her return to France, and in the following year, perhaps because of his German origin, he was made one of the escorts for Blanche, the king's daughter, on her journey to Germany to be married.[106] A few years before this, in September 1400, his wife had died. He was granted custody of her heir, with the prospect of political and financial gains that this offered.[107] But in 1405 he landed a much richer prize: the hand of Reginald Braybrooke's widow, Joan. The marriage was to be short lived, however. Nicholas died only two years later, in 1407.[108] Like his predecessor, he was brought for burial at Cobham; and there, in the chancel, his widow honoured him with what Waller considered 'about the finest military brass of the time' (fig. 19).[109]

At the beginning of 1408 Joan married again. Her next husband—her fourth—was a Herefordshire knight, Sir John Oldcastle of Almeley. The match may well have been arranged by the Prince of Wales. In 1400 Owen Glendower had sparked a massive rebellion against the English in Wales, and John had actively assisted the prince in restoring order; it is possible that Joan's hand was his reward.[110] John's paternal inheritance in Herefordshire was a small one, consisting of little more than the manor of Almeley. However, by his coup in securing Joan's hand his prospects were transformed. Joan herself had only shortly before succeeded to the Cobham estates, and John was summoned to parliament in her right as Lord Cobham. His career to this time had been marked chiefly by soldierly prowess and zeal. But alongside his militarism went a deeply heterodox piety. Herefordshire and the Marches were strong Lollard country. Several Lollard proselytizers had been active there, and a supporting network had developed among the gentry. Oldcastle had almost certainly embraced Lollardy by the time of his marriage: it has been suggested that he derived his beliefs from William Swinderby, who had

---

[106] Waller, 'The Lords of Cobham', 90. [107] *CPR 1399–1401*, 424.

[108] In consequence, Hawberk made little or no impact on Kent landed society. His arms were not included in the grand armorial of the cloister vault of Canterbury cathedral.

[109] Waller, 'The Lords of Cobham', 91; for the date of the brass, see below, 114. The two early fifteenth-century tournament helmets which hang in the chancel at Cobham are usually associated with Braybrooke and Hawberk. For these, see below, 100, n. 71.

[110] Accounts of Oldcastle's career are found in W. T. Waugh, 'Sir John Oldcastle', *EHR*, 20 (1905), 434–56, 637–58; K. B. McFarlane, *John Wycliffe and the Beginnings of English Nonconformity* (London, 1952); and, most recently, *House of Commons*, iii, 866–9.

preached at Almeley while he was a boy.[111] By the autumn of 1410 he was in active correspondence with some of the leading reformers in Bohemia; he even wrote to the Bohemian king himself urging resistance to the Antichrist. By 1410, however, the authorities were becoming aware of his activities. In April of that year Archbishop Arundel had sent word to the prior of Rochester that a Lollard chaplain was living with Oldcastle at Cooling and preaching heresy in the churches of Cooling, Halstow, and Hoo. A ban was imposed on the preacher, but a little oddly two days later it was lifted, perhaps to allow the marriage of Oldcastle's step-daughter, Joan.[112] In March 1413 Oldcastle found himself in more serious trouble. During a search of an illuminator's shop in London a number of heretical tracts belonging to him were uncovered. On 23 September he was put on trial in St Paul's and, being confirmed as obdurate, was excommunicated and handed to the secular arm for burning. His former patron the prince, now Henry V, was, however, still hopeful of a change of heart. At his especial request, the authorities granted Oldcastle a forty-day respite, during which he was confined in the Tower. But on the night of 19 October, apparently with outside help, Oldcastle escaped. He found refuge with a Smithfield bookseller's, and from his hide-out plotted a hare-brained scheme to capture the king on the night of 9–10 January at Eltham. News of his plans leaked out, and the rising was nipped in the bud. On Twelfth Night, as the rebels converged on St Giles Fields, royal troops rounded them up. Oldcastle himself escaped, and for the next few years lived a life on the run in Herefordshire. He was finally arrested in September 1417 near Welshpool and taken to London and burned.

Joan's fifth and last husband was another soldier. This was Sir John Harpedon, scion of a Poitevin noble family and probably a descendant of the Sir John Harpedon who had been seneschal of Saintonge in the 1380s.[113] In the absence of a previous connection between Joan and her husband, it is likely that royal patronage again explains the match. Harpedon was a well connected man and appears to have had ties with the court; Duke Humphrey of Gloucester was one of his feoffees.[114] Like Joan's earlier husbands, Harpedon was practised in arms. In 1415 he served on the Agincourt campaign, and in 1417 he joined Henry V's invasion of Normandy.[115] A lengthy spell in France appears to be implied by

---

[111] *House of Commons*, iii, 867.   [112] i.e. Joan Braybrooke. For the marriage, see below, 31.
[113] For his career and possible kinship ties, see below, 216–19.   [114] PRO, C139/86/28.
[115] N. H. Nicolas, *History of the Battle of Agincourt* (London, 1833, repr. 1971), 380; PRO, E101/51/2.

his virtual absence from English records of the 1420s. John survived his elderly wife by a little over four years. The latter died on 13 January 1434, and her husband in May 1438.[116] John was sufficiently distinguished—or sufficiently well connected—to be buried in Westminster Abbey, where his brass remains (fig. 41).[117]

Joan had numerous issue by her first three husbands, among them a couple of sons by Braybrooke and another by Hawberk. However, only one of the brood survived to adulthood: Joan, a daughter by Braybrooke, who became her mother's heiress. The responsibility of finding a husband for her was undertaken by Oldcastle. By an agreement made on 20 February 1410 Joan was contracted to marry the son of a west-country knight, Thomas Brooke. Thomas's father, another Thomas, gave an undertaking to pay Oldcastle 1,300 marks on the day of the wedding, which was to take place before Whit Sunday, and in return the Brookes were assured that Joan Braybrooke, who was aged six, would inherit her mother's possessions.[118] Accordingly, on her mother's death a quarter of a century later Joan took the Cobham and de la Pole estates to her husband, who from then on was styled Lord Cobham *jure uxoris*.

The Brookes were to be the lords of Cobham for the next 170 years. For most of the first half of that time their association with Cobham, indeed with Kent generally, was much looser than their predecessors'. They chiefly resided at their traditional seats, Holditch and Weycroft, in east Devon. Thomas's continuing west-country ties are indicated by his office-holding appointments: he was a justice of the peace in Somerset from 1422 to 1433 and in Devon from 1431 till his death; and he was a tax assessor in Devon in 1436.[119] Not surprisingly, when he died he was buried in the west country—in the parish church at Thorncombe (Dorset), close to his parents' tomb.

Thomas's son and heir Edward, the 2nd Lord, played no more prominent a role in Kent life than his father had. The focus of his interests remained in the west country. In 1439 and 1442 he was an MP for Somerset, and in the 1450s he was an active supporter of the earl of Devon in his campaign against his local rival, William, Lord Bonville.[120]

---

[116] PRO, C139/86/28: not 1458, as Waller, 'The Lords of Cobham', 99.
[117] For discussion of the brass, see below, 219.
[118] Nichols, 'Memorials of the Family of Cobham', 392; *House of Commons*, ii, 375–6.
[119] Ibid. 375.
[120] J. C. Wedgwood, *History of Parliament, 1439–1509: Biographies* (London, 1936), 115–16; R. L. Storey, *The End of the House of Lancaster* (London, 1966), 89. In his youth he had fought in France: he had been on the coronation expedition of 1430: PRO, E404/46/226.

In his later years he identified strongly with the Yorkists.[121] It was only in the time of Edward's son and successor, John, that the Brookes took a closer interest in their Kent inheritance. John's social and marital ties led him to look eastwards: his two wives came from the eastern counties. Moreover, he was involved in Kent political life: from 1483 he was a justice of the peace in the county.[122] Interestingly, he was the first of the Brooke line to be buried at Cobham: in 1506 he commissioned a brass there to himself and his second wife (fig. 21). After a break of some sixty years the link between Cobham and its lords had been re-established.

Although, by the fifteenth century, the main line of the Cobhams had died out, the 'Cobham' surname was to live on in the junior branches. Until the 3rd Lord's time the Cobhams had been a prolific brood. In every generation there had been three, four, or more sons. It seems to have been usual in the family for the younger sons to be endowed with land. It is true that in 1276 John Cobham 'the younger' had sought to limit subdivision and to preserve the core inheritance intact by securing a royal charter disgavelling his lands in Kent.[123] None the less, he appears to have been willing to partition any gavelkind lands which he acquired subsequent to the charter—as his successors were to do after him.[124] It is also noticeable that partitions continued to be made of the gavelkind lands held by collateral branches. In 1359 and 1362 multiple partitions were made of the lands of the Cobhams of Randall.[125] So long as the Cobham clan acquired new lands—which they did for most of the period—it was possible for younger sons' expectations to be fulfilled.

Several of the Cobham junior branches became distinguished in their own right. The successful establishment of these branches owed much to marriage to heiresses. Two of the younger sons of Sir John de Cobham

---

[121] In 1452 he was involved in York's attempted *putsch* and was in the duke's retinue when the latter presented his petition to the king at Dartford. In late Jan. 1461 he was included in a list of Yorkist-inclined lords which the Yorkists compiled for their short-term political purposes. Six months before, in July, he had been involved with Salisbury in the Yorkists' assault on the Tower: R. A. Griffiths, *The Reign of King Henry VI* (London, 1981), 692–700, 863; C. Richmond, 'The Nobility and the Wars of the Roses. The Parliamentary Session of January 1461', *Parliamentary History*, 18 (1999), 261–9.

[122] His first wife was Eleanor, daughter of—Anstell, of Suffolk, and his second wife, Margaret, daughter of Edward Nevill, Lord Abergavenny (*Complete Peerage*, ii, 346–7). He served, with Abergavenny, as a JP in Kent for most of the reigns of Richard III and Henry VII (*CPR 1476–85*, 562–3; *1485–94*, 490; *1494–1509*, 644); he was also a commissioner of array in 1490 (*CPR 1485–94*, 322).

[123] The charter is *CChR 1257–1300*, 198; copied in Hatfield House, MS 306, fos. 29ᵛ–30ʳ.

[124] Nichols, 'Memorials of the Family of Cobham', 330.   [125] Ibid. 335, 340.

'the elder' (d. *c*.1251) did particularly well for themselves. Henry, John's second son by his first marriage, married Joan, one of the two Penchester coheiresses, and in so doing acquired a substantial inheritance based on Allington, near Maidstone.[126] Reginald, a younger son by John's second marriage, won the hand of Joan de Hever, heiress to the Sterborough estate in Lingfield.[127] Henry and Reginald both established long-lived lines. Henry's branch based itself at Randall in Shorne, near Cobham. Henry himself was an active figure in Kent affairs, serving as sheriff of Kent in 1314 and, before that, as keeper of the coasts.[128] Stephen, his son, made a name for himself nationally and was the receipient of a summons to the Lords from 1326 to his death.[129] Later generations failed to maintain Stephen's position among the peers, but were still active locally. John (d. 1361) served as a Member of Parliament several times and his son Thomas (d. 1394) as both a sheriff and Member of Parliament.[130] The family flourished in the male line until the 1420s, when their estates passed to the Moresbys.

The story of the Cobhams of Sterborough, in broad trajectory, resembles that of the Cobhams of Randall.[131] The Sterborough Cobhams, like their kinsmen of Randall, were for a while numbered among the lesser peerage. Reginald, the distinguished war captain of Edward III, received regular summonses to parliament as a lord; and his son briefly received summonses in the 1370s. Later generations, however, failed to maintain their predecessors' distinction, and the family fell back into the gentry. For the most part, the Sterborough branch were less productive of sons than the other Cobham branches. None the less, they kept going in the male line for nearly three centuries. On the death of Thomas, the last male, in 1471, a daughter carried their estates to the Burghs of Gainsborough (Lincs.).[132]

The longest surviving of the junior branches was one which never attained the fame and distinction of these others—the Cobhams of Beluncle. Henry, 1st Lord Cobham, had granted the manor of Beluncle,

---

[126] G. O. Bellewes, 'The Cobhams and Moresbys of Rundale and Allington', *AC*, 29 (1911), 154–63.

[127] *VCH Surrey* (4 vols.; London, 1902–12), iv, 304; see below, 123.

[128] Moor, *Knights of Edward I*, i, 218.

[129] Ibid. 219; *Complete Peerage*, iii, 351–2. He died in 1332.

[130] Bellewes, 'The Cobhams and Moresbys of Cobham and Allington', 156–7; *House of Commons*, ii, 608–9; F. Hull and R. A. Keen, 'English Politics and the Sheriff of Kent, 1378', *AC*, 71 (1957), 206–13.   [131] The family are discussed below, Ch. 6.

[132] Anne married Sir Edward Burgh.

in Hoo St Werburgh (Kent), to Thomas, his second son, probably in the 1320s.[133] The endowment was not large: apart from Beluncle itself, it probably only comprised lands in West Chalk.[134] The inadequacy of the endowment led to tension between Thomas and his elder brother on Henry's death. Thomas, keen to augment his holdings, laid claim to the manor of Chisbury and the advowson of Clyffe Pypard (Wilts.), which his brother had inherited; indeed, he appears to have occupied Chisbury. John fiercely resisted his brother's claims. In a statement which he drew up of his case, he maintained that his marriage to Joan Beauchamp had been contracted on the condition that the core inheritance was preserved intact—adding, for good measure, that Henry had given Thomas a £10 annuity to supplement his landed income.[135] The case was submitted to the arbitration of Reginald, Lord Cobham of Sterborough, the prior of Rochester, 'and other good men', and settled, so it appears, largely in John's favour.[136] Thereafter, relations between the two families became more amicable. Members of the Beluncle line frequently interacted with, or appeared alongside, their kinsmen of Cobham. Reginald, the rector of Cooling, was commonly employed as a Cobham feoffee, and his elder brother, less often, as a charter witness.[137] Unlike the other Cobham collaterals, the Cobhams of Beluncle were never active in county affairs. Perhaps their modest landed endowment made it difficult for them to be so.[138] In the 1470s Thomas Cobham served as a justice of the peace and a commissioner of array, and a century later one John Cobham as a justice of the peace and commissioner of sewers.[139] But from the mid-fifteenth century their activities centred increasingly on the

[133] The earliest reference to Thomas Cobham's presence at Hoo is provided by a charter of 16 Edw. II (1322–3): Nichols, 'Memorials of the Family of Cobham', 333.

[134] CKS, U601/T11; U601/T13/1 and 2. By the fifteenth century the family also had lands at Frindsbury, near Strood: BL, Harley Ch. 47 H 49.

[135] BL, Harley Roll C 27: a statement of John, Lord Cobham's grievances against his brother. John says that payment of the marriage portion of £300 (not £400 as in Nichols, 'Memorials of the Family of Cobham', 325) was conditional on preservation of the inheritance.

[136] The statement of John's grievances in BL, Harley Roll C 27, is endorsed: 'Et acorde fust devaunt Mons Reynald de Cobham le priour de Roucestr' et aultres bones gentz par assent le dit Sr Thomas (Cobham) qe le dit Johan deveroyt avoir restitucioun de biens lour piere auxi com dite due aly.' This is a reference to one of John's subsidiary complaints—namely, that he had been distrained by the bailiffs of the sheriff of Kent for debts which, in his view, were owed by his brother. Clearly the decision on this matter had gone in his favour. No reference is made to the main issue at stake—the tenure of Chisbury and the advowson of Clyffe Pypard. Chisbury, however, descended to John's son, John, the 3rd Lord (CIPM, xix, no. 364).

[137] BL, Harley Chs. 48 E 24; 48 E 36; Nichols, 'Memorials of the Family of Cobham', 335, 338.

[138] Although the family had acquired lands at Frindsbury, near Strood, their endowment was still small (BL, Harley Ch. 47 H 49).

[139] CPR 1467–77, 352, 618; 1560–3, 438; 1563–6, 23; 1569–72, 225.

city of Rochester. In 1459–60 Thomas Cobham served as a warden of Rochester bridge, and in the 1570s a descendant of his was entrusted, alongside others, with enquiring into, and repairing, the bridge's structure.[140] In the 1620s John Cobham, the last of his line, was an alderman and mayor of Rochester. The family's links with Cobham itself had become a thing of the past.

With John's death in the 1630s the line established by Serlo, the freeholder of Cobham, came to an end.[141] In their heyday, in the thirteenth and fourteenth centuries, the Cobhams had been one of the most active and important families in Kent. Their skill and versatility as administrators had enabled them to establish themselves in landed society. In the absence of a secular magnate of consequence locally, they quickly assumed a leading role in county affairs. Thanks to their abundance of male issue, they established a remarkable network of cadet branches. By the fourteenth century, after the cadets themselves had sprung sub-branches, the family had acquired the character of a clan. Through the operation of gavelkind, proprietorship in Kent was anyway widely dispersed; and among the Cobhams partitioning continued by mutual consent, even after the disgavelling of the family's estates. The distinct clannishness of the Cobhams was reinforced by a high degree of cohesion between the various kin. Intra-family disputes were rare; and, when they occurred, they were quickly settled. Solidarity, not division, was the hallmark of their mutual relations.[142] The burial in the mausoleum at Cobham, alongside each other, of so many Cobham kinfolk affords powerful witness to the cohesion of the family and their assumption of a group identity.

---

[140] Nichols, 'Memorials of the Family of Cobham', 334; *CPR 1569–72*, 225, 278; *1572–5*, 194.
[141] Hasted, *History of Kent*, iv, 171–2.
[142] In this respect they were like the early Nevilles: Young, *Making of the Neville Family*, 3, 142.

⇨ 3 ⇦

Cobham Church and College

THE association between the Cobham family and the village from which they took their name was a very close one. Even after the 3rd Lord had moved his residence to Cooling, which he had done by the 1380s, it was to Cobham that the Cobhams were invariably brought for burial.

The clearest expression of this atavistic tie between family and village is to be found in Cobham parish church. With its array of family brasses and its rich chancel fittings provided by the 3rd Lord, Cobham church comes across strongly as the Cobhams' church. But it needs to be asked whether the Cobhams presence here was always so strong. After all, the Cobhams were a family of relatively late origin. When did their association with the church begin? And how far is their influence to be seen in its architectural development?

Cobham church, as we see it today, is a large, dignified building (fig. 1). Its stateliness is enhanced by its lofty setting. Situated at the highest point of the churchyard, it dominates the western approach to the village. From the north it presents a particularly distinguished aspect. Tower, porch, chancel, and aisle come together in a bold grouping of masses. The dominant impression is one of length. The chancel extends to four bays. The nave appears low by comparison; unusually for a Kent church it has a clerestory, but this is hidden behind the steeply pitched aisle roof. At the western end, a vertical corrective is provided by the boldly projecting tower, with its corner turret, and the north porch. The porch, which is of two storeys, the lower one vaulted, affords the main entrance.

The origins and early history of the church are obscure. If, as may have been the case, there was a pre-Conquest church on the site, no trace of it is visible above ground. The oldest part of the present fabric—an arch with an austere impost which was discovered south of the chancel arch in 1860—is probably twelfth century in date.[1] In 1133 Henry I granted the church to the Cluniac foundation of Bermondsey.[2] It is likely that Bermondsey substantially rebuilt the church on taking possession. There are signs that the new structure was of some size. The fact that the arch discovered in 1860 was off-centre suggests that it provided access to an aisle. If that was the case, the nave could have been as large as its later-medieval successor. It is possible that we should envisage another patron lending support to the work: perhaps a layman. Generally in Kent, church-building was associated with the presence or establishment of manorial lordship; and this may have been the case at Cobham. Unfortunately, it is not known if there was an early medieval manorial dwelling near the church, but it is conceivable that there was; the later history of the site certainly lends support to the idea. In the 1370s John, 3rd Lord Cobham, arranged for his new chantry college to be built immediately to the south of the church; and simultaneously he embarked on the construction of a new residence at Cooling, five miles to the north: a coincidence of timing which suggests that the reason for the building of Cooling could have been the loss of his property at Cobham.[3] By the mid-sixteenth century the focus of lordship at Cobham had moved to the other end of the village, to the site of the present-day Cobham Hall. The fabric of this splendid house dates entirely from the mid-sixteenth century and later. There is no evidence of a high-status residence on the site in the Middle Ages. The balance of probability must be that in the twelfth century or earlier the lord had lived a mile or so to the west, near the church. Church and manor house could have stood together as twin symbols of secular and ecclesiastical authority.

Much the most memorable part of Cobham church is the chancel (fig. 2). This striking composition is a high-quality work of thirteenth-century Gothic. It is grandiose in conception—some 50 ft long and over 20 ft wide. Inside, it is airy and spacious.[4] Laterally, it is lit by five single

[1] The reused Roman brick jamb at the east end of the south aisle may indicate a date as early as the eleventh century for the south-eastern corner of the nave. I am very grateful to Tim Tatton-Brown for this observation. [2] *Registrum Roffense*, 229.

[3] At least part of the site of the college was represented by the parish cemetery. We know this because, when the building of the college was planned, the master and chaplains petitioned Bermondsey priory for permission to build on the cemetery (see below, 46). However, this does not mean that the entire site was taken from the cemetery. Part could have been demesne land.

[4] The present appearance of the chancel does not entirely correspond to its appearance in the thirteenth century. The likelihood is that, when the chancel was first built, it had a steeply pitched roof. It seems that the walls were raised, and the present low-pitched roof installed, in the late fourteenth or the fifteenth century.

FIG 1. Cobham church from the north

lancets and at the end by a group of three lancets; a connecting hood links the side windows. The materials used are flint with Caen and Reigate stone dressings (and Kent ragstone for later embellishments).[5] As Larry Hoey has shown, large-scale chancels are a characteristic of Kent architecture in the late twelfth and thirteenth centuries.[6] There are particularly fine examples at Westwell, Cheriton, Stockbury, and Eastry.[7] Many of these chancels were commissioned by ecclesiastical patrons. Christ Church, Canterbury, was responsible for the one at Westwell and the archbishop of Canterbury for that at Eastry. It may be that monastic

[5] In the course of building work on the chancel in 1999 blocks of tufa were also found to be incorporated in the exterior north wall; this presumably represents reused material. Tufa is quarried in Kent in the Leeds–East Malling area. A curiosity of the chancel is that, whereas on the north side it is supported by five external buttresses, on the south there are none. From the late fourteenth century support was provided by the archway and east wall of the college. But these structures were not present in the previous century when the chancel was built. Could some now demolished structure have abutted? I am grateful to Bill Pritchett for these observations.

[6] L. R. Hoey, 'Style, Patronage and Artistic Creativity in Kent Parish Church Architecture: c. 1180–c. 1260', AC, 115 (1995), 45–70.

[7] A scarcely inferior example is very close to Cobham, at Cooling. Here the lower parts of the chancel walls are decorated with a series of arches on marble shafts springing from marble benches. On the south side the arches run straight on with three trefoiled sedilia and a fine double piscina. A date of c.1260 is suggested: Newman, West Kent and the Weald, 239.

FIG 2. Cobham church: interior of the chancel, looking west to the nave

patronage accounts for the scale of the Cobham chancel. The Cluniacs, who formed the Bermondsey community, had a distinct penchant for architectural splendour. On the other hand, there are aspects of the design which raise questions about monastic involvement. Although the chancel is spacious, it lacks the richness of some of the chancels associated with the monasteries. It had a fine double piscina with dog-tooth ornament (later replaced), but there were apparently few other lavish fittings. A monastic patron would probably have looked for something richer in effect. Conceivably, the spur to rebuilding came less from the Bermondsey community than from a local proprietor, perhaps one of the Cobhams. Whether or not such a suggestion convinces depends on the view taken of the likely date of the work. The shortage of architectural details makes precise dating difficult. It is conceivable that the fabric was begun as early as c.1220. On the other hand, as Tim Tatton-Brown has suggested, it could be as late as the 1240s or 1250s.[8] If the earlier date is accepted, then the Cobhams' involvement can probably be ruled out, for the family would not have been rich enough by that time. However, if the later date is preferred, then family involvement is a possibility—but only a possibility. The task of maintaining the chancel in this

[8] Lecture at Cobham church, 2 May 1998.

period was held to lie with the clergy, and any layman wishing to leave his mark on a fabric would be more likely to have built a side chapel or aisle. Although there are thirteenth-century grave slabs in the chancel today, these probably came from another part of the church.[9] There is no evidence that, at the time of rebuilding, the chancel was conceived as a mausoleum.

The rebuilding of the chancel formed part of a much larger programme of works on the church. Shortly after the chancel was finished, work began on the nave. A relatively modest arcade of four bays was built, probably on the old foundations (fig. 2). The work is humbler in scale than the earlier work in the chancel, and is presumably by a different mason. There are low round piers and arches with two hollow chamfers. The north arcade appears to be earlier than the south. The aisles, the outer walls of which were later rebuilt, appear to be of the original width. The north aisle is wider than the south. At the east end of the south aisle is a thirteenth-century piscina. This feature points to the possibility of a family chapel here. A family like the Cobhams is more likely to have been involved in the rebuilding of this part of the church than the chancel.[10]

By the early fourteenth century the condition of parts of the fabric was deteriorating. In March 1327 there was a meeting in the church at which the prior of Bermondsey was ordered by the bishop of Rochester, Hamo de Hethe, to undertake all necessary repairs to the chancel and to remedy its deficiency in books and vestments.[11] Sir John de Cobham, Henry's son and heir, and other parishioners attended the meeting.[12] It may have been on Cobham's initiative that a programme of embellishment was initiated in the chancel. In the nave vestry at Cobham is a series of fragmentary sculptures—three large female heads and eight smaller incomplete figures—found in the south-east corner of the chancel at the restoration of 1860.[13] Some of the sculptures are to be associated with John, 3rd Lord Cobham's, embellishment of the church in the 1380s. Others, however, have an earlier look. The three female heads, which are particularly fine, are comparable in character to corbel heads in the nave

[9] The slabs are discussed below, 81.

[10] Another possibility is the north aisle. This is very wide, suggesting that it replaces an earlier chapel at the east end of its predecessor.

[11] *Registrum Hamonis de Hethe*, i, 172. The letter refers to the prior of 'Levesham' (i.e. Lewisham). This is clearly a mistake for Bermondsey.

[12] Henry himself was still alive, but elderly and apparently living in retirement in Somerset. John was already assuming leadership of the family.

[13] For the 1860 restoration, see *The Ecclesiologist*, 24 (1863), 314.

of St Albans Abbey datable to c.1325.[14] It seems likely that they came from a reredos which included tabernacle work with figures of various sizes under canopies. John, the future 2nd Lord, is not otherwise known as a patron of art, and for much of his career he was relatively inactive.[15] But it is possible that he is to be associated with the programme of minor embellishment and improvement initiated in the 1320s.

Despite Sir John de Cobham's involvement in the meeting in 1327, the Cobham family had no proprietary rights over the church; nor were they accorded a formal role in its life. The church was a property of Bermondsey priory; and the priory appointed the vicar and collected the great tithes. The Cobhams' commitment to the church may well have been increasing at this time, and family burials may have been made in the side aisles.[16] None the less, it was not until 1362 that the family's relationship with the church was to undergo a fundamental change. In this year John, the 3rd Lord, founded Cobham college.

A college was a form of chantry. The purpose of foundations of this sort was to provide perpetual post-obit intercession for the souls of the deceased and their kin.[17] Since the twelfth century, the belief had increasingly gained favour that the regular celebration of masses could shorten the sufferings of the soul in purgatory. Accordingly, it became the practice for those who could afford it to endow masses for their benefit. The less affluent would generally establish a small endowment for a chaplain for a term of years, while the better-off would offer a more lavish endowment for a chantry in perpetuity—and would probably provide a chapel to go with it. Lord Cobham, being a wealthier patron, planned on the very grandest scale. He endowed not one priest but a whole community: a college, in other words. The terms 'chantry' and

[14] J. Alexander and P. Binski (eds.), *Age of Chivalry: Art in Plantagenet England, 1200–1400* (London, 1987), no. 508. See also E. S. Prior and A. Gardner, *An Account of Medieval Figure Sculpture in England* (Cambridge, 1912), 360, where a date of c.1320 is suggested and the sculptures are compared to those on the Rochester chapter doorway of c.1340.

[15] For this John, see above, 20.

[16] Joan de Cobham's brass of c.1305 (M.S. I) now lies in the chancel with the others, but it is conceivable that this brass and the now lost brass of her husband were originally laid elsewhere in the church and moved to the chancel by the 3rd Lord. This matter is discussed below, 80.

[17] For medieval chantries, see K. L. Wood-Legh, *Perpetual Chantries in Britain* (Cambridge, 1965); G. H. Cook, *Medieval Chantries and Chantry Chapels*, 2nd edn. (London, 1963); C. R. Burgess, '"A Fond Thing Vainly Imagined"', in S. Wright (ed.), *Parish, Church and People* (Leicester, 1988), 56–85; idem, '"For the Increase of Divine Service": Chantries in the Parish in Late Medieval Bristol', *JEH*, 36 (1985), 48–65; P. W. Fleming, 'Charity, Faith, and the Gentry of Kent, 1422–1529', in T. Pollard (ed.), *Property and Politics: Essays in Later Medieval English History*, (Gloucester, 1984), 36–58.

'college' were used interchangeably in the letters patent issued in his favour.[18]

Lord Cobham initiated the establishment of his college in 1362. In November that year he obtained letters patent from the king allowing him to found a chantry community and to assign for its maintenance the manor of West Chalk.[19] John had succeeded to his inheritance seven years earlier. The spur to his action was probably the death in October 1361 of his cousin Reginald, 1st Lord Cobham, of Sterborough.[20] Reginald was one of the most distinguished members of the Cobham line. He had enjoyed a brilliant career in France; he was a close associate of the king and the Black Prince, and he had been rewarded with election to the Order of the Garter. John, Lord Cobham, whose career was to follow a similar course, probably greatly admired him. The two branches of the family were on cordial terms. Very likely it was the sense of loss caused by Reginald's death which prompted John to think of commemoration. The college was to be Reginald's memorial (although he was himself interred at Lingfield).

However, there may well have been a secondary reason for John's action. In the previous generation the Cobhams of Cobham had been eclipsed in fame by their Sterborough kin. John's father, the 2nd Lord, had enjoyed a distinctly lacklustre career. He had taken only a small part in the French war; and his record of service in Scotland had been undistinguished. Only in the final years of his life was he summoned to parliament as a peer. Beside Reginald he cut a sadly unimpressive figure. John's decision to establish the college may have been undertaken partly at least to bolster his family's honour and prestige. It was an act consciously magnificent in conception. The depth and intensity of John's piety need hardly be doubted; but as so often with the gentry, that piety was suffused with worldliness. By presenting himself as a founder he believed he was adding to the family's stock of honour and fame.

Lord Cobham's plans for his foundation were highly ambitious. Generally, a lord of his rank would be content to endow a chaplain or two to celebrate masses in a transept or side chapel. But what Cobham called into being was a monastery in miniature. It is conceivable that Cobham was influenced by Edward III's grandiose foundation of the college of

---

[18] 'Chantry' is used in *CPR 1361–4*, 265; *1364–7*, 387; *1367–70*, 250, 277, 282–3; *1370–4*, 122; *1377–81*, 373; *1391–6*, 698; and 'college' in *CPR 1367–70*, 98, 218; *1374–7*, 117, 381; *1377–81*, 383, 543; *1381–5*, 276; *1388–92*, 131, 221–1; *1391–6*, 184. The term 'college' appears to become the more commonly used one.

[19] *CPR 1361–4*, 265.   [20] Reginald's career is discussed in detail, below, Ch. 6.

St George at Windsor.[21] Cobham, who had been a royal banneret earlier in his career, was close to the court and would have been familiar with the king's plans.[22] His original scheme of 1362 was for an establishment of five chaplains, one of whom was to be warden or 'master'.[23] But gradually over the years the size of the establishment was increased. In 1389, following the acquisition by the college of more lands, the five priests rose to seven, with two chaplains temporal and two servers in addition.[24] Later still, the number of priests rose to eleven. The master was to undertake the duties of the former vicar.[25]

Lord Cobham's initial endowment of the community was modest. For a man of baronial standing, his estates were by no means large.[26] The most valuable property which he made over was his manor of West Chalk, on the Thames near Cobham, and this was supplemented by lands and rents in Cobham itself, East Chalk, and Hoo St Werburgh. The income from these properties, which probably amounted to some £60, was soon found to be insufficient, however, for declining rents and the rising cost of labour eroded their value.[27] Accordingly, in 1367 the college obtained a licence from the king to acquire further lands and rents to the value of £40 per annum.[28] A number of purchases were made in consequence of this grant. In 1369 the college acquired a tract of marsh in Upchurch and some lands in Shorne, and two years later some areas of pasture and woodland in Shorne.[29] But from the mid-1370s there was a gradual shift from the buying of land to the acquisition of advowsons. In 1376 Lord Cobham paved the way by obtaining a licence from the king to alienate any two advowsons in his possession.[30] A couple of

---

[21] According to the statutes of 30 Nov. 1352, the clerical establishment was to consist of a warden and 12 other canons, 13 priest vicars, and 4 clerks. Six choristers, 26 poor knights, and a verger completed the foundation (A. K. B. Roberts, *St George's Chapel, Windsor Castle, 1348–1416: A Study in Early Collegiate Administration*, Windsor, 1947, 6–7).

[22] PRO, E101/392/12, fo. 40ᵛ.

[23] The foundation deed has not survived, but much of its text appears to be reproduced in a formal letter of Bishop Brinton of Rochester of 23 Mar. 1388: A. A. Arnold, 'Cobham College', *AC*, 27 (1905), 64–95.

[24] The chaplains temporal were of a different status from their peers. While performing much the same duties as the other chaplains, they served only at the will of the master and senior chaplains and had no say in the affairs of the college. The 'aquibajuli', or holy-water servers, were scholars who studied at the school attached to the college (Arnold, 'Cobham College', 65–6). It is tempting to see the hierarchy of chaplains as imitative of Windsor.

[25] The master was nominated by the prior and convent of Bermondsey: ibid. 64.

[26] For a discussion of the Cobham estates, see below, Appendix.

[27] In a petition to the pope, the master and chaplains complained of diminished income brought about 'by pestilence and other misfortunes': *Records of Gravesend*, i, ed. W. H. Hart (Gravesend, 1878), 44.

[28] *CPR 1364–7*, 387.   [29] *CPR 1367–70*, 277, 282–3.   [30] *CPR 1374–7*, 381.

years later he made over the advowson of Horton Kirby, a church some five miles to the west of Cobham, which he had earlier purchased from the Kirby family;[31] and in 1380 he made a complex set of arrangements for the college to acquire the church (as well as the manor) of Chalk by means of an exchange with Norwich cathedral priory.[32] In 1383 he also secured for the college the church of Rolvenden (Kent), which belonged to the Sussex knight Sir Richard de Poynings and his feoffees, appropriation being completed in 1389.[33] In November of this latter year he made over to the college what was probably his final grant—that of the church of East Tilbury (Essex), which he acquired from the Essex knight Sir William Coggeshall.[34] All these grants, with various others, received confirmation in royal letters patent in 1390.[35]

The gradual rise in the college's income can be traced in the scattered accounts which survive from these years. In the early days of its existence the college had an annual income of some £80; in 1365–6 the precise figure was £83. 18s. 10d.[36] The greater part of these receipts was represented by rents and farms from the manor of West Chalk, which came to £44—with sales of marshland adding another £6. Forty years later, however, the picture was very different. By 1402–3 the college's annual income had risen to over £200.[37] The profits of the appropriated churches accounted for the greater part of this. Cobham church was worth £11, Horton Kirby £31, Chalk £24, Tilbury £19, and Rolvenden £26; altogether, the churches produced some £110 a year. The college's income from its rents at West Chalk and elsewhere was still high at £92; sales of corn accounted for another £15, and cash in hand another £12. In the early 1400s the college's income probably reached its peak. Twenty years later, it was beginning to decline. In 1425 the profits of churches came to only £86, and rents and farms to £62. Total receipts barely

---

[31] *CPR 1377–81*, 373; *Records of Gravesend*, 44. Appropriation was completed in the following year.
[32] *CPR 1377–81*, 543; *Records of Gravesend*, 51. In the 1370s Lord Cobham had granted his manor of Martham (Norfolk) to the college, and the college now surrendered this to Norwich cathedral priory in return for the advowson of Chalk, which the priory held.
[33] *CPR 1381–5*, 276; *Records of Gravesend*, 46; BL, Harley Ch. 54 I 32.
[34] *CPR 1388–92*, 131; *Records of Gravesend*, 45. William Coggeshall was an associate of Cobham. Cobham paid £124 to him for the benefice: *House of Commons*, ii, 617. Tilbury, although on the opposite bank of the Thames, is immediately opposite Gravesend and is thus not very far from Cobham as the crow flies.
[35] Ibid. pp. 221–2.   [36] BL, Harley Roll C 20.
[37] BL, Harley Roll C 22. Total receipts in the account came to £231. 0s. 10d., but of this £12. 8s. 3d. was represented by 'arrears'. 'Arrears' might be cash in hand rather than 'arrears' in the modern sense.

exceeded £165.[38] In the later fifteenth century, income levels were almost certainly some way below those of earlier years; on the eve of the Disso-lution gross receipts were a mere £142.[39] On the other hand, there is no evidence that the college was ever afflicted by serious indebtedness. The chaplains, it seems, managed to live within their means. Cobham college, while hardly a wealthy institution, was never an encumbered one.

In the early days of the college the chaplains probably lived in the building to the north-east of the churchyard known as 'the Stone House'. Although much altered in the eighteenth century, this is essen-tially a late medieval hall-house with flanking wings. However, as the size of the community grew, the accommodation within its walls proved insufficient. Accordingly, in 1370 the master and brethren applied to Bermondsey priory to build 'suitable houses and dwellings' on the site to the south of the church occupied by the parish cemetery. The prior acceded to their request subject to the proviso that 'the processional way on the south of the church is for ever preserved for the parishioners, especially at the time of Matins, Mass and Vespers'.[40] When the college buildings were erected, a space was duly left. The route in question was presumably the one followed by the parishioners in the processions of Holy Week, Rogationtide, and other feast days.[41] Christopher Hussey suggested that, as they made their way round the churchyard, people sprinkled holy water on the graves of the deceased.[42]

The buildings of the former college are now occupied by the almshouses of the so-called 'New College' of Cobham. This was the foundation established by the will of William Brooke, Lord Cobham, in 1597. Lord Cobham clearly stated his wish to see the old medieval struc-tures 're-edified', as he put it—turned into dwellings for the relief of the poor;[43] and the builders who undertook the work took trouble to respect his wishes. Not only did they incorporate much of the medieval fabric in the new, preserving the medieval south wing almost in its entirety; they ensured that their own work as far as possible matched the appearance of the old. Indeed, where appropriate, features such as windows and door-ways from the old fabric were incorporated. As a result, the medieval and later buildings form a harmonious blend.

---

[38] BL, Harley Roll C 23.   [39] *VCH Kent*, ii, 231.

[40] A. Vallance, 'Cobham Collegiate Church', *AC*, 43 (1931), 137.

[41] For the importance of Rogationtide processions, see E. Duffy, *The Stripping of the Altars. Traditional Religion in England, 1400–1580* (New Haven and London, 1992), 136–8.

[42] C. Hussey, 'Cobham, Kent-III. A Medieval Parish', *Country Life*, 4 Feb., 1944, 200–3.

[43] P. J. Tester, 'Notes on the Medieval Chantry College at Cobham', *AC*, 79 (1964), 110.

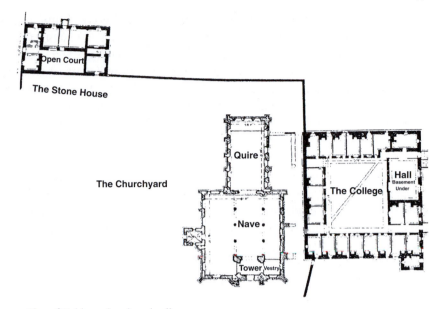

FIG 3. Plan of Cobham church and college

The 'old' college of John, Lord Cobham, took the form of an uneven quadrangle or courtyard measuring externally 110 by 100 feet (fig. 3).[44] The signs are that the courtyard in the centre was cobbled or paved. Around three sides there was a pentice or covered walk 8 feet 8 inches wide: a set-off on the north wall of the south range 9 feet from the ground strongly suggests this. Originally the east and west ranges were probably wider than they are now. On the inner wall of the south range is a weathered string-course which terminates 6 feet from the almshouses on the east side, suggesting that when the side ranges were rebuilt they were set back by that amount. Whether there was originally a range on the north, as there is today, is unclear, but it seems that there probably was not: no medieval stonework survives in the internal wall. Quite possibly, the courtyard was closed by the wall now forming the northern limit along the processional route. To the south of the hall range there was an outer courtyard which contained a kitchen and probably, too, domestic offices. It appears that this was served by a separate entrance. No significant remains of this range are visible today.

[44] This discussion of the college buildings largely follows Tester, 'Notes on the Medieval Chantry College'. Also of value still is C. Hussey, 'Cobham, Kent-IV: Cobham College', *Country Life*, 11 Feb., 1944, 244–7.

Peter Tester has attempted a reconstruction of the chaplains' rooms and other accommodation around the main courtyard. He suggests that the master's lodgings probably occupied the eastern range. The evidence which points to this is the partly blocked Perpendicular window, with holes for the attachment of a grille, in the outer wall. It is conceivable that this window formed the east window of a chapel; however, the presence of the holes for the former grille suggests otherwise, for grilles were only supplied when windows were unglazed. It is altogether more probable that the window illuminated a high-status room of secular use—in other words, the parlour or hall of the master. If it is accepted that the master occupied the east range, then it is likely that the chaplains occupied the west. The evidence suggests that they had separate rooms on the ground floor and sleeping quarters above, the former being connected by a passage on the quadrangle side. The main room on the south side, then as now, was the hall, the most complete surviving of the medieval buildings. The roof-opening shows that this was originally heated by an open hearth. To the east side of the hall was a small room, which was probably the buttery.

As in other early colleges, there was no accentuated entrance to the main courtyard. Peter Tester, indeed, suggests that the courtyard could only have been entered via the buildings themselves.[45] There appears to have been one entrance at the north end of the east range, presumably for the master's use, and another at the equivalent end of the west range for the chaplains. It is likely that there was a separate entrance to the south or outer court, probably on the east side near to the kitchen.

Half a century ago Christopher Hussey suggested that the distinguished royal master mason Henry Yevele was probably Cobham's consultant architect for the college.[46] From the late 1370s, Yevele was involved in a professional capacity with Cobham on a variety of projects. Between 1380 and 1382 he acted as quantity surveyor, and probably too as overall architect, of Cobham's castle of Cooling on the Hoo peninsula, and in 1381 he supplied the 'devyse', or design, for the new south aisle and porch which Cobham built at St Dunstan-in-the-East, London.[47] From March 1383 he also worked with Cobham in arranging the reconstruction of Rochester bridge.[48] Considering his close co-operation with

[45] Tester, 'Notes on the Medieval Chantry College', 115–16.

[46] Hussey, 'Cobham College-III'.

[47] The aisle and porch were actually built by Nicholas Typerton: BL, Harley Ch. 57 B 8.

[48] J. H. Harvey, *English Medieval Architects: A Biographical Dictionary down to 1550*, 2nd edn. (Stroud, 1984), 361–2.

Cobham in these projects, it seems not unreasonable to assume his responsibility for the design of the college. What remains, and is visible, of the college's external fabric strongly supports such a hypothesis. The preference for plain ragstone surfaces and the use of simple Perpendicular tracery in the hall windows are consistent with Yevele's known style.[49] The plan of the college may have owed something to Yevele's contemporary design for the London Charterhouse. As John Harvey has observed, the idea of arranging the separate units around a courtyard bears an obvious similarity to the arrangement of the cells around the cloister garth of a Carthusian monastery.[50] However, there are grounds for supposing that a more direct model was the accommodation provided for the vicars choral at the secular colleges and cathedrals.[51] This accommodation, in common with its counterpart at Cobham, was generally arranged as separate units. In 1348 the bishop of Wells, Ralph of Shrewsbury, commenced building the well-known Vicars' Close at Wells—a structure which, in planning terms, was effectively a stretched-out courtyard.[52] A few years later, in the 1350s, the dean and canons of Windsor built the Canons' Cloister immediately to the north of St George's Chapel at Windsor. This latter cloister may have been an especially strong influence on Cobham. Significantly, it was conceived as a set of timber-framed units around a garth—precisely the model to be followed at Cobham. The fact that Yevele was wholly familiar with the royal works would make the choice of the Windsor model for Cobham understandable.

Further evidence of Yevele's involvement is to be seen inside the church. Unlike other founders in this period whose plans were ambitious—for example, the earl of Arundel at Arundel—Cobham did not undertake a complete rebuilding of the fabric. The chancel, functionally the heart of the building, already offered more than enough space. In consequence, Cobham deemed it sufficient to commission new fittings for the chancel and to make some additions at the west end. It is possible that in the longer term he envisaged reconstructing the nave. However, if that was the case, he did not accomplish it. Lack of means may well have stood in his way.[53]

[49] The West Gate at Canterbury, a Yevele work of *c*.1380, affords a good local parallel.

[50] J. H. Harvey, *Henry Yevele, c.1320 to 1400: The Life of an English Architect* (London, 1944), 30, 58. Harvey restated the connection in *The Perpendicular Style, 1330–1485* (London, 1978), 67, 107.   [51] I am grateful to Tim Tatton-Brown for this suggestion.

[52] W. Rodwell, 'The Buildings of Vicars' Close', in L. S. Colchester (ed.), *Wells Cathedral: A History* (Shepton Mallet, 1982), 212–13. The houses seem to have been finished by 1363.

[53] See below, 54; Appendix.

The craftsmen whom Cobham employed on the church included some of the leading figures of the day. A major new set of stained glass windows was commissioned from John Brampton, the king's glazier.[54] Brampton was one of the most active glaziers in the capital and supplied windows for Sheen Palace and St Stephen's chapel, Westminster;[55] unfortunately very little of his glass at Cobham survives.[56] A magnificent new set of ashlar fittings for the chancel was commissioned from Yevele's workshop. Two of the fittings still remain—the piscina and the sedilia; a third, the altar reredos, was largely destroyed at the Reformation. All three fittings were executed in Kent ragstone. The two fittings that survive are works of the very highest beauty and craftsmanship (fig. 4). The piscina is almost shrine-like in its richness. The bowl containing the drain is like a small font. Running along its upper edge, and continuing along the sides, is a narrow band of quatrefoils. Above and behind the bowl is a recess, the three faces of which are ornamented with cinquefoiled panelling, giving it the character of a blind oriel window. Crowning the recess is a set of three canopy gables, each crocketed and finialled and enclosing a trefoil. The recess ceiling, under the canopy, is ribbed to imitate vaulting, while framing the sides are buttresses enclosing trefoil panels and ending in canopies which range with those of the recess. The sedilia, immediately to the west, consist of three seats with projecting edges, chamfered, under tall canopies. The three canopies are identical, with crocketed pediments which rise rapidly to the finials. The shafts dividing the recesses are enriched with slender buttresses set diagonally, in the manner of those found on canopied brasses. The two furnishings are works of consummate elegance. The major elements in their design mirror those of the grander brasses of the period. Micro-architecture, monumental art, and stained glass design all drew on essentially the same motifs.[57] Ideas and motifs were readily transferable.

A curiosity of the Cobham chancel is the newel staircase in the south-eastern corner discovered by Scott in the restoration of 1860. The staircase entrance had been blocked at the Reformation, but Scott reopened it. The stairs rise some seven or eight steps from the floor, take a half-

---

[54] BL, Harley Ch. 48 E 47 (a receipt of John Brampton, glazier of London, for 30s. received from John, Lord Cobham, dated 6 Feb. 1383).

[55] R. Marks, *Stained Glass in England during the Middle Ages* (London, 1993), 30, 47, 48, 93.

[56] There are only a few fragments in the porch.

[57] V. J. B. Torr, 'The Sedilia and Altar-Drains', *AC*, 43 (1931), 156–60.

FIG 4. Cobham church: piscina and sedilia with, above the sedilia, one of the fifteenth-century tournament helms

turn and then come to the face of the wall again to the west. Vallance suggested that the stairs belonged to a night staircase erected for the convenience of the chaplains when the church became collegiate. He believed that the archway across the processional path outside carried a bridge which connected the chancel with the chaplains' sleeping-quarters in the college to the south.[58] However, as he also conceded, the south-east corner of the chancel is a decidedly unusual place to find a night staircase. Moreover, there is no evidence of the staircase giving access to any structure externally; the only access which it offers is to the interior. Peter Tester and, before him, Waller both suggested more plausibly that it gave access to a gallery along the top of the reredos.[59] Its

[58] Vallance, 'Cobham Collegiate Church', 134–6.
[59] Tester, 'Notes on the Medieval Chantry College', 118.

position in the south-east corner would certainly suggest this. In the late Middle Ages galleries or walkways were often placed along the tops of the grander reredoses. Choristers and musicians assembled on these to perform on feast days. The presence of a gallery at Cobham would be entirely consistent with the founder's concern to promote liturgical magnificence.

The medieval reredos probably stood some way to the west of its present-day Victorian successor.[60] The splendid Renaissance tomb of George Brooke, Lord Cobham (d. 1558), may well occupy its site. Conceivably, Brooke, like his Protestant contemporary, the earl of Hertford, in Salisbury Cathedral, claimed the altar position for his tomb to effect a symbolic break with the past.[61] The character of the medieval reredos can only be guessed at. One possibility is that it was a smaller and simpler version of the celebrated 'Neville' screen which Yevele supplied for Durham Cathedral—in other words, a rich pinnacled work with niches containing statues. Against this possibility, however, has to be set the fact that parts of the earlier reredos were retained. Among the fragmentary figure sculpture found in the blocked-up staircase were pieces of early fourteenth-century date which had evidently survived from the earlier reredos.[62] It is possible that Yevele retained the image screen of the earlier structure while embellishing it with new statuary; in any event, it is clear that he did not entirely replace it. Work was also carried out in the area behind the reredos. In March 1381 Nicholas Typerton, a mason, acknowledged receipt from Lord Cobham of £2. 17s. 8d. for the making of a passage ('chemin') behind the reredos of the high altar of the church.[63] The 'chemin' appears to have been the space between the reredos and the east window. What Typerton did in this area is unclear. It is possible that he simply refurbished the area: he could have supplied wall panelling, for example, although none survives. However, it is likelier that he did something more. The so-called 'chemin' probably served

---

[60] The present reredos was installed by Scott in the 1860 restoration.

[61] I am grateful to the vicar of Cobham, Revd Steve Davie, for venturing this suggestion. George Brooke, Lord Cobham, was one of the earliest and closest associates of Archbishop Cranmer among the evangelical gentry of north Kent. He proclaims his 'defence of the Gospel' on his tomb epitaph. (The tomb was erected in 1561.) His brother Thomas joined Cranmer's household staff and married his niece (D. MacCulloch, *Thomas Cranmer: A Life*, New Haven and London, 1996, 203). Other examples of tombs on the sites of former altars are the grandiose Gorges and Hertford tombs in Salisbury Cathedral. [62] See above, 41.

[63] BL, Harley Ch. 57 B 8. Typerton was the mason whom Cobham employed to build the new aisle and porch at St Dunstan-in-the-East under Yevele's direction: Harvey, *English Medieval Architects*, 304.

as a sacristy—the function of a similar space behind the high altar at Tideswell (Derbyshire) today.[64] However, the character of the area was not simply utilitarian; it was in some measure ceremonial, for it formed part of the chaplains' processional route. When the chaplains made their way around the church on feast days, they would have entered the 'chemin' through one door and left it through the other, censing the high altar as they went.[65] The two doors could have been openings in the actual reredos, as in the later examples at Westminster or Winchester; or, alternatively, if the reredos extended less than the chancel's full width, they could have been openings in a wall behind it. When it is recalled that Yevele was merely reconstrucing an earlier reredos, it becomes possible to imagine that the latter could have been the case. In other words, Typerton's task would have been to construct a transverse wall backing onto the reredos. His engagement to carry out work of this kind is altogether more plausible than to suppose he was upgrading an existing wall—a task for which Yevele's workshop would anyway have been engaged.

In addition to equipping the chancel with new fittings, Lord Cobham initiated, or carried out, other work on the fabric. It is very likely that he was responsible for commissioning the splendid north porch. To judge from its grandeur and size, this edifice, like the 'chemin', may have been conceived with the needs of feast-day processions in mind. It is a two-storey structure with a stone vault on the ground floor. The upper room, which served as a parvise chamber, is approached through a staircase from the north aisle. There was stained glass in the small side windows, and various fragments of this remain. It is reasonable to suppose that Yevele was again called on to advise on the porch's design.

How far Lord Cobham was involved in carrying out other work on the fabric is unclear. John Newman has suggested that he may have rebuilt the tower, aisles, and nave clerestory at the same time.[66] It is true the western parts of the church, with the exception of the nave arcades, are all late medieval work. However, stylistically they have little in common with Yevele's work in the chancel; they belong to a later phase in the operations. Evidently, a lengthy programme of works was

---

[64] The arrangements at Tideswell, also late fourteenth century, probably afford the nearest indication of what the east end of the Cobham chancel would have looked like. A low reredos runs the full width of the chancel a little way to the west of the end wall, creating behind it the space for a small sacristy. For discussion of this and other examples, see F. Bond, *The Chancel of English Churches* (London, 1916), 53.

[65] For processions of this kind on Sundays at High Mass, see Duffy, *Stripping of the Altars*, 124–5.

[66] Newman, *West Kent and the Weald*, 218–19.

undertaken in stages in the fifteenth century. The first of these was probably the rebuilding of the tower. This appears to date from the early years of the century: the large moulded plinth is a characteristic of this period; possibly the masons moved straight onto this project after finishing the porch. Half or three-quarters of a century later, a series of works was carried out in the nave. A cluster of references in wills provides evidence of this. In 1471 one Thomas Wright left the sum of 13s. 4d. for the cost of lead for the nave roof. Twenty years later, in 1494, one Richard Tonnok left a more modest 3s. 4d. for the repair of the tower. Then in 1503 Robert Holt left 3s. 4d. for repair of the nave.[67] Taken together, these references point to a connected series of works in the west of the church. From Wright's bequest it can be inferred that the clerestory had been built and that work had begun on the roof. The present nave roof, a low-pitched king post design, very likely dates from this time.[68] Shortly after work on the roof was finished, the aisles were extended west to embrace the tower; originally, the tower had been detached at the sides. A late fifteenth-century date for the aisle extensions is suggested by the square-headed windows and the use of ashlar (fig. 1).[69] It may be significant in this context that much of the woodwork in the church dates from the fifteenth century. The screen fragments from the former chancel screen, now in the nave, appear to be mid- to late fifteenth century in date.[70] The signs are that Lord Cobham lacked the resources to carry through his scheme for the church in full. In addition to endowing the college, he was also rebuilding Cooling Castle and paying for an aisle to be added to St Dunstan-in-the-East. There are indications that by the 1390s he was falling into debt. In 1396 he is found negotiating the repayment of a £500 loan to two London merchants.[71] It is fairly clear that the fitting-out of the chancel was unfinished at his death. In 1436 one Elena James bequeathed the sum of 6s. 8d. for the making of stalls in the church: which is presumably a reference to the stalls in the chancel.[72] After the founder's death the completion of the church evidently became a communal endeavour. Where the founder had left off, it fell to the parishioners to pick up and complete.

[67] *Testamenta Cantiana: A Series of Extracts from Fifteenth and Sixteenth Century Wills: West Kent*, ed. L. L. Duncan (London, 1906), 13.

[68] The roof was restored in the 1930s, apparently using the original timbers.

[69] The walls further east are flint and rubble.

[70] The presence of this screen across the chancel entrance would have reinforced the sense of the chancel as a private space.

[71] BL, Harley Ch. 48 F 5. For discussion of Lord Cobham's finances, see below, Appendix.

[72] Rochester Bridge Trust, Rochester, T8, calendared in Historical Manuscripts Commission Report 20714, 3–4 (the Darnley Collection).

FIG 5. Cobham M.S. XII: William Tanner, master of the college, d. 1418

The later history of Cobham college is ill documented. The brief run of masters' accounts, which are so valuable for its early years, end in the 1420s, and the sources thereafter are few. Fortunately, it is possible to compile a list of masters from the Rochester episcopal registers and the Harley charters.[73] The men who served in the office of master are all rather shadowy figures, in most cases mere names. Only a few were graduates. The earliest masters followed one another in quick succession—William de Newton, Edward de Standlake, John Wetwang, and Walter Shuldham all served in the 1370s and '80s. William Tanner was the first to serve for any length of time. Appointed in 1390, he held office until his death in 1418; his memory is preserved by a brass in the chancel (fig. 5).[74] John Gladwin, who succeeded him, served for even longer—for over thirty years. Like his predecessor he is commemorated by a brass,

---

[73] The list is given in *VCH Kent* (3 vols.; London, 1908–32), ii, 231.

[74] Tanner was promoted from within: he was a chaplain of the college: Arnold, 'Cobham College', 66. His epitaph says: 'His iacet Willelmus Tannere qui primus obiit Magister istius Collegii . . .' The sense here is that he was the first master to die in office, not that he was the first master.

FIG 6. Cobham M.S. XV: John Gladwin, master of the college, engraved c.1450

FIG 7. Cobham M.S. XVI: William Hobson, master of the college, d. 1473

now in the nave aisle (fig. 6).[75] Gladwin was succeeded by William Bochier (or Bourchier), who held office till 1458, and he in turn by William Hobson (d. 1473), who was also commemorated by a brass (fig. 7). Hobson's successor was John Holt. Holt was succeeded by John Bycroft, and Bycroft by Thomas Lindley, who held office only briefly.[76] Next came John Sprotte, probably a Londoner by birth, who died in 1498 and was commemorated by a brass (fig. 8).[77] John Alan, John Baker, George Cromer (later archbishop of Armagh), and John Bayly carried the succession through to the Dissolution.

A little can be learned of the internal regime of the college from an

[75] Since no date of death is given, he presumably commissioned it in his lifetime.

[76] Lindley is probably to be identified with the man of that name who was successively bursar and sub-warden of Merton College, Oxford, and was rector of Chiddingstone (Kent) in 1487–8 and of Chelmsford (Essex) from 1489 to his death in 1492: A. B. Emden, *A Biographical Register of the University of Oxford to A.D. 1500* (3 vols.; Oxford, 1957–9), ii, 1194.

[77] In 1436 one Alexander Sprotte was a taxpayer in London; forty years before that, John, Lord Cobham, had been engaged in financial dealings with Hugh Sprotte, citizen of London (S. L. Thrupp, *The Merchant Class of Medieval London (1300–1500)*, Chicago, 1948, 384; BL, Harley Ch. 48 F 5). By the fifteenth century there were Sprottes in Kent. In the chancel of Crundale church, near Canterbury, there is an incised slab to John Sprotte, rector (d. 1466).

FIG 8. Cobham M.S. XVII: John Sprotte, master of the college, d. 1498

inventory of its goods compiled in 1479.[78] This gives the impression that the sacristy was well stocked. There were ample vestments—copes, chasubles, tunicles, albs, and so on: some of them being for 'ordinary wear' and some for feast days. There were also plenty of ornaments ('jocalia') and altar vessels. Books, however, appear to have been relatively few in number. Most of those dozen or so listed were service books. Various of the volumes were described as 'worn and old'. The most surprising volume was one 'treating of difficult words in the lectionary and

---

[78] Printed in *Registrum Roffense*, 239–41, and translated in an appendix to Vallance, 'Cobham Collegiate Church', 147–52.

Missal'. The presence of this book may indicate that by the late fifteenth century the intellectual attainments of the chaplains were few.

Late medieval colleges rarely attained distinction as centres of learning, but there is evidence that Lord Cobham initially entertained rather higher expectations of his chaplains. When an inventory was compiled of the college's possessions in 1400—towards the end of the founder's lifetime—a larger and more varied collection of books was recorded than was to occur later.[79] The books listed were for the most part not service books; indeed, beyond a few psalters, service books were absent. They were books of devotion, doctrine, and history—a couple of copies of Peter Lombard's *Sentences*, an 'old book of prophecies', a copy of Higden's *Polychronicon*, several 'books of saints', a book 'of John Chrysostom', a copy of St Bernard's meditations, Giovanni d'Andrea's commentaries, several volumes of sermons, a decretal collection, a work by the canonist Hugh of Pisa, Gregory the Great's *Moralia* (a commentary on Job), and a number of other works by Gregory.[80] It is likely that most, probably all, of these books were the gift of the founder. Cobham's bookish interests are well attested. He was a man of letters, and he enjoyed the friendship of such *litterati* as Gower.[81] He made provision for a school to be attached to the college: a 'schoolhouse' is mentioned in 1383.[82] Possibly some of the works were to be used by the chaplains in instructing the young. But most of them were probably not; they were for a distinctly highbrow readership. The only use to which they could have been put was the chaplains' own edification.

The end of the college came in 1537. Unlike most other chantry colleges, that at Cobham did not suffer the fate of forcible suppression by the crown. Thanks to the close tie between the college and patron, there was a peaceable transition. The master of the college and his fellows, foreseeing the ruin which threatened, voluntarily sold everything to Lord Cobham. A confirmatory deed was made in the following year, and Lord Cobham's rights were secured by Act of Parliament. Lord Cobham had no use for the buildings, which gradually fell into disrepair. But forty

---

[79] BL, Harley Roll C 18, briefly noted by J. O. Halliwell in *Archaeologia*, 28 (1840), 455.

[80] I am grateful for the assistance of Fr. Jerome Bertram in interpreting the list.

[81] See above, 25. For the bequest to Joan Cobham, the family heiress, of a book which had once belonged to her grandfather, see Margery Nerford's will, in E. Freshfield, *Wills, Leases and Memoranda in the Book of Records of the Parish of St Christopher Le Stock* (London, 1895), 8–9. I am grateful to Dr C. M. Barron for this reference.

[82] BL, Harley Ch. 48 E 46. For comment, see N. I. Orme, *English Schools in the Middle Ages* (London, 1973), 186–7. It is possible that the building referred to is the much-altered late medieval house at the north-eastern corner of the churchyard.

years later they were put to a new use. William Brooke, Lord Cobham, took them over for his 'new college'—a set of almshouses for the poor. It is this charitable foundation which makes use of the college to this day.

The establishment of Cobham college provides the background to, and context for, the commissioning of the brasses in the church. According to the founder's wishes, the chaplains of the college were charged with praying in perpetuity for the souls of the Cobham dead; and the purpose of placing the brasses in their midst was to remind them of their task. Lord Cobham conceived of his college on the grandest scale. He saw it as a jewel in the family's crown. The most famous master mason of the day, Henry Yevele, was consulted on matters of design, while sculptors of the highest quality were employed on the fittings in the chancel. None the less, the founder's ambitions outran his means. The refurbishment of the church remained unfinished at his death. Cobham collegiate church became a monument to overoptimistic planning. All the same, the process of intercession for the deceased had been set in motion. A series of brasses was commissioned to assist the clergy in their task. Given the founder's ambition, it was only appropriate that the brasses should be among the finest of their day.

⇥ 4 ⇤

The Market for Brasses

I N the 1380s, when the 3rd Lord Cobham was commmissioning the fittings for the Cobham chancel, the art of brass engraving in England was already a century old. There is evidence that brasses were being produced in London by the 1280s or earlier, and that effigial incised slabs were being made well before that. By Lord Cobham's time brasses had become much the most popular form of funerary monument, and in the marblers' workshops around St Paul's churchyard in London there was something approaching mass production. How is the popularity of brasses to be explained? And where was the demand for them coming from?

Brasses had first become a popular commemorative medium around the mid-thirteenth century. The earliest surviving brass effigies are to be found in Germany. The oldest of all is a remarkable plate covering the grave of St Ulrich (d. 973) in a vault at St Ulrich and St Afra's, Augsburg. Engraved in 1187, this is actually a brass by circumstance rather than design since it was the work of goldsmiths who subsequently did not specialize in this medium. It is lightly engraved in copper and bears the bearded figure of the saint.[1] The earliest brass effigy in the generally accepted sense is probably that of Bishop Yso von Wolpe (1231) at St Andrew's, Verden. This was laid not in a vault but in the body of the church and was exposed to view. Like the St Ulrich plate, it shows the bishop in pontifical vestments—although on this occasion holding not a crosier but representations of his church and the city which he fortified. From later in the century come a second episcopal brass at Hildesheim, to Bishop Otto von Brunswick, and a Virgin and Child commemorating a grant of indulgence at Halberstadt.[2]

It is virtually certain that brasses were being produced in considerable

---

[1] The brass is discussed by Norris, *Monumental Brasses: The Craft*, 30, and illustrated, fig. 7.
[2] Norris, *Monumental Brasses: The Memorials*, i, 3–4.

number in France at this time, too. However, the almost total loss of medieval French brasses makes reconstructing developments here very difficult. For our knowledge of French brasses of the period we are almost entirely dependent on the drawings made in the seventeenth century by François-Roger de Gaignières. At Sens Cathedral de Gaignières records a series of five brasses to archbishops of the Cornut family, the earliest commemorating Archbishop Gautier Cornut, 1241, while at Poissy he illustrates a brass to two sons of Louis VIII, engraved 1230–50, and at Joyenval one to Nicholas de Roye, bishop of Noyon, 1240.[3] The majority of these early French brasses were probably made in workshops at Paris, although it is possible that a few could have come from Tournai, later a major production centre, or its vicinity.

A third significant cluster of early brasses comes from the eastern fringe of the German world, in Silesia. At the abbey of Lubiąz there was a series of four brasses from c.1290–1300, three commemorating dukes of Silesia or Steinau, and the fourth a knight, Martin Buswoyz. All of these brasses, now in Wrocław Museum, bore large, vigorously engraved, figures under low canopies. Duke Conrad was shown in a surplice and hooded cloak, and the others in armour.[4] The brasses have various features in common with other Silesian monuments of the period and were almost certainly engraved in Wrocław.

The stylistic variety and wide geographical range of these early brasses makes it highly unlikely that they were of common origin. The signs are that the German examples originated as two-dimensional versions of the low-relief bronze effigies which had been produced there since the eleventh century. The prototype for the series has long been recognized as the effigy of Rudolf of Swabia at Merseburg (c.1080),[5] but it is likely that the tradition can be traced further back to the remarkable mid-century slabs of a series of abbesses at Quedlinburg.[6] To the west of the Rhine the line of evolution was almost certainly different. Here the evidence points to brasses originating as a by-product of stone incised slabs. By the thirteenth century these slabs—flat engraved gravestones—

---

[3] For these brasses, see Norris, *Monumental Brasses: The Memorials*, i, 1–2; N. Rogers, 'English Episcopal Monuments, 1270–1350', in J. Coales (ed.), *The Earliest English Brasses: Patronage, Style and Workshops, 1270–1350* (London, 1987), 9–10.

[4] The Polish brasses are discussed in Norris, *Monumental Brasses: The Memorials*, i, 4–7; illus. idem, *Monumental Brasses: The Craft*, figs. 113–16.

[5] E. Panofsky, *Tomb Sculpture: Its Changing Aspects from Ancient Egypt to Bernini* (London and New York, 1964), 51–2; fig. 197.

[6] J. Bertram, *Brasses in Germany: Some Reflections upon Recent Discoveries* (privately published, Oxford, 1997), 1–2.

were being inlaid with resins, alabasters, or metals to give a richer quality to the composition.[7] Increasingly, the inlay used was 'latten'—brass: an alloy chosen for its durability.[8] Bodily features such as the head or hands might be inlaid; eventually, and after experimentation, the entire figure was. When that stage had been reached, the brass may be said to have 'arrived'.

The role of the incised slab is of crucial importance to understanding the origins and early history of brasses in England. Almost certainly, the earliest engravers of brasses were first and foremost makers of incised or relief slabs. Huge numbers of these slabs were produced in the thirteenth century. Generally, they took the form of tall or elongated crosses with foliate terminals to the arms, but effigial designs were used as well. By the late thirteenth and early fourteenth centuries, brass inlays were introduced, as on the Continent—the slab of a priest at Westwell (Kent) provides a good example[9]—while separate brass letters were used for inscriptions. From these innovations it was but a small step to using brass for the entire composition. This was the stage reached in such attractive cross brasses as those at Caverswall (Staffs.) and Hatley Cockayne (Beds.).[10] A common variant was for a brass head or bust of the commemorated to be placed in or above the head of the cross, as at Chinnor (Oxon.) or Merton College, Oxford. The tiny head of a priest at Ashford (Kent), which is now considered to be the earliest extant brass (c.1280), is probably a survival from such a composition.[11]

The late thirteenth century saw the production of the earliest big effigial brasses. The first patrons of these appear to have been the bishops and senior ecclesiastics. The design source for the memorials was probably to be found in the shrine-like tombs commissioned by some of the bishops mid-century. At Lincoln Bishop Grosseteste, who had died in 1253, was commemorated by a large tomb chest with cast-metal effigy surmounted by a gabled canopy.[12] The engravers simply translated this pattern into a two-dimensional medium. One of the earliest episcopal

---

[7] Norris, *Monumental Brasses: The Craft*, 29; W. J. Blair, 'English Monumental Brasses before 1350: Types, Patterns and Workshops', in Coales (ed.), *The Earliest English Brasses*, 136.

[8] Most medieval brasses were composed of roughly 78–80 per cent copper, 15 per cent zinc, 3–4 per cent tin, and 2 per cent lead.

[9] Illus. Blair, 'English Monumental Brasses before 1350', fig. 155.

[10] Illus. ibid. figs. 145–6. These brasses are now lost but can be visualized from their indents.

[11] The brass is illustrated in *The Earliest English Brasses*, fig. 114, where it is dated to c.1340. For the revised date, see S. Badham and M. Norris, *Early Incised Slabs and Brasses from the London Marblers* (London, 1999), 151–6; below, 65, 68.

[12] Rogers, 'English Episcopal Monuments', 20.

brasses appears to have been that of Bishop Henry de Sandwich (d. 1273) at St Paul's, although this is now lost. The earliest of which the slab (together with a fragment of the brass) survives is that of Bishop Thomas de Cantilupe at Hereford. This is known to have been in position by 1287, when it is mentioned in connection with a reported miracle at the tomb. To judge from the surviving indents, the bishop was depicted in full pontificals, turned slightly to the left, under a crocketed canopy. Flanking his head were two small figures, that on the right being of St Ethelbert, while surrounding the whole was a marginal epitaph.[13] The brass was a highly professional product suggesting that the engravers had long experience of their craft. Several other episcopal brasses were laid in the next two decades. Those which can be associated with surviving slabs are the memorials to William de Luda (Louth) at Ely (1298), Oliver Sutton at Lincoln (1299), and Walter de Haselshaw at Wells (1308); there were also several large brasses of abbots. Many of these early brasses have a number of characteristics in common: notably, crocketed single-gable canopies with cusps of varying elaboration; thin canopy shafts; and marginal inscriptions of fillet or separate-letter form. These tell-tale characteristics point to a common workshop source, and it seems very likely that this was the capital. Evidently by the turn of the thirteenth and fourteenth centuries London had gained what it was for so long to retain: a national dominance in the design and manufacture of brasses.

Although it was the bishops and senior abbots who pioneered the use of large-scale figure brasses, other groups soon followed in their wake. The class, or estate, most heavily represented in extant early brasses are the gentry—the knights and the esquires and their wives. Some of the early knightly effigies are to be numbered among the finest ever engraved. The sheer scale, and the sheer quality of the engraving, of such effigies as those of Sir John d'Abernon at Stoke d'Abernon (Surrey) and Sir Robert de Bures at Acton (Suffolk) raise them to the level of works of art. The dating of these knightly brasses and, by implication, the chronology of the popularization of brasses among knightly patrons, presents problems. Very few of the pre-Black Death knightly brasses are firmly attributed. In many cases the inscriptions are lost; and even where these survive the date of death is not given. For long, dating and attribution were decided largely by reference to the armour in which the commemorated was shown attired; and because the armour included the mail

---

[13] Rogers, 'English Episcopal Monuments', 29–32.

hawberk, and mail, it was thought, was being covered by plate in the fourteenth century, a date of before the early fourteenth century was preferred. In the 1960s and '70s, however, these assumptions were called into question. Close study of the lives of the commemorated, in particular of Sir Robert de Bures and Sir Roger de Trumpington, combined with stylistic analysis of the brasses themselves, led to the conclusion that the figures all dated from a generation or two later than supposed. The brass of Sir John d'Abernon was redated from 1277 to c.1330 and that of Sir Robert de Bures from 1302 to c.1331; none of the figures was allowed a date before 1300.[14]

The most recent work on the early workshops, however, undertaken by Badham and Norris, has suggested the need for further revision still.[15] Badham's and Norris's researches into the principal series of late thirteenth-century London-made incised slabs has highlighted similarities between these memorials and some early brasses, in particular the bust of a priest at Ashford (Kent) and the knightly effigy at Gorleston (Suffolk). The characteristics which the co-authors show that the two memorial types have in common are a sketchy engraving style and a somewhat immature feel to the design. In Badham's and Norris's view, there can be little doubt that both incised slabs and brasses were produced in the same workshop; and the co-authors further argue, on the evidence of the distribution of the extant examples, that this workshop could only have been based in London. The implications of Badham's and Norris's researches for the chronology of early brass engraving are far-reaching. On the co-authors' own evidence there can be little doubt that brasses were being made in the London workshops by the 1280s, and perhaps earlier. In these closing years of the century, the manufacture of incised slabs was almost certainly the principal business of these workshops—the engraving of brasses being no more than a sideline. However, in the early 1300s the output of brasses appears to have rapidly increased, and by c.1310 the production of substantial knightly figures had become common. Badham's and Norris's conclusions, which are amply supported by the evidence they cite, can also be justified on a priori grounds. It seems highly unlikely that such high-quality brasses as those at Stoke d'Abernon and Acton could have been produced in a vacuum; those responsible for them must have had some previous experience. As Nicholas Rogers has shown, brasses were being commissioned by the

---

[14] For a survey of the literature, see M. W. Norris, 'Views on the Early Knights, 1786–1970', in Coales (ed.), *The Earliest English Brasses*, 1–7.
[15] Badham and Norris, *Early Incised Slabs and Brasses*.

bishops and senior clergy from at least the 1280s and 1290s.[16] It is only natural to suppose that, once the popularity of the new medium caught on, the engravers should have extended their figure repertory to include brasses for the laity.

The recent re-examination of the early brasses and London-made incised slabs has highlighted the sheer scale of activity in the London workshops by 1300. In contemporary parlance, the men who made slabs and brasses were known as the 'marblers'. They were identified by this name because brasses made in London were set in marble—Purbeck marble. The connection between brass and marble had been forged back in the early to mid-thirteenth century, when the fashion developed of inlaying marble slabs with separate-letter inscriptions. By the 1250s a number of marblers were being attracted to London as a result of Henry III's rebuilding of Westminster Abbey—a prestige work which made use of the stone widely fashionable. Around 1280 the occupational name 'marbler' begins to figure more often in London records, with the appearance of John the Marbler, Godfrey the Marbler, and Walter the Marbler.[17] The most successful of this group, and someone who can be shown to have been deeply involved in brass manufacture, was one Adam of Corfe, alias Adam the Marbler.[18] Adam—whose toponymic is a clear pointer to his origins—had settled in London by 1305 and shortly afterwards set up business as a marbler. In 1313 he contracted to pave four bays of the choir of St Paul's and in 1321 he supplied £40 worth of marble to the shrine of St Thomas Cantilupe at Hereford. His will of 1331 casts some light on the organization of his business. He disposed of properties and rents in London, and also tenements in Corfe. Evidently his operation had two arms—one at Corfe controlling the quarry materials and the other in London for the manufacture and retailing of his wares. Adam was a wealthy man: he could endow a chantry in London for the benefit of his soul. It is clear that he had the resources to run a major business. John Blair has pointed out that his death (probably in November 1331) coincides with an end to stylistic uniformity in London-made brasses. As his will indicates that his business did not survive him, it is likely that the two phenomena were related. In the early 1300s Adam established himself as the leading marbler of his day. The circumstantial

---

[16] Rogers, 'English Episcopal Monuments'.
[17] Blair, 'English Monumental Brasses before 1350', 140.
[18] Ibid. 166–9. See also, J. Harvey, *Medieval Craftsmen* (London, 1975), 130.

case for seeing him as the engraver of the so-called 'Camoys' series of brasses seems strong.[19]

Although Adam's workshop dominated the market for brasses in the south and south-east of England, regional workshops satisfied much of the demand in other areas. On the evidence of despoiled slabs it seems that there were three main centres of production in the north-eastern counties and a scatter of small ill-defined workshops in the Midlands and south. The most prolific of the regional workshops was the one at York. This was probably operative by the late thirteenth century, and its output was more diverse in style and design than that in London. Archbishop Greenfield's brass in York Minster (c.1315) is probably the best-known example of this school's work. The other north-eastern workshops were probably based at Lincoln and Newcastle. That at Lincoln had a substantial output from the 1270s into the next century, while Newcastle operated in a small way around 1300–20.[20] In the west of England the most active workshop was that at Exeter. The executors' accounts for a dean of Exeter, Andrew de Kilkenny, suggest that his brass was made in the city.[21] Kilkenny's despoiled slab survives, and a number of other west-country slabs have close affinities with it. The signs are that the Exeter workshop was active from 1302 to 1316. Around the same time there appear to have been workshops at Shrewsbury and somewhere in the north-west, in or near Carlisle.[22] Clearly the demand for brasses was sufficiently widespread and sufficiently buoyant to sustain production centres in many different parts of the country.

However, around the middle of the fourteenth century, there was a radical shift in the geography of the engravers' trade. One by one, the regional ateliers went out of business. The last Lincoln brasses were made in the 1340s, while production at most of the other regional centres had ceased well before then. Probably only at York was output sustained into the fifteenth century. The reasons for the decline in the regions were several. One was obviously the effect of the Black Death (1348–9):

---

[19] For the 'Camoys' series, see below, 68. The series of pre-Black Death London-made brasses are generally named after the earliest brass in the series to survive. So 'Camoys' is named after the brass of Margaret de Camoys at Trotton (Sussex), one of its earliest products.

[20] For the northern workshops in this period, see Badham, *Brasses from the North East*, 2–8.

[21] Blair, 'English Monumental Brasses before 1350', 162. The workshop's methods were different from those common in London. A plain slab was ordered, presumably in Corfe, and brought to Exeter to be inlaid by one Master John the Painter. It is interesting to note a possible time-lag between the commemorated's death and the laying of his brass. Dean Kilkenny died in 1302; the executor's accounts were closed c.1316.   [22] Ibid. 164–6.

sudden and heavy mortality would have disrupted production more severely in a small workshop than in a larger one where losses of man-power could have been absorbed. The second, and perhaps more impor-tant reason, was the sheer prestige and authority of the London-made brasses. Not only did they enjoy the patronage of the nation's secular and ecclesiastical élites; they offered assured standards of workmanship and design. The smaller workshops could hardly compete with them. York survived because of its distance from London; locally, its products could undercut London prices. Not until the middle of the next century, however, was there a general revival in regional manufacture. London's dominance of the market became a near monopoly.

The growth of a mass, nation-wide, market in brasses encouraged methods approximating to mass production. Medieval English brasses were nearly always engraved according to stock designs. That is to say, the same conventions, the same ways of representing particular features, were used by the engravers over and over again. As a result of this, by analysis of the conventions it is possible to reconstruct the product series of the main workshops. Before the Black Death four main series appear to have been produced in London.[23] The first of these is known as the 'Basyng' style, after its earliest datable product, the incised slab of Prior Basyng (1295) in Winchester Cathedral; there is a strong probability that the brass of Bishop Cantilupe at Hereford was produced in this work-shop. The second is referred to as the 'Ashford' style, after the brass of a priest at Ashford (Kent), which is its earliest identifiable product. The brass of Roger Bacon esquire, c.1305, at Gorleston (Suffolk) is the only full-length example of this workshop's output. Both the 'Basyng' and 'Ashford' ateliers, as Badham and Norris have shown, specialized chiefly in the making of incised slabs. At around the time that 'Ashford' was scaling down, the third of the series, Adam of Corfe's workshop, entered production. Adam's products are often referred to as the 'Camoys' style, after the brass of Margaret de Camoys at Trotton (Sussex), c.1305–10, which stands near the beginning of his output. The earliest of the Cobham brasses, that of Joan de Cobham (fig. 9), is a product of Adam's workshop.[24] After Adam's death, and the consequent break-up of his business, the fourth and last of the pre-Black Death workshops came into being—the so-called 'Seymour' style, which takes its name from the brass of Lawrence Seymour at Higham Ferrers (Northants.). This atelier,

[23] Badham and Norris, *Early Incised Slabs and Brasses*; P. Binski, 'The Stylistic Sequence of London Figure Brasses', in Coales (ed.), *The Earliest English Brasses*, 94–132.

[24] This brass is discussed in detail below, 82–7.

which flourished into the 1340s, also produced such notable brasses as those of Sir John and Lady de Creke and his wife at Westley Waterless (Cambs.).

In the aftermath of the Black Death there was a sharp fall in output from the workshops and a rise in imports, particularly from Flanders. However, by the 1360s production levels had largely recovered and two main London workshops are found dividing the market between them.[25] The first of these, known as workshop 'A', which produced M.S. II–V at Cobham and M.S. II at Lingfield (figs. 10–13, 28), may have absorbed engravers from the old 'Seymour' workshop: the brasses of the two series had a number of characteristics in common, in particular a taste for depicting noses in profile. The brasses of 'A''s main rival, style 'B', represented by most of the rest of the Cobham brasses, by contrast, exhibit few if any affinities with those of the earlier period. 'B''s elegant, if somewhat austere, products, economical in their use of ornament, mark a radical shift in aesthetic from the richer, more exuberant pre-Black Death work: a change which can be compared with that from 'Decorated' to 'Perpendicular' in architecture. The output of both 'A' and 'B' was prolific: their products penetrated into every corner of the land. Series 'B' was the longer lived. Beginning in the 1350s, it flourished for well over a century until the mid- to late 1460s. The first marblers whose work can be associated with 'B' are Richard and Henry Lakenham, who were almost certainly father and son. A contract which Henry made in 1376 identifies him as the supplier of the tomb of Sir Nicholas Loveyne in St Mary Graces, London, which had affinities with 'B' work.[26] Henry died in 1387 and the signs are that his business was taken over by his apprentice William West.[27] William's connection with the series is proved by his appearance—shown as a child and described as a marbler—on the 'B' brass to his parents at Sudborough (Northants.). On William's retirement, perhaps well before his death in 1453, the business was taken over by John Essex. A John Essex, marbler, contracted to supply the brass epitaph for the tomb of Richard Beauchamp, earl of Warwick, at St Mary's, Warwick, and this is in 'B' script. After Essex's death in 1465 the series went into decline.[28]

[25] For the stylistic sequence of London-made brasses from the 1360s, see Kent, 'Monumental Brasses: A New Classification of Military Effigies', 70–97.

[26] W. J. Blair, 'Henry Lakenham, Marbler of London, and a Tomb Contract of 1376', *Antiquaries Journal*, 60 (1980), 66–74; see also below, 109–10.

[27] Henry Lakenham refers to West as his apprentice in his will: ibid. 67.

[28] Emmerson, 'Monumental Brasses. London Design *c.*1420–1485', 50–78, esp. 65–9. See also, Harvey, *Medieval Craftsmen*, 130–1.

During the long years of the 'B' ascendancy, a number of other significant workshops were producing brasses. 'B''s main rival for business in London was the workshop responsible for series 'D', represented by Eleanor Cobham's brass at Lingfield (fig. 29). The earliest 'D' brasses are datable to shortly after 1410 and the series continues until the 1480s. The rise of 'D' follows sharply on the demise of 'A', and it is possible that the two events are connected: conceivably, 'D' is the older workshop under new management. Like those of 'A', 'D''s brasses are fairly ornate: they form a contrast with the austere, economical 'B' products. 'D''s output was again large: at its height in the 1430s and 1440s it came close to rivalling 'B''s. At intervals, a number of smaller workshops are found in the market. From c.1380 to 1408 there was a workshop designated style 'C'. This atelier produced a series of highly distinctive brasses notable for their decorative richness and the sour expressions of their figures. A number of Richard II's chamber knights patronized the series. In the second quarter of the fifteenth century a workshop known as 'E' was operating. The brasses of this series can be recognized by the strongly defined mouths and staring eyes of the figures. In the middle of the century, workshops in various regional centres either entered the market or increased their production. New or revived ateliers were established at Norwich, Cambridge, and Bury, while much higher production levels were recorded at York.[29] The growing affluence of the lesser proprietors probably sustained a buoyant local demand. The work of the smaller or regional workshops is not, however, represented among the Cobhams' brasses.

The conformity which characterizes the brasses of the main series was maintained, it appears, principally by workshop tradition. The lack of any precise correspondence between such tell-tale details on brasses as drapery hems or veils indicates that designs could hardly have been traced or pricked from templates. A reasonable hypothesis would appear to be that the engravers were trained to follow particular models. Robin Emmerson has suggested that these models could have been drawn on translucent material, and the occasional appearance of designs in mirror-image seems to point to this.[30] The effect of these working methods was to encourage stylistic conservatism. Patterns of armour and costume were certainly updated from time to time. However, well-engrained habits of design died hard. In the 'B' workshop no major design changes were

---

[29] For an overview of regional work, see Norris, *Monumental Brasses: The Memorials*, i, ch. 13.

[30] Emmerson, 'Monumental Brasses: London Design'.

introduced from *c.*1458 till shortly before the firm's virtual collapse around 1470.

Paradoxically, the trend to stylistic conformity after the Black Death was accompanied by greater flexibility on the part of the engravers in matters of size and composition. Brasses were increasingly tailored to individual patrons' requirements. A rich patron might order an elaborate de luxe brass with life-size figures under a double canopy with shields at the top and a marginal inscription surrounding the whole. A middling patron might order a couple of smaller figures and a foot inscription, while a tenant farmer could order a simple two-line inscription, or—one better—an emblem and inscription. Patrons could effectively ask for what they wanted. Costs were broadly related to the scale and complexity of the product. A large canopied brass generally cost £12–13 upwards, a smaller one £2–3 or even less.[31] Carriage could add to the bill. If little or no carriage was involved, a smallish brass could be obtained very cheaply. By the late fourteenth century quite humble folk were commissioning such brasses. At Brightwell Baldwin (Oxon.) a four-line inscription of *c.*1370 commemorates a village tenant, John the Smith.[32] At Fletching (Sussex) an inscription with a pair of gloves commemorates Peter Denot, a glover. As Paul Binski has observed, brasses in the late Middle Ages became a domesticated phenomenon.[33] They reflected the aspirations and self-image of the middling-to-lesser ranks of English society.

One of the reasons for the wide dissemination of the English brass was its use of the 'separate-inlay' technique. On the Continent brasses generally took the form of large rectangular plates engraved all over. The best of the continental brasses—pre-eminently, those made in Flanders in the fourteenth century[34]—were virtuoso displays of the engraver's art—vast, decorative, and exuberant. But for precisely that reason they were hugely expensive. They were beyond the reach of most non-élite purchasers. English brasses were different. Being made up of separate pieces, they could be put together in different ways. Pieces could be

---

[31] For some examples of cost, see Norris, *Monumental Brasses: The Craft*, 52–3. More extensive evidence is to be found in the large corpus of unpublished wills.

[32] For information from the Magdalen College archives on John the Smith's standing, see W. J. Blair, 'John Smith of Brightwell Baldwin', *MBS Bulletin*, 81 (May 1999), 431.

[33] P. Binski, 'Monumental Brasses', in J. Alexander and P. Binski (eds.), *Age of Chivalry: Art in Plantagenet England 1200–1400* (London, 1987), 172.

[34] Examples of Flemish brasses in England are those of Abbot Thomas de la Mare at St Albans (*c.*1360) and of Adam de Walsoken and his wife (1349) and Robert Braunche and his two wives (1364), both at St Margaret's, King's Lynn.

included or left out, as appropriate. An arms and inscription could be offered to a humble esquire, a half-figure in mass vestments with an inscription to a village parson, and a life-size figure to a wealthy knight. Responsiveness to market conditions is indicated by the success of the regional workshops. There was a huge demand among the clergy of the northern and eastern counties for the little chalice brasses mass-produced in Norwich and York. Medieval English brasses were certainly less showy than continental ones, and they never attracted much custom abroad. However, they faithfully reflected the aspirations of an increasingly prosperous and self-conscious clientele at home.

In the light of these observations it is possible to answer an obvious question raised by a study of the Cobham brasses. Why did the Cobhams so consistently patronize brasses? Or to put it the other way round: why did they not patronize relief monuments?[35] Among the titled nobility, stone or alabaster monuments were highly esteemed; indeed, the grandest of the nobility seem to have preferred them. So, how do we account for the Cobhams' enthusiasm for brasses?

The answer to this question should by now be clear. Brasses were widely favoured at all levels of society. They appealed to the magnates and parliamentary peerage as much as to the gentry or sub-gentry. Among the senior nobility commemorated by brasses were the duke and duchess of Gloucester at Westminster Abbey (1399 and 1400), the earl and countess of Warwick at St Mary's, Warwick (1401), the duke and duchess of Buckingham (c.1480) at Pleshey (Essex), and the earl and countess of Essex (1483) at Little Easton in the same county. Brasses were never considered inferior or second-best. The highest-ranking ecclesiastics continued to patronize them in the fourteenth and fifteenth centuries just as they had before. Archbishops and bishops were commemorated by brasses in almost every English cathedral.[36] Clerks in the king's

---

[35] There are two full-relief monuments to Cobhams at Lingfield (Reginald, 1st Lord Cobham, and his grandson). However, all the pre-Reformation monuments to the family at Cobham are brasses.

[36] Most of these are now lost, but the indents survive. At Canterbury in the late Middle Ages the following archbishops were commemorated by brasses, all now lost: Simon Islip (d. 1366), William Whittlesey (d. 1374), John Stafford (d. 1452), John Morton (d. 1500), and Henry Dean (d. 1503); William Courtenay (d. 1396), a kinsman of the Cobhams, was commemorated by a brass at his collegiate church at Maidstone: C. Wilson, 'The Medieval Monuments', in P. Collinson, N. Ramsay and M. Sparks (eds.), *A History of Canterbury Cathedral* (Oxford, 1995), 470–1, 481, 487; A. G. Sadler. *The Indents of Lost Monumental Brasses in Kent, Part I* (privately published, 1975; copy in Society of Antiquaries Library), 15–23, 73. At least four of the priors of Canterbury were commemorated by brasses: Richard Oxenden (d. 1338), Robert Hathbrand (d. 1370), Thomas Chillen-

service were also significant patrons. Some of the finest late fourteenth-century brasses commemorated high-level clerks, like Peter de Lacy, keeper of the privy seal, and John Sleford, keeper of the wardrobe, at Northfleet (Kent) and Balsham (Cambs.) respectively. The market among the country gentry was becoming particularly buoyant.[37] Friends or acquaintances of the Cobhams commemorated by brasses included Sir John de Northwood and his wife at Minster in Sheppey (c.1320), Sir Richard Attelese and his wife at Sheldwich (1394), Sir William de Brien (1395) at Seal, and Sir Arnald Savage (c.1420) at Bobbing.[38] Outside the south-east there were extensive series of brasses to gentry patrons at Astley (Warks.) and Letheringham (Suffolk).[39] By the 1360s people of lesser standing such as franklins and minor esquires were also choosing brasses. There was thus a well-established tradition of commemoration by brasses by 1400. Moreover, there is evidence of consistency of taste running in particular families. The Malyns's of Chinnor and the Wing-fields of Letheringham were all commemorated by brasses. Thus the interest shown by the Cobhams in brasses is hardly unusual. It can be fitted into a recognizable pattern of gentry patronage at this time.

The general popularity of brasses was obviously a major influence on the Cobhams' commemorative choice. But there was a second factor at work—and one which was to become increasingly important with time. This was the pressure on space in the chancel at Cobham. The chancel, built in the thirteenth century, was highly ambitious in conception.[40] But even so, as the number of family burials increased, shortage of space

den (d. 1411), and William Selling (Wilson, 'The Medieval Monuments', 491–3). At Rochester Cathedral at least four of the bishops were commemorated by brasses: Thomas Trilleck (d. 1373), Thomas Brinton (d. 1389), Richard Young (d. 1418), and William Wells (d. 1444) (although the attributions are not certain): A. G. Sadler, *The Indents of Lost Monumental Brasses in Kent, Part II* (privately published, 1976; copy in Society of Antiquaries Library), 7–19. Doubtless, a similar picture would emerge from an examination of the evidence for other cathedrals. The choir aisles of Lincoln and Ely are paved with fifteenth- and early sixteenth-century indents of unidentified ecclesiastics.

[37] This was presumably accounted for by proximity to the London workshops.

[38] For these, see R. Griffin and M. Stephenson, *A List of Monumental Brasses remaining in the County of Kent in 1922* (Ashford and London, 1922), 144, 166, 167, 64; W. D. Belcher, *Kentish Brasses* (2 vols.; London, 1888–1905), i, 15, 84, 96; ii, 18, 121. Roger de Northwood and William de Septvans were witnesses to a Cobham indenture in 1344: Nichols, 'Memorials of the Family of Cobham', 333; for John de Northwood, see also, below, 87. For dealings between the Cobhams and various members of the Savage family in the fourteenth and early fifteenth centuries, see Nichols, 'Memorials of the Family of Cobham', 336, 342.

[39] W. Dugdale, *The Antiquities of Warwickshire*, 2nd edn. (2 vols.; London, 1730), i, 118; J. Blatchly, 'The Lost and Mutilated Memorials of the Bovile and Wingfield Families at Letheringham', *Proceedings of the Suffolk Institute of Archaeology*, 33 (1974), 168–94.

[40] See above, 39.

could have become a problem. Now a particular attraction of brasses was that they were the least inconvenient form of commemoration. Because they could be laid on the floor, they caused little physical obstruction. Tomb chests, by comparison, were highly inconvenient; they not only took up the space needed for stalls and wall fittings; they interfered with the free flow of processions. Sir William de Burgate's huge tomb at Burgate (Suffolk), right in front of the high altar, illustrates the problem.[41] In a collegiate foundation, like Cobham, it was vital to ensure the adequate provision of floor space in the high altar area. The founder attached high importance to liturgical splendour. Among the new fittings which he provided were a piscina and sedilia.[42] In such circumstances, tombs projecting from the wall would have been awkward and inappropriate. Brasses, on the other hand, were ideal, for they could be integrated into their surroundings. In this respect, the Cobhams' commemorative tastes were consistent with the general aesthetic of the age. The fashion in church design was for greater unity. A Perpendicular church was meant to be viewed and interpreted as a whole, not as a catalogue of individual parts as a Decorated church had been. What mattered was the overall discourse. The fact that floor brasses were unobtrusive made them peculiarly suited to the realization of this vision. Doubtless it was practical considerations that figured highest in the Cobhams' priorities. But the aesthetics of piety may have counted for something. John, the 'founder' had a powerful visual sense as his artistic and architectural patronage at Cobham and elsewhere shows.

[41] Norris, *Monumental Brasses: The Craft*, fig. 36.   [42] See above, 50–1.

⇢ 5 ⇠

The Brasses at Cobham

COBHAM boasts a collection of no fewer than twenty medieval brasses, the majority of them, mainly those of the Cobham family and their kin, in the chancel, and the remainder in the nave aisles. There is one important Renaissance monument, the splendid alabaster and marble tomb of the Cobhams' descendant George Brooke, Lord Cobham (d. 1558), in front of the high altar. There are also memorials to the Brookes' successors, the Bligh earls of Darnley, in the vault beneath the chancel.

The growth of the Cobham mausoleum strikingly illustrates the phenomenon of secular intrusion into sacred space in the later Middle Ages.[1] Before the close of the twelfth century the sacred character of the chancel had generally been respected. Burials had been confined to the churchyard or nave or, in the case of monasteries, to the chapter house—the chancel being preserved as a functionally distinct area, dedicated to the Holy Sacrament and decorated to evoke a vision and image of heaven. However, from the end of the twelfth century the long-standing conventions were breached. A major campaign was launched, with the bishops in the forefront, to extend chancel burial rights. As early as the 1230s bishops were being buried in the eastern parts of the cathedrals of Wells, Exeter, and Worcester. A little later, the clergy's example was followed by royalty and members of the higher nobility. By the 1260s princely mausoleums were being created in France in the eastern parts of the abbeys of Royaumont and St Denis, and in England in the same areas of Westminster; while a couple of generations later mausoleums of near-comparable splendour were created for the magnate families of Despenser in the choir of Tewkesbury, and Berkeley at St Augustine's, Bristol. Before the late thirteenth and the fourteenth centuries, the

---

[1] A. Martindale, 'Patrons and Minders: The Intrusion of the Secular into Sacred Spaces in the Late Middle Ages', in D. Wood (ed.), *The Church and the Arts* (Studies in Church History, 28; 1992), 143–78.

gentry were still generally buried in recesses along the nave aisles or in a side chapel or transept. However, from the early 1300s proprietors of gentry rank began adopting the habits of their superiors. Tombs or brasses to gentry figures appeared in the chancels of Little Shelford (Cambs.), Stoke d'Abernon (Surrey), and Letheringham (Suffolk).[2] From the middle of the fourteenth century, gentry burials in chancels became more common. Usually such interments were undertaken with sensitivity. Indeed, on occasions, as at Hawton and Beverley minster, they were integrated into the liturgical furnishings. The novelty of the Cobham mausoleum lay in the sheer scale of the intrusion. Not only was the family's take-over of the sacred area more blatant than in any parish church before; the role accorded to the monuments—in this case, brasses—in securing commemoration was appreciably greater. Admittedly, the preference for floor brasses over tomb chests minimized the intrusion into the area of liturgical celebration. But the scale and boldness of the take-over clearly indicated the character of gentry ambitions to come.

The stimulus to this funerary intrusion came from a variety of factors. The underlying cause was a theological development—the growth of the doctrine of purgatory. Growing popular acceptance of purgatory not only stimulated a desire for tombs generally; it encouraged, in particular, a demand for tombs in the chancel to act as *aides-mémoires* to the celebrant clergy at Mass. Connected with this development was a second, and related, factor—a growing preference by the socially influential to be buried immediately next to the high altar. The high altar was considered *ad sanctos*—close to the saints and under their protection; and it was widely believed that burial in the vicinity of the altar would speed the soul's passage through purgatory. But there was also a change in ecclesiastical attitudes influencing burial choice. In the late Middle Ages the hierarchy of the Church became more willing to accommodate lay influence in church affairs. In the twelfth century the aspirations of the laity had been strongly resisted by the clerical reformers. A century or two later the emphasis had shifted to compromise. The changing climate was

---

[2] For these, see respectively N. Pevsner, *Cambridgeshire*, 2nd edn. (Harmondsworth, 1970), 348; M. Stephenson, *A List of Monumental Brasses in Surrey* (Bath, 1970), 480–3; Blatchly, 'The Lost and Mutilated Memorials of the Bovile and Wingfield Families at Letheringham', 168–93. Other examples include Edvin Ralph (Heref.). Here there are two tomb recesses in the chancel. Almost certainly the effigies of a knight and his wife, and a knight and two wives, currently under the tower, belong to these: N. Pevsner, *Herefordshire* (Harmondsworth, 1963), 127; G. Marshall, 'The Church of Edvin Ralph and Some Notes on Pardon Monuments', *Transactions of the Woolhope Naturalists' Field Club* (1924–6) 40–55.

reflected in attitudes to seating. In statutes at Worcester and Lincoln patrons and others of high rank were exempted from the rule which had hitherto disqualified them from taking seats in the choir.[3] A clerical willingness to accept the presence of the laity in the chancel may have contributed to the spread of monuments there. A growing number of influential laity asked to be buried by their accustomed seat in the chancel. In 1374 one Alan of Alnwick requested burial by his seat in the chancel of St Michael le Belfry, York, while in 1456 Alexander Neville specified interment in Old St Mary's, York, 'before the stall where I sitt at mese'.[4] A tomb was in a sense a substitute for the presence of the person himself. Where the person had once been, the tomb now was.

By the late fourteenth century a growing number of parochial chancels were being taken over for lay burials. Bunbury, Wingfield, and Etchingham afford particularly good examples; Chinnor and Stoke d'Abernon are others. What is remarkable about the Cobham experience, apart from its relatively early date and the sheer number of the brasses, is the self-consciousness of it all. The brasses are spread out in two parallel lines in front of the high altar. The arrangement has a distinct look of artificiality: it seems too tidy to be authentic. Can the series really have grown in this way? Or do we detect in it the hand of the Victorian restorer?

The documentary and antiquarian record can offer some assistance in resolving these issues. The earliest documentary evidence is provided by a couple of wills. The first is that of Sir Thomas Cobham of Beluncle, who died in 1367 and whose brass is on the north side. Thomas's will is brief and unspecific: it merely requests burial in the church of St Mary Magdalene at Cobham, and no particular position is specified.[5] The second will is that of the esquire Ralph Cobham of Chafford, who died in 1402. This document is more precise: Ralph asked to be buried 'in the chancel of Cobham collegiate church, namely in the choir, in front of the master's stall'.[6] By coincidence, Ralph's brass is one of the few known to have been moved. Today it is at the northern end of the west row; before 1781, however, it lay on the south side, a little to the west of the main

[3] M. Aston, 'Segregation in Church', in W. J. Sheils and D. Wood (eds.), *Women in the Church* (Studies in Church History, 27; 1990), 245. The Lincoln statutes date from the episcopate of Grosseteste (1235–53); they related to earlier provisions of Walter Cantilupe at Worcester.

[4] Aston, 'Segregation in Church', 245–6. For other examples, see R. Dinn, '"Monuments Answerable to Mens Worth": Burial Patterns, Social Status and Gender in Late Medieval Bury St Edmunds', *JEH*, 46 (1995), 248.

[5] Lambeth Palace Library, Register of Archbishop Langham, fo. 115ᵛ.

[6] PRO, Reg. Marche: PROB 11/2A, fo. 21ʳ.

series; very likely, this was its original location.[7] The post-medieval journeyings of the brass remind us of the constant rearrangement to which church fixtures and fittings are subjected. However, what is important in the present context is the evidence of positioning afforded by Ralph's will. Ralph specifically asked for burial in the chancel. By this time, it is clear, the chancel had become the family's accustomed place of burial.

From the later sixteenth century, the evidence of the antiquaries helps to fill out the picture. In Elizabeth's reign, when there was a growing interest in genealogy, the Cobham brasses attracted considerable attention from the antiquaries, who valued them for their heraldry and epitaphs. The first authority to make a detailed record was Robert Glover, Somerset Herald, who wrote in 1574. Glover's main interest was in the epitaphs. Although he did not directly comment on the arrangement of the brasses, their mutual relation can be inferred from the order in which he recorded them. This order was as follows: John, 2nd Lord Cobham; Margaret de Cobham; Maud, Lady Cobham; Margaret, Lady Cobham; John, 3rd Lord Cobham; Sir Thomas de Cobham; Joan de Cobham; Sir John de Cobham 'the younger' (now lost); John Brooke, Lord Cobham; Sir Nicholas Hawberk; Joan, Lady Cobham; Sir Reginald Braybrooke; Thomas Brooke, Lord Cobham; Ralph Cobham; and Reginald Cobham, rector of Cooling.[8] The order of Glover's notes is recognizably the order of the brasses today. Glover began at the southern end of the east row, worked his way northwards, and then started again at the southern end of the west row, again working his way north. The only brasses whose location is uncertain are the last two—Ralph's and Reginald's; the former, as we have seen, was moved in 1781, while the latter's is not in the chancel at all; it is in the nave.

In the next half century, two other antiquaries made on-site records of the brasses. The first was William Smith, Rouge Dragon, who made a beautifully executed series of drawings of them in 1597.[9] Smith's drawings appear in the same order as Glover's list—starting with John, the 2nd Lord, continuing with the brasses in the east row, then moving onto John Brooke's and continuing with those in the west row; Ralph's and

---

[7] Gough, *Sepulchral Monuments in Great Britain*, i pt 2, 148; ii pt 2, 11. The move was occasioned by the creation of the Darnley vault. The brass of John Sprotte, master of the college, 1498, was moved at the same time: ibid. ii pt 2, 51; and possibly too that of John Gladwin, master of the college, now in the nave: ibid. Gough dated his remarks on Cobham to 7 Aug. 1783: ibid. i pt 2, 148.

[8] Glover's notes are printed in Lack, Saul, and Whittemore, *Monumental Brasses in St Mary Magdalene, Cobham*, 39–40. [9] BL, MS Lansdowne 874, fos. 60^v–61^v.

Reginald's brasses are noted separately, presumably as outliers. The second antiquary to make a record of the brasses was John Weever, writing in the 1630s.[10] Weever's witness is notoriously unreliable—he was slipshod in recording dates and was apt to confuse names; but on this occasion his witness can probably be relied on. Weever lists the brasses in exactly the same order as his two predecessors, starting with the 2nd Lord and working along the two rows. In Weever's case, as in Glover's and Smith's, the natural assumption must be that the order of recording corresponds to that on the ground.

The first authority to make an explicit record of the brasses' location was the Rochester antiquary, John Thorpe. Thorpe, a doctor of medicine turned collector of epitaphs, visited Cobham some time between 1715 and 1750.[11] In his *Registrum Roffense* (1769) he noted the positions of the brasses very carefully. He described them thus: in the eastern row, going from north to south, Joan de Cobham; Sir Thomas de Cobham of Beluncle; John, 3rd Lord Cobham; Margaret, Lady Cobham; Maud, Lady Cobham; an unidentified Cobham lady; and John, 2nd Lord Cobham; and in the western row, John Brooke, Lord Cobham; Sir Nicholas Hawberk; Joan, Lady Cobham; Sir Reginald Braybrooke; and Thomas Brooke, Lord Cobham. Thorpe's arrangement again reproduces Glover's and Smith's—except that in the case of the east row it is in reverse: where the earlier two had started at the southern end, Thorpe started at the northern. The arrangement is essentially that found in the church today. The row to the east, in fact, corresponds exactly. The western row has grown a little in the mean time. Two brasses have been added: Ralph Cobham's (M.S. IX), moved in 1781, and that of a master of the college, John Sprotte (M.S. XVII);[12] and William Tanner's (M.S. XII) has been placed a little to the west. What the antiquarian evidence thus indicates is that the arrangement of the brasses goes back to Elizabeth's reign; and if it goes back that far, to the period well before the fashion for reordering church interiors, it is reasonable to suppose that it goes back to the Middle Ages.

How the tidy arrangement came to be arrived at can only be a matter of guesswork. It is tempting to find a clue in the placing of the two earliest brasses at the sides—Joan de Cobham's on the north, and the 2nd Lord's opposite it on the south. Quite possibly, these first two brasses were laid at the sides to reduce the pressure on space, and then gradually,

[10] J. Weever, *Ancient Funerall Monuments* (London, 1631), 327–9.
[11] *Registrum Roffense*, 764–6.   [12] See above, 78 n. 7.

as more and more brasses were laid, the groups expanded until they met in the middle. In very general terms, this seems a reasonable reconstruction. However, there are indications that from time to time in the Middle Ages rearrangements were made. The first such rearrangement was probably made in the 1360s by John, the 3rd Lord. It was the 3rd Lord, the founder of the college, who effectively appropriated the chancel for the Cobhams' burials. Before his time it seems likely that members of the family were buried elsewhere in the church. John 'the younger' and his wife were probably buried in one of the nave aisles—this being the usual burial place for members of the gentry at this date.[13] If this was in fact the case, then John's and his wife's brasses were almost certainly moved to the chancel in the 1360s, when the college was founded. There is also reason to believe that rearrangements were made on at least two later occasions. The fittingly appropriate location of the brass of Joan, the family heiress (M.S. XIII), between those of her husbands (M.S. X, XI) presumably dates from after her death in 1434—for the two husbands' brasses, ordered twenty-five years earlier, would surely have been placed together.[14] The present position of all three brasses in the middle of the west row must be the result of a further rearrangement. Chronologically, the brasses are the earliest in the row. It is reasonable to suppose, in that case, that originally they lay at the side. Their relocation to a position in the middle must have occurred in the sixteenth century when the brass of John Brooke, Lord Cobham, on the south side, was added (M.S. XVIII).

The self-consciousness of the Cobham layout is thus very much a product of the Middle Ages. The Cobham family, in remarkably deliberate fashion, took over the parochial chancel. But when did the tradition of family burial in Cobham church begin? Were earlier members of the family buried there before the period of brass-laying? Or did the foundation of the college mark a turning-point in the family's policy?

The earliest firmly attested family burial in the church is that of Sir John 'the younger', Joan's husband, who died in 1300. The burial places of earlier members of the family are unrecorded. Pope Urban V in his letters of 1362 authorizing establishment of the college referred to Cobham as

[13] As argued above, 41, there is no evidence that the chancel, although spacious, was built with lay burials in mind. Gentry figures were usually buried in the nave aisles or side chapels before the fourteenth century; see above, 76.

[14] The husbands are Sir Reginald Braybrooke and Sir Nicholas Hawberk (see above, 27–8). Their brasses are M.S. X and XI.

the place 'where John's ancestors had sought burial'.[15] But whether they actually had been buried there is unclear. In the heyday of monasticism, in the twelfth century, it had been fashionable for members of the gentry to seek burial in local or honorial monasteries with which they had ties, and this may have been the case with the Cobhams. Henry, the founder of his line, enjoyed amicable relations with St Andrew's, Rochester, and Christ Church, Canterbury, and his sons at least with the latter.[16] It is conceivable that either he or they could have been buried in monastic surroundings. On the other hand, there is evidence that high-status burials were taking place at Cobham by the thirteenth century. In the chancel, near the high altar, there survives a set of four high-quality cross slabs. Memorials of this sort are normally associated with members of the clergy. However, it is conceivable that in this instance they are to be identified with the local gentry family—the Cobhams.[17] The finest of the four, an elegantly worked piece with a floriated head and sprigs of stiff leaf at the base, is datable to *c*.1225–*c*.1250: in other words, contemporary with the death of Henry de Cobham (d. *c*.1230). Unfortunately, there are no epitaphs on the chamfers of the slabs; or, if there were, they are now lost; and as a result, identifications are uncertain. But when, as at Cobham, the incumbents were only vicars, and by implication of little means, it is tempting to identify the memorials with high-status laity. The possibility that the slabs may commemorate some of the early Cobhams cannot be ruled out.[18]

In the century after 1300 the pattern of the family's burials becomes clearer. The majority of the family was buried in local parish churches. The parent line, resident at Cobham, was buried at Cobham itself and their Sterborough kinsfolk at Lingfield;[19] the early Cobhams of Randall were buried at Shorne. The main exception to this pattern was provided by the later Cobhams of Randall, who were buried at Boxley—a Cistercian priory near Maidstone. Various of the lesser Cobham branches were buried in parish churches near their estates—the Cobhams of Gatwick at Charlwood (Surrey), for example. But interestingly a number of them chose burial at Cobham itself. There was a sense in which Cobham

---

[15] *Registrum Roffense*, 234.   [16] See above, 12–13.

[17] For descriptions, see *Church Monuments Society Newsletter*, 14 pt 1 (Summer 1998), 22–3.

[18] The slabs are not in their original positions. It is doubtful even if they belong to the chancel. It was usual for slabs of this sort to be fitted into wall recesses—and there are no such recesses in the Cobham chancel. Evidently the slabs came from the nave—which strengthens the case for their identification with laity.

[19] Henry, 2nd Lord Cobham, was, however, buried in the manorial chapel at Stoke-sub-Hamdon (Som.), where he died. See above, 19.

served as a mausoleum not just for one branch of the family but for the whole clan.

The taste for commemoration by brasses developed in similarly irregular fashion in the course of the fourteenth century. A couple of brasses were laid c.1305–10 for John 'the younger' and his wife, but after these there were no more for half a century. At Shorne, near Cobham, John's half-brother Sir Henry was commemorated by a stone effigy.[20] It was only in the second half of the century that there emerged a pattern of sustained patronage of brasses by the family; and for this, John, the 3rd Lord, was largely responsible.

Today, it is Joan de Cobham's brass which inaugurates the series, her husband's being lost. Appropriately, this is a very high-quality memorial, one of the finest of its time. It was produced by the 'Camoys' atelier (M.S. I; fig. 9). The female effigy is over 5 ft long, and the entire composition nearly 8 ft. The quality of engraving is bold. Joan is depicted in a loose gown with demi-sleeves, over a close-fitting kirtle, her head covered by a veil, and a wimple enveloping the neck and lower portion of her face. Above, supported on two slender columns (restored), is a canopy of pedimental form enclosing a trefoil arch with foliated spandrels. Around the margin is an inscription in Lombardic lettering promising forty days' pardon to any who pray for her soul.[21]

The lost brass of Joan's husband was probably of similar scale and quality. A description by Robert Glover in 1574 gives a clear idea of its character. 'The stone whereon appeareth the place where the brass of an auncyent knight hath ben wth a lyon under his foot and at the upper end the arms of Cobham with the lyons and the lyk on his brest in a great scucheon of brass'.[22] Glover's description is consistent with the idea of a figure similar to that of the elder Sir John d'Abernon at Stoke d'Abernon, another high-quality 'Camoys' product. His reference to a heater-shaped shield—'on his brest a great scucheon of brass'—certainly aligns it with Stoke d'Abernon rather than with the contemporary effigies at Trumpington and Chartham, on which the shield is curved around the body.

[20] Newman, *West Kent and the Weald*, 503; A. V. B. Norman, 'Two Early Fourteenth Century Military Effigies', *Church Monuments*, 1 pt 1 (1985), 10–19.

[21] The canopy shafts, shields, and individual letters of the epitaph, all lost by the eighteenth century, were replaced by Waller in the restoration of 1865–6.

[22] Waller, 'The Lords of Cobham', 56; Lack, Saul, and Whittemore, *Monumental Brasses in St Mary Magdalene, Cobham*, 39–40. Glover does not mention a canopy, but that does not mean that none existed: heralds were chiefly interested in noting details of heraldic significance.

FIG 9. Cobham M.S. I: Joan de Cobham, engraved c.1305

The dating of these first two Cobham brasses has generated debate. Sir John died in March 1300, and his wife a couple of years earlier. However, the 'Camoys' workshop is unlikely to have been in full production until c.1304–5, and the series of effigies associated with Sir John d'Abernon's is usually assigned to the years c.1320–30. The brass closest in appearance to Joan de Cobham's is that of Margaret de Camoys at Trotton, one of the earliest in the sequence, which is usually dated to c.1310.[23] There are clear indications that Joan's brass is to be ranked with Margaret's among the atelier's earliest products. The canopy pediment has close affinities with that on the tomb of Aveline de Forz in Westminster Abbey, which is datable to c.1290–5: the broad trefoil arch, foliage crockets, and foliage sprays are all derived from this source.[24] Thus a date of c.1305–10 for the brass, roughly contemporary with that at Trotton and reflecting the wider dissemination of the courtly style, would be perfectly plausible. But if a date of that order is accepted, then a difficulty arises over the date of the husband's brass. The figures to which this memorial most closely corresponds are datable to some fifteen to twenty years later. Theoretically it is possible that the brasses of Joan and her husband were commissioned at different times—Joan's first and her husband's later. However, on balance, this seems unlikely. The couple died within a few years of each other, and it would be natural to suppose that the memorials were ordered together. A resolution of this difficulty can be found in Badham's and Norris's reassessment of early incised slab and brass production in London. Badham and Norris have shown that the production of incised slabs in London was on a far larger scale before 1300 than previously supposed, and that for much of the time the two biggest workshops were also producing brasses.[25] Badham herself has separately argued that the brass of an armed figure at Gorleston (Suffolk), formerly assigned to the 1320s, is more likely to be a product of the 'Ashford' workshop, which was operating earlier, and should accordingly be given a date of c.1305.[26] Badham's and Norris's chronological revision makes it possible to allow for the production of large-scale armoured effigies in the 'Camoys' workshop around the

[23] Illus. in *The Earliest English Brasses*, fig. 62.

[24] Binski, 'The Stylistic Sequence of London Figure Brasses', 82, 101. For discussion of the tomb, see P. Binski, *Westminster Abbey and the Plantagenets: Kingship and the Representation of Power, 1200–1400* (New Haven and London, 1995), 113–15.

[25] Badham and Norris, *Early Incised Slabs and Brasses*. The two workshops which produced brasses were those known as the 'Basyng' and 'Ashford' styles.

[26] See above, 65.

beginning of the century. The time-lag once thought to have existed before the appearance of the big armoured figures is thus eliminated. That being the case, there can be no objection to supposing that John de Cobham's brass was engraved at the same time as his wife's. Both are likely to have been engraved around 1305.

A second question in that case arises: who commissioned the two brasses? In the years around 1300 brasses were still rather avant-garde for the country gentry. In the period to the 1290s, brasses had been commissioned mainly by the bishops and the senior clergy. Major courtly clerks like Bishops Burnell of Wells and de Luda of Ely had been commemorated by brasses;[27] and so too had leading monastic functionaries like Abbot John of Berkhamstead at St Albans. In the early years of the new century, however, the market began to broaden out. Brasses were laid to leading members of the judiciary, like Elias de Beckingham, a colleague of John de Cobham's, at Bottisham (Cambs.) and Ralph Hengham, another of his colleagues, at St Paul's.[28] A few well-to-do knights such as Sir Edmund Gascelin of Marholm (Northants.) were commemorated by brasses too.[29]

In general, the task of commissioning a memorial was assumed by the executors or the immediate kin of the deceased. Thus, the person responsible for the Cobhams' brasses is likely to have been someone either very close to them or related to them. One possibility is that it was a member of the important local gentry family of Septvans, to whom the Cobhams were related. The Septvans's were among the earliest lay patrons of brasses. Sir Robert de Septvans was commemorated by the fine knightly brass of c.1306–10 at Chartham, while Robert's son, Sir William, was commemorated by a brass, now lost, at Canterbury cathedral.[30] Sir John

[27] Rogers, 'English Episcopal Monuments', 46, 50.

[28] Ibid. figs. 54, 63, for illustrations. Beckingham was a justice of common pleas from 1290 till his death in 1306: *Select Cases in the Court of King's Bench under Edward I*, i, pp. cxxxvii–cxxxix. Hengham, a king's bench justice, was one of the architects of Edward I's legal reforms: M. Prestwich, *Edward I* (London, 1988), 292–3. He was dismissed for corruption in 1289.

[29] Gascelin's brass was in Peterborough cathedral: Binski, 'The Stylistic Sequence of London Figure Brasses', fig. 125.

[30] The Chartham brass is illustrated in J. G. Waller and L. A. B. Waller, *A Series of Monumental Brasses from the 13th to the 16th Century* (London, 1864, repr. 1975), no. 4. P. Binski dated the brass to the early years of the century in 'Chartham, Kent, and the Court', *TMBS*, 13 pt 1 (1980), 73–9; however in 'The Stylistic Sequence of London Figure Brasses', 86–90, he revised his views, favouring a date in the 1320s. The earlier date is to be preferred, partly for the reasons that Binski originally set out, and partly because the revisionist work on the early brasses shows that the London workshops were almost certainly producing large military effigies by the period c.1305–10. This means that it is likely to represent Sir Robert, Joan de Cobham's brother. For the descent of the Septvans family, see R. Tower, 'The Family of Septvans', *AC*, 40 (1928), 105–30.

'the younger's' wife, Joan, was a Septvans by birth.[31] There is an obvious case, in the light of the family's patronage, for supposing that one of the Septvans's was involved in arranging their kinsfolks' commemoration at Cobham.

However, the Septvans's were not the only people likely to have been involved in the commission. Someone much closer to the commemorated may have been. This was John and Joan's third son—Thomas, a clerk. Thomas de Cobham was one of his father's executors.[32] More significantly still, he was a person of very similar background to the other early patrons of brasses. He was a highly successful lawyer and civil servant. He had been educated at the universities of Oxford, Cambridge, and Paris. From the 1290s, in the manner of the careerist, he began accumulating benefices: he picked up, in rapid succession, the rectories of Boxley, Hackney, and Rotherfield, and in 1301 he became archdeacon of Lewes. His expertise in law brought him major political responsibilities. In 1305 and 1312 he was despatched on embassies to France, and on several occasions he served as a commissioner for the repair of truces. His legal and diplomatic services brought him further ecclesiastical preferment. In 1299 he became a canon of Hereford and of Wells, and in 1306 a canon of St Paul's. In 1313 he was elected archbishop of Canterbury, only to be set aside in favour of Walter Reynolds; four years later, however, he was appointed to Reynolds's previous see of Worcester.[33] Thomas's high-flying career is obviously comparable to those of the other early clerical patrons of brasses. He was someone who regularly attended court. He was in close contact with advanced, metropolitan taste. He had convenient access to the businesses of the capital: his cathedral of St Paul's,

For the outline of a Chartham-like brass on an outside wall at Canterbury, see F. A. Greenhill, 'On the Ghosts of Some Brasses Formerly in Canterbury Cathedral', *AC*, 65 (1952), 137–9. Its attribution to William de Septvans, suggested by Greenhill, is uncertain, but there was a tradition of Septvans burials in the cathedral: Wilson, 'The Medieval Monuments', 509 n. 258.

[31] Joan de Cobham is identified as a Septvans in the genealogy in Society of Antiquaries MS 728/3, fos. 17ᵛ–18ʳ.

[32] Thomas is named as one of John's executors in Winchelsey's register (*Registrum Roberti Winchelsey Cantuariensis Archiepiscopi A.D. 1294–1313*, ed. R. Graham, 2 vols.; Oxford, 1952, i, 384). The other executor was Thomas de Chartham, a clerk—his name indicating the Septvans connection.

[33] For Thomas's career, see E. H. Pearce, *Thomas de Cobham, Bishop of Worcester, 1317–1327* (London, 1923); Emden, *Biographical Register of the University of Oxford*, i, 450–1; idem, *A Biographical Register of the University of Cambridge to 1500* (Cambridge, 1963), 145–6. (This last adds a few details omitted from the earlier Oxford volume.) For his burial place in his cathedral and his monument (a relief effigy), see Hon. Mrs O'Grady, 'Bishop Cobham 1317–1327. His Monument and Work in Worcester Cathedral', *Reports and Papers of the Associated Architectural Societies*, 26 (1902), 232–40.

indeed, was close to the marblers' ateliers in St Paul's churchyard. And he came from a knightly family, like such other early clerical patrons as Adam Bacon.[34] Thomas is the obvious person to see as the contractor for his parents' brasses;[35] clerks of his background were regularly ordering brasses. Where it is conceivable that he was an innovator was in ordering not for himself but for others—for members of the laity. It is in this respect that the first two Cobham brasses may be seen as occupying a position of some importance. The effigies of John and Joan are among the earliest surviving to members of the laity. Hitherto, brasses had been chiefly patronized by the clergy. From now on, they were to find a much wider market, particularly among the gentry. Gentle-born clerical patrons, like Thomas, may well have been instrumental in promoting brasses among their lay relatives, and in this way encouraging their use more widely. It may not be coincidental that, in the wake of the Cobham commission, another Kent knight and his wife were to be commemo-rated by brasses—Sir John de Northwood and his wife at Minster in Sheppey.[36] The Northwoods had many dealings with the Cobhams;[37] indeed, they may have numbered them among their executors. It is con-ceivable that the influence of the Cobham commission was felt more widely still. Ralph Hengham, the judge, who was commemorated by a brass in St Paul's Cathedral, was closely associated with John Cobham 'the younger'. Not improbably, his executors' decision to lay a brass to his memory owed something to his colleague's example. The brass was engraved only a couple of years after Cobham's own.

In the Cobham circle itself the precedent set by the brasses of Sir John and his wife was not immediately followed. Sir Henry de Cobham of Randall was commemorated by a stone effigy at Shorne, while Henry, the 1st Lord, John's heir, who was buried at Stoke-sub-Hamdon, is not honoured by an extant monument at all. The next member of the family for whom a brass was laid at Cobham is John, the 2nd Lord, who died in 1355 (fig. 10). John's was the first in the sequence to be laid on the south

---

[34] Adam Bacon was commemorated by a brass, now lost, at Oulton (Suffolk); the Bacons were an important East Anglian knightly family. Another clerk of knightly background commemo-rated by an early brass is Laurence Seymour, at Higham Ferrers (Northants.).

[35] The assumption that Thomas ordered the brass also helps to account for the inclusion of a pardon on the epitaph. Permission for pardons would normally be obtained from the local dioce-san—in this case, the bishop of Rochester. For a discussion of the pardon in the context of the Cobhams' piety, see below, 244.

[36] These brasses, however, are probably of French workmanship: illus. in Norris, *Monumental Brasses: The Craft*, pls. 109, 110. Sir John de Northwood died in 1319.

[37] Nichols, 'Memorials of the Family of Cobham', 333, 340, 342 (bis), 346 (bis); *CPR 1313–17*, 152.

FIG 10. Cobham M.S. II: John, 2nd Lord Cobham, d. 1355, engraved c.1367

side. Like most of the Cobham brasses it consists of a single figure under a canopy. The effigy itself is gracefully drawn; it exhibits the swaying posture characteristic of styles of the 1340s. The armour illustrates the later stages of the transition from full mail to plate. John is shown in a mail haubergeon stretching to his hips, over which he wears a jupon. On his arms and legs the mail is supplemented by plate defences—'schynbalds' and poleyns on the legs, vambraces, couters, and spaudlers on the arms and shoulders. Around his hips is slung an elaborate belt, from which the sword hangs, looped at the end. The pendant aventail is suspended from the lower edge of the bascinet (restored). Over the figure rises an elegant single canopy, and a marginal inscription completes the composition.

A major English figure brass datable to the 1350s is a distinct rarity. In the aftermath of the Black Death output from the London workshops went into sharp decline and the production of large-scale figure brasses virtually ceased. The most commonly found products of these years are simple inscriptions, or shields and inscriptions, and floriated crosses with small figures in the head.[38] The brass at Cobham cannot be accommodated to this pattern. Is it in fact a product of the 1350s? A closer analysis of the memorial is needed to answer this question.

In one significant respect, the brass wears a distinctly conservative look. The jaunty hip-shot stance of the figure is evocative of mannerisms of the 'Seymour'-style brasses of the 1330s and '40s. But in virtually every other respect the brass looks forward to the styles of the 1360s. The elegant proportions and general economy of line are paralleled in the designs of that decade. More specific features point to connections with 'A''s output in the later years of the decade. Particularly significant here are the letter forms and the decoration of the epitaph. These are almost identical to those on the rest of 'A''s output of those years. Moreover, the inscription is punctuated by a four-petalled rose which also appears on the other 'A' brasses at Cobham—those of the 3rd Lord and Sir Thomas Cobham of Beluncle, both of c.1367.[39] Suggestions of a link with the other Cobham 'A' brasses are reinforced by similarities in the depiction of the armour. Cuisses studded with rivets, just visible beneath the 2nd Lord's hauberk, are clearly visible on the other two; while the central longitudinal keel of the poleyns is shown on all three in the same way—

---

[38] S. Badham, 'Monumental Brasses and the Black Death. A Reappraisal', *Antiquaries Journal*, 80 (forthcoming).
[39] A cross also appears at the beginning of the inscription on all three brasses, but as this is a Waller restoration it is less reliable as a guide to date and style.

with two curved lines and a trefoil top and bottom. Moreover, the brasses have certain artistic mannerisms in common. On all three, the rows of mail on the aventail disappear towards the middle bottom. Cumulatively, the parallels between the 2nd Lord's brass and those of his nephew and son are so strong as to make only one conclusion possible—that the 2nd Lord's dates not from the 1350s, but from the same time as the others. The brass is a retrospective commission.

The spur to this belated commemoration was almost certainly provided by the 3rd Lord's establishment of Cobham college. In 1362 the 3rd Lord obtained licence from the king to alienate an endowment to the college, and by the end of the decade he was taking the first steps to providing his community with accommodation.[40] In his letters of foundation, he placed a perpetual duty on the clerks to pray for his good estate while living and for the safe repose of the souls of his kinsfolk and forebears in death. Around this time, he commissioned a brass to his own memory (fig. 11), and it is likely that he commissioned that to his father to go with it. The purpose of laying the brasses was to remind the clerks of their intercessory task. His own brass makes the point clearly. John is shown holding a stylized representation of his church, and the inscription honours him as the 'founder of this place'. A close parallel is to be observed with the slightly earlier memorial of Sir John de la Riviere, c.1345, at Tormarton (Gloucs). John de la Riviere, like Cobham, had established a chantry in his church and had memorialized the deed on his brass. In an elaborate composition showing him in the head of a cross, he is depicted holding a stylized representation of the chantry, a tall pinnacled edifice like Cobham's.[41] De la Riviere appears to have commissioned his brass shortly before leaving England for the Holy Land and joining the Dominicans.[42] It seems likely that the comparable event prompting Lord Cobham's commission was the death of one of his kinsmen. On 20 December 1367 his cousin and close associate, Sir Thomas de Cobham of Beluncle, died. Sir Thomas is himself commemorated by a brass (fig. 12). On stylistic grounds, all three can be dated to around the late 1360s. Very likely it was this bereavement that made Lord Cobham think about honouring his kin.

[40] See above, 42–3.
[41] The brass, which like Cobham's was of style 'A', is now lost, but the indent survives; for illustrations, see Haines, *Manual of Monumental Brasses*, p. cxxiv; H. F. Owen Evans, 'Tormarton, Glos.', *TMBS*, 11 pt 4 (1972), 288–90. For the foundation of the chantry in the early 1340s, see *CPR 1340–3*, 9; *CPR 1343–5*, 44; *Calendar of Papal Registers. III, 1342–62*, 300–1.
[42] He obtained licence to go to the Holy Land in 1346: *CPR 1345–8*, 128. For his career there and subsequently, see C. Tyerman, *England and the Crusades 1095–1588* (Chicago, 1988), 259, 289.

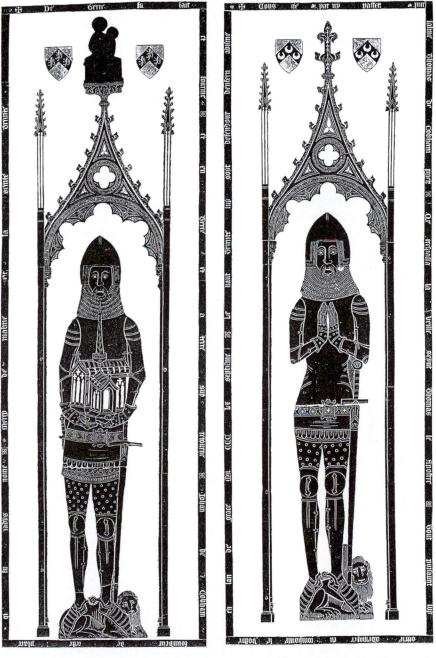

FIG 11. Cobham M.S. III: John, 3rd Lord Cobham, d. 1408, engraved c.1367

FIG 12. Cobham M.S. IV: Sir Thomas de Cobham, d. 1367, engraved c.1367

The brasses of the 3rd Lord himself and his Beluncle cousin, though contemporary with the 2nd Lord's and products of the same workshop, are strangely inferior in quality to his. The elegant single canopies exhibit the same sleekness, but the figures themselves are clumsy. The shoulders are hunched, the facial expressions naïve and the limbs ill proportioned. A likely explanation for these unsatisfactory features is to be found in the patterns used. In the 1360s the knightly figures of style 'A' were heavily influenced by the wall paintings of two military saints formerly in St Stephen's Chapel, Westminster. The influence of the two saints' figures is clearest on two other brasses of the same stylistic group, those of Thomas Cheyne at Drayton Beauchamp (Bucks.), and Sir John de Mereworth at Mereworth (Kent):[43] the studding on Cheyne's greaves and the pendant bells below his knee are obviously derived from St Mercurius' figure.[44] The figures in St Stephen's were hunched because they were painted on narrow piers between the window bays. However, the significance of this physical context was lost on the style 'A' engraver, who simply reproduced the artificially compressed image. These presentational problems appear not to have arisen in the retrospective commission for the 2nd Lord because the engraver, here required to design a figure in the styles of a decade earlier, had to think more independently.[45] The same repertory of motifs was used, but the result was aesthetically a happier product.

One other brass needs to be considered in the context of this group—that of Margaret de Cobham, a canopied single figure of a lady with marginal inscription, on the south side (fig. 13). This is much the most heavily restored of the Cobham brasses. Before Waller's attentions it was a wreck: the inscription, canopy, shields, and most of the sinister arm of the figure, had all gone.[46] Unfortunately Waller had little evidence to guide him while effecting his restoration: the slab was almost effaced, and the outlines of the lost portions were gone. For his replacements he had to resort to guesswork, and all too easily his guesswork turned to

[43] The knight at Freshwater (I.o.W.), can also be connected with this group.

[44] Rogers, 'Brasses in their Art-Historical Context', 154.

[45] Another possibility is that the engraver of this brass was a different man from the engraver of the other two. A busy workshop like 'A' would have employed a whole team of engravers—probably in 'A''s case, loosely supervised. There are strong indications that in the larger workshops the engraving of inscriptions was the work of specialists: see S. Badham, 'Techniques for Incising Inscriptions', *MBS Bulletin*, 78 (May 1998), 370. If the inscriptions were engraved by one person and the figures by another, we would have an explanation for the close similarity of the inscriptions on brasses with such different figures.

[46] For the pre-restoration condition of the brass, see Lack, Saul, and Whittemore, *Monumental Brasses in St Mary Magdalene, Cobham*, 50–1.

FIG 13. Cobham M.S. V: Margaret de Cobham, wife of Sir Matthew Fitzherbert, d. 1357, engraved c.1367

invention.[47] He designed a completely new canopy based on those of adjacent brasses of different style.[48] Worse still, he provided a new inscription, the wording of which lacked any foundation in the documentary sources he claimed to have used. Thus the dating of the brass is problematical, and the identification of the lady commemorated by it open to question. Consideration of both issues must be undertaken anew.

The inscription, in the fragmentary state in which it was recorded by the sixteenth-century antiquaries, provides the essential starting-point for any discussion. According to Robert Glover in 1574, it read:

Icy gist dame Margarite de Cobham iadis femme/ a . . . chevalier qui morust le 4 jour de Septembre lan/ de grace M° CCC LXXV de qui/ alme dieu pour sa pitie ait merci amen.[49]

Glover's transcription is confirmed in its essentials by the later witness of Smith and Weever—except that Smith gives the date as 1475.[50] Smith is clearly in error here because the lady is dressed in the attire of the fourteenth century; presumably in the process of transcription an unwanted 'C' crept in. The lady commemorated may thus be said to have been a Margaret (or Margery) de Cobham, who married a knight, now unidentified, and was living in the mid-fourteenth century. Can such a person be traced in the documentary record?

Waller, in his epitaph, identified her as the wife of Sir William Pympe of Nettlestead (Kent).[51] In his article on Cobham in *Archaeologia Cantiana* he cited as his authority Glover's record of the lost original.[52] But Glover does not actually say what Waller implies that he said. Glover left a gap in his notes for the name of the husband, just as Weever and Smith were to do, and the names 'Monsr Will'm Pympe ch'r/ Monsr Mathw Fitzherbert' were his editorial insertions, presumably representing his guesses as

---

[47] Lack, Saul, and Whittemore, *Monumental Brasses in St Mary Magdalene, Cobham*, 23–4. Waller also carried out an unscholarly restoration on the brass of Maud, Lady Cobham (M.S. VI): see N. H. MacMichael, 'Kentish Items. Cobham and Goudhurst', *TMBS*, 9 pt 9 (1962), 477–84.

[48] i.e. it is of style 'B' and not of style 'A'.

[49] Lack, Saul, and Whittemore, *Monumental Brasses in St Mary Magdalene, Cobham*, 39.

[50] BL, Lansdowne MS 874, fo. 60ᵛ.

[51] The Pympes were a family closely associated with the Cobhams: Thomas Pympe witnessed a Cobham charter in 1348 (BL, Harley Ch. 52 I 29), while his half-brother Sir William, Margaret's putative husband, was a regular charter witness for the family in the 1360s and '70s (BL, Harley Chs. 48 E 25, 53 A 46; *CCR 1364–8*, 65; *CCR 1374–7*, 207, 456; *Records of Gravesend*, i, 39, 40, 43).

[52] Waller, 'The Lords of Cobham', 68. Waller simply says 'the inscription ran thus:'. His wording, and his use of the past tense, indicate his use of the antiquarian record.

to the husband's possible identity.[53] Waller added to the confusion by supposing that the two names were those of successive husbands of the same lady: and thus in his article he wrote that Margaret de Cobham 'was married twice—first, to Matthew Fitzherbert, and secondly, to Sir William Pympe'. On this particular matter there can be little doubt that he was in error. Glover was referring to the marriages of quite separate ladies. According to the heralds' pedigree of the family of the 1590s, there were two Cobham ladies called Margaret. One was Margaret the wife of Sir William Pympe, who lived in the early years of the century, and the other, her namesake and probable niece, the wife of Sir Matthew Fitzherbert of Hampshire. The lady commemorated by the brass is to be identified with the second of these. Margaret, Sir William Pympe's wife, lived too early: she died in 1337. Matthew Fitzherbert's wife, the 2nd Lord's sister, lived a generation later, which makes a better fit chronologically.[55] All the same, a problem remains: according to her inquisition post mortem Margaret died in 1357, whereas according to the record of her epitaph she died in 1375.[56] The problem can be resolved by supposing that there was an error in the heralds' transcription. If the final two digits of the date noted by the heralds are transposed, then 1375 becomes 1357. In the sixteenth and seventeenth centuries the heralds were notoriously sloppy in their transcription of dates: even the scholarly Dugdale made errors.[57] The problem of identity, potentially difficult, is neatly resolved if we suppose that an error of this sort occurred here. The evidence is not strong enough to be wholly conclusive, but the case for connecting the brass with Margaret Fitzherbert seems overwhelming.

The identification of the brass with Margaret reinforces the connection, already clear, between the laying of the brasses and the foundation of Cobham college. Margaret's brass, like that of the 2nd Lord her brother, was a retrospective commission. It was one of a block-order of

---

[53] Lack, Saul, and Whittemore, *Monumental Brasses in St Mary Magdalene, Cobham*, 39–40 (where the relevant extract from College of Arms, MS Philpot E.1 is printed). Significantly Glover prefaced the two names with the word 'quere'.

[54] W. E. Ball, 'The Stained Glass Windows of Nettlestead Church', *AC*, 28 (1909), 166, 248, 278. Moreover, it is recorded that she was buried at Nettlestead.

[55] The marriage took place in 1339. Margaret took a portion of £280. 6s. 8d. to her husband (Nichols, 'Memorials of the Family of Cobham', 320).

[56] Margaret's inquisition is *CIPM*, x, no. 370. Her heir was said to be John de Cobham 'of Chisbury', presumably John, the 3rd Lord. Her husband had died in the previous year. For his inquisition, which lists lands in Hampshire, Gloucestershire, and Yorkshire, see ibid. no. 317.

[57] This is shown by his treatment of the Peytos of Chesterton. In his pedigree of the family he correctly gave Edward Peyto's date of death as 1488, but in his transcription of the epitaph he gave 1438 (MCCCCXXXVIII): in other words, he omitted the 'L': Dugdale, *Antiquities of Warwickshire*, i, 477.

four which the 3rd Lord placed in the late 1360s—the others being those
to the 2nd Lord, Sir Thomas de Cobham of Beluncle, and the 3rd Lord
himself. The commissioning of series of retrospective tombs and brasses
is a feature particularly associated with the endowment of chantries. In
1420, when Sir Arnald Savage ordered a brass to his parents at Bobbing,
near Faversham, it was in conjunction with the foundation of a chantry.[58]
What is remarkable about the Cobham brasses is less the fact of retrospective commemoration itself than the scale on which it was carried out.
It was not just one—or even a couple—of brasses that were ordered, but
a whole series. The Cobham mausoleum was launched with bravura. The
3rd Lord wanted nothing but the best for his family.

A noteworthy characteristic of the 3rd Lord's brasses is the highly personal nature of their epitaphs. At the time when the brasses were laid, the
content of epitaphs was settling into a routine. Generally, the epitaphs
were brief and to the point. They would begin with 'Hic iacet . . .' or
'Orate pro anima . . .' if the language was Latin, or 'Ici gist . . .' or 'Priez
pur lalme . . .' if it was French, while almost invariably they would end
with a plea for God's mercy. What is striking about the Cobham epitaphs
is that they depart from the norm; they exhibit a personal, even idiosyncratic, touch. In their character, almost certainly, can be detected the taste
and influence of the patron.

The most remarkable of the epitaphs is that to John, the 2nd Lord.
This reads:

+ Vous qe passez icy entour priez pur lalme le cortays viaundour Qe Johan de
Cobham avoit a noun Dieux luy face verray pardoun Qe trespassa lendemayn
de seint Mathi Le puisaunt otrie a demorer ove ly en lan de grace Mil CCC L
qatre Ces enemis mortels fist abatre.

In these poorly rhymed lines the traditional elements of the epitaph—a
request for prayers and plea for divine mercy—are combined with a celebration of the values of lordship. It is striking that Lord Cobham's hospitality is honoured: he is said to have been a 'courteous host' ('cortays
viaundour'). The reason for this is that hospitality was a key attribute of
nobility. The same attribute was celebrated on a later Cobham brass, that
of Reginald, 2nd Lord Cobham, at Lingfield (d. 1403): Reginald was

---

[58] *The Register of Henry Chichele, Archbishop of Canterbury, 1414–1443*, ed. E. F. Jacob (4 vols.;
Oxford, 1943–7), ii, 205–6; Griffin and Stephenson, *Monumental Brasses in Kent*, 64. The younger
Arnald's father was Arnald Savage, the Speaker of the Commons.

described as 'dapsilis in mensis' (having a sumptuous table);[59] while much later, the idea occurs on the brass of Richard Manning, 1605, at St Mary Cray, Kent:

Houskeper good and joyed moch to welcome frem [stranger] and frynd.

Equally striking are the concluding words of the epitaph: John's mortal enemies are said to have been laid low. This passage can be read at two levels. At one level, the 'mortal enemies' might be hell, sin, and death: in which case John is portrayed as enjoying a posthumous conquest, triumphing over the devil and his friends. But, at another, the references could be to this world: John is applauded for seeing off his enemies on earth. There may be an allusion here to John's tribulations in the 1330s and '40s: in other words, to his poor military record, his dismissal from office as admiral, and the eclipse of his family by the Sterborough line. It is possible that his son, who was very likely the main influence on the epitaph, was vindicating his father's name in death.

Hardly less remarkable than this epitaph are two others—those to the 3rd Lord himself and his cousin, Sir Thomas Cobham of Beluncle. The epitaph to Sir Thomas is similar to that of the 2nd Lord. It reads as follows:

+ Vous qe par icy passez pur lalme Thomas de Cobham prietz Qe trespessa la veille seynt Thomas le Apostre Tout puisaunt luy ottrie a demorer en companie le vostre en lan de grace M CCC LX Septisme le haut Trinite luy soyt defendour denfern abisme.

The opening words directly parallel the opening words of the 2nd Lord's brass, which likewise appeal for the passer-by's intercession. The middle passage, while curiously constructed, is fairly standard in form, consisting of the deceased's date of death and a plea for the Almighty's mercy. But the final section is again exceptional: Thomas makes an appeal for the protection of the Holy Trinity. The idea of concluding the epitaph with a bold flourish is a feature of the 2nd Lord's brass. But whereas the 2nd Lord's last thoughts had been concerned with his 'mortal enemies', Thomas's were with the trials to come: with the fires and torments of hell. Thomas appeals for the intercessory prayers of the faithful; however, his deepest hopes were placed in the saving power of the Trinity.

---

[59] There are echoes here of Chaucer's almost contemporary description, in the *Canterbury Tales*, of the Franklin's table loaded with bread, ale, wine, baked-meat pies, and other dainties.

The reference to the Trinity almost certainly reflects the influence of the 3rd Lord. The 3rd Lord was particularly devoted to the cult of the Trinity. On his own epitaph he appeals to the Trinity to have mercy on his soul. The 3rd Lord's epitaph is the third and last of this highly distinctive series. In some ways it is similar to the others; yet in others it is *sui generis*. The text of it reads:

+ De Terre fu fait et en Terre et a terre suy retourne Johan de Cobham foundeur de ceste place qi fu jadis nomme Mercy de malme eit la seinte Trinite.

In both structure and form the epitaph differs considerably from the others—for the obvious reason that it commemorates someone still alive. Elements commonly included, such as the date of death, are omitted. What is left has less the character of a funerary epitaph than a statement of personal belief. The key element in it is John's description of himself as 'founder of this place'. At one level this can be read as an explanatory gloss, accounting for the peculiar form of the brass, with its depiction of the commemorated holding the church; while at another it can be seen as a personal declaration: a declaration that this act was more vital to the commemorated than any other.[60] For John, the establishment of Cobham college was not merely an expression of belief in the power of intercessory prayer; it was also a witness to the connection in his mind between piety and lineage. Religion for John was inseparably connected with the things of this world: with status, buildings, and a sense of his family's position in the world. Religion for him centred on the visible and the tangible.

But other elements in the epitaph hint at a much deeper piety. There are pointers to the highly ascetic cast of his mind. Particularly significant here is the opening line, 'De terre fu fait . . .' ('from earth to earth..'). This passage had its origins in God's curse on Adam in the Bible (Gen. 3: 19). In a similar form it was used in the Ash Wednesday liturgy and the Office of the Dead.[61] The wording is found on a handful of other brasses, three of them extant—those of Hawise Botiller at Norbury (Staffs.), Sir John

[60] It is no coincidence that his granddaughter, when she commissioned the brasses to her two husbands, Braybrooke and Hawberk, in *c*.1409 identified herself as 'heir of Sir John de Cobham founder of this college'. It was as founder that he wished to be remembered.

[61] It may have been popularized by Pope Gregory the Great's epitaph, quoted by Bede: 'Suscipe, terra, tuo corpus de corpore sumtum . . .': *Bede's Ecclesiastical History of the English People*, ed. B. Colgrave and R. A. B. Mynors (Oxford, 1969), 132. See also the early medieval texts quoted by F. Paxton, *Christianizing Death: The Creation of a Ritual Process in Early Medieval Europe* (Ithaca, N.Y., 1990), 54–5, 147, 178.

de Mereworth (d. 1366) at Mereworth (Kent), and Sir William de Etchingham (d. 1388) at Etchingham (Sussex)—and one now lost, at Birdbrook (Suffolk). These all date from the period c.1360–c.1390.[62] The popularity of the form of words at this time is a mark of the puritanical, anti-worldly, streak in contemporary piety, which probably had its origins in the writings of the mystic Richard Rolle.[63] Rolle's work stimulated in his readers a sense of their personal unworthiness. Evidence of the appeal of his writing is found in the anti-carnal language of a number of contemporary wills. The Yorkshire knight Sir Brian Stapleton, for example, in 1394 referred to his 'caitiff body', while Gerard Braybrooke in 1429 described himself as a 'wretch'.[64] Similarly ascetic tastes are evidenced by the prohibition of funerary pomp in a scattering of wills. William Stourton, a Wiltshire knight, for example insisted on a simple burial for his 'putrid body, naked as it came into the world except for a linen cloth', while Sir Ralph Hastings of Yorkshire asked for his body to be brought to Selby abbey in a simple cart.[65] Seen in the context of these wills, the highly ascetic tone of Lord Cobham's epitaph becomes a manifestation of an increasingly fashionable lay piety. There are signs that the 3rd Lord's tastes may have been inherited by members of his family. A number of his, and his granddaughter's, connections were with men and women of similar outlook. John Prophet, the keeper of the privy seal and dean of York, who left Joan Cobham a bequest, referred in his will to his

[62] N. E. Saul, *Scenes From Provincial Life: Knightly Families in Sussex 1280–1400* (Oxford, 1986), 155–6; M. Norris (ed.), *Monumental Brasses: The Portfolio Plates of the Monumental Brass Society* (Woodbridge, 1988), no. 38. For the reference to Birdbrook I am grateful to Sally Badham. The text may, of course, have been used on other brasses now lost. It is significant that the four brasses are of different styles—Norbury, Cobham, and Mereworth of 'A', and Etchingham of 'B'; so evidently a variety of workshops were using the text.

[63] For Rolle's influence on late fourteenth-century piety, see J. Hughes, *Pastors and Visonaries: Religion and Secular Life in Late Medieval Yorkshire* (Woodbridge, 1988), esp. ch. 2; J. I. Catto, 'Sir William Beauchamp between Chivalry and Lollardy', in C. Harper-Bill and R. Harvey (eds.), *The Ideals and Practice of Medieval Knighthood, III* (Woodbridge, 1990), 39–48.

[64] K. B. McFarlane, *Lancastrian Kings and Lollard Knights* (Oxford, 1972), 215, 217. For further discussion, see J. A. F. Thomson, 'Knightly Piety and the Margins of Lollardy', in M. Aston and C. Richmond (eds.), *Lollardy and the Gentry in the Later Middle Ages* (Stroud, 1997), 95–111.

[65] Thomson, 'Knightly Piety', 215; M. G. A. Vale, *Piety, Charity and Literacy among the Yorkshire Gentry, 1370–1480* (Borthwick Papers, 50; York, 1976), 13. Wills enjoining funerary austerity are more common in the north than in the south of England—perhaps a mark of Rolle's influence, for he lived at Hampole (Yorks). Another example is afforded by the will of Thomas Neville, Lord Furnival, who in 1407 requested burial in Worksop priory 'mediocriter et sine vana gloria mundi': *Testamenta Eboracensia: Selection of the Wills from the Registry at York*, iii, ed. J. Raine (Surtees Society, 45; 1864), 40–1. A connected train of thought led to an insistence on simple commemoration, or none at all. William Waltham, canon of York and Lincoln, requested burial in Lincoln cathedral without anything over his grave other than the stone of the pavement (ibid. 56–7).

'putrid body'.[66] The Cobhams' kinswoman, Margery Nerford, who died in 1417, made a will which, with its many references to books, is suggestive of more than conventional piety.[67] In the context of these ties, Joan Cobham's fourth marriage to Sir John Oldcastle, the Lollard, may well have had more than a purely political significance. Although it was arranged to reward a hard-working and loyal soldier knight, it is possible that it was underpinned by a shared outlook in matters religious.

All this evidence—John's interest in the Trinity, the very personal nature of his epitaph, and the pride in the foundation of the college—points to the exceptional nature of his piety. A number of similarities are to be noticed between John's piety and that of his friend the Black Prince and his circle. As Richard Barber has shown, the prince was a keen devotee of the cult of the Trinity. The earliest portrait of him, a lead badge, shows him kneeling before the Trinity, while a tester painted with the Trinity was placed above his tomb at Canterbury.[68] It is also apparent that both men had a leaning to religious austerity. The prince lent his patronage to an austere order, the Bonshommes, while John was sympathetic to the Carthusians: he is said to have retreated into a Carthusian house in his old age.[69] It is likely that John's religion had its origins in broadly the same set of beliefs as the fashionable courtly *devots*.[70] Where it differed was in its emphatic rejection of heterodoxy. John's piety was never other than mainstream orthodox. John shunned the *devots'* self-conscious preoccupation with feelings of contrition and personal guilt. Although his tastes were personally austere, he showed no interest in funerary austerity. When his wife Margaret died in August 1395, he laid on the most lavish funeral for her at Cobham.[71] For John, there was no

[66] *Testamenta Eboracensia*, iii, 53–5. The phrase is 'corpus meum putridum'. Prophet, who was secretary 1402–5 and keeper of the privy seal 1406–15, asked to be buried at Pocklington or York, if he died in the north, or Leighton Buzzard or Ringwood, if he died in the south. In the event he was buried at Ringwood, where his brass, probably commissioned by his executors, remains.

[67] 'Introduction', in *Lollardy and the Gentry in the Later Middle Ages*, ed. Aston and Richmond, 16–18. Among the bequests in the will was one 'to Lady Cobham, the wife of John Oldcastle, (of) my book which once belonged to Lord Cobham'.

[68] R. Barber, *Edward, Prince of Wales and Aquitaine* (London, 1978), 240–1; J. Vale and M. Vale, 'Knightly Codes and Piety', in N. E. Saul (ed.), *Age of Chivalry: Art and Society in Late Medieval England* (London, 1992), 24–6.

[69] Barber, *Edward, Prince of Wales and Aquitaine*, 241; D. Knowles, *The Religious Orders in England*, i (Cambridge, 1962), 202. For John Cobham's withdrawal to a Carthusian house, see above, 23.

[70] For the piety of the prince and princess of Wales and the knights in their service, a number of whom were Lollards, see Saul, *Richard II*, 297–300.

[71] He ordered four sets of heraldic banners and 100 pennons from a London painter: BL, Harley Ch. 54 G 48. It is evident from this that the church was to be decked out with all the emblematic display of lineage and descent; for a discussion of such funerals, see Hughes, *Pastors and Visionaries*, 30. A legacy of the Cobhams' ceremonious funerals is the two fifteenth-century

conflict between personal religious austerity and elaborate funerary rituals. Neither was there for the Black Prince—whatever his possible sympathy with Wycliffism. In his will of 1376 the prince, while carefully prescribing an unworldly epitaph, insisted on the grandest possible obsequies.[72] For both men religion was at once introspective and yet suffused with deeply chivalric values and ritual. It was entirely appropriate that their funerary monuments should exhibit both aspects. In each case, the inscription dwelled on mortality, while the effigy attested worldly splendour. The two aspects stood in essential counterpoint.

In the half century or so from the 1370s it became usual for the Cobhams to be commemorated at Cobham by brasses. As many as seven memorials were laid to members of the family in this period. The first two commemorated ladies—Maud, the wife of Sir Thomas Cobham of Randall (d. 1380) (fig. 14),[73] and Margaret, daughter of Hugh Courtenay, earl of Devon, and the 3rd Lord's wife (d. 1395) (fig. 15). After these came the small half-figure of Ralph Cobham of Chafford, who died in 1402 (fig. 16),[74] and the elegant bracket composition, also of 1402, to Reginald Cobham, rector of Cooling (fig. 17). After these came the two magnificent brasses of the second and third husbands of Joan the family heiress, Sir Reginald Braybrooke and Sir Nicholas Hawberk (figs. 18, 19), and finally that of Joan herself (fig. 20). The brasses of Ralph Cobham and Reginald the rector apart, these were all conceived in the traditional

tournament helms now in the Royal Armouries at Leeds, replicas of which hang in the chancel at Cobham. These were probably carried at the funerals of Braybrooke and Hawberk and bequeathed to the church afterwards. See C. Blair, 'The Funeral Helms at Cobham', *Monumental Brass Society Bulletin*, 79 (Sept. 1998), 392–4.

[72] *Collection of the Wills of the Kings of England*, ed. J. Nichols (London, 1780), 66–70. The inscription was inscribed on his tomb almost exactly as laid down in the will: 'Tu qe passez ove bouche close par la ou cist corps repose, / Entent ce qe te dirray, sicome te dire le say. / Tiel come tu es, je autiel fu; tu seras tiel come je su; / De la mort ne pensay je mie, tant come javoy la vie. / En terre avoy grand richesse, dont je y fys grand noblesse, / Terre, mesons et grand tresor, draps, chivalx, argent et or, / Mes ore su je povres et cheitifs, profond en la terre gys. / Ma grande beaute est tout alee, ma char est tout gastee. / Moult est estroite ma meson. En moy na si verite non. / Et si ore me veissez, je ne quide pas qe vous deissez, / Qe je eusse onqes hom este, si su je ore de tout changee. / Pur Dieu pries au celestien roy, qe mercy eit de l'alme de moy. / Tout cil qi pur moi prieront, ou a Dieu m'acorderont, / Dieu les mette en son paradys, ou nul ne poet estrechetifs.' Obvious parallels are to be observed here with the sentiments in Lord Cobham's epitaph. The source of the prince's epitaph was a twelfth-century collection of narratives, the *Disciplina Clericalis* of Petrus Alphonsi: D. B. Tyson, 'The Epitaph of Edward, the Black Prince', *Medium Aevum*, 46 (1977), 98–104.

[73] For the identity of this lady, see MacMichael, 'Kentish Items: Cobham and Goudhurst', 477–84. She was the daughter of Thomas Morice, a London lawyer. Waller, wrongly supposing her to be Sir William Pympe's daughter, supplied a shield bearing the Pympe arms.

[74] For this brass, see below, 118.

FIG 14. Cobham M.S. VI: Maud, daughter of Thomas Morice, wife of Sir Thomas Cobham of Randall, d. 1380

FIG 15. Cobham M.S. VII: Margaret, daughter of Hugh Courtenay, earl of Devon, wife of John, 3rd Lord Cobham, d. 1395

FIG 16. Cobham M.S. IX: Ralph Cobham, d. 1402

FIG 17. Cobham M.S. VIII: Reginald de
Cobham, rector of Cooling, d. 1402

FIG 18. Cobham M.S. X: Sir Reginald Braybrooke, d. 1405,
engraved c.1408

FIG 19. Cobham M.S. XI: Sir Nicholas Hawberk, d. 1407,
engraved c.1408

FIG 20. Cobham M.S. XIII: Joan, Lady Cobham,
d. 1434

Cobham mould. They were large, usually elaborate, compositions, consisting of elegant single figures under canopies, with shields of arms at the top or at the sides. A few exhibit innovatory design features. Three, for example, remarkably for their date, depict children. Overall, however, the influence of client or patron is less noticeable than on the earlier commissions. Inscriptions are invariably less personal; on most, standard formulae like 'Icy gist' and 'lalme de quy dieux eyt mercy' are used. But occasionally marks of personal piety are included. On the brasses of Margaret Cobham and Joan's two husbands the figures of patron saints are included. Sometimes, too, there is evidence of client influence in composition or design. Thus Reginald, the rector of Cooling, is commemorated by a bracket brass—a type often associated with members of the clergy; while the modest size of Ralph's half-figure reflects his lowly position in the family hierarchy.

In one highly significant respect the brasses of these years are to be distinguished from those of the previous generation: they were produced in a different workshop. Whereas the brasses ordered by the 3rd Lord were of London style 'A', these are from 'B', 'A''s main rival for business in the capital. From this time until the mid-fifteenth century all the brasses at Cobham were to be 'B''s work. This was a decisive shift in patronage: indeed, the only one to occur in the Middle Ages at Cobham. What were the considerations that brought it about?

The factor least likely to have had a bearing was aesthetics. There is very little evidence to suggest that medieval patrons chose monuments for their attractiveness to the eye.[75] As the numerous instructions given in wills show, the matter of most concern to customers was accurate depiction of heraldry and the marks of status.[76] Judged by this criterion the 'A' brasses at Cobham would have appeared perfectly satisfactory: the Cobham arms were appropriately differenced, and the marks of cadency correctly shown. Moreover, the engraver even faithfully reproduced the founder's idiosyncratic epitaphs. It is doubtful if the clumsiness of two of the male figures would even have been noticed. Attractiveness to the eye is a relative concept. What is considered attractive by one generation may be utterly unattractive to another.

The main influences behind the change of workshop are likely to have been personal and social. In other words, what was of greatest moment to

[75] For useful comment on the factors influencing taste, see R. Emmerson, 'William Browne's Taste in Brasses', *TMBS*, 12 pt 4, (1978), 322–5.

[76] Norris, *Monumental Brasses: The Craft*, 90–1; S. Badham, 'Status and Salvation', *TMBS*, 15 pt 5 (1996), 413–65.

the Cobhams was the taste of their kinsfolk and business associates. There is plenty of evidence from the fourteenth century to indicate the role played by social and business networks in influencing choice. The brasses of style 'C', for example—one of the minority workshops in London— found a ready market in a closely knit group of Richard II's courtier knights in the 1390s.[77] In the same period style 'B' was patronized by a no less closely knit group of government clerks who served each other in the office of executor and arranged the laying of each others' memorials.[78] It is altogether plausible to see networking of this sort as lying behind the Cobhams' switch to 'B'. The switch has the appearance of being a switch by the whole family. A batch of three or four Cobham commissions was given to 'B' at this time. The grandest of these was the big triple canopied brass at Chrishall (Essex) to Cobham's daughter, Joan, and her husband, Sir John de la Pole (fig. 36). A second, and scarcely inferior, memorial was the elegant figure of Elizabeth, the first wife of Reginald, Lord Cobham, at Lingfield (fig. 27); and the third was the more modest brass to Sir Henry de Cobham, a member of the Beluncle line, at Clyffe Pypard (Wilts.) (fig. 38). It is tempting to see a single hand initiating these commissions. Indeed, there is evidence to support such an idea. The brass at Lingfield bears an uncanny resemblance to that of Maud, Lady Cobham (M.S. VI), at Cobham (fig. 14). On both brasses there is a distinctive fur flounce on the lower part of the dress. There can be little doubt that the two memorials were commissioned simultaneously—indeed, were commissioned by the same patron. So, who could this influential and well-connected figure have been? And why did he, or she, go to style 'B'? To answer these questions, it is necessary to look for a moment at the men in charge of the 'B' workshop at this time.

From roughly the 1360s to 1387 London style 'B' was run by two generations of the Lakenham family, Richard and Henry, who were probably father and son. Henry Lakenham's involvement in tomb-making is established by a contract which he made to supply a tomb to Sir Nicholas Loveyne in St Mary Graces, London.[79] The core of Lakenham's business was almost certainly represented by the production of tombs and brasses for sale directly to the market, but it is likely that he was also engaged in engraving inscriptions for tombs by the mason, Henry Yevele, who was a

---

[77] N. E. Saul, 'The Fragments of the Golafre Brass in Westminster Abbey', *TMBS*, 15 pt 1 (1992), 19–32.
[78] The clerks were William Ermyn, John Sleford, and William Fulbourne, commemorated respectively at Castle Ashby (Northants.), Balsham (Cambs.), and Fulbourne (Cambs.).
[79] Blair, 'Henry Lakenham, Marbler of London', 66–74.

marbler himself.[80] In the later 1380s Yevele secured a prestigious contract to make the tomb chest for Cardinal Langham's monument in Westminster Abbey; and around the chamfered edge of this is an inscription in 'B' lettering.[81] A few years later Yevele and his partner Lote secured the still more prestigious contract for the monument to Richard II and his queen, again in Westminster Abbey, for which Broker and Prest were to supply the effigies; and around this too is an inscription in 'B' lettering.[82] What these two cases suggest is that the arrangements for making big late fourteenth-century tombs closely resembled those adopted for the monument of Richard Beauchamp at St Mary's, Warwick, some fifty years later. Beauchamp's monument was the responsibility of a whole team of craftsmen—the marbler John Borde supplied the tomb chest, John Massingham carved a wooden model of the effigy, the goldsmith Bartholomew Lambespring prepared the effigy for gilding, and William Austen, a founder, undertook the casting.[83] Yevele—or Yevele and Lote, who is once described as a 'latoner'—were probably involved in not dissimilar arrangements.[84] Jointly they assumed the overall responsibility for supplying the tomb chest; however, for particular tasks beyond their competence they, or their successors, drew on the services of others; and for the engraving of epitaphs they turned to Lakenham, or his apprentice West, whose premises were nearby.[85] John Harvey has suggested that Yevele was responsible not only for the tombs of Richard II and Langham but also for those of Edward III, again at Westminster, and of the Black Prince at Canterbury; and it is interesting to note that these too carry latten inscriptions with 'B' lettering.[86] As Harvey and others have demonstrated, Yevele ran a wide-ranging busi-

[80] Yevele's will has a reference to 'all my marble and latten goods and my tools therein': Harvey, *English Medieval Architects*, 365.   [81] Harvey, *Henry Yevele*, 49.

[82] T. Rymer, *Foedera, Conventiones, Litterae etc.*, vii, ed. G. Holmes (20 vols.; London, 1704–35), 795–6, 797–8; Alexander and Binski (eds.), *Age of Chivalry: Art in Plantagenet England*, no. 446. In this case, the responsibility for supplying the epitaph lay with Broker and Prest. According to the contract, they were to base the effigies on a 'patron' shown to them: which suggests that someone else was providing the designs. This could have been Yevele.

[83] These were the principal figures engaged, but there were others. The most recent discussion of the tomb is P. Lindley, *Gothic to Renaissance. Essays on Sculpture in England* (Stamford, 1995), 62–6.

[84] For Lote as a 'latoner', see Harvey, *English Medieval Architects*, 188.

[85] Yevele's premises were in St Paul's churchyard, and Lakenham is known to have lived not far from there in St Faith's parish; Lakenham also requested burial in St Paul's churchyard (Harvey, *English Medieval Architects*, 365; Blair, 'Henry Lakenham, Marbler of London', 67). William West, Lakenham's apprentice, appears to have taken over his business on his death: Emmerson, 'Monumental Brasses. London Design', 66–7.

[86] Harvey, *English Medieval Architects*, 361, 364. Part of the inscription of the Black Prince's tomb is illustrated in Norris, *Monumental Brasses: The Memorials*, ii, pls. 69, 70. The tomb of Yevele's friend and patron Sir John Beauchamp, formerly in St Paul's cathedral, is also in his style (Harvey, *English Medieval Architects*, 365).

ness, with interests not only in sculpture but in the design and construction of buildings and the supply of building materials. It would be entirely natural, given the scale of his operations, if he chose to devolve areas of specialized work to others. The evidence suggests that it was generally to Lakenham that he turned for the supply or the engraving of epitaphs.

Yevele's business relations with Lakenham have a relevance to the brasses at Cobham in the context of Lord Cobham's own relations with Yevele. Cobham employed Yevele as either an architect or an architectural consultant intermittently over a period of some twenty years. The two men very likely first met when they were employed in royal service in the 1360s. Yevele had by then established himself as a mason and was the obvious man for Cobham to approach for his works at Cobham. The first commission which Cobham entrusted to him was probably that for the remodelling of Cobham church and the construction of the buildings of Cobham college.[87] Later, as Cobham's appetite for building grew, other commissions followed. Around 1380 Cobham employed him as consultant architect for his new castle at Cooling, and in 1381 he commissioned designs from him for a new aisle at St Dunstan-in-the-East, London.[88] But Cobham was not only a major source of patronage to Yevele; he was also a frequent associate on public works in Kent. In 1383 the king commissioned the two of them to rebuild Rochester bridge and a couple of years later they were employed in surveying Canterbury's city walls.[89] The length and closeness of the association between the two makes it likely—indeed, virtually certain—that it was Yevele who introduced Cobham to 'B'. Indeed, it is conceivable that Cobham employed Yevele and Lakenham together at Cobham: the sedilia on the south side of the chancel have canopies very similar to those on 'B' brasses. The series of links between Cobham, Yevele, and Lakenham have an obvious bearing on the switch to 'B' for the Cobhams' brasses. The change was almost certainly one initiated by the 3rd Lord himself. It is unfortunate that we cannot be certain which, or how many, of the brasses he was personally responsible for. There is a fair likelihood that he commissioned his wife's brass, for she died in 1395. However, it is possible that he ordered several more. Two obvious candidates are the brasses of the two ladies of c.1380.[90] Around this time Cobham was closely involved with Yevele: he had just begun the building of Cooling castle, and work was

[87] See above, 48.   [88] Ibid. 361–2; see above, 48.
[89] *CPR 1381–5*, 221; *CPR 1385–9*, 103; Harvey, *English Medieval Architects*, 361–2.
[90] Maud Cobham at Cobham; Elizabeth, wife of Reginald, 2nd Lord Cobham at Lingfield.

well under way on the college. It would be entirely natural if he had approached Yevele with an order for the brasses. If he became less involved later as he grew older, he had at least indicated where business was to go in future.

Cobham's switch to 'B' brought the family's patronage into line with that of most of the other higher nobility and gentry commemorated by brasses at this time. By 1390 'B' had established a fairly secure grip on this affluent, well-connected market. Among the nobility, for example, the earl of Warwick at St Mary's, Warwick, and Lords Berkeley and Ferrers at Wotton-under-Edge and Merevale respectively went to 'B'. The Cobhams' preference for this workshop thus fits into a much broader pattern of patronage. A couple of decades earlier, however, Cobham had given his business to style 'A'. So what lay behind the change? What led him to switch from one workshop to another?

Cobham's abandonment of 'A' is symptomatic of a much wider problem which workshop 'A' appears to have faced: a loss of customers at the top end of the market. 'A' was still very active. Among its more high-status clients were a Cobham—Reginald, 2nd Lord Cobham of Sterborough, commemorated at Lingfield (fig. 28)—and civil servants like John Prophet, keeper of the privy seal, at Ringwood (Hants.), and Henry de Codington, master of chancery, at Bottesford (Leics). The majority of its clients, however, were drawn from the middling or lesser country gentry and the parish clergy; courtly figures and magnates were few. Generally, the quality of its output was no worse than before; indeed, in some cases it was better.[91] So how can the loss of these higher-ranking customers be explained?

The most likely reason is that there was a change of management. In a business like funerary sculpture in which personal contact counted for so much, a break in the continuity of contact could be disastrous. Unfortunately, the lack of evidence for style 'A''s personnel makes it difficult to identify the succession of their main engravers, but a document from the Cobham archive casts a valuable shaft of light. In the Centre for Kentish Studies at Maidstone is a receipt for a delivery of wheat given to Lord Cobham in April 1371 by one John Thornton, executor of 'John Ramsey,

---

[91] The quality of style 'A' brasses was highly variable. Among their brasses of the 1390s, those of Thomas and Richard Gomfrey at Dronfield, Derbys., stand out as mediocre, while that of John de Swynstede at Edlesborough, Bucks., is simply superb (respectively, *Monumental Brasses: The Portfolio Plates of the Monumental Brass Society*, nos. 90, 82). The quality of 'B''s output, by contrast, was more consistent. The variability in quality of 'A''s work may be attributed to weaker workshop control.

lately marbler of London'.[92] Ramsey was a member of the prolific London-based family which produced a number of master masons in these years; from 1343 to 1348 he served as warden of the masons at St Stephen's, Westminster, and in the 1360s he supplied marble for the cloisters in the upper bailey of Windsor Castle.[93] The receipt shows Cobham to have been selling grain either to or through him, and it is possible that, like Yevele, he had a sideline in victualling.[94] It is naturally tempting to wonder if Cobham's dealings with him in one capacity could have led to dealings with him in another: in other words, if Ramsey could have been the man with whom Cobham placed his orders for brasses in the 1360s. An idiosyncracy in the design of 'A''s knightly figures lends some support to the idea. In the mid- to late 1360s the 'A' engravers usually showed their knights with studded cuisses, a feature rarely found on 'B' brasses. It is very likely that the design source for this oddity was the figure of St Mercurius (c.1351–60) in St Stephen's chapel, Westminster, where the Ramseys had worked.[95] The connection with a project in which the Ramseys were involved greatly strengthens, if it does not altogether clinch, the case for linking Ramsey with workshop 'A'. The receipt in the Cobham archive shows that by 1371 Ramsey was dead. A decade or so later, when Cobham was next ordering brasses, he went to a different marbler. There can be no certainty, of course, that it was Ramsey's death which prompted the change, but the evidence certainly points to this being the case.

The brasses ordered by the Cobhams from workshop 'B' in the 1380s and later are to be numbered among the outstanding memorials of their age. Overall, they are of far higher quality than 'A''s of the 1360s. The engraving is bold and incisive; the figures are well proportioned, and the canopies endowed with admirable lightness and elegance. The two most eye-catching of the series are those of Braybrooke and Hawberk (figs. 18, 19); Waller, indeed, considered Hawberk's the finest military brass of its age.[96] The two memorials are very similar. Each consists of a single figure under a canopy with enclosing inscription. Braybrooke's brass is marginally the simpler. The knight is shown in full armour, with the greater part of his body protected by plate, but a mail aventail covering the neck.

---

[92] CKS, U601/E7.   [93] Harvey, *English Medieval Architects*, 241.

[94] In 1359 Yevele was granted a licence to discharge victuals at Calais: ibid. 359.

[95] See above, 92. Work began on the internal decoration of St Stephen's chapel at the east end in 1351 and is documented until at least 1360 (R. A. Brown, H. M. Colvin, and A. J. Taylor, *The History of the King's Works: The Middle Ages* 2 vols.; London, 1963, i, 518–19).

[96] Waller, 'The Lords of Cobham', 91.

Alongside him are miniature representations of his two sons on pedestals. Over him rises an elegant triple-arched canopy, at the apex of which, between two shields, is a Trinity under an enclosing super canopy. Hawberk's figure is virtually identical to Braybrooke's except that his head is shown resting on a helmet and crest. Alongside him is a representation of his son, the boy being shown on a pedestal like Braybrooke's boys. The canopy is this time of exceptional splendour. Like Braybrooke's, it is of triple-arched design, but in addition to the Trinity in the centre are figures of the Virgin and Child on the dexter side and St George spearing the dragon on the sinister. The shields, displaced from the canopy spandrels, are relocated on the side buttresses.

These superb brasses are so similar to each other that there can be little doubt that they are by the same hand and of the same date. A *terminus a quo* for the date of engraving is afforded by the inscriptions. As Waller noted, the deceased's wife in each case is referred to as 'Lady Joan, Lady of Cobham, heir of John de Cobham, the founder of this college'.[97] Since Joan could not be styled 'Lady of Cobham' until after her grandfather's death in 1408, it follows that the brasses must have been laid after that year. Braybrooke had died in 1405, and Hawberk two years later. It is a reasonable supposition that their brasses were ordered around 1409. This was another of the multiple orders that are a characteristic of the Cobham series.

A notable feature of the two brasses is their inclusion of children. The little boys on their pedestals—two of them on Braybrooke's brass, and one on Hawberk's—are among the earliest youngsters to be shown on brass. Before the mid-fourteenth century, brasses—indeed, monuments generally—had rarely included subsidiary figures. Monuments were laid principally to elicit prayers for the commemorated; thus by definition no figures other than the commemorated's were needed. Around the second quarter of the century, however, attitudes had begun to change.[98] Weepers, or earthly mourners, among whom the deceased's kin might be numbered, began to be placed around the sides of tombs. On John of Eltham's tomb in Westminster Abbey, an early example (1337), there was a gallery of weepers who included his parents.[99] On Edward III's tomb of

[97] Waller, 'The Lords of Cobham', 89.

[98] For this subject, see J. Page-Phillips, *Children on Brasses* (London, 1970), esp. 14–15. Badham sees the interest in children beginning a little earlier on the Continent, and perhaps influencing developments in England: 'Status and Salvation', 426.

[99] Illustrated in L. Southwick, 'The Armoured Effigy of Prince John of Eltham in Westminster Abbey and Some Closely Related Military Monuments', *Church Monuments*, 2 (1987), fig. 1.

half a century later weepers were included representing the king's twelve children.[100] This three-dimensional idea of weepers was reduced to two-dimensional form in 1347 on the brass of Sir Hugh Hastings at Elsing (Norfolk). Here eight weepers—four on either side and chiefly his companions-in-arms—were placed vertically in the side shafts of the canopy.[101] A broadly similar arrangement was found on the exceptional brass, now lost, of Thomas of Woodstock, duke of Gloucester, in Westminster Abbey (c.1400).[102] In this example, the central figure of the duke was surrounded by smaller figures of his parents and his eleven brothers and sisters, some of them on pedestals. At the same time, and perhaps as a response to the impact of child mortality from plague, the idea of representing children separately on brass began to emerge. The first extant brass to commemorate children alone is that to Raulin and Margaret Brocas, c.1370, at Sherborne St John (Hants.), an attractive composition of two small half-figures. From twenty years later comes the remarkable brass, now lost, of the sons of Sir John Salisbury, at Marlow (Bucks.), showing them below a Resurrection scene.[103] A little later, the idea of employing miniature figures to represent children on the brasses of their elders entered the engravers' repertory. An important transitional example is the brass of John Corp and his granddaughter, at Stoke Fleming (Devon), where the granddaughter is shown three-quarters size and raised on a pedestal to achieve visual balance.[104] The employment of diminutive figures in the proper sense is found for the first time at Cobham. The inspiration for these little figures was probably twofold: the use of pedestals was almost certainly derived from the Westminster and Stoke Fleming examples, while the diminutive figure form was borrowed from earlier weeper figures. The 'child type' pioneered at Cobham passed before long into more general use. At Trotton (Sussex), 1421, the figure of a little boy nestles in the ample folds of his mother's dress, while a child, probably a boy, stands beside his mother at Furneaux Pelham (Herts.).[105] At Weston Colville (Cambs.), in 1427, Richard Leverer's son is

---

[100] For these tombs, see L. Stone, *Sculpture in Britain: The Middle Ages*, 2nd edn. (Harmondsworth, 1972), 162, 193; pls. 123, 149. [101] Ibid. 164–5.

[102] The brass was illustrated by F. Sandford, *Genealogical History of the Kings and Queens of England* (London, 1677), 230, and reprod. in J. S. N. Wright, *The Brasses of Westminster Abbey* (London, 1969), 12; Page-Phillips, *Children on Brasses*, fig. 6.

[103] See Page-Phillips, *Children on Brasses*, figs. 1, 2.

[104] Ibid. fig. 4. The brass is dated 1391.

[105] Illus. respectively in Stone, *Sculpture in Britain*, 199, and *Monumental Brasses: The Portfolio Plates of the Monumental Brass Society*, no. 134. The figure of the child on the Furneaux Pelham brass is lost, but the indent remains. On stylistic grounds the brass can be dated to c.1420.

placed equidistant between his parents.[106] Shortly before this time, the first groups of children had been shown on brass. The earliest extant examples are probably those on the Stokes brass at Ashby St Ledgers (Northants.), 1416.[107]

In general terms, the representation of children on brasses can be taken to mark a change in the character of the monument. The brass, instead of being, as it had been, essentially retrospective in character, now became prospective. It looked to the future; its imagery celebrated the survival and continuance of the family line. However, the earliest representations of children were rarely if ever rooted in such thinking. When children entered the commemorative repertory, it was usually because they had died young. Richard, the young heir shown on the Camoys brass at Trotton, had clearly predeceased his parents: in 1421 it was a grandson who succeeded.[108] The two Brocas children must likewise have succumbed to early death, for otherwise a separate memorial to them would have been unnecessary. The story is repeated at Cobham. Failure, and not success, was the spur to representation. Joan, the family heiress, who commissioned her husbands' brasses, was reflecting on the frustration of her hopes. After three marriages she had still not borne a healthy son. Her two boys by Braybrooke had both died in early youth, while her one son by Hawberk was stillborn or had died in infancy. There is a definite poignancy in the boys' appearance on the brasses. The boys' names are given: Reginald and Robert on Braybrooke's (the elder boy being named after his father), and John on Hawberk's. For once the coldly impersonal nature of these stylish 'B' brasses is broken. The sadness of the bereaved parent is felt; the brass is stamped with the bitter imprint of disappointment. These are deeply expressive memorials. Joan, the unhappy mother, was pouring her innermost feelings into her instructions for their composition and design.[109]

The theme of hopes disappointed is picked up in Joan's own brass, which lies between those of her husbands (fig. 20). Superficially the memorial, which was laid after her death in 1434, is a celebration of

---

[106] Illus. in W. Lack, H. M. Stuchfield, and P. Whittemore, *The Monumental Brasses of Cambridgeshire* (London, 1995), 244.

[107] Illus. in *Monumental Brasses: The Portfolio Plates of the Monumental Brass Society*, no. 124. The chronology for the depiction of children as diminutive figures in stained glass is broadly the same: see Marks, *Stained Glass in England*, 13.

[108] *Complete Peerage*, ii, 508.

[109] For an assessment of medieval attitudes to children emphasizing the complexity of those attitudes, see S. Oosterwijk, '"Litel Enfaunt that Were but Late Borne". The Image of the *Infans* in Medieval Culture in North-Western Europe' (University of Leicester Ph.D. thesis, 1999).

lineage. The dominant feature is the dazzling array of shields—six in all, three on each side. Together, these provide an epitome of the family's history. Reading from the top, the arms are, on the dexter side: Cobham; Peverel quartering de la Pole and impaling Cobham, for Joan's father and mother; and Braybrooke impaling Cobham; and on the sinister side, Cobham impaling Courtenay, for her grandparents; Cobham quartering de la Pole; and Brooke, for Joan's son-in-law, impaling Cobham. This grandiose array of arms, more numerous than on any other Cobham brass, bears powerful witness to the family's connections and, more particularly, to their success in the marriage market. But the brass can be interpreted in another sense: as a study in disappointment. Alongside the figure and above the inscription are two groups of children—ten in all, six sons and four daughters. These groups are among the earliest of their kind on brass: probably only those at Ashby St Ledgers (Northants.) predate them.[110] The patron's purpose in commissioning them is clear: to create an impression of Joan the fecund mother, the begetter of a great brood. Yet the reality of her experience was very different. Not only is it highly unlikely that she ever bore ten children—the plates were presumably stock issue—but not one of the boys she bore survived to manhood. When she died in 1434 her heir was her daughter by Braybrooke: which accounts for her identification as Braybrooke's wife on the epitaph ('uxor domini Reginaldi Braybrook militis'). So this remarkable brass, with its intense interest in children and virtuoso display of heraldry, is at one level a celebration of lineage, but at another a study in the concealment of failure. After six generations the Cobham line had ended; yet not a hint of that sad outcome is given here.

Joan's was the last of the Cobham brasses to be laid at Cobham. Although junior branches of the family flourished for some time to come at Randall and Beluncle, their members were buried, and commemorated, elsewhere—at Boxley priory, generally, in the case of the former line, and at Hoo St Werburgh in the case of the latter. With the extinction of the senior line, Cobham was no longer the preferred burial-place of the wider kin. Nor, at least in the short term, does it seem to have been that of their immediate successors, the Brookes. Joan's son-in-law, and probably too her grandson, were buried at Thorncombe in the west country. Only early the next century, in John's time, did the Brookes start commissioning brasses to lie alongside the Cobhams'.

[110] The Ashby St Ledgers groups—four boys and twelve girls—are strikingly similar to those at Cobham; in each case they gaze upwards.

It was probably the presence of so many Cobham brasses in the chancel floor that disposed the Brookes to favour this form of memorial. Commemoration by the same medium as the Cobhams stressed continuity; it presented the Brookes as the Cobhams' legitimate successors. But the Brookes' brasses were very different in appearance from their predecessors'. They were double brasses. Two brasses were commissioned by the family in the early sixteenth century—one for John in 1506, and the other for his son in 1529 (figs. 21, 22). On each of these the commemorated was shown with his wife. The Cobhams had never adopted the double-figure form. They had invariably chosen single figures. This was the pattern which had been established in 1300 for the brasses to John and Joan de Cobham, and it was maintained in the years that followed. Not once was a double brass laid, despite the growing popularity of the form.

The consistency of the Cobhams' taste is one of the most remarkable things about their brasses. The many generations of the family buried and commemorated at Cobham all favoured much the same type of brass—one composed of a full-length effigy, a single canopy and a marginal inscription. Over a period of a century and a quarter, only two members of the family (or their executors) favoured a different form. These were Reginald and Ralph (figs. 16, 17): Reginald, the rector of Cooling, was commemorated by a bracket brass, a type very popular with the clergy, while Ralph was commemorated by a small half-figure showing him holding his epitaph. Ralph's brass is closely comparable to the similar half-figure of Robert Gower at Brabourne, near Maidstone (now lost but recorded by Philpot), in which the commemorated is shown holding a shield (fig. 23).[111] The brasses are roughly contemporary with each other, and either could have provided the model or inspiration for the other.

The uniformity of the Cobhams' commemorative tastes, together with their remarkable keenness to be buried at Cobham, afford clear evidence of the family's sense of solidarity. Cobham church was more than a family mausoleum; it was a mausoleum for the wider kin. The Cobhams of Cobham, the Cobhams of Randall, the Cobhams of Beluncle, the Cobhams of Chafford: representatives of all these branches were

---

[111] For Philpot, and his importance as a recorder of monuments now lost, see H. S. London, 'John Philipot, M.P., Somerset Herald, 1624–1645', *AC*, 60 (1947). A notable feature of Gower's brass is the presence of an orle on the bascinet. The orle is relatively rare on brasses, and it is not found on the brass of Ralph Cobham. The one Cobham brass on which the orle does appear is that of Reginald, Lord Cobham at Lingfield. For further discussion, see below, 172 n. 110.

FIG 21. Cobham M.S. XVIII: John Brooke, Lord Cobham (figure lost), d. 1512, and his second wife Margaret, d. 1506, engraved c.1506

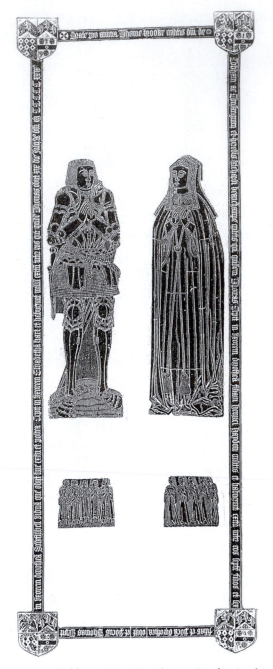

FIG 22. Cobham M.S. XIX: Thomas Brooke, Lord Cobham, d. 1529, and his first wife Dorothy.

FIG 23. Philpot's drawing of the lost brass of Robert Gower at Brabourne (Kent). (BL, Harley MS 3917, fo. 77^r)

brought to Cobham for burial. The founder's consciousness of a kin-network reaching beyond the nuclear family is shown by the arrangements which he made for his wife's obsequies in 1395: he commissioned an extravagant series of banners and pennons showing his own arms, those of Cobhams of Sterborough and of other families to which he was related.[112] It goes without saying that on occasion the Cobhams could be competitive as well as co-operative: the argument between the heirs of Henry, the 1st Lord, over the division of the family lands shows that.[113] But more striking overall is the evidence of their willingness, at least on

---

[112] BL, Harley Ch. 54 G 48. Cobham also wanted the arms of Edward Courtenay, earl of Devon, of other members of the Courtenay family, and of Lord Grey of Codnor, who was related to the Cobhams of Sterborough. [113] See above, 34.

matters in which they had a common interest, to strike an accord. A good example of the family's disposition to compromise is provided by the arrangements made to difference their coats of arms. Without some agreement on differencing, identifying members of the family armorially would have been virtually impossible. At some stage—it is not clear when—a series of conventions was introduced: the Cobhams of Beluncle were to display three crescents on their arms, the Cobhams of Chafford three crosslets, and so on.[114] Co-operation of this sort was a characteristic of the Cobhams' 'clan' identity. And it is precisely that 'clan' identity which is illustrated by the conformity of their taste in memorials. Over a century or so there were few deviations from the preferred norm; time after time, large canopied single-figure brasses were ordered. In death as in life, harmony reigned in the family. The group identity triumphed; individual identities were subsumed within the collective. Over the period as a whole only one branch of the family successfully fashioned a separate commemorative identity for themselves, and that was the Cobhams of Sterborough. The mausoleum which they created at Lingfield is a witness to their own distinct sense of their worth in the world.

[114] In the mid-seventeenth century, in his commentary on Upton, Edward Bysshe interestingly cited the differencing of the Cobham arms as a remarkable example of the use of heraldry within the family: *Nicholai Uptoni de Studio Militari Libri Quatuor*, ed. E. Bysshe (London, 1654), 3–4. I am grateful to John A. Goodall for this reference.

→ 6 ←

The Cobhams of Sterborough

THE monuments of the Cobhams of Sterborough constitute the finest and most numerous to any branch of the Cobham family outside Cobham. In their burial church at Lingfield are tomb effigies to two members of the family and brasses to three others. The Cobhams of Sterborough were for over a century the most successful of the Cobham collateral branches. Reginald, Lord Cobham, the second of his line, who died in 1361, was one of the outstanding figures of his day: a brilliant war captain and a respected royal councillor. He and his son were both summoned to parliament as peers. But the family's ascendancy did not last: after two generations their star faded and they sank back into the gentry. The Sterborough line's changing fortunes are vividly reflected in their monuments. A brief overview of the family's rise and decline will allow us to set those monuments in their context.

The Cobhams of Sterborough were descended from Reginald, a younger son of Sir John de Cobham 'the elder' by his second wife, Joan Neville. The success which the family later enjoyed was partly attributable to their auspicious beginnings. Reginald was fortunate in his marriage. The Cobhams had a well-to-do tenant, William de Hever of Prinkham in Lingfield, whose coheirs were his two daughters. Reginald's half-brother, John 'the younger', as head of the family claimed the daughters' marriages for his kin. Joan, the younger of the two, was married to Reginald, while her elder sister was given to Reginald's elder brother, William.[1] On William de Hever's death, according to the terms of the partition, Reginald acquired Prinkham, which he

---

[1] That a double marriage alliance was arranged can be inferred from the later evidence. Reginald's marriage to Joan is well attested: it is proved by his succession to Sterborough. That William was married to the other coheiress is proved by the fact that at his death he held lands once held by the de Hevers (*CIPM*, vi, no. 260); the de Hevers' lands are listed in a grant of free warren: *CChR 1257–1300*, 246. It was stated in his son-in-law's inquisition that two of his manors (East Shelve and Austin) were held from the Cobhams: *CIPM*, vi, no. 260.

was shortly to rename Sterborough.[2] In 1321 his brother died without issue, and he took over his lands.[3] He thus gained possession of the whole of the de Hever estate. Besides Prinkham, or Sterborough, he held East Shelve, Austin, and Chiddingstone, all in Kent.

For a man so relatively affluent, Reginald remains a shadowy figure. He figured little in local administration; nor is there any indication that he involved himself in family affairs. Possibly, the greater part of his adult life was spent outside the south-east. Sometime in the 1290s he entered the service of Roger Bigod, earl of Norfolk. He appears as one of the earl's knights in a list of his retainers in 1297, and in the following year he fought with him at Falkirk.[4] But in December 1306 the earl died and he lost his patron. There is no evidence that he joined the service of another lord as some of the earl's other retainers did. Indeed, his later years are obscure. The last reference to him comes from 1307. In that year he sought release from prison for his involvement in an attack on the manor of Penshurst, a property of Stephen de Penchester's widow, Margaret, whose daughter Joan was the wife of Henry de Cobham of Randall.[5] Penshurst lay only a few miles from his brother's manor of Chiddingstone, and possibly the two of them had some residual claim to it.

By his marriage to a coheiress Reginald had gained a substantial endowment for his heirs. But the family's political and social ascent really began in the next generation. Reginald II, the 1st Lord Cobham of Sterborough, was an altogether grander figure than his father. Not only was he a highly successful soldier—a 'good' and 'valiant' knight, 'who caused the French sore loss';[6] he also showed the qualities of 'sagesse' and intellect that made him a respected royal counsellor. By his ability and varied achievements he won for himself and his heir a position in the parliamentary peerage.

Reginald first appears in the records in 1328. On 9 June that year he was sent on a mission by Edward III to treat with the duke of Brabant

---

[2] The name was probably derived from the family of Richard Sterr', who is mentioned in 1312: in J. E. B. Gover, A. Mawer, and F. M. Stenton (eds.), *The Place-Names of Surrey* (English Place-Name Society, 11, 1982), 331. But could the preference for the name over Prinkham have been encouraged by play on the 'estoilles' (stars) on the family's arms?

[3] *CIPM*, vi, no. 260.

[4] *Documents Illustrating the Crisis of 1297–98 in England*, 157; *Scotland in 1298*, ed. H. Gough (London, 1888), 16, 20, 40.　　　　　　　　　　　　　　[5] *CCR 1307–13*, 13.

[6] These are the admittedly conventional tributes of Chandos Herald, the Black Prince's biographer: *The Life of the Black Prince by the Herald of Sir John Chandos*, ed. M. K. Pope and E. C. Lodge (Oxford, 1910), ll. 132, 571, 1312.

and the cities of Brabant and Flanders.[7] Evidently he was already to be numbered among the king's closest associates, and there is every likelihood, since he does not appear among the household staff, that he was retained in the chamber.[8] In 1334 he figured for the first time in the wardrobe books as a knight of the household, and in January 1336 he became a banneret.[9] His entry into the household is probably the single most significant factor in accounting for his early ascent. Not only did it give him a foothold on the ladder of advancement; it won him immediate access to royal patronage and greatly enlarged the range of his associates. How he secured this privileged position is unclear. The Cobhams had no obvious connections with the new king and his close entourage. In the later years of the previous reign their record had been one of co-operation with the discredited Edward II and his agents. Henry, the 1st Lord, had been constable of Rochester, while his kinsman Sir Stephen Cobham of Randall had fought on the royalist side at Boroughbridge;[10] at an earlier point John, the future 2nd Lord, had served in the Despenser retinue.[11] It is possible that by the mid-1320s the family had become disillusioned with Edward's tyrannical regime and the dominance of the two Despensers. Other gentry families alienated by the Despensers had opened secret communication with the queen and her son.[12] Conceivably the Cobhams had done the same; Reginald's entry into the young Edward III's household could have originated in such an initiative. But, if it did, the details and timing of the manoeuvre are unclear.

Reginald quickly established himself as an intimate of the young king. In May 1329 he was included in the retinue that Edward took with him to Amiens to perform homage to Philip of France.[13] Edward was at this time still under the tutelage of his mother. However, at a council meeting at Nottingham in October 1330 he ordered her to be arrested along

---

[7] *CPR 1327–30*, 300.

[8] Strangely, he does not appear in the lists of royal household staff in 1328 and 1330 printed in *Calendar of Memoranda Rolls (Exchequer) Michaelmas 1326–Michaelmas 1327* (London, 1968), 373–85.

[9] C. Shenton, 'The English Court and the Restoration of Royal Prestige, 1327–1345' (University of Oxford D. Phil. thesis, 1995), 51; *CPR 1334–8*, 346.

[10] For Henry: see above, 18–19; for Stephen: Moor, *Knights of Edward I*, i, 219. See also N. Fryde, *The Tyranny and Fall of Edward II* (Cambridge, 1979), 183. The Cobhams' long tradition of administrative service to the crown would have predisposed them to continued involvement in government.   [11] Apr. 1321 in Glamorgan: *CPR 1317–21*, 575.

[12] N. E. Saul, 'The Despensers and the Downfall of Edward II', *EHR*, 99 (1984), 1–33, esp. 20, 30.

[13] *CPR 1327–30*, 300, 317; J. W. Flower, 'Notices of the Family of Cobham of Sterborough Castle, Lingfield, Surrey', *SAC*, 2 (1864), 119.

with her lover, Mortimer. His main accomplices in the coup and his closest associates in the years ahead were a group of young household knights—notably William Montagu, Edward Bohun, and Robert Ufford—with all of whom Reginald Cobham was intimately associated.[14] In the wake of the Nottingham coup the king embarked on a programme of reasserting royal authority, a key element of which was the promotion of the court as a centre of companionship and honour. Tournaments and jousting now became regular features of courtly life. Reginald Cobham jousted at Carlisle and Dunstable in 1334.[15] The chivalric atmosphere of the court fully accorded with his temperament and tastes. In his employment at court he found the ideal setting in which to develop his talents.

In the summer of 1333 Edward reopened his grandfather's war against the Scots. Since 1331 Edward Balliol, the son of the pretender to the Scottish throne, had been resident in England and was urging Edward to resume the struggle against Bruce. In 1332 Edward offered him limited financial support, and the pretender's forces inflicted a surprise defeat on the Scots at Dupplin Moor. In the following year Edward launched a foray of his own, defeating the Scots at Halidon Hill and driving David Bruce into exile. For the next three years English armies were regularly deployed in the north. The wardrobe books show that Reginald Cobham was involved each season. In the winter of 1334–5 he served with one knight, Sir Stephen de Cossington, and five esquires.[16] In the following year, when he accompanied the king to Perth, he again served with Cossington, one of his most loyal followers, this time with a company of seven esquires.[17]

In the summer of 1337 the focus of activity shifted to the continent. On 24 May 1337 Philip of France had confiscated the English-held duchy of Aquitaine and Edward had retaliated by renouncing his oath of homage to the French and preparing for war. In 1338, after receiving a grant of taxation from parliament, the king crossed to the Low Countries at the head of a large army. As was usual at the time, the household contingent formed the core of the force. A number of the household retinues were very large. At one point Reginald Cobham had over two dozen men

---

[14] It is possible that Cobham was involved in the coup, but there is no evidence to clinch this.

[15] *English Medieval Rolls of Arms, I, 1244–1334*, ed. R. W. Mitchell (Heraldry Society of Scotland; 1983), 448, 459.

[16] BL, Cotton MS Nero C VIII, fo. 234ʳ.

[17] Ibid. fo. 238ʳ. For Cossington, see below, 164–7.

under him, at least five of whom were knights.[18] The thrust of the king's strategy was a massive invasion of France from the north-east. In 1339 there was a stand-off between the English and French at Buironfosse; for some three days the two sides gazed at each other suspiciously, but neither was prepared to engage. In the following year the French mounted a challenge to the English at sea. King Philip ordered a massive fleet to be assembled in the Zwin estuary near Sluys. On 23 June Cobham and two others put ashore at Blankenberg to spy out the Sluys anchorage.[19] As a result of their intelligence, Edward and his counsellors decided to delay an engagement until the next day when the wind and tide would be in their favour. On the afternoon of 24 June the English attacked. The result was one of the most convincing victories of the war, and three-quarters of the French fleet were captured. Edward, however, lacked the strength to follow up his unexpected success at sea. In late July he decided on operations on land instead. In a manoeuvre aimed to lure the French into the field, he invested the city of Tournai. By mid-August he had completely cut off the town, and Cobham and others ravaged the surrounding country.[20] But, as the weeks went by, he ran short of money and had to submit to a truce. In November he returned to England, angry and disappointed. According to Geoffrey le Baker, Reginald Cobham accompanied him.[21] Many of the household staff had been away continuously, or with only a short break, for two years. Cobham had been drawing wages since May 1338.[22]

In the 1340s, in response to the disappointment of these campaigns, Edward changed tactics. Instead of deploying a single large force, as he had in Flanders, he now deployed several smaller ones, with the aim of dividing and distracting the enemy until the knock-out blow could be delivered. Intervention in regional disputes in Flanders and Brittany provided him with the bases from which to strike into the French heartland. Since his strategy was necessarily decentralized, he had a particular need for able field commanders; and, because of this, soldiers of the calibre of

[18] *The Wardrobe Book of William de Norwell, 12 July 1338 to 27 May 1340*, ed. M. Lyon, B. Lyon, and H. S. Lucas (Brussels, 1983), no. 305.

[19] *Knighton's Chonicle*, 28–9. The Lanercost writer's version is that Cobham and the bishop of Lincoln went ashore to rouse the Flemings against the French: *Chronicon de Lanercost*, ed. J. Stevenson (Maitland Club; Edinburgh, 1839), 333.

[20] *Chronica Adae Murimuth et Roberti de Avesbury*, ed. E. M. Thompson (Rolls series; 1889), 316. Avebury says that Cobham was marshal of the English army.

[21] *Chronicon Galfridi le Baker de Swynebroke*, ed. E. M. Thompson (Oxford, 1889), 72.

[22] *Wardrobe Book of William de Norwell*, ci, no. 252.

Cobham came into their own. The first local struggle in which Edward intervened was that in Brittany, where a succession dispute was being fought between a pro-English and pro-French claimant. In September 1342 Edward crossed with a force and quickly took control of the duchy. Reginald Cobham accompanied him with a force of six knights, forty-two esquires and forty-seven mounted archers. No pitched battle was fought, but even so Reginald lost his best warhorse, worth 100 marks.[23] Four years later Edward crossed to France as part of a larger series of operations. The king and his son, the prince of Wales, launched a major assault on Normandy, while his cousin Henry, earl of Derby, ravaged the area south of the Loire. Edward and the prince enjoyed remarkable early success. In July they took Caen, looting and ravaging the town and despatching the plunder to England. From Caen they headed inland, but they encountered difficulty crossing the rivers because so many of the bridges were destroyed. On 24 August they finally forded the Somme at Blanchetaque. Knighton says that Cobham and the earls of Warwick and Northampton led the advance guard and routed a French force on the other side.[24] A day or two later the decisive engagement with the main French army was fought at Crécy. Edward dismounted his men-at-arms to fight. He entrusted the prince, who was on the right flank, to the care of the earl of Warwick, Sir John Chandos, and Sir Reginald Cobham.[25] The French put their faith in a massed cavalry charge, but the advancing knights were mown down by the English archers. It was another remarkable English victory. At the end of the day, according to Froissart, Cobham was one of those appointed to compile an inventory of the French dead.[26] After their triumph the English continued their march north and laid siege to Calais. The operations there were difficult and lasted for nearly a year. By late July, however, with no relief offered, the burgesses offered to submit. Cobham was involved in the negotiations.[27] Calais finally surrendered on 3 August. The king and his forces returned home in triumph two months later.

Shortly after these victories, the Black Death swept across Europe, bringing a temporary halt to major operations on land. There was still activity at sea, however. In 1350, in an engagement off Winchelsea, an

---

[23] PRO, E36/204, fos. 87^r, 106^v, 108^v.
[24] *Knighton's Chronicle*, 60. For discussion, see J. Sumption, *The Hundred Years War: Trial by Battle* (London, 1990), 523–4.
[25] For Cobham's retinue, see *Crecy and Calais*, 195.
[26] J. Froissart, *Chronicles*, ed. T. Johnes (2 vols.; London, 1862), i, 163, 168.
[27] *Chronica Adae de Murimuth et Roberti de Avesbury*, 392.

English force under the prince of Wales, and including Cobham, triumphed over a fleet of Castilian galleys.[28] The next major expedition to France which Cobham joined was the prince's expedition to Aquitaine in 1355–6. The king was ready by now to intensify the pressure on the French. In 1355 he put two expeditions in the field, one under the prince south of the Loire and the other under Henry, duke of Lancaster, north of it. In the summer of 1355 the prince led a devastating *chevauchée* in the direction of Narbonne and the Mediterranean. In the winter he and his men ravaged the Garonne valley, and Cobham was involved in taking Castelsagrat.[29] In August the following year, encouraged by his earlier success, the prince decided to strike deep into France. The marshal of his host was Cobham.[30] The prince's main objective may have been to take Bourges. As he and his men approached the Loire basin, however, they found their way blocked by the French and had to turn back. On the return march, the French constantly dogged the prince's footsteps, and at Poitiers he decided that he would have to give battle. He arranged his men in the usual three formations, and Cobham and other leading knights were with him in the main body.[31] The result was another crushing English victory. Among the many French captives was King John himself. Froissart tells that the prince despatched Cobham and the earl of Warwick to rescue the king from the English and Gascon men-at-arms who were quarrelling over their prize.[32] For Cobham himself it was a highly profitable encounter: he took a valuable French prisoner, the count of Longueville, from whose ransom he was to earn 6,500 florins.[33] Cobham's role in the Poitiers campaign led to him becoming one of the prince's most trusted intimates. A couple of years later the prince in a display of affection gave him a fine bascinet.[34]

Although now approaching sixty, Cobham enlisted for service again

---

[28] Barber, *Edward, Prince of Wales and Aquitaine*, 100.

[29] *Chronica Adae Murimuth et Roberti de Avesbury*, 446, 448.

[30] *Register of Edward, the Black Prince* (4 vols.; 1930–43), iv, 338. Cobham had earlier acted in the office of marshal in 1340: *Chronica Adae Murimuth et Roberti de Avesbury*, 316.

[31] H. J. Hewitt, *The Black Prince's Expedition of 1355–1357* (Manchester, 1958), 115.

[32] Froissart, *Chronicles*, i, 224.

[33] *CPR 1358–61*, 167: an acknowledgement by the king to Cobham of a debt of 6,500 florins for the part of Longueville's ransom falling to Cobham. According to Froissart, *Chronicles*, i, 223, Cobham was responsible for slaying the celebrated French knight Sir Geoffrey de Charny, the author of the *Livre de Chevalerie*. Charny was bearing the *oriflamme*, the sacred banner of the French kings. Presumably, as a matter of honour, he preferred death to capture.

[34] *Black Prince's Register*, iv, 246. The relationship between Cobham and the prince, however, went back a long way. In the winter of 1337–8 the king had appointed Cobham one of his son's councillors: T. F. Tout, *Chapters in the Administrative History of Medieval England* (6 vols.; Manchester, 1920–33), v, 322.

in October 1359 when the king planned yet another major expedition to France. Earlier in the year the negotiations for King John's release had broken down. Edward decided to bring pressure to bear on the French by besieging the city of Rheims, where the French kings were crowned. Reginald enlisted with a retinue of eight knights, thirty-one esquires, and forty archers.[35] The expedition quickly ran into difficulties. Edward failed to take Rheims and fell back on ravaging the Ile de France. By this time, however, the wintry weather was claiming a heavy toll: Reginald lost eighteen of his appraised warhorses.[36] In May 1360 Edward decided to negotiate a settlement with the French at Bretigny and return home.[37] The settlement was subsequently ratified at Calais. The expedition to Rheims in 1359–60 marked the end of an era: for many, indeed, the end of a way of life. In the following year—providentially—Reginald died, probably a victim of pneumonic plague.[38]

Reginald Cobham's successful career is attributable to a variety of factors. First and foremost, he was a gifted soldier. He had a distinguished record of service in Scotland and on the Continent stretching over some thirty years. On the campaign trail he displayed both daring and cunning; and in battle he proved a resourceful combatant. He showed himself capable of independent command. In May 1344 he was appointed admiral of the fleet in the west.[39] Promotion at court—and in the field—followed hard on his military success. In 1348, after Crécy, he was summoned to parliament for the first time as a lord, and four years later he was elected a Knight of the Garter.[40] His career was broadly comparable to those of his fellow knights, Bradeston and Berkeley.[41] He throve on the opportunities created by war. The particular character of the English strategy—the combination of decentralized command with use of *chevauchées*—created ideal conditions for him to thrive in. But although he excelled in arms, he was more than a mere soldier. He showed his mettle in other ways. He was a valued royal counsellor. In the late 1330s in Flanders he was one of the small inner circle which advised Edward on tactics.[42] He remained a valued adviser and confidant after his

[35] PRO, E101/393/11, fo. 80ᵛ.   [36] Ibid.
[37] Cobham was a member of the delegation, most of them knights of the Garter, which received the oath of the regent Charles (the future Charles V) to the terms at Bretigny: *Chronica Johannis de Reading et Anonymi Cantuariensis, 1346–1367*, ed. J. Tait (Manchester, 1914), 283.
[38] He died 5 Oct. 1361 (*CIPM*, xi, no. 59).   [39] *CPR 1343–5*, 259.
[40] W. A. Shaw, *The Knights of England* (2 vols.; London, 1906), i, 2.
[41] For Bradeston and Berkeley, see below, 133.
[42] The members of the council are named in letters patent issued at Antwerp in November 1339 authorizing the terms of an alliance with William, marquis of Juliers: *CPR 1338–40*, 374.

return. In 1340 he was one of the justices appointed to investigate malad-ministration in the shires.[43] At intervals in his career he was entrusted with diplomatic duties. Between 1338 and 1340, when Edward was in the Low Countries, he was appointed to commissions to treat with local princes about alliances or to discuss the disposal of wool with the merchants.[44] In 1343 he served on an important embassy to the papal *Curia*.[45] In 1347, as the siege of Calais was drawing to a close, he was a member of the delegation that negotiated the town's surrender with the cardinals.[46] Towards the end of his career, in 1359, he was sent on a mission to Calais with the bishop of Norwich to discuss possible peace terms with the French.[47] Edward valued him as much for his political and diplomatic skills as for his prowess in arms.

But talent alone is scarcely sufficient to account for the scale of Reginald's success. The ties which he forged with the nobility played a role too. In the late 1320s, when he entered the royal household, a whole new world of clientage was opened to him. Early on, he forged a close liaison with the important Gloucestershire family of Berkeley. Probably his closest associate in the 1330s was the young up-and-coming knight Sir Maurice de Berkeley of Uley, who entered the household a year or two before he himself did.[48] Maurice and Reginald were of similar age and outlook and their careers ran in parallel: Maurice became a banneret in 1330 and Reginald six years later; and they both fought at Crécy and Calais. Only premature death robbed Maurice of a place in the peerage. Maurice's elder brother Thomas, Lord Berkeley, enjoyed particular favour in the opening years of the reign: Roger Mortimer, Queen Isabella's lover, was his father-in-law. Mortimer's fall greatly weakened his standing at court, but he quickly recovered favour and was later active on military service. Cobham's close relations with the Berkeleys bore fruit in 1343 in his marriage to Lord Berkeley's elder daughter Joan.[49] Another Gloucestershire associate of Reginald's was the Berkeleys' close friend and ally, Thomas Bradeston of Breadstone. Bradeston's property lay very close to the Berkeleys', and he and Maurice de Berkeley were

---

[43] *CPR 1340–3*, 111.

[44] *Foedera*, iv, 745; *CPR 1338–40*, 388; *CCR 1337–9*, 127.

[45] *Foedera*, v, 374–5.

[46] *CPR 1345–8*, 562; Barber, *Edward, Prince of Wales and Aquitaine*, 77.

[47] PRO, E101/312/39.

[48] Maurice de Berkeley first appears on the books of the household in 1328: *Calendar of Memoranda Rolls (Exchequer) Michaelmas 1326–Michaelmas 1327*, no. 2270 (iii).

[49] J. Smyth, *The Berkeley MSS. I and II, The Lives of the Berkeleys: III, The Hundred of Berkeley*, ed. J. Maclean (Gloucester, 1883–5), i, 348.

regular companions-in-arms.[50] As young esquires the two neighbours entered the king's household together and fought on the same campaigns. Cobham quickly became an associate of theirs and shared in their successes—as in their occasional failures: in October 1345 he lent his assistance to Bradeston when the latter was seeking his son's release from captivity in Italy en route to the Holy Land.[51] Cobham's connections in the king's household also extended to the families of the north midlands. In the 1340s he is found associating with the senior household banneret, Robert Ferrers of Chartley.[52] In September 1343 he and Ferrers were granted joint custody of the Beauchamp of Hatch estates in Somerset.[53] Almost certainly it is the Ferrers connection which explains the marriage in the next generation between Reginald's son and John Ferrers's widow, Elizabeth.[54]

Reginald's seniority and his extensive connections at court made him ideally placed to advance his own and his family's interests. In his heyday in the 1340s the fortunes of the senior branch of the family at Cobham were anyway in eclipse: John, the 2nd Lord, lacked vigour and distinction and was only a reluctant soldier.[55] Reginald was now the family's main sponsor at court and in government. There is no evidence that the 2nd Lord and his kin viewed him with jealousy. On the contrary, such indications as there are point to mutually supportive relations between the two branches. In 1338, on the eve of his departure for Antwerp, Reginald nominated Lord Cobham as one of his attorneys, and the latter's kinsman, John Cobham of Randall, enlisted as an esquire in his retinue.[56] A few years later Reginald acted as an arbitrator in the dispute between Lord Cobham and his kinsman Thomas over the manor

---

[50] For Bradeston, see *Complete Peerage*, ii, 273; N. E. Saul, *Knights and Esquires: The Gloucestershire Gentry in the Fourteenth Century* (Oxford, 1981), 76–7. [51] *CCR 1343–6*, 659.

[52] Ferrers is listed as a banneret of the household in the 1340s: PRO, E36/204, fo. 86ʳ. For his career, see *Complete Peerage*, v, 310–12. Till the fall of Calais (1347) he fought in all the same campaigns as Cobham—the Low Countries, Brittany, Crécy.

[53] *CCR 1343–6*, 182, 183. The Beauchamps of Hatch had a kinship tie with the main branch of the Cobhams. John, 2nd Lord Cobham, of Cobham, was married to Joan, sister of Sir John Beauchamp of Hatch—custody of whose heir Reginald and his colleague obtained. The 2nd Lord was also a beneficiary under Sir John Beauchamp's will (BL, Add. Ch. 40616: transcript made for the 2nd Lord). It is a mark of the 2nd Lord's lack of influence and, correspondingly, of Reginald's ascendancy that it was to the latter and his colleague that the wardship was granted.

[54] *Complete Peerage*, v, 313–14. John Ferrers was Robert's son and heir. Elizabeth was daughter of Ralph, earl of Stafford. Her brass is the earliest of the Lingfield series: see below, 168–70.

[55] See above, 20.

[56] *CPR 1334–8*, 416; *Treaty Rolls, II. 1337–1339*, ed. J. Ferguson (London, 1972), nos. 416–18.

of Chisbury, while John Cobham of Randall served at Reginald's suggestion as a justice of oyer and terminer in a case relating to a property of
his.[57] In the long term, probably the most valuable service which Reginald performed for his kin was brokering the match between Joan, the
3rd Lord's only daughter and heiress, and Sir John de la Pole.[58] Ultimately, this match was to secure for Lord Cobham's granddaughter possession of the rich de le Pole estates, although in the short run the
prospects looked more favourable for the de la Poles, who gained the
hand of an heiress. The territorial interests of the de la Poles lay chiefly in
the east midlands, Cambridgeshire, and Essex. The founder of this
branch of the family was Richard de la Pole (d. 1345), the elder brother of
William de la Pole, the controversial wool merchant and financier. There
is no evidence that the de la Poles were acquainted with the Cobhams
before the marriage: their estates lay in different parts of the country and
they had few associates in common. The initiative for the match almost
certainly came from Reginald. Reginald was known to the de la Poles
through their involvement in war finance in the 1330s. But he was also
linked with them by a more precise connection: Robert Bradeston, the
son of his friend Thomas, Lord Bradeston, was married to Isabel Peverel,
whose brother-in-law and sister were William and Margaret de la Pole,
John's parents.[59] Reginald was therefore particularly well placed to
sponsor a deal. Detailed terms were agreed in 1362 when a couple of
indentures were enrolled.[60] Reginald himself had died a few months
before this. But there can be little doubt that the responsibility for the
match was his.

In a sense, Reginald appears to have been more successful at advancing his family's interests than his own. Certainly, his own marriage, to
Joan Berkeley, served him well: Joan came not only with a portion of
£2,000 but with the reversion of the manor of Langley Burrell (Wilts.).[61]
Where he experienced disappointment was in securing landed endowment from the king. Normally, when granting money fees to his staff, the
king pledged himself to early replacment of these with lands of comparable value. This was the case in 1336 when he raised Reginald to the
rank of banneret. Reginald at that time received an annuity of 100 marks

---

[57] BL, Harley Roll C 27; *CPR 1348–50*, 177. It is possible that the 'John de Cobham' named as
one of Reginald's executors in a document of the 1360s is John, Lord Cobham of Cobham: CKS,
U601 E3.

[58] For the de la Poles and the marriage, see below, 193–206.

[59] Nichols, 'Memorials of the Family of Cobham', 327–8; *Victoria County History of Northamptonshire*, iv, ed. L. F. Salzman (London, 1937), 233.

[60] *CCR 1360–4*, 425–6.   [61] Smyth, *Lives of the Berkeleys*, i, 348.

as a bachelor; and Edward now added to this a grant of an extra 300 marks annually with the promise that the entire sum would be exchanged for lands and rents of the same value.[62] The problem, however, was that the king lacked the resources to make good his promise. The story of Reginald's trials bears this out. In May 1337, in part-fulfilment of the usual pledge, Reginald was given the manor of Cippenham (Bucks.), which was worth £64 per annum, for his life, and a year later £55 from the farm of Great Yarmouth and £140 out of the profits of the shrievalty of Surrey and Sussex.[63] But for every advance that he made there was a step back. In 1339 Reginald was required to surrender Cippenham to a local landowner, Sir John Molyns, who had rights over it in tail male which the king had overlooked.[64] In 1340 Reginald was awarded another grant by the king—this time of the manor of Strood (Kent), which Margaret, countess of Pembroke, held for life. However, a couple of years later this grant too was revoked, oddly as a favour by the king to the countess, who was a lady-in-waiting to his daughter Joan.[65] The king's failure to provide adequate endowment for Cobham resulted in a substantial debt to him by the exchequer by 1341. In an attempt to provide temporary satisfaction, the king assigned to him some of the money due from the abbot and convent of St Albans, along with the sale of 100 sacks of wool. But in 1343 he still counted as a royal creditor, and the grant of the Beauchamp of Hatch wardship represented yet another attempt to offer him satisfaction. Four years after this he was granted the reversion of West Cliff (Kent), a property into which he shortly entered.[66] This was to be the last grant which the king made in his favour.

Despite these difficulties and disappointments, Reginald died a reasonably rich man. According to his inquisition, he held property in five counties: the manors of Oxted and Sterborough in Surrey; Hever, East Shelve, Bowzell, Aldington, Hiltesbury, and Austin in Eynsford, all in Kent; Northey in Sussex; Leigh Delamare and Langley Burrell in Wiltshire, and various tenements in these counties.[67] It is hard to say how much in total these properties were worth, for the extents in inquisitions only give rental value and not yearly income. However, since in theory they represented the value in land of a fee of 400 marks, they must have been worth approximately that amount. To his landed income, Reginald could add his income from the profits of war—principally,

[62] CPR 1334–8, 346.   [63] CPR 1338–40, 152.   [64] Ibid. 310–11.
[65] Ibid. 511; CPR 1340–3, 461.   [66] CPR 1345–8, 250.   [67] CIPM, xi, no. 59.

booty and money from ransoms. He is known to have taken at least one valuable prisoner, the count of Longueville, whom he captured at Poitiers, and doubtless he took others. By mid-career Reginald had the means extensively to remodel Sterborough Castle. The new structure was highly ambitious in conception, consisting of a large courtyard with angle towers within a moat.[68] Reginald was evidently living there in comfort. Unfortunately his will, if he made one, does not survive, and the range and value of his moveable wealth are thus lost to view. However, there is every possibility that in his chamber at Sterborough he had a store of jewellery and plate to match those of other captains of the age.

Reginald was buried in his local parish church at Lingfield. The splendid monument on the north side of the chancel commemorating him dates from shortly after his death.[69] In the wake of his death, his widow or executors decided to enlarge the church. On initial inspection, Lingfield appears almost entirely a mid fifteenth-century structure—the tower and broach spire over the south aisle being the only obvious survivors from an earlier fabric. However, the appearances are deceptive: incorporated in the building is a good deal of fourteenth-century work.[70] The most telling evidence is provided by the moulding profiles of the piers. Two types of pier are employed. Those in the nave are of a standard post-Yevele London type and date from the mid-fifteenth century. Those in the chancel, however, are almost certainly earlier: they employ alternating convex and concave curves in an idiosyncratic way to create an illusion of four shafts and four hollows (fig. 25). The design is without precedent and is clearly the work of a mason unfamiliar with the canons of Perpendicular being established in London. A clue to the likely date of the work is provided by an entry in the register of Bishop Wykeham of Winchester. In 1369 the bishop gave permission for 'the newly rebuilt chancel' to be reconsecrated following an act of sacrilege.[71] The piers are almost certainly part of the rebuilding to which the bishop refers.

---

[68] Licence to crenellate was granted in 1341: *CPR 1340–3*, 304. Nothing remains of the castle, which was slighted after the Civil War, although the line of the moat is still visible. An attractive eighteenth-century folly occupies the site. A precisely observed drawing by Hollar, *c.*1640, shows the castle to have been of standard quadrangular design. Maxstoke (War.) and, on a smaller scale, Hever (Kent) convey an idea of how it would have looked. Including the moat, the area covered was an acre and a half (O. Manning and W. Bray, *The History and Antiquities of the County of Surrey*, 3 vols.; London, 1804–14, ii, 346–7).

[69] For discussion of the tomb, see below, 149–68.

[70] What follows is largely derived from S. Pratt, 'The Collegiate Church of St Peter, Lingfield, Surrey' (University College, London MA thesis, 1993), esp. 15–24. I am grateful to Mrs Pratt for allowing me to draw on her work.

[71] *Wykeham's Register*, ed. T. F. Kirby (Hampshire Record Society; 2 vols.; 1896–9), ii, 94.

Presumably a pair of side chapels was added north and south of the chancel to create extra burial space. It is possible that Reginald junior, Reginald's son and heir, could have commissioned the work. However, it is more likely, given his youth, that his mother was responsible.

In 1361 the signs were that Reginald Cobham had won a secure place for his family in the peerage. Through his achievements in the field he had eclipsed the senior branch of the family in fame, while through his eminence at court he had been able to increase his family's wealth. And with the birth around 1350 of a son, Reginald junior, the continuance of the line seemed assured. Yet within two generations his family had fallen back into the gentry. Reginald's son only received occasional summonses to parliament, and his grandson none at all. The later Cobhams were ordinary knights. How is the family's lapse from nobility to be explained?

In the fourteenth century the lower ranks of the peerage were still ill defined. Families on the borderline between the gentry and the nobility tended to oscillate between the two, with one generation being honoured with a summons and another not. Entitlement to a parliamentary summons depended on a variety of factors, principally landed wealth, possession of royal favour, and military achievement. Reginald Cobham owed his summonses mainly to the last two: his position in the royal household gave him access to the king's ear, while his prowess in the field raised him in honour and esteem. In terms of military rank Reginald Cobham was a banneret—in other words, an élite knight entitled to carry a square banner rather than a pennon in battle.[72] In the mid-fourteenth century the bannerets counted as a rank in the peerage. C. Given-Wilson has commented that the majority of new men summoned to parliament under Edward III were of banneret rank: a mark of the importance of military attainment in determining selection.[73] In the final decades of the century, however, the distinctiveness of the banneret rank was gradually being eroded. The richer and more prominent bannerets were absorbed into the ranks of the barons, while the lesser fell back into the gentry. By the mid-fifteenth century, the bannerets' rank had virtually disappeared. The main reason for the pressure to which the bannerets succumbed appears to have been the lessening of military activity

[72] For the bannerets, see Tout, *Chapters in the Administrative History of Medieval England*, iii, 296; Saul, *Knights and Esquires*, 8.

[73] C. Given-Wilson, *The English Nobility in the Late Middle Ages* (London, 1987), 61.

in the second half of Richard II's reign. Prowess in the field now counted for much less than it had previously done among the criteria for promotion. At the same time, other factors counted for more. Especially important were political prominence, loyalty to the crown, and standing at court. In the fourteenth century the Cobhams of Sterborough had had little trouble in satisfying these criteria. A generation or two later, however, this was not the case. So what had gone wrong?

The answer is partly to be found in some accidental factors. It was particularly unfortunate that in 1361 Reginald Cobham left a son under age. Minorities in the Middle Ages were invariably damaging to a family's prospects. Not only was the momentum built up in the previous generation, or generations, quickly lost; the power represented by the family's lordship over land fell into abeyance. In the Cobhams' case the period of minority was lengthy—almost nine years. Reginald junior did not come of age until 1370.[74] Custody of the family's estates was granted by the king to his queen, Philippa, a notoriously exacting landlord.[75] The degree of administrative disruption may have been reduced by continuity in local administrative personnel. Nevertheless, it is likely that Reginald entered into a depleted inheritance.

In addition to this, Reginald encountered problems at the national level. Although he was of distinguished parentage, he could not expect automatic recognition from the king: he needed first to establish his worth. It was particularly unfortunate for him that in his most active years the opportunities for him to do so were fewer than they had been for his father. In the 1360s, in the wake of the settlement at Bretigny, England was at peace with the French, and in the 1370s, after hostilities were resumed, the tide of war distinctly favoured the enemy. On the English side there were serious deficiencies of leadership: the king was growing old, and his son, the Black Prince, suffering from dysentery. On the French side a new generation of leaders was emerging with imaginative new thinking on tactics. Instead of directly engaging the enemy in battle, as they had, they harried and harassed them; the war was turned into a guerrilla war. The new strategy was highly successful. By the mid- to late 1370s the French had recovered virtually all the lands they had lost at Bretigny. And, to do so, they had had to fight hardly a battle. For the younger generation of English knights, like Cobham, the results

---

[74] *Complete Peerage*, iii, 353.
[75] Queen Philippa was granted custody on 15 Oct. 1361: *CPR 1361–4*, 86. For her proprietorship of her estates in Sussex in the 1350s, see N. E. Saul, *Scenes From Provincial Life: Knightly Families in Sussex, 1280–1400* (Oxford, 1986), 23–4.

were disastrous. With fewer battles to fight, they had fewer opportunities to win fame and fortune. Even the major *chevauchées* were disappointing. John of Gaunt's great expedition of 1373, while bravely defiant, brought little material reward. The leading English commanders were angry and frustrated. Yet in a sense the fault was partly theirs. They had failed to fashion a convincing response to the Fabian tactics of their foes. In their desire to emulate the past, they had become prisoners of the past.

The decline in English military fortunes posed particular problems for the banneret class. For the bannerets, distinction in arms held the key to continued membership of the peerage; without it they risked loss of dignity. A number of banneret lineages weathered the threat and survived. In general, these were the wealthier ones. Among their number were the Zouches of Harringworth, the Greys of Codnor, and Ferrers of Chartley—families with incomes of £400 a year or more. Judged by their tally of manors, the Cobhams of Sterborough might be thought to have had the money to survive. However, the tally by itself is deceptive. Many of the Cobhams' manors were small. Oxted and Langley Burrell were probably the two biggest—being coincident with vills. In the inquisition on Reginald's death Oxted was given a value of 20 marks per annum and Langley Burrell rather less. Northey in Sussex was also valuable, at £20 per annum.[76] Most of the others were outliers of villages or subsidiary settlements. Austin in Eynsford, Bowzell in Chevening, Filston in Shoreham, Sharnden in Eaton Bridge, Hiltesbury in Lullingstone all fell into this category.[77] These manors were not only small; they were difficult to organize economically. In reality, the financial position of the Sterborough Cobhams was less secure than it looked.

So how was the younger Reginald to safeguard his claim to nobility? Naturally he looked for what advantage he could in war. He had had his first experience of arms while still a youth. In the 1360s, well before inheriting his estates, he was performing military service in Gascony, probably in a border garrison.[78] The first major expedition which he joined was John of Gaunt's *chevauchée* across France in 1373–4. The purpose of this venture was probably to divert the French from attacking

---

[76] PRO, C135/158; *Wiltshire Inquisitions Post Mortem from the Reign of King Edward III*, ed. E. Stokes (Index Library, 48; 1914), 281–2.

[77] For these manors, see Hasted, *History of Kent*, ii, 531, 547; iii, 8, 183, 205, 222.

[78] His mother refers to him being in Gascony in her will of 1369 (printed in Flower, 'Notices of the Family of Cobham of Sterborough', 170–6).

Brittany.[79] Gaunt disembarked at Calais, swept south-east past Rheims, and then pressed west to Bordeaux. Reginald Cobham enlisted as a member of the earl of Warwick's retinue; he entered the king's wages in June and was discharged in April the following year.[80] At the beginning of Richard II's reign Reginald saw service in arms again. Shortly after the king's coronation, the minority council organized a naval expedition to challenge French dominance at sea. Reginald Cobham enlisted with a retinue, as did his kinsman John, Lord Cobham.[81] The expedition sailed in November under Thomas of Woodstock's command with two objectives—attacking a Franco-Italian fleet off Sluys and relieving the English garrison at Brest; but a week or two after embarkation the fleet was dispersed by a storm and had to return to port. A decade later, during the ascendancy of Richard's opponents, the Appellants, Reginald Cobham saw active service for the fourth and last time. In March 1387 Richard, earl of Arundel, headed a naval expedition to intercept and destroy the French fleet on its return from Bordeaux. Cobham joined with a substantial retinue of four knights and several dozen esquires.[82] The expedition was wholly successful: Arundel encountered the French fleet off Cadzand and, deploying superior armament, destroyed it.[83] Cobham was almost certainly present for the victory, although his account with the exchequer notes him as returning early.

Reginald's record of military service was a perfectly respectable one for a knight of his rank. He was a regular campaigner at a time when knightly participation in warfare was declining, and the retinues he assembled were generally sizeable. However, the opportunities given to him to distinguish himself were few, and there is no evidence that his experience in arms added to his repute—or to his wealth. In consequence, his father's route to success had little to offer him. There were other ways, however, in which he could improve his fortunes. An obvious one was through marriage—to win the hand of a rich widow or an heiress. In this area Reginald enjoyed more evident success. He married twice. His first wife was a well-dowered widow, Elizabeth, the daughter of Ralph, 1st earl of Stafford. Elizabeth had survived two previous

---

[79] There is no certainty as to the purpose of the expedition: perhaps to ease the French pressure on Brittany, but alternatively to promote Gaunt's claim to the crown of Castile. For discussion, see G. Holmes, *The Good Parliament* (Oxford, 1975), 23–8; A. Goodman, *John of Gaunt: The Exercise of Princely Power in Fourteenth-Century Europe* (London, 1992), 232–3.

[80] PRO, E101/32/39.   [81] PRO, E101/36/29.   [82] PRO, E101/40/33.

[83] *Westminster Chronicle*, 180–2; J. J. N. Palmer, *England, France and Christendom, 1377–99* (London, 1972), 93.

husbands. Her first had been Fulk, Lord Le Strange of Blackmere, who had died, probably of the plague, in 1349, and her second another mid-lander John, Lord Ferrers of Chartley, who died in 1367.[84] Elizabeth probably married her third husband around 1368.[85] The dower lands which she brought with her were extensive. According to the inquisition taken on her death in 1375, she held a string of manors across six counties, including a life interest in the main Ferrers seat of Chartley itself.[86] Reginald married his second wife probably in late 1380.[87] This lady was even wealthier than his first—she was Eleanor, the daughter and coheiress of John, Lord Maltravers of Lytchett (Dorset). Like Elizabeth, Eleanor was a widow. Her first husband, whom she had married in 1365, was Sir John Arundel, younger brother of Richard Fitzalan I, earl of Arundel. John Arundel was renowned as a soldier and captain. A battle-hardened veteran of the wars, he was appointed marshal of England in 1377.[88] His career ended disastrously two years later, when he was given command of an expedition to assist the duke of Brittany. The fleet set off too late in the season and ran into storms in the Channel; virtually all on board, including Arundel himself, were drowned.[89] Cobham must have married Eleanor soon after the tragedy. He needed to remarry to father an heir. How the match was arranged is a mystery. Cobham and his bride apparently had little or no previous association; and there is no evidence of affection between them, and none developed. In her will Eleanor never once refers to her husband, and throughout she styles herself 'Eleanor Arundel'.[90] For Reginald, however, she was a valuable catch. She brought with her half of her father's wide estates and a handful of dower manors from her marriage to Arundel. Her landed possessions were spread over five counties.[91] In the latter part of his life Reginald was an extremely wealthy man. His landed income must have been almost twice his father's. He doubtless anticipated that his wealth would earn him eventual summons to the Lords. However, this was not to be the

---

[84] *Complete Peerage*, iii, 353.
[85] There is a fair likelihood that the marriage was arranged by Reginald's mother, who died in 1369: Reginald senior had known John Ferrers's father, Robert, through their employment in the king's household together: see above, 132.
[86] *CIPM*, xiv, no. 105.   [87] *Complete Peerage*, iii, 354.   [88] Ibid. i, 259–60.
[89] The most vivid account of these events is Walsingham's: *Chronicon Anglie, 1328–1388*, ed. E. M. Thompson (Rolls series; 1874), 247–53. Walsingham interpreted the disaster as retribution for the soldiers' violation of a local nunnery before embarkation at Plymouth. For the background and the political sequel, see Saul, *Richard II*, 43–4.
[90] The will is printed by Flower, 'Notices of the Family of Cobham of Sterborough', 186–90. Throughout, Eleanor styles herself 'Eleanor Arundel', not 'Eleanor Cobham'.
[91] *CIPM*, xviii, nos. 1115–22. For a list of her manors, see Appendix.

case. He was only summoned twice, and then at the beginning of his career—in 1371 and 1372.[92] Strangely, no summonses followed his later acquisition of wealth. The reason for the lack of recognition appears to have been largely political. Richard II associated him with the group of Appellant lords who had opposed him in 1387–8. Reginald had served at sea with the Appellant earl of Arundel in 1387; his wife was connected by marriage with the Arundel family; and his own kinsman, John, Lord Cobham of Cobham, had been one of the continual councillors of 1387.[93] Reginald, in Richard's eyes, was tarred with the Appellant brush.[94] It was probably for much the same reason that he was denied a role in local government. After 1392 he was not even appointed to the commission of the peace in Surrey: a position which he had every reason to expect, given his means.

Reginald Cobham died in July 1403 and his wife eighteen months later.[95] His heir was their only surviving son, Reginald III. On the surface, the prospects for the new lord were promising. The downfall of Richard II in 1399 and the accession of Henry of Lancaster heralded an end to the family's isolation. Reginald had many connections with the ruling élite. He enjoyed the patronage and sponsorship of Thomas, the new earl of Arundel;[96] and his daughter was a lady-in-waiting to the duchess of Gloucester.[97] He had had experience of service abroad: in 1415 he was at Agincourt.[98] However he was never once summoned to parliament. His family's descent into the gentry now became irreversible. The reason for the denial of a summons to him was probably his reduced means. On the death of his father he lost possession of his mother's estates. His father had held these by right of his wife; after his death they were resumed by

[92] *Complete Peerage*, iii, 353.

[93] Shakespeare in *Richard II* (2. 1. 279) confused Reginald with John Cobham. The error is repeated in M. Stephenson, *A List of Monumental Brasses in Surrey* (Bath, 1970), 342.

[94] Yet on one occasion the king invited a 'Lady Cobham' to spend time with him at court. The invitation is referred to in a letter to her sister which survives in the All Souls formulary book; the letter is undated but appears to be of Richard II's reign. The 'Lady Cobham' can only be Eleanor Cobham of Sterborough since the other 'Lady Cobham'—Joan Cobham of Cobham—lacked siblings. Eleanor's sister, Joan, was well connected at court: her late husband was the royal chamber knight, Sir Robert Rous. Eleanor clearly owed her invitation to her sister and not to her husband—who, interestingly, is not mentioned in the letter (*Anglo-Norman Letters and Petitions*, ed. M. D. Legge, Anglo-Norman Text Society, 3; 1941, no. 343; *Complete Peerage*, viii, 586).

[95] *CIPM*, xviii, nos. 760–70, 1115–22.   [96] *CPR 1413–16*, 389.

[97] The daughter was Eleanor, who was to become Gloucester's second wife. For the accusations of witchcraft against her in 1441, and her subsequent trial and imprisonment, see R. A. Griffiths, 'The Trial of Eleanor Cobham: An Episode in the Fall of Duke Humphrey of Gloucester', *Bulletin of the John Rylands Library*, 51 (1968–9), 381–99.

[98] Nicolas, *History of the Battle of Agincourt*, 378.

his widow, and on her death in turn they reverted to her first husband's son.[99] None the less, he still had ample wealth to play a major role in local affairs; yet strangely the evidence for his involvement in these matters is slight. The only public responsibility given to him was custody of one of the most valuable prisoners from Agincourt, Charles, duke of Orléans.[100] It is possible that he lacked the ability or know-how for office-holding; it is possible too that he had had a misspent youth.[101] But a likelier explanation is that he was considered too exalted for such work. Many of the most affluent gentry in the late Middle Ages were never appointed to local office. The Willoughbys in Nottinghamshire, the Dinhams in Devon and Cornwall, and the later Bradestons in Gloucestershire were similarly inactive. Two centuries before, the same was true of Bartholomew of Thurleigh in Bedfordshire.[102] Detachment from office-holding was a mark of status; the exalted stood above the fray.

Reginald's lasting memorial was the foundation of the college at Lingfield. The inspiration for the idea probably came from the similar foundation at Cobham. The Sterborough Cobhams had been buried in Lingfield church for at least a century. Reginald's father and grandfather were both commemorated by tombs there; so too was Eleanor, Reginald's first wife. The church, however, was purely parochial in character; and the Cobham family had no special place in its life. Accordingly, on 16 March 1431, Reginald, jointly with his wife Anne, obtained licence to reconstitute it as a college. The community was sizeable. There were to be a provost or master, five other chaplains, four clerks, and thir-

---

[99] *CIPM*, xviii, nos. 1115–22. By her first marriage to Sir John Arundel, she had a son, John junior, who was named as her heir in all of the inquisitions.

[100] Nicolas, *History of the Battle of Agincourt*, 178. See also Flower, 'Notices of the Family of Cobham of Sterborough', 146, where, however, Orléans is wrongly identified. It is possible that Reginald held the constableship of Pevensey Castle, but the identification of the Reginald Cobham who was replaced in this office in 1446 is by no means certain: BL Add. Ch. 30720 (a grant of the constableship to Sir James Fiennes in place of Reginald Cobham).

[101] Could he have been the Reginald Cobham who, at the end of Richard II's reign, was accused of bigamy? In a petition to Bishop Stafford, the chancellor, one Margaret Grimsby of 'Straesburgh' in Germany complained that Reginald Cobham had married her, affirming that he was 'Lord Cobham's son' and heir to a great inheritance, but later abandoned her saying that he was already married—though not before making off with her goods (PRO, C1/3/49). Which member of the Cobham clan was this? The Christian name and the reference to 'Lord Cobham's son' are suggestive of Reginald III, of Sterborough. But it is not clear whether or not Reginald III was married by this time—or how, indeed, he could have come into contact with the obscure Margaret Grimsby. The Christian name 'Reginald' is also found in the Randall and Chafford branches of the family at this time. Unfortunately, no light is shed on the case by other sources.

[102] K. H. Faulkner, 'Knights and Knighthood in Early Thirteenth-Century England' (University of London Ph.D. thesis, 1998), 43.

teen 'poor persons': all of them praying for the good estate of the founders and their kin, and their souls after their death.[103] Lands to the value of £40 per annum were assigned by the founder to support them.[104] At the same time, the church itself was enlarged and partly rebuilt. The new structure was essentially a hall-church (fig. 24).[105] The continuous central vessel of nave and chancel was flanked on the north side by a broad aisle and a chapel of the same height, giving the impression of a double-naved building. The earlier tower and spire were incorporated on the south side, and to the east of them a new chapel was built. The church was lavishly provided with fittings. The stained glass windows and the wooden parclose screens were all of the highest quality.[106] Heraldry figured prominently, particularly in the glazing.[107] To the west of the church was erected the clerks' residential accommodation. Although long demolished, this appears to have taken the form of a courtyard block, like the similar range at Cobham, the ground floor being of stone, and the upper of brick.[108] The cost of this extensive building programme must have been considerable—the equivalent of several years' income from the Cobham lands; but Reginald could well afford it. Indeed, such conspicuously lavish spending constituted a valuable affirmation of status.

Reginald died in 1446. In his will he requested burial in his new church.[109] His eldest son, another Reginald, having predeceased him, he was succeeded by his second son, Thomas, who was shortly knighted. Thomas took little part in national affairs, but was more active locally

[103] *VCH Surrey*, ii, 127–8; *CPR 1429–36*, 146–7.

[104] G. Leveson-Gower, 'Inventories of the College of Lingfield', *SAC*, 7 (1880), 229. Further endowments followed in 1449, when Reginald's widow, Anne, granted to the college the manors of Haxted and Billeshurst in Lingfield: *CPR 1446–52*, 240–1.

[105] Pratt, 'The Collegiate Church of St Peter, Lingfield'; Harvey, *The Perpendicular Style*, 172, 279; I. Nairn and N. Pevsner, *Surrey*, 2nd edn. (Harmondsworth, 1971), 347–8.

[106] For the remains of the glazing scheme, now gathered in the south-east window of the chancel, see A. V. Peatling, *Ancient Stained and Painted Glass in the Churches of Surrey*, ed. F. C. Eeles (Surrey Archaeological Society, 1930), 55–7. There was also a fine series of wall paintings. In the chancel three half life-size standing figures and some angels were uncovered by L'Anson in 1845: E. L'Anson, 'Mural Paintings Formerly Existing in Lingfield Church', *SAC*, 1 (1858), 71–2.

[107] The arms of Cobham and Bardolph appeared in the glass: ibid. According to Aubrey, who visited the church in the 1670s, the arms of the Gaynesford family also appeared: J. Aubrey, *Natural History and Antiquities of the County of Surrey* (5 vols.; London, 1718–19, repr. 1975), iii, 59. The Gaynesfords were a local gentry family: see below, 186. Coats of arms figured on the chancel misericords. On the first return stall on the south side are the arms of Cobham of Sterborough; on the first on the north side, a turbaned soldan's head, for Cobham; and on the second, the arms of Bardolph.

[108] Aubrey, *Natural History and Antiquities of the County of Surrey*, iii, 64.

[109] *Testamenta Vetusta*, i, 246–7.

FIG 24. Lingfield church: exterior from the north

than his father had been. He was a justice of the peace in Surrey for twenty years from 1452 and sheriff of the county in 1455–6.[110] Moreover, his strong sympathies with the Lancastrian court ensured his appointment in other counties: he served as sheriff of Essex and Hertfordshire in 1453–4 and as sheriff of Norfolk in 1460–1.[111] It was a mark of his relative distinction that he married well. His first wife was Elizabeth, widow of Lord Fitzwalter, and his second, whom he married around 1461, Anne, the daughter of Humphrey Stafford, duke of Buckingham, and widow of Aubrey de Vere, the earl of Oxford's son.[112] Thomas Cobham was to be the last of his line. He sired a bastard, Reginald, but no legitimate son. When he died between April and July 1471, he was succeeded by a daughter Anne, who carried her inheritance in marriage to Sir Edward Burgh of Gainsborough, Lincs.[113] With the extinction of the

---

[110] *CPR 1452–61*, 678–9; *CPR 1461–7*, 573; *CPR 1467–77*, 632; *CFR 1452–61*, 144. He was also a commissioner of array in the county: *CPR 1452–61*, 557.

[111] *CFR 1452–61*, 74, 289.

[112] *Complete Peerage*, iii, 355. His marriage brought him lands in Essex and other eastern counties which provided him with the qualification for office-holding there.

[113] For Thomas's will of 1466, see H. J. Cooper, 'Some Surrey Wills in the Prerogative Court of Canterbury, I', *SAC*, 51 (1950), 83–4. He requested burial at Lingfield and made a bequest of £20 to the church for repairs. He made other pious bequests to St Thomas's, Tower Royal, London, the priories of Merton and Dunmow, and Stonebridge church, Kent.

Sterborough line, the Cobhams of Beluncle were the only branch of the Cobhams surviving.

The story of the rise and fall of the Cobhams of Sterborough is one with many parallels among the English medieval lesser nobility. The fourteenth and fifteenth centuries saw a remarkable flowering of noble cadet branches. In many cases this was attributable to the workings of the 'use' and the consequent division of family estates. However, although partible inheritance was practised on the Cobham family's Kent lands to the 1270s, the rise of the Cobhams of Sterborough is not to be explained in this way. Theirs was for the most part a story of self-assertion. Reginald was one of the outstanding war captains of his day. He owed his rise to his prowess in arms and to his place in Edward III's affections. His many achievements won for him election to the Order of the Garter and a place in the peerage. But his family's standing was dangerously dependent on continuing success in arms. When each of the next two lords failed to match their forebear's brilliance and prowess, the family sank back into the gentry.

The changing fortunes of the family are mirrored in their monuments in Lingfield church. A pride in the brotherhood of arms is the dominant characteristic of the first Reginald's tomb, while bombast in the face of decline is proclaimed by his grandson's. These are forceful, eloquent monuments. They are every bit as instructive as their counterparts at Cobham.

The Brasses and Monuments at Lingfield

T HE historical development of the mausoleum at Lingfield stands in sharp contrast to that at Cobham. At Cobham, the whole commemorative scheme was informed by the defining vision of one highly influential figure: John, 3rd Lord Cobham. While it is true that the two dozen or so brasses at Cobham cover a period of 150 years, it is the vision and ambition of John, Lord Cobham that dominate. At Lingfield the position is very different. At Lingfield there was no presiding genius of comparable importance to the 3rd Lord: no one who was equally influential in shaping the development of the mausoleum. In consequence, a greater variety of taste is to be found in the monuments. The remarkable consistency which characterizes the memorials at Cobham is absent. Brasses alternate with full-relief effigies. Some of the brasses are canopied, while others are not. Identifying and isolating the various influences at work is less straightforward than at the sister church.

The setting of the brasses also distinguishes the Lingfield mausoleum from that at Cobham. At Cobham the brasses are marshalled in two great rows in front of the altar; one or two outliers are found in the north aisle, but it is the chancel brasses that dominate. At Lingfield, on the other hand, the brasses and monuments are more scattered. Some of them are in the Lady chapel, and others in the chancel; some are on tombs, and others on the floor. The aesthetic effect is more diffuse, and the impact less concentrated.

At Lingfield the brasses also stand in different chronological relation to their surroundings from those at Cobham. At Cobham the brasses were essentially accommodated in an existing fabric. The chancel, built in the thirteenth century, offered space enough for burials, and there was no need to enlarge it; even after the 3rd Lord had founded the college, alterations were confined to upgrading the fittings.[1] At Lingfield, however, the original church was much smaller. Consequently, when it was adopted by the Cobhams as their burial-place, it had to be enlarged. The work was carried out in stages. In the 1360s, after the death of the 1st Lord, chapels were added each side of the chancel to provide space for monuments; in the fifteenth century, when the college was founded, the nave and aisle were rebuilt. At Lingfield, in contrast to Cobham, church and mausoleum grew together. There is a closer, more organic, relationship between building and monuments than in the sister church.

A final introductory point needs to be made about the Lingfield monuments. As at the sister church, the brasses have suffered much from mutilation and neglect. A number of the brasses have been wholly or partially lost. That of Isabel Cobham of Gatwick was already lost when Aubrey visited the church in the early eighteenth century.[2] Others were lost during the century that followed. Aubrey records brasses commemorating two priests and a lady which are now missing.[3] Moreover, a number of the extant brasses have suffered damage. The elegant brass of Eleanor, first wife of Sir Reginald Cobham, was a wreck by the 1850s: the figure was mutilated, and the shields, the banner, and the evangelistic symbols at the corners all missing.[4] Sizeable portions were lost from the brass of Elizabeth, Lady Cobham, close by. Losses were still occurring as late as the mid-nineteenth century: a section of the inscription on the 2nd Lord's brass disappeared sometime between the 1840s and 1870.[5] L'Anson's restoration of the church in the mid-nineteenth century did little to help. In the course of repairing the floor and altering the floor levels, l'Anson moved a number of the brasses. Those of Isabel Cobham and Katherine Stoket were shifted from the north or Lady chapel to the chancel, while others, mainly of clergy, were moved to the same location from the Turton chapel.[6] The lengthy process of loss and decay was only arrested by Waller's major restoration of the monuments in 1865–6.[7]

---

[1] See above, 49–50.

[2] Aubrey, *History and Antiquities of the County of Surrey*, iii, 50.   [3] Ibid. iii, 60–1.

[4] See the illustration opposite Flower, 'Notices of the Family of Cobham of Sterborough', 146.

[5] J. G. Waller, 'Notes on the Monuments of the Cobham Family at Lingfield', *SAC*, 5 (1871), 192.   [6] Ibid. 193, 198.

[7] See Lack, Saul, and Whittemore, *Monumental Brasses in St Mary Magdalene, Cobham*, 24–5. Waller's restorations at Lingfield were generally of higher quality than those at Cobham. He made some slips. For example, on the inscription to the brass of Eleanor, Lady Cobham (d. 1420), he employed majuscule letter forms more appropriate for a style 'A' brass of twenty years earlier. A problem that Waller faced at Lingfield was the lack of an antiquarian record comparable to that for Cobham, so that he could not replace epitaphs or coats of arms. Where these were missing and he lacked an authority, he generally inserted metal blanks.

Missing portions were then replaced, and the brasses which had been removed from the Lady chapel were returned there. As at Cobham, the cost of the work was borne by Francis Capper Brooke of Ufford Hall, Suffolk.[8]

The earliest of the monuments at Lingfield is the monument of the effective founder of the line, Reginald, 1st Lord Cobham KG (d. 1361). This still remains in its original position under the arch separating the chancel arcade from the north chapel (fig. 25).[9] The monument consists of an embattled tomb chest with a recumbent effigy in armour on top. The chest is of Caen stone and the effigy of local Reigate stone.[10] Reginald is shown in a typical suit of mid-fourteenth-century armour. His chest and torso are enclosed in a jupon, on which his arms are emblazoned. Beneath the jupon is worn the mail haubergeon, which is partly visible at the armpits and below the bottom of the jupon. The shoulders and arms are defended by spaudlers and vambraces. Around the hips is slung a fine sword belt, looped towards the end. Over the upper legs are worn cuisses of brigandine work, to which poleyns are attached, and on the lower legs metal greaves; the feet are protected by laminated sabatons. Reginald's head is protected by a bascinet from which a mail aventail is suspended. Beneath, and offering support to, the head is a fine helm adorned with the crest of a Moor's head, alongside which are two youthful male figures. Under the feet is a 'soldan', or turbaned figure, shown in reclining position, with his right arm supporting the head, and the left extended to an upraised knee.[11] The whole effigy was richly decorated. According to Waller, the mail was represented in stucco and applied with a hair pencil, and it is possible that the garter on his left leg was represented in the same way.[12] The studs, or rivets, of the cuisses and the studs

---

[8] SHC, 2399/7/3 (Lingfield vestry minute book, meeting of 10 Aug. 1868).

[9] In its present condition the tomb lacks an identifying inscription. It is likely that this was painted on the chamfer beneath the battlemented parapet and has since been lost. There can be no doubt about the identity of the commemorated, however: the heraldry (discussed below, 152–67) leaves no doubt. Moreover, it was usual for a founder's tomb to be placed on the north side.

[10] The use of different materials in medieval monuments is not unusual. John of Eltham's monument in Westminster Abbey has an effigy of alabaster and a chest of freestone inset with panels of alabaster and blackstone. Edward II's monument at Gloucester has a canopy of freestone, an effigy of alabaster, and a chest of Purbeck marble. At a less exalted level, the first of the de Vere monuments at St Stephen's chapel, Bures, consists of an effigy of clunch, a chest of Caen stone, and a plinth of Purbeck marble (Probert, 'The Riddles of Bures Unravelled', 58–9).

[11] The 'soldan' is referred to as such in Joan Cobham's will (Flower, 'Notices of the Family of Cobham of Sterborough', 178).

[12] Waller, 'Notes on the Monuments of the Cobham Family', 187.

FIG 25. Lingfield: tomb of Reginald, 1st Lord Cobham, d. 1361

of the spur straps were made of lead. The entire effigy was brightly coloured. The jewelled work of the sword-belt appears to have been represented by a kind of varnish over blue-black, while the thigh armour was probably deep red and the studs picked out in gilt. The gauntlets, poleyns, and sabatons were all gilded, and the rest of the armour black. The present colour scheme, the work of modern restorers, is probably a fair copy of the original.[13]

The monument with its relief effigy differs fundamentally from any at Cobham, where after 1300 brasses were always preferred. The choice of a tomb chest and relief effigy must reflect non-Cobham influences. There can be little doubt that the key influence was that of the deceased's Berkeley kinsfolk. Reginald and his father-in-law Thomas, Lord Berkeley, had died within a few weeks of each other: Reginald on 5

---

[13] The Cobham tombs were 'cleaned and renovated' in 1947 at a cost of £20: SHC, 2399/9/4 (Lingfield PCC, finance committee minutes). Cleaning and renovation probably entailed repainting.

FIG 26 Berkeley, Gloucestershire: tomb of Thomas, Lord Berkeley, d. 1361, and his wife

October 1361, and his father-in-law three weeks later on 27 October.[14] Thomas Berkeley, like Reginald, was commemorated by a fine tomb chest with, in his case, effigies of him and his wife. The monument is still in Berkeley church (fig. 26). Its similarity to Cobham's is obvious. Both chests are adorned with battlemented parapets; and both have panelled sides with quatrefoils containing shields of arms. There are one or two differences. Lord Berkeley's monument is of alabaster, and not stone; and on the Berkeley tomb chest there are decorative embellishments, notably blue-glass strips between the panels, which are absent from Cobham's. None the less, the similarity between the two monuments is obvious. It is reasonable to suppose that they were both produced in the same workshop, probably a workshop in London. It is conceivable that the two widows handed in their orders together; alternatively, one could have been responsible for both. At any rate, the evidence for close liaison between the two families is clear.

[14] *CIPM*, xi, no. 59; Smyth, *Lives of the Berkeleys*, i, 357.

A striking characteristic of the tomb is the series of coats of arms around the sides. Heraldry was a common decorative embellishment in English fourteenth-century art. Galleries of arms are found in a variety of secular and ecclesiastical settings. On the gatehouses of castles and abbeys such elaborate displays brought a fantasy element to the design. At Kirkham priory (Yorks.) the arms of the house's patrons were shown over the gate, while at Butley priory (Suffolk) those of the leading county gentry occupied almost an entire side of the façade. Inside buildings, arms were displayed on walls, in stained glass windows and on tombs. A number of these armorials were very large. At his newly built church at Shottesbrooke (Berks.) Sir William Trussell had some forty or so shields of arms displayed in the windows of the nave and transepts, while in the refectory of the Austin friars, Bristol, there was a gallery of over fifty.[15] The purpose of these armorials varied considerably according to their setting. In monasteries like Kirkham their purpose was clearly to honour the patron and chief benefactors. However, in churches with which the gentry were associated they were concerned primarily to honour the patron's mesne lord, associates, and kin. At Etchingham (Sussex) Sir William de Etchingham's glazing scheme included, in the chancel, the arms of his noble patrons, and, in the nave, those of his associates, neighbours, and in-laws. In a few armorials, careers in arms were celebrated. At Elsing (Norfolk) Sir Hugh Hastings's distinguished career in France was memorialized on his magnificent brass of c.1347.[16] In a particularly grandiose armorial, that of the Gloucester east window, it was an event that was celebrated—the battle of Crécy: at the foot of the window are the arms of the English commanders in the battle.[17] Into which of these schemes are the shields of arms on Reginald's tomb to be fitted? On what principles were they selected?

As they appear on the tomb today, the shields may be identified as follows: on the west, Cobham of Sterborough, and Berkeley; on the north: Cobham impaling Stafford; Badlesmere; Ros; Pavely; on the south: Mortimer; Bohun; Vere; Arundel; and to the east: Cossington and

[15] For Shottesbrooke, see N. E. Saul, 'Shottesbrooke Church. A Study in Knightly Patronage', *Medieval Art and Architecture in the Windsor and Reading Region* (British Archaeological Association; Leeds, forthcoming); for Bristol, idem, 'The Religious Sympathies of the Gentry in Gloucestershire, 1200–1500', *Transactions of the Bristol and Gloucestershire Archaeological Society*, 98 (1980), 107–8.

[16] In the canopy shafts are figures of his companions in arms, each identified by a heraldic jupon: Norris, *Monumental Brasses. The Memorials*, 18–19.

[17] C. Winston, 'An Account of the Painted Glass in the East Window of Gloucester Cathedral', *Archaeological Journal*, 20 (1863), 319–30.

Valognes. In their present brightly coloured condition, the blazons are obviously the product of nineteenth-century repainting.[18] It is possible that l'Anson could have undertaken the work in the 1840s. However, it is more likely that Waller did so a generation later: Waller was keenly interested in heraldry and in 1871 published an account of the blazons suggesting identifications.[19] Unfortunately, there is nothing to indicate how faithful the nineteenth-century restoration was to the original.[20] Waller gave no authority in his article, and it is conceivable that in places he resorted to invention. Waller's reconstruction has been followed in all subsequent accounts. However, an earlier, and hitherto unnoticed, account in Powell's notes of his visits to Surrey churches in January 1806 gives a different version of two of the blazons.[21] According to Powell, the arms on the first shield on the north side were those of Cobham impaling Berkeley, and not Stafford, while those on the last shield on the south were Burghersh, and not Arundel. Powell's version of the blazons is obviously to be preferred to Waller's, since it is based on earlier observation. All the same, it is not without problems of its own. Much of the paintwork was already decayed when Powell wrote. A sketch by Edward Blore, dating from a decade or two later, shows no colouring on the shields at all.[22] Powell's witness may not be completely beyond challenge; on the other hand, it is much the most valuable that we have. As recorded in Powell's notes, the blazons on the tomb were as follows:

On the west:
Gules on a chevron or, 3 estoiles sable: Reginald, Lord Cobham;
Gules, a chevron between 10 crosses formy, six in chief, four in base, argent: Thomas, Lord Berkeley;
On the north, from the west:
Gules on a chevron or, 3 estoiles sable impaling *Gules, a chevron between 10 crosses formy, six in chief, four in base, argent*: Cobham of Sterborough impaling Berkeley;
Or, a fesse between 4 gemelles, gules: Giles, Lord Badlesmere;
Azure, 3 water bougets, argent: William, Lord Ros of Hamlake;

---

[18] There was probably also some repainting in 1947: SHC, 2399/9/4.
[19] Waller, 'Notes on the Monuments of the Cobham Family'.
[20] By the early nineteenth century only one of the shields on the south side was still decipherable: Manning and Bray, *History and Antiquities of Surrey*, ii, 359.
[21] Minet Library, Camberwell, MS 1/713 O.S. I am very grateful to John A. Goodall for drawing this document to my attention. There is no evidence that Waller was aware of Powell's notes.
[22] BL Add. MS. 42012, fo. 49 (wrongly attributed to the 2nd Lord Cobham).

Azure, a cross fleury, with a martlet in the first quarter: Sir Walter Pavely;
On the south, working from the west:
Azure, three bars or in chief, between 2 esquires based, 2 pales of the second: Roger
  Mortimer, earl of March;
Azure, a bend argent cotised and six lions rampant, or: Humphrey de Bohun,
  earl of Hereford;
Quarterly, gules and or, in the first quarter a mullet, argent: John de Vere, earl of
  Oxford;
Gules a lion rampant tail-forked or: Bartholomew, Lord Burghersh;
On the east:
Azure, three roses or: Sir Stephen de Cossington;
Paly wavy, or and gules, in a bordure ermine: Sir Waresius de Valognes

A wide spectrum of the English knightly élite was represented on the
tomb. Socially, they ranged from the highest nobility through the ranks
of the baronage to the gentry. The earls of March and Oxford ranked
among the parliamentary nobility, Ros and Badlesmere among the middling baronage, and the two knights Cossington and Valognes among
the gentry. The geographical spread of those represented was equally
wide. William, Lord Ros's interests lay chiefly in the north midlands
and Yorkshire, Hereford's and March's in the Welsh border counties,
and Cossington's and Valognes' more locally in Kent.

The obvious point at which to begin considering the heraldry is at the
head of the tomb. Here, in the position of honour, were placed the two
shields of the deceased and his wife—Reginald's on the north side and
his wife's family's on the south. It was usual on tombs for the arms of the
deceased and his spouse to be shown in this position. Sometimes the two
blazons were impaled; here, however, because of the width to be filled,
they were shown separately. The blazons were a celebration of marriage,
of the union of the two families. The themes of kinship and marriage
were picked up on the first shields on the sides. On the south side, the
Mortimer blazon honoured the ancestry of Joan, Lady Cobham, for her
mother, Thomas Berkeley's wife, was Margaret, daughter of Roger Mortimer, earl of March. Originally, the shield on the equivalent position on
the north side represented Cobham impaling Berkeley, repeating the
arms on the west side (though today it shows Cobham impaling
Stafford).[23] Surprisingly perhaps, these are the only blazons on the tomb

---

[23] Cobham impaling Stafford would have celebrated Reginald II's marriage to Elizabeth
Stafford. It would have been an extremely improbable shield, since the marriage probably did
not take place till after Reginald I's death.

which attest the network of Cobham kin. Members of other Cobham lines are unrepresented. It is possible that this is because Reginald attached a relatively low importance to his relations with the other Cobhams.[24] But a likelier explanation is that the tomb was commissioned by his widow—a Berkeley—and her Berkeley kin.

The remaining shields on the tomb illustrate ties of association. The blazons are all those of Reginald's friends and companions. For the most part, the men honoured were soldiers—the most 'strenuous' of the knightly class, the commanding élite of Edward III's armies. Probably the most active of the group was John de Vere, earl of Oxford. Oxford's career followed a broadly similar course to Cobham's.[25] Like Cobham, he served his military apprenticeship in Scotland. In 1333 he fought at Halidon Hill and in 1335 he joined the king's assault on Perth. In 1338, when Edward crossed to the Low Countries, he was given responsibility for defending London against possible French assault, but in the following year he sailed with the king to Flanders. In the next two decades his and Cobham's careers overlapped repeatedly. In 1342 they enlisted for Edward's campaign in Brittany. Four years later they took part in the victory at Crécy and were present at the siege of Calais.[26] In 1355 they accompanied the Black Prince on his *chevauchée* in Aquitaine; and finally, in the autumn of 1359, they joined in the king's last expedition to France—the ambitious offensive which, after failing to take Rheims, ended with the peace settlement at Bretigny.[27]

Hardly less active than Oxford was another lord represented on the tomb, Bartholomew, Lord Burghersh.[28] Burghersh was a slightly younger contemporary of Cobham's. He belonged to a family whose estates lay principally in Kent and east Sussex.[29] His father, towards the end of his life, was Edward III's chamberlain of the household. The

---

[24] Counter to this is both the evidence of good relations between the Sterborough Cobhams and other branches of the Cobham family and the likelihood that Reginald sponsored the Cobham interests generally at court: see above, 132.

[25] *Complete Peerage*, x, 222–4.

[26] Oxford was one of the commanders of the prince of Wales's division: *Crecy and Calais*, 31.

[27] The earl died in 1371 and was buried at Earl's Colne priory. The tomb which is probably his is now in St Stephen's chapel, Bures.

[28] For Burghersh, see *Complete Peerage*, ii, 426–7; *DNB*, vii, 334–5. His uncle was Henry Burghersh, bishop of Lincoln, chancellor 1328–30 and treasurer 1334–7.

[29] The name Burghersh is represented by the modern Burwash in east Sussex. Between the 1330s and the 1360s the family greatly added to their holdings. The younger Bartholomew at his death held a string of manors in Suffolk, Wiltshire, and Herefordshire: *CIPM*, xii, no. 322. The family held a manor close to Sterborough at Chiddingstone (Kent), which the younger Bartholomew demised for life to another knight represented on the tomb, Sir Walter Pavely. See below, 160.

younger Burghersh's career began in 1339 when he accompanied the king to the Low Countries. In the winter of 1342–3 he was again in the king's service on a sortie into Brittany. Four years later he played a leading role in the major expedition to France; he fought under the prince's banner at Crécy, with Cobham one of his companions, and he was active in the siege of Calais.[30] From this time on, his career and Cobham's, like Oxford's and Cobham's, constantly overlapped. In July 1347 the two men were associated in the negotiations for the surrender of Calais. In 1355–6 they were companions on the Black Prince's expedition to Aquitaine, Burghersh acquitting himself with particular distinction at Poitiers.[31] And in 1359–60 they served for the last time on Edward III's ambitious, if disappointing, expedition to Rheims.[32] In his years of retirement, after Cobham's death, Burghersh was extensively engaged in diplomacy. In 1364 he attended on the king of France at Dover and two years later he went on an embassy to the pope.[33] He died in 1369.[34]

Another active campaigner represented on the tomb was Roger Mortimer, earl of March.[35] The positioning of this man's arms adjacent to

---

[30] After Crécy he returned to England, but in May 1347, with others, was summoned back to Calais: *Black Prince's Register*, i, 79–80.

[31] Burghersh captured the Seigneur de Pompadour: Hewitt, *The Black Prince's Expedition*, 134. For his earlier exploits on the raid to Narbonne and the Mediterranean, see *Chronicon Adae Murimuth et Roberti de Avesbury*, 436, 439.

[32] For his role in the capture of Cormicy, near Rheims, see Barber, *Edward, Prince of Wales and Aquitaine*, 162.

[33] In 1364, King John, to atone for the escape of his son Louis of Anjou, one of the hostages for the payment of his ransom, voluntarily returned to captivity. Burghersh was one of the nobles appointed to receive him at Dover and to conduct him to Edward's presence at Eltham.

[34] He requested burial at Walsingham, in the chapel before the image of the Virgin Mary (*Testamenta Vetusta*, i, 76–7). The skeleton of an elderly man uncovered in excavations there in the 1960s is generally assumed to be his; the skeleton was enclosed in a substantial tomb, but there was no sign of an effigy or brass (C. Green and A. B. Whittingham, 'Excavations at Walsingham Priory, Norfolk, 1961', *Archaeological Journal*, 125, 1968, 267, 277–8). At Lincoln Cathedral, on the north side of St Catherine's chapel, is a monument to a member of the Burghersh family with a series of shields on the sides, one of which bears the arms of Cobham of Sterborough. The tomb is usually said to be that of the elder Bartholomew (d. 1355) (Crossley, *English Church Monuments*, 67). However, according to a list of sixteenth-century burials in the church of the Grey Friars, London, Bartholomew the elder was buried there: Nichols, 'Register of the Sepulchral Inscriptions in the Church of the Grey Friars', 286. The confusion over burial-places is odd. The heraldry on the Lincoln tomb points unmistakably to a member of the Burghersh family. The paintwork today is renewed, but Gough, writing in the eighteenth century, recorded the blazons of Bohun, earl of Northampton, Mortimer, Vere, Badlesmere, Ros of Helmsley, and Cobham of Sterborough: all lords with whom the Burghershs were associated (Gough, *Sepulchral Monuments*, 1 pt 2, 108). A date of c.1350–60 would be consistent with the design of the tomb. Unfortunately, the effigy presently on the tomb does not belong, the original being lost, and there is no epitaph. Despite the presence of the Cobham arms on this monument, there can be little doubt that it was the younger Burghersh who was honoured by the blazon at Lingfield. Not only did the two men's careers overlap; they were both knights of the Garter: see below, 159.

[35] *Complete Peerage*, viii, 442–5; *DNB*, xxxix, 144–5.

Cobham's own suggests that he was included chiefly on grounds of kinship. All the same, from the mid-1340s he was heavily involved in the king's enterprise in France. He was a boy of three when his grandfather, Isabella's lover, was executed in 1330. He first came to popular attention when he distinguished himself in a tournament at Hereford in 1344. Two years later he played a conspicuous role in the English invasion of France. He was knighted alongside the prince of Wales and other tiros when Edward and his army landed at La Hogue, and at Crécy he fought, with Cobham, under the prince's banner; in the next year he was involved in the siege of Calais. In 1355 he enlisted with the duke of Lancaster's expedition to Normandy but experienced disappointment when the expedition had to be cancelled as a result of bad weather; later in the season he joined the expedition led by the king himself. In 1359 he enlisted for the king's final expedition to France, the bid to take Rheims: as constable of the army, he crossed over with the advance guard and raided the coast around Boulogne.[36] Later, he distinguished himself in combat at Rheims. After the lifting of the siege, he accompanied the king on his foray into Burgundy, but died in February at Rouvray.

Another younger lord represented by a blazon on the tomb was William, Lord Ros of Helmsley.[37] Like March, Lord Ros had his first experience of active service on the Crécy campaign, and in common with many other tiros he was knighted by the king at La Hogue. In August 1350 he served in the fleet which defeated the Castilians in the naval engagement off Winchelsea. In 1351 he was preparing to go overseas again; and he was almost certainly overseas in the following year when he died. Forty years later his nephew William was to marry the younger Reginald Cobham's step-daughter, Margaret.[38]

One other magnate with a possible claim to be included in this group is Humphrey de Bohun, earl of Hereford. Hereford, who came from an ancient and distinguished lineage, was hereditary constable of England and fought in the Scottish wars of the 1330s. However, in his middle and later years he was inactive. He never fought in France, and he did not serve on the council; he remained unmarried. It has been suggested that he may have been physically incapacitated.[39] In the light of his inactivity, it is conceivable that the man whose arms were depicted on the tomb was

[36] K. Fowler, *The King's Lieutenant: Henry of Grosmont, First Duke of Lancaster, 1310–1361* (London, 1969), 202.

[37] *Complete Peerage*, xi, 99–100. The Ros's of Helmsley are often referred to as of Hamlake, another of their estates.

[38] Ibid. 103; *Wykeham's Register*, ii, 456. The marriage took place at Sterborough.

[39] G. A. Holmes, *The Estates of the Higher Nobility in Fourteenth-Century England* (Cambridge, 1957), 20–1.

not the earl but his younger brother, William, earl of Northampton. Northampton's arms were very similar to his brother's, but differenced with three mullets. Bearing in mind the deterioration of the paintwork by the 1800s, it would be understandable if the restorers had mistaken the arms for his brother's.[40] Northampton was one of the most vigorous and successful commanders of his day.[41] A member of the king's inner circle of knights, he served regularly on campaigns both in Scotland and France. He gained his first experience of arms on the Scottish expeditions of the 1330s. After the outbreak of war on the Continent, he crossed to the Low Countries and stayed there for nearly two years. In the 1340s he was given an independent command in Brittany, scoring a significant victory over the French at Morlaix. Four years later he was in the forefront of the king's invasion of France. On 24 August he and Cobham led the forcing of the Somme at Blanchetaque, and two days later he played a leading role in the victory of Crécy.[42] In 1350 he led a retinue in the naval engagement against the Castilians off Winchelsea and in subsequent years he was heavily involved in the defence of the north. In 1355 he joined in the renewed campaigning in France, seeing action in Artois, and between 1357 and 1359 he was in Gascony. Like his friends and companions-in-arms Oxford and Cobham, he enlisted for the last time on the Rheims expedition of 1359–60.[43]

The importance of military experience as a characteristic linking those represented on the tomb is self-evident. The point can be appreciated

---

[40] Powell's notes of 1806 show the medieval paintwork in varying stages of decay. The stars on Reginald's own coat, for example, were almost gone; so too were the tinctures on the coats of Badlesmere, Ros, Burghersh, Cossington, and Valognes: Minet Library, Camberwell, MS1/713 O.S.

[41] For his career, see *DNB*, v, 310; Holmes, *Estates of the Higher Nobility*, 22–3; A. Ayton, 'Edward III and the English Aristocracy at the Beginning of the Hundred Years War', in M. Strickland (ed.), *Armies, Chivalry and Warfare in Medieval Britain and France* (Stamford, 1998), 173–206. He was granted his earldom in Edward III's mass creation of earls in 1337.

[42] *Knighton's Chronicle*, 60; see above, 128. Northampton may have been the person responsible for the tactical ploys which contributed to the English victory at Crécy. At this battle, for the first time in a major engagement with the French, the English men-at-arms were dismounted and pit-traps were dug in the approach to the English lines. These were tactics that Northampton had earlier used at Morlaix. For Morlaix, see T. F. Tout, 'The Tactics of the Battles of Boroughbridge and Morlaix', *Collected Papers of Thomas Frederick Tout* (3 vols.; Manchester, 1932–4), ii, ch. 8; Sumption, *Hundred Years War: Trial by Battle*, 402.

[43] *Complete Peerage*, ix, 664–7; *DNB*, v, 310. Cobham's association with the Bohun family is further attested by the appearance of his arms in the Bohun Psalter (BL, MS Egerton 3277) of c.1361–73, at fo. 129. L. F. Sandler, *Gothic Manuscripts, 1285–1385* (2 vols.; London, 1986), ii, 153, noting this, describes Reginald as the captor of the king of France at Poitiers and implies an association with an earlier pictorial reference to the English triumph at the battle. There is no evidence that Reginald was the actual captor of the king, and the inclusion of his blazon is better explained in terms of general companionship in arms.

from another angle. At least three of the knights, besides Cobham, were knights of the Garter. These were the earl of March, Bartholomew, Lord Burghersh, and someone not yet mentioned, Sir Walter Pavely. The Order of the Garter had been instituted around 1348—the exact date of foundation is not known—as an élite company of knights. Its origins are thought to have lain in the tourneying activities of two teams, one headed by the king and the other by the prince.[44] Burghersh, March, and Pavely were among the founder knights. All three were ambitious young knights who enjoyed strong links with the prince. Burghersh had seen action at Crécy as a member of the prince's retinue and had quickly risen in his trust: a decade later he was to be with him at Poitiers.[45] March, like Burghersh, had shared in the triumph of Crécy, fighting under the prince's banner, and had risen quickly in his favour; in 1349 he assisted the prince in thwarting an attempt to betray Calais to the French.[46] The third Garter knight, Sir Walter Pavely, was a man of less exalted birth than his fellows. A scion of a middling gentry family with estates in Wiltshire and Kent, he quickly gained a formidable reputation for prowess. He fought in all the main campaigns of the day.[47] In 1342 and 1345 he served in Brittany and in 1343 in Aquitaine. In 1346 he fought at Crécy, like the two others, in the prince's division, and in 1355 he joined the prince's expedition to Aquitaine. After a further spell in Brittany in 1358, he accompanied the prince to Aquitaine and remained in his service in the duchy for much of the 1360s.[48] He died in June 1375.[49] Pavely owed his election to the Garter partly to his military record and partly to his association with the prince. The prince regarded him highly enough to pay him a fee of 100 marks per annum.[50] Like Burghersh and March,

---

[44] For discussion of the origins of the Order, see J. Vale, *Edward III and Chivalry: Chivalric Society and its Context, 1270–1350* (Woodbridge, 1982), ch. 5.

[45] In Nov. 1351 the prince appointed him his steward of the honor of Wallingford, and two years later justice of Chester: *Black Prince's Register*, iv, 32; iii, 128. For gifts by the prince to Burghersh indicating favour, see ibid. ii, 78; iv, 69, 70, 108, 146, 230, 253.

[46] *Chronicon Galfridi le Baker*, 104. It is worth adding that a subsidiary factor in March's election may have been the king's desire for reconciliation following his grandfather's execution for treason in 1330. Until 1354 he was actually 'Sir Roger Mortimer': he was not restored to the earldom until that year.

[47] For Pavely's career, see *DNB*, xliv, 100–1, largely following E. Ashmole, *The Institutions, Law and Ceremonies of the Order of the Garter* (London, 1672), 708. Ashmole identified his father as Sir Walter Paveley the elder, who in 1316 held the manor and hundred of Stowting, and the manors of Boughton Aluph, Biddenham, and Cranbrook, all in Kent (Ashmole, *Institutions*, 708; Moor, *Knights of Edward I*, iv, 15; *Feudal Aids*, iii, 11).

[48] *CPR 1361–4*, 489.   [49] *CIPM*, xiv, no. 184.

[50] *Black Prince's Register*, iv, 384. There were other marks of the prince's favour: in 1346 he gave him a 'nouche' adorned with pearls and diamonds and in 1349, when they were in Normandy, a charger called 'Morel More'.

Pavely was also well known to Cobham. The two men held properties close to each other: Pavely's manor of Chiddingtone was only a few miles from Cobham's at Sterborough.[51] Pavely was also related in blood to some of Cobham's close associates. His mother Maud was Bartholomew Burghersh's cousin, while his sister Isabel was Thomas, Lord Bradeston's, wife.[52] There is reason to believe that the arms of a fourth knight of the Garter were emblazoned on the tomb—those of William, earl of Northampton, if the coat currently Hereford's is indeed his. Northampton was elected to the Order in around 1349 as one of the first replacement knights. His membership of the Order and association with this circle of knights strengthens the case for identifying the shield with the Bohun lions as his.

The dominant impression given by the blazons so far considered is the sense of companionship and pride felt by Edward III's military élite. The lords represented here were the king's leading associates and commanders: the men in the forefront of the war in France and the principal agents of his rule at home. They were Cobham's own close associates. A further connection between them can be found in their shared experience at Crécy: March, Oxford, Northampton, Burghersh, Pavely, and Ros had all been present at the battle. In a sense, the tomb can be interpreted as a celebration of victory, a tribute to the achievement of the knights involved. A celebration of Crécy was identified by Charles Winston as a major theme in the heraldry of the east window at Gloucester.[53] It is possible that the scale and importance of that mighty victory encouraged a bond between those who had fought there which united them even in death.

But there was one person represented on the tomb who does not fit into this scheme; and that is Giles, Lord Badlesmere. Badlesmere never took part in, nor even lived through, the victories of the Hundred Years War: he had died in 1338. He was only twenty-four years old then, and was the last of his line. The Badlesmeres were a baronial family. Their estates, mostly in the south-east, were extensive. In Kent they held the manors of Badlesmere, from which they took their name, Erith,

---

[51] E. Hardcastle, 'Chiddingstone', *Aspects of Edenbridge*, v (1983), 27. Pavely was a tenant of Burghersh in the manor. Pavely's other manors were in Kent—Boughton Aluph, Stowting, and Sifflington and Brampton (in Ditton): *CIPM*, xiv, no. 184.

[52] Moor, *Knights of Edward I*, iv, 15. Burghersh appointed Pavely one of his executors: *Testamenta Vetusta*, i, 77; he was already one of his feoffees: *CIPM*, xii, no. 322. For the Bradeston connection, see PRO, C81/1760/69. In this petition Bradeston says that Paveley, his 'brother-in-law', received robes from him.

[53] Winston, 'An Account of the Painted Glass in the East Window of Gloucester'.

Chatham, Snodhurst, Wilderton, Whitstable, Kingston, Sibton, Blean, Ringwold, and Chilham: Chilham being their chief seat.[54] Giles's father, Bartholomew, had been a leading figure in the politics of Edward II's reign.[55] In the early years of the reign he had been an associate of Gilbert de Clare, earl of Gloucester, but after the latter's death at Bannockburn in 1314 he had entered the king's service and had risen quickly in his favour.[56] In 1318 he was appointed steward of the king's household and for two years was active on royal diplomatic and administrative business. Increasingly disenchanted by the Despensers' avarice, however, he had joined the opposition and had fought on the baronial side at Borough-bridge. He was captured after the battle and on 14 April executed at Canterbury. His son was still under age when his father died but was given early livery of his lands in 1328.[57] He was summoned to parliament in 1336 and 1337, and mid-decade performed military service in Scotland and Ireland.[58] In or before June 1338, however, he died. His premature demise prevented him from sharing in the battle honours won by his contemporaries. Yet nearly a quarter of a century later he was to be honoured on Reginald, Lord Cobham's tomb. Why?

The answer is principally to be found in the local importance of the Badlesmere barony. In their heyday in the early years of the century the Badlesmeres were one of the wealthiest families in Kent. They were richer by far than the Cobhams, and their lands stretched across more than a dozen counties.[59] Moreover, through the sub-tenancies which they created they exercised a major influence on Kent social and political life.[60] Reginald Cobham, for example, was a tenant of the Badlesmeres in his manors of Lullingstone and Hever in Kingsdown.[61] The Badlesmeres' natural importance in Kent and Cobham's tenurial connections with them go a long way to explaining the appearance of the arms on the tomb.

---

[54] *CIPM*, viii, no. 185.

[55] For Badlesmere's career and attitudes towards him, see *Complete Peerage*, i, 371–2; J. R. Maddicott, *Thomas of Lancaster, 1307–1322* (Oxford, 1970), 182, 193, 223–5, 231–3, 272–3, 293–4; J. R. S. Phillips, *Aymer de Valence, Earl of Pembroke, 1307–1324* (Oxford, 1972), 12, 136–9, 144–7, 216–17.

[56] Gilbert de Clare held the lordship of Tonbridge (Kent).

[57] i.e. after Edward II's fall.

[58] *Complete Peerage*, i, 372–3; *CPR 1334–8*, 489, 495. His arms appear on the Carlisle roll of 1335: *English Medieval Rolls of Arms, I, 1244–1334*, 452.

[59] Hasted says that Bartholmew was 'styled the rich Lord Badlesmere of Leeds': Hasted, *Kent*, vii, 272. On one occasion Giles Badlesmere witnessed a charter of the Cobhams of Cobham: Nichols, 'Memorials of the Family of Cobham', 336.

[60] Bartholomew Badlesmere had the important royal castle of Leeds, near Maidstone, by grant of the crown: *CPR 1317–21*, 46.

[61] Hasted, *Kent*, ii, 481, 547; *Feudal Aids*, iii, 48.

However, there is another factor which has a bearing on the matter. In addition to the tenurial bond between Cobham and the Badlesmere barony, there was a tie of kinship between Giles Badlesmere himself and some of Cobham's knightly associates who were honoured on the tomb. Giles Badlesmere left as his coheiresses four sisters—Margery, who was married to William, Lord Ros of Helmsley; Maud, who was married to John de Vere, earl of Oxford; Margaret, who was married to Sir John Tiptoft; and Elizabeth, the widow of Sir Edmund Mortimer and later the wife of William de Bohun, earl of Northampton.[62] Two of these husbands are represented on the Cobham tomb—the earls of Oxford and Northampton (assuming the Bohun coat to be Northampton's); and so too is the son of a third, William, Lord Ros.[63] It is unlikely that the inclusion of these men's arms is a coincidence. By right of their wives they were major proprietors in Kent and the south-east. Cobham would have been in regular contact with them through the normal workings of feudal tenure. On Giles Badlesmere's death and the succession of the coheiresses and their husbands, he automatically became a tenant of the earl of Oxford in Lullingstone and of Lord Ros and the earl of Northampton in Hever in Kingsdown.[64] Some of his retainers stood in similar relation to other of the Badlesmere coheiresses' husbands. Sir Stephen de Cossington, for example, was a tenant of Lord Ros at Cossington and Acrise.[65] Cobham's connection with the Badlesmeres, and subsequently with their successors, is crucial to understanding the selection of blazons on the tomb. The connection can also be used to explain another odd characteristic of the armorial. Hardly any of the lords represented were Cobham's near-neighbours; Ros was essentially a northerner: his main territorial interests lay in Yorkshire, and he had only a loose connection with the royal household; the earl of Oxford resided chiefly in Essex, while the earl of Northampton's main interests were in the midlands. All of these lords, however, had acquired territorial stakes in Kent through marriage. And some of them had acquired very considerable stakes: Ros, for example, took over the former Badlesmere *caput*

[62] Moor, *Knights of Edward I*, i, 32; Holmes, *The Estates of the Higher Nobility in Fourteenth-Century England*, 30.

[63] There can be little doubt that the member of the Ros family whose arms are on the tomb is the younger William, and not his father, the husband of the coheiress. The latter never fought alongside Cobham: *Complete Peerage*, xi, 97–100.

[64] *CCR 1341–3*, 150; Hasted, *Kent*, ii, 481. Hever in Kingsdown (in the North Downs) is not to be confused with the better-known Hever near Edenbridge.

[65] *Feudal Aids*, iii, 31, 45. It is possible that the Cossington arms, *azure three roses or*, involved a pun on the name of Ros. For Cossington, see below, 164–7.

of Chilham.[66] Tenurial politics were as decisive in determining inclusion as companionship in arms.

Two other shields on the tomb remain to be considered. These are the pair at the eastern end. End positions on tombs were usually reserved for the foremost associates or kinsfolk of the deceased. Yet here, anti-climactically, the position at one end is occupied by two relatively obscure knights—Sir Stephen de Cossington and Sir Waresius de Valognes. The natural presumption must be that they were men particularly esteemed by Lord Cobham. In fact, as an analysis of their careers shows, they were his most trusted companions-in-arms—the lieutenants who accompanied him regularly on campaign after campaign.

Waresius was the less notable or substantial of the two. He appears to have been a ruffianly type, an adventurer who lived on his wits. He sprang from a relatively well-to-do gentry family based at Hougham, near Dover.[67] In 1327 he served as admiral of the Cinque Ports, and later he was appointed to a few commissions.[68] A taste for violence appears to have disfigured his and his family's behaviour. In 1323 Waresius and his kinsman Sir Henry were accused of attacking the earl of Pembroke's property at Brabourne, while in 1331 his son was involved in a homicide and was himself the victim of homicide three years later; and simultaneously his father was accused of rape.[69] On the reopening of the war with France in the 1330s, Waresius found an outlet for his violence on campaign. In 1338 he crossed to Flanders with Cobham and he appears

---

[66] Hasted, *Kent*, vii, 272. A later Ros married the step-daughter of Reginald Cobham II: *Wykeham's Register*, ii, 456. The Ros arms appear on the early fifteenth-century vault of the cloister of Canterbury Cathedral: Griffin, 'The Heraldry in the Cloisters of the Cathedral Church of Christ at Canterbury', 520.

[67] Waresius's place in the family genealogy cannot be established precisely. Since the family did not hold their lands in chief, there are no inquisitions post mortem. His kinsman Sir Henry, however, seems to have been head of the family in the 1330s (Hasted, *Kent*, viii, 190). In 1340 Waresius had a grant of free warren in his manors of Hougham, Elmsett, and Otham (Kent): *CChR 1327–41*, 467. The other manors held by the family were: Cheriton, Seene, and Beechborough in Newington, Ford in Godmersham, and Great and Little Repton in Ashford (Hasted, *Kent*, vii, 323, 531, 532; viii, 190, 202, 204): all in south Kent. The Valognes' contacts with the Cobhams went some way back. In the thirteenth century Reginald de Cobham had married Maria de Valognes, while in 1291 Laderyna de Valognes had sold the advowson of Worplesdon (Surrey) to Sir John de Cobham of Cobham: *VCH Surrey*, iii, 395.

[68] *CPR 1327–30*, 101; *CPR 1343–5*, 100, 169, 171.

[69] *CPR 1321–4*, 384; *CPR 1330–4*, 148, 579; PRO, C260/47/64. There were other incidents. In Aug. 1324 Prior Eastry of Canterbury had to write sternly to Sir Henry expressing concern at his riotous assemblage of retainers and warning him that complaints were being made about his behaviour: *Literae Cantuarienses*, ed. J. B. Sheppard (3 vols.; Rolls series; 1887–9), i, 120–2. Relations between various members of the Valognes family were occasionally uneasy. In 1323 Sir Waresius incurred the anger of his brother for taking the homage of a tenant who belonged to him: ibid. 94–5.

to have served there for the greater part of the next two years.[70] In 1341 he was sent on a diplomatic mission to France and in the following year he served in Scotland.[71] Later he served on various minor commissions in Kent.[72] The last reference to him occurs in 1345 and by the following year he had died.[73]

His companion knight, Sir Stephen de Cossington, was an altogether more substantial figure. While, again, largely a soldier-adventurer, he was also a busy man of affairs. His long career took him to realms as far apart as Germany and Castile, and he enjoyed the trust not only of Cobham but of the prince of Wales and Henry, duke of Lancaster.

Stephen was born into a local knightly family which took its name from the manor of Cossington, near Aylesford.[74] His immediate forbears had figured only intermittently in public affairs, and Stephen was to show himself the most vigorous of his line.[75] His connection with Reginald Cobham stemmed from the fact that they were both tenants of the Badlesmere barony: Stephen being a Badlesmere vassal in two of his three manors.[76] Stephen's lengthy career in arms began at Halidon Hill in 1333[77]—although it is not known in whose retinue he served then. The first occasion on which he and Cobham are found together is in Edward's expedition to Scotland in 1335: Cossington's arms are next to Cobham's on the roll of arms of the muster at Carlisle;[78] and according to the wardrobe book, he served in Cobham's retinue from 28 June to

[70] PRO, C76/15 m. 20.   [71] PRO, C76/16 m. 13; C71/22 m. 14.

[72] CPR 1343–5, 100, 169, 171; PRO, C76/19 m. 15.

[73] In 1346 his wife Isabella is referred to as his widow: *Feud. Aids*, iii, 40. Waresius also had links with the Cobhams of Cobham: in 1344, with his kinsman Henry, he attested a Cobham charter (Nichols, 'Memorials of the Family of Cobham', 346).

[74] The family held three manors: Cossington, Acrise, and South Barton, all in Kent: *CChR 1327–41*, 302. The family's arms appear on the cloister vault of Canterbury Cathedral: Griffin, 'The Heraldry in the Cloisters of the Cathedral Church of Christ at Canterbury', 481, 501, 527 (shields 124, 263, 488).

[75] The descent of the family is obscure. Stephen's father could have been either Sir Stephen de Cossington the elder or Sir William de Cossington; both appear in the records of the previous generation. Sir William's arms correspond exactly to Stephen's—*azure, 3 roses or*—which seems to point to his paternity. On the other hand, in the Parliamentary Roll of Arms of c.1311 William is listed under Wiltshire and Hampshire, not Kent; so there is room for doubt (Moor, *Knights of Edward I*, i, 240). His father was probably dead by 1316: in that year the manor of Acrise was held by one Roysia de Cossington, presumably a widow (*Feud. Aids.*, iii, 11).

[76] *Feud. Aids*, iii, 31, 45; *CCR 1341–3*, 150; see above, 162. In the previous generation Sir William de Cossington had witnessed an inspeximus of Katherine de Leybourne alongside Bartholomew Badlesmere (*CPR 1307–13*, 387).

[77] In July 1333 he received a grant of free warren in all his demesne lands in recognition of his recent service in Scotland: *CChR 1327–41*, 302.

[78] *English Medieval Rolls of Arms. I, 1244–1334*, 448.

30 September.[79] Cossington continued to serve with Cobham after the opening of hostilities on the Continent. In July 1338, when Cobham crossed to Flanders, Cossington accompanied him, and he appears to have remained in his service until 1340.[80] The bond which the two men forged in arms was sustained in peace. On several occasions, they served together in local government: in 1342, for example, they were jointly commissioned to seize the procurations imposed by the papal envoys and deposited in Faversham abbey.[81] The two men worked together in other capacities. In 1347, for example, they sat with the earls of Lancaster and Huntingdon as judges in the court of chivalry in a dispute over ownership of arms.[82] Given their long record of co-operation, it is perhaps surprising that Cossington did not accompany Cobham on the Crécy campaign of 1346. However, in the previous summer he had contracted to serve with the king's cousin Henry of Lancaster, earl of Derby, in Aquitaine.[83] Derby, whose campaign was spread over two seasons, was still serving in the duchy when Edward and his force embarked for Normandy. Cossington probably returned to England with Derby on the latter's surrender of his lieutenancy in January 1347.[84] In the meantime the English army had begun the task of reducing Calais. The town, which was strongly defended, put up tough resistance, and by early spring rumours were circulating that French relief was on hand. Summonses were sent to England for reinforcements. Cossington was among those who responded in late May.[85] With their ranks refreshed the English tightened their grip on the town, and in August the inhabitants surrendered. In September most of the English army returned home, and Cossington joined in the celebratory tournaments at Canterbury.[86] From now on Cossington's fortunes, like Cobham's, were increasingly bound up with those of the Black Prince.[87] In 1350 Cossington and

[79] Ibid.; BL, Cotton MS Nero C VIII, 238[r].   [80] *Treaty Rolls, II, 1337–9*, nos. 416–18.

[81] *CCR 1341–3*, 390. The procurations, which had been imposed in 1339, were contentious and led to disputes with the king: W. E. Lunt, *Financial Relations of the Papacy with England, 1327–1534* (Cambridge, Mass., 1962), 632–5.

[82] G. D. Squibb, *The High Court of Chivalry* (Oxford, 1959), 14.

[83] Wrottesley, *Crecy and Calais*, 128.

[84] Fowler, *The King's Lieutenant*, 70; J. H. Ramsay, *The Genesis of Lancaster, 1307–1399* (2 vols.; Oxford, 1913), i, 337.

[85] *Black Prince's Register*, ii, 79–80, 81; Barber, *Edward, Prince of Wales and Aquitaine*, 76.

[86] Ibid. 93. For the hastiludes at Canterbury in 1348 the king attired his knights in harnesses worked with Cossington's arms: a personal compliment (N. H. Nicolas, 'Observations on the Institution of the Most Noble Order of the Garter', *Archaeologia*, 31, 1846, 42).

[87] Cossington was formally retained by the prince in 1355, when he was granted an annuity of 100 marks. This was increased to £100 'on the day of Poitiers' (*Black Prince's Register*, iv, 555).

Cobham served under the prince in the engagement against the Spaniards off Winchelsea.[88] Four years later they enlisted with him for service in Aquitaine, and Cossington's role in the army was recognized in the Canterbury chronicle.[89] Cossington remained in the prince's service long after Cobham's death. In the 1360s he played an active role in the government of Aquitaine and he was retained on the prince's council.[90] In 1367 he enlisted for the prince's expedition to Spain and was appointed one of the marshals of the army. According to Chandos herald, at the battle of Najera he fought in the right wing with Chandos and Devereux.[91] Najera was the veteran campaigner's last big engagement. He was now in his late fifties, and around 1371 after the prince's surrender of the duchy he returned to England. He spent his last years in local administration, serving as a justice of the peace in Cornwall, one of the prince's lordships.[92] Sometime in early 1377 he died.

Cossington's career shows him to have been an able and energetic man. Chandos Herald in his *Life of the Black Prince* paid tribute to him as a 'noble person', and a man 'with a noble heart'.[93] His qualities were many. First and foremost, he was a gifted soldier, and his greatest asset was a strong right arm. But he was also a man of wider accomplishments. He was a skilful envoy and diplomat. The prince entrusted him with a number of delicate missions. In 1361 he named him one of the commissioners to take possession of the duchy of Aquitaine, and in 1363 he entrusted him (and others) with taking a treaty of alliance with Castile to the Castilian king, Pedro.[94] Cossington was a familiar figure in southern Aquitaine: indeed, in 1366 he became a liegeman of King Charles of Navarre.[95] His sterling qualities earned him recognition from his own king. In 1348 Edward entrusted him with accompanying his daughter, Joan, to Castile to marry King Alfonso, and in 1364 he sent him on an embassy to Flanders.[96] His good offices were taken up by senior members of the nobility. By the late 1340s he had become a close associate of Henry of Lancaster, whom he had earlier served in Aquitaine. In the winter of 1349–50 he contracted with the duke to serve on a second

---

[88] Ibid. 100.   [89] *Chronica Johannis de Redyng*, 196.
[90] Barber, *Edward, Prince of Wales and Aquitaine*, 171. Cossington is referred to as a member of the prince's English council as early as 1351: *Black Prince's Register*, iii, 32.
[91] *Life of the Black Prince*, l. 3237.   [92] *CPR 1370–4*, 388; *1374–7*, 139, 332.
[93] *Life of the Black Prince*, ll. 2282, 4200.   [94] *CPR 1361–4*, 299.
[95] B. Leroy, *Le royaume de Navarre à la fin du Moyen Age. Gouvernement et société* (Aldershot, 1990), 94. I am grateful to Prof. Michael Jones for this reference.
[96] *CPR 1348–50*, 343. Joan never arrived, however: she died of the plague at Bordeaux. For Flanders: *CPR 1361–4*, 489.

expedition to bring aid to the duchy.[97] Twelve months later, he was acting on the duke's behalf in his quarrel with Duke Otto of Brunswick. Lancaster had been informed that Otto intended to waylay him as he went on crusade to Prussia, and at Cologne he issued a formal challenge to meet him in a duel. However, a bitter dispute arose over who was the injured party, and Lancaster sent Cossington and three others to Paris to argue his case in front of Otto. A formal hearing was fixed for 1 September 1352 before the king of France, and Cossington and a colleague acted as the duke's proctors. After heated debate the French king declared in Lancaster's favour and a date was fixed for a duel. Cossington had evidently presented his case ably, but in the end the French king imposed a settlement on the disputants himself.[98] Lancaster's confidence in Cossington is shown by the generosity of his reward: he gave him a life grant of the manor of Hartley Mauduit (Hants.).[99]

It is thus apparent from their careers that the two knights honoured on the east face of the tomb were no ordinary knights. Rather, they were to be numbered among Cobham's most intimate associates. Waresius de Valognes was Cobham's companion in the early part of his career, while Stephen de Cossington was with him right to the end. They were both veteran campaigners. The loyal service each gave provided ample justification for his inclusion in the armorial.

How can the series of arms on the tomb as a whole be characterized? Several layers of meaning can be uncovered. At one level, the dominant theme is that of companionship among the military élite. Most of the lords represented had served alongside each other in the French wars, and a number of them before that in Scotland. A notable feature of the blazon is the high representation of protagonists at Crécy and Calais. It is possible that Cobham's widow had specifically asked for the Crécy victory to be celebrated on the tomb. The inclusion of several of the founder knights of the Garter would appear to suggest as much. As Juliet Vale has shown, virtually all the founder knights had fought in the battle.[100] However, there is evidence of another theme running through the armorial: that of the partition of the Badlesmere inheritance. The arms of Giles Badlesmere himself are included, and so too are those of

---

[97] A. Ayton, *Knights and Warhorses: Military Service and the English Aristocracy under Edward III* (Woodbridge, 1994), 59. He evidently campaigned in style. Before he left Aquitaine in 1350, he sold his horses; his destrier fetched 100 marks, and his other three horses £43. 6s. 8d. combined. [98] Fowler, *The King's Lieutenant*, 106–9.
[99] *CPR 1361–4*, 50.   [100] J. Vale, *Edward III and Chivalry*, ch. 5.

some of the coheiresses' husbands. This heraldic evidence points to the continuing importance of tenurial bonds in the structuring of gentry society. Mesne lords (or overlords) still remained very much a focus of service and loyalty for their tenants. In Cobham's case, they were also a source of companionship. Some of the coheiresses' husbands, the earl of Northampton for example, were to be numbered among his closest comrades in arms. The multiple levels of reference on the tomb thus intermingled and overlapped. The arms selected mirrored the seamless merging in Reginald's mind of local associations with those of the campaign trail and the life of the court.

Nearly fifteen years were to elapse before another Cobham was brought to Lingfield for burial—Reginald's widow being buried at South-wark.[101] In 1375 the younger Reginald's first wife, Elizabeth (*née* Stafford), was interred in the church. This lady was commemorated by the first in the series of brasses. In its complete state, Elizabeth's must have been a superb memorial (fig. 27). Austere, but boldly engraved, it consisted of the near life-size figure of the deceased with a pair of shields of arms at the top and a marginal inscription. By the nineteenth century it had suffered a number of losses: the shields and the inscription had all gone, and the figure itself had suffered damage.[102] Waller's restorations of the 1860s, however, allow us to appreciate it in something of its original splendour.[103]

The brass is an excellent example of the work of London style 'B'. Its similarity to the style 'B' brass of Maud, Lady Cobham, at Cobham has already been noted.[104] There can be little doubt that the two memorials were engraved from the same model or pattern. Not only do they exhibit the same gently swaying posture; they depict the commemorated in virtually identical attire—a closely fitting kirtle, sideless cote-hardi and mantle, with the distinctive flounce at the bottom of the cote-hardi. The two brasses were presumably commissioned around the same time. Elizabeth died in August 1375 and Maud, Lady Cobham, just five years later. There is a fair likelihood that the Cobham paterfamilias, John, the 3rd Lord, was involved in both commissions.[105] The 3rd Lord was in regular

---

[101] Where she lived in retirement. For her brass in St Mary Overy, which is known from her will but is now lost, see below, 220–3.

[102] The cushions and coiffure surrounding the head had gone; these were replaced by Waller on the evidence of the surviving indent.

[103] For illustrations of the lady's head before and after restoration, see *MBS Bulletin*, 79 (Sept., 1998), 389.   [104] See above, 109.   [105] See above, 111.

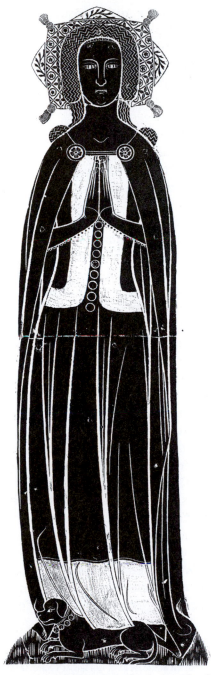

FIG 27. Lingfield M.S. I: Elizabeth, wife of
Reginald, 2nd Lord Cobham, d. 1375, engraved c.1380

contact at this time with the distinguished mason and tomb-maker Henry Yevele, and Yevele placed his orders for lattenwork with Henry Lakenham, whose workshop can be identified with 'B'. Admittedly, the evidence for Lord Cobham's involvement is only circumstantial: none the less it is compelling. There can be little doubt that the influence of this man on the family's commemorative taste extended far beyond Cobham itself.

The arrangements for Elizabeth's commemoration contrasted sharply with those for Reginald I nearly fifteen years earlier. On Reginald's death it had been the family's Berkeley kinsfolk who had been drawn into the business of arranging commemoration; on this occasion it was the collateral Cobhams. Cobham influence on taste shows in a number of ways—in particular, in the choice of a brass rather than a relief effigy, and in the similarity of the two ladies' costume. But there is evidence that Elizabeth's husband and executors were involved in advising on the commission too. Their influence is evident in compositional matters. At Cobham the brasses were all canopied, whereas Elizabeth's, although ambitious, was not. At Cobham it was usual for religious imagery to be included on the memorials; yet, no such imagery appears on Elizabeth's. The instructions which Reginald junior gave for his wife's brass evidently reflected his own tastes as much as his kinsmen's.

A similar balance of influences is evident in the next monument in the series, that of Elizabeth's husband, the 2nd Lord himself (fig. 28). This monument dates from within a couple of years of the subject's death in 1403. It consists of a stone tomb chest with a brass, two shields, and a marginal inscription on top. The choice of a brass for the monument obviously suggests a general indebtedness to Cobham. However, as with Elizabeth's brass, the Cobham influence is neither straightforward nor direct. Other influences can be felt, the strongest being that of the older Reginald's tomb close by.[106]

The younger Reginald's tomb is of similar size and character to his father's. Originally it was free-standing in the chancel, but when the church was rebuilt it was moved to the Lady chapel.[107] It is of standard London design. The sides are panelled with quatrefoils containing shields of arms—four on the long sides and two on the shorter, exactly

[106] Reginald, the 2nd Lord's tomb provided the model for the chest; no tomb chests were employed at Cobham before the sixteenth century.
[107] Reginald asked to be buried at the head of his father's tomb (Flower, 'Notices of the Family of Cobham of Sterborough', 183). Presumably his tomb was in the way of the new stalls placed in the chancel when the college was founded.

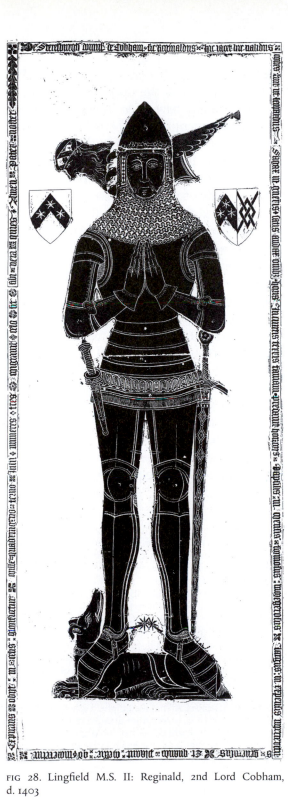

FIG 28. Lingfield M.S. II: Reginald, 2nd Lord Cobham, d. 1403

as on the earlier commission. The slab on top is of Purbeck marble. Strangely, it lacks a chamfer on the upper side, which suggests that a floor position may originally have been intended.[108] Reginald's brass is near life size and superbly engraved.[109] His body armour, typically for the period, consists of a breastplate with skirted fauld over the mail haubergeon, vambraces on the arms and greaves and cuisses on the legs. Around the hips is slung a richly decorated belt supporting the sword and dagger, the scabbards of which are also richly worked. Protecting the neck and shoulders is the mail aventail. The bascinet is encircled near the crown by a jewelled orle, and supporting the deceased's head is a helm which is surmounted with the family crest of the Moor's head. A shield of arms is placed on each side of the figure, and a marginal inscription surrounds the whole.[110]

The brass is an excellent example of the work of London style 'A'. All the familiar 'A' hallmarks are present: the widely flared nostrils, the upward thrust of the dog's head, and the distinctive letter forms of the epitaph (notably the ornate, curvy capital D). London 'A' had been the workshop which the 3rd Lord Cobham had patronized at Cobham in the 1360s: the series of brasses which he had ordered after the foundation of the college had all been 'A' commissions. In the 1380s, however, after he had established contact with Yevele, he turned to 'B'. All the later Cobham brasses are 'B'; and so too is Elizabeth's at Lingfield. The choice of 'A' for Reginald's brass is thus somewhat surprising. It is hard to say who could have placed the order. Reginald's widow can be ruled out: she is not even mentioned in his will.[111] And not one of the seven executors

---

[108] The slab also looks too heavy for its position: it is two and a quarter inches thick.

[109] Reginald is shown alone. His first wife was already commemorated in the church, and his widow, who anyway bore him no affection, was to seek burial elsewhere: see above, 140.

[110] The head of the crest, the two shields, and parts of the inscription are all Waller restorations. The most distinctive feature of Reginald's figure is the jewelled orle around his head. The orle, though rarely featured on monuments (there are examples at Methley, Yorks., and Spilsby, Lincs.), was a popular fashion accessory at the turn of the fourteenth and fifteenth centuries. A number of the donors in the St Albans Book of Benefactors (c.1380) are shown wearing them with civilian attire: BL, MS Cotton Nero D. VII, fos. 108ʳ (Sir Thomas Fitling), 110ʳ (Thomas of Woodstock, duke of Gloucester), 112ᵛ (Sir John Eynsford). Inclusion of the orle on Reginald's brass is a mark of the sumptuousness of its detail. The brass is one of a group of 'A' military figures which are all very similar. The others are Thomas St Leger at Otterden (Kent), John Hawley and wife at St Saviour's, Dartmouth (Devon), John Wilcotes at Gt Tew (Oxon.), and the two de Freville couples at Little Shelford (Cambs.). All but the Lingfield example can be dated to c.1408–10. Reginald died in 1403. A date some five years earlier than the rest leaves his memorial a little out of line; so c.1405–7 may be more plausible. Even so, the depiction of the armour is strikingly state-of-the-art. The skirted fauld had only just come in by this time. The two 'B' effigies at Cobham nearest in date (M.S. X and XI; c.1408–9) are in very old-fashioned armour by comparison, with no skirted fauld at all.   [111] The two were not close: see above, 140.

named had traceable links with 'A'.[112] The senior executor, Archbishop Arundel, a confidant of Henry IV, would have been too busy with the affairs of government to be involved. By default, the task almost certainly fell to the lesser figures—John Woodcock, a London mercer, Thomas Yokefleet, Thomas Blast, and William Furby. Blast was a Surrey attorney in the service of the Fitzalans who would have known his way round the capital.[113] It is likely, although it cannot be proved, that he and the Londoner, Woodcock, bore the main responsibility for placing the commission.

The most striking feature of the tomb before the loss of the paintwork would have been its display of heraldry. The use of shields of arms in quatrefoils on the sides mirrored the similar feature on Reginald, Lord Cobham's tomb. In the late Middle Ages, a formal system of panelling was virtually *de rigueur* on the work of the London tomb-makers. On the grander tombs, it was becoming popular to substitute niches with weepers for shields of arms, but on the more routine products shields held sway. The purpose of including an armorial on this tomb was obviously to stress continuity with the earlier monument. In a sense, Reginald junior was being associated with his father's connections and achievements. Unfortunately the painted blazons on the shields are lost, and no antiquarian record of them survives. So it is impossible to say exactly whose arms were depicted. However, some reasonable guesses can be made. It is likely that the arms of the two Cobham families would have figured, along with those of Stafford for Reginald's first wife. If the pattern of the earlier tomb were repeated, a number of lords with whom the deceased had social or military ties would also have been represented—the earl of Arundel, perhaps, under whose banner Reginald had fought, and the Greys, into whom his sister had married.[114] But beyond that it is probably unwise to go.

Nearly two decades later, the next brass in the series was laid, that of Eleanor Culpeper, first wife of Reginald's son, Reginald III (d. 1420) (fig. 29). In one respect, this brass is very much the exception in the Lingfield series: it is canopied. But it is unusual in another way. It is the only example in the Cobham series of style 'D''s work. Characteristically for 'D', it is a striking and ornate composition. Eleanor is shown full face,

---

[112] For the executors, see Flower, 'Notices of the Family of Cobham of Sterborough', 184–5, 186. [113] Saul, *Scenes From Provincial Life*, 47.
[114] Joan married Henry, son and heir of John, Lord Grey of Codnor, who predeceased his father: *Complete Peerage*, vi, 127. She was still alive in 1393, when she was the subject of an action for debt: PRO, C131/210/5. Other families whose arms might have been represented are the Le Stranges and Ferrers, for his first wife's first and second husbands respectively.

FIG 29. Lingfield M.S. IV: Eleanor, first wife of Sir
Reginald Cobham, d. 1420

wearing a close-fitting kirtle with tight sleeves and over it a mantle held in position by a cord passing through two brooches. Her head-dress is of the horned variety favoured by 'D', and there are two lap-dogs at her feet. Over her figure rises a square-headed canopy consisting of a cusped arch supporting an entablature of pierced quatrefoils with battlements above.[115] The spandrels of the arch are filled with tracery, and the band along the top is ornamented with roses. From the battlement rises a banner charged with the arms of Cobham of Sterborough impaling Culpeper. Above and below the canopy are shields of arms, and surrounding the whole is a marginal inscription.[116]

Eleanor was born into the important and prolific Kentish family of Culpeper. Her father was the wealthy landowner Sir Thomas Culpeper of Upper Hardres and Bayhall (Kent), while her brother, John, who resided at Exton (Rutland), was several times Member of Parliament and sheriff for Rutland.[117] But for all the honour and distinction of her own lineage, it is the interests and aspirations of the Cobhams that dominate. Heraldry, as always, is a major feature. Not only is there the customary quartet of shields at the corners; a banner rises prominently above the canopy entablature. The banner is a highly unusual feature. The only known earlier examples are on the brasses of the countess of Athol at Ashford (Kent) and Bartholomew, Lord Bourchier, at Halstead (Essex). However, a decade or two later, there were to be banners on the brasses of Hugh Halsham at West Grinstead (Sussex) and Edmund Ingolsthorp at Burrough Green (Cambs.).[118] The justification for including the banner was almost certainly the Cobhams' need to reinforce their claim to banneret status. Reginald, the 1st Lord, had been raised to the rank of

---

[115] The square-headed canopy is unusual. It is best interpreted as a type of super-canopy brought down in place of the usual canopy pediment. The model for the design may have been the flat three-dimensional canopy or tester sometimes placed over tomb chests—for example, that formerly over the tomb of Thomas Beauchamp, earl of Warwick (d. 1401) at St Mary's, Warwick (illustrated in Dugdale, *Antiquities of Warwickshire*, i, 404).

[116] The symbols of the evangelists at the corners, the banner and the four shields, the head of the figure, and the bases of the canopies are all restorations by Waller. For an illustration of the brass in its pre-restoration state, see Flower, 'Notices of the Family of Cobham of Sterborough', facing 146. Waller based the symbols of the evangelists on those on the brass of Nicholas Carew and his wife, 1432, at Beddington, Surrey: Lack, Saul, and Whittemore, *Monumental Brasses in St Mary Magdalene, Cobham*, 25.

[117] Stephenson, *List of Monumental Brasses in Surrey*, 346. For her brother, see *House of Commons*, ii, 710–11.

[118] These brasses are illustrated in, respectively, Suffling, *English Church Brasses from the 13th to the 17th Century*, 339; *Monumental Brasses: Portfolio Plates of the Monumental Brass Society*, no. 121 (indent of banner); M. Clayton (ed.), *Catalogue of Rubbings of Brasses and Incised Slabs*, 2nd edn. (London, 1968), pl. 20; *Monumental Brasses of Cambridgeshire*, 15. The brass at Burrough Green is now lost.

banneret in 1336. For the next fifty years he and his son, after him, ranked as bannerets in the social and military structures of the realm. However, in the fifteenth century, as the gulf between the lords and knights gradually widened, the position of the bannerets began to look vulnerable. A process of sorting-out, segregation, and definition took place. The greater bannerets were absorbed into the ranks of the lords, while their lesser comrades slipped down into the gentry.[119] Sir Reginald III, who commissioned this brass, was to be numbered among the losers; he was never summoned to parliament as a lord. Hence his concern to display the banner on the memorial. The banner was a mark of status, a symbol of his family's standing. Entitlement to carry it distinguished his line from their lesser neighbours. In a sense, it stood for everything that his family cherished and yet was in danger of losing.

A desire to impress is also noticeable in Reginald's own tomb in the middle of the chancel (fig. 30). Reginald left instructions for his tomb in his will of 1445. He asked to be buried before the high altar of the college with 'a tomb of alabaster for my monument'.[120] His widow and executors followed his instructions to the letter. The monument was placed immediately before the chancel altar, and the effigies, as requested, are of alabaster. The quality of the effigies is superb. Reginald is shown in a suit of elegant Milanese armour. The cuirass, or body armour, is of the most up-to-date design. The breastplate, once single, is now cut in two, with the upper part ending at the waist, and its lower part overlapped by a lower-breastplate which curves up to a point in the centre. The besagews are fashionably elongated, and the tassets are attached to the fauld. This is state-of-the-art armour. The other defences are generally more conventional. The vambrace and leg harness are of usual late medieval form except that the couters are slightly larger. On the legs the side-wings of the poleyns are clearly visible. Unusually, the head and hands of the knight are uncovered. Reginald's head reclines on a helm surmounted by the Cobham crest, the turbaned 'soldan', while under the feet is a 'nebok', or sea-wolf.[121] Reginald's widow is also carefully depicted. She is shown, appropriately for her condition, with a

---

[119] See above, 136–7.

[120] Lambeth Palace Library, Register of Archbishop Stafford, fo. 142ʳ. The will is summarized in *Testamenta Vetusta*, i, 246–7.

[121] The 'nebok' is a mythical heraldic beast, approximating to a sea-wolf. Its appearance on this tomb is hard to explain: on the tombs of his father and grandfather the Cobham 'soldan' had been shown. The 'nebok' is very rare in heraldry. Its only other recorded appearance is on the banner of William Fitzwilliam, earl of Southampton (d. 1542). I am grateful to John A. Goodall for advice on this.

FIG 30. Lingfield: tomb of Sir Reginald Cobham, d. 1446, and his second wife, Anne

widow's veil and a barbe covering her chin. Over her kirtle she wears a long mantle emblazoned with her paternal arms *azure three cinquefoils or* for Bardolph. Beneath her head is a pillow or cushion *semée*, or powdered, with cinquefoils. The heraldic theme is picked up on the sides of the chest. Shields of arms alternate in the quatrefoil panels with heraldic beasts. Blazons pertaining to the Cobhams are placed on Reginald's side, and ones pertaining to Bardolph on his wife's.[122] On the pairs of shields at each end the families' arms are impaled. A latten inscription (renewed) around the chamfered edge honours Reginald and Anne as founders of the college.[123] The tomb was originally brightly coloured, and some of the lesser details were picked out in gilt. There are also indications that metal inlays were used for enrichment. Reginald's

[122] The 'nebok' again appears for Reginald.
[123] The inscription was probably lost by Aubrey's time, since he does not record it. The section on the south side was restored by J. G. Waller in 1865–6: J. M. Blatchly, 'Further Notes on the Monumental Brasses of Surrey and the Collection of Rubbings at Castle Arch', *SAC*, 68 (1972), 36; the rest is now represented by blank metal.

figure may well have exhibited a livery collar as the studs for fixing remain, and it is likely that the lady had a cordon to her mantle.[124] The tomb was conceived on the grandest scale: it measures 103 in. by 68 in.; and, doubtless as intended, it dominates the chancel. As founders of the college, Reginald and Anne were naturally entitled to prestigious commemoration. But, even so, this is a tomb of exceptional magnificence. It exudes bombast and pride. Through a combination of symbolism and show it affirms status in the face of decline.

This mighty tomb could have been produced in either London or one of the midlands workshops. It is tempting to associate the effigies with the alabasterers based at Chellaston (Derbys.). However, the tomb chest on which the effigies rest is of fire-stone, a local Surrey material. Big alabaster tombs are relatively rare in the southern counties at this time, because of the distance from Chellaston. In the 1370s, John Orchard's workshop in London was apparently holding supplies of alabaster, because it was responsible for producing the alabaster figures of Edward III's children for Westminster Abbey.[125] If Orchard's successors were carrying alabaster stocks still in the fifteenth century, then the Lingfield monument could be of London origin. Such an hypothesis would certainly account for the use of a local material for the chest; it would also help to explain the choice of alabaster by a Surrey patron.

The lead in commissioning the tomb was in all probability taken by Reginald's widow. Not surprisingly, her interests and tastes are reflected in the monument as much as her husband's. Anne was one of the two daughters and coheirs of an important Suffolk knight, William Phelip, Lord Bardolph.[126] Bardolph had died in 1441, only a few years before

---

[124] These suggestions were first made by Waller, 'Notes on the Monuments of the Cobham Family at Lingfield', 194–5. Waller thought that the collar was probably the Yorkist device of suns and roses, but this is unlikely: the date of the tomb is too early, and Reginald had no traceable connection with the house of York. The tomb has suffered losses into modern times. In 1936 one of Reginald's gauntlets was broken off and had to be replaced: SHC, 2399/9/1 (Lingfield PCC, finance committee minutes).

[125] A. Gardner, *Alabaster Tombs of the Pre-Reformation Period in England* (Cambridge, 1940), 7.

[126] William Phelip was the son and heir of Sir William Phelip of Dennington by Julian, daughter of Sir Robert Erpingham. Before 1407 Phelip had married Joan, one of the daughters and coheirs of the Norfolk lord, Thomas, Lord Bardolph. Bardolph joined the Percies' rebellion against Henry IV in 1408, was killed at Bramham Moor and his lands subsequently seized. His heirs quickly recovered the greater part of his property, but Phelip and his wife had to wait until 1437 before recovering the major lordship of Wormegay (Norfolk). From Nov. 1437 Phelip appears in the council minutes and elsewhere as 'Lord Bardolph', although he was not summoned to parliament as a lord in the only subsequent parliament of his lifetime in 1439 (*Complete Peerage*, i, 420–1; J. E. Powell and K. Wallis, *The House of Lords in the Middle Ages*, London, 1968, 467). He was a distinguished soldier, serving at Agincourt and in the Normandy campaigns, and c.1419 he was elected a knight of the Garter.

Cobham, and was commemorated by a magnificent tomb at Dennington (Suffolk). As Waller noted, the Dennington monument bears a close resemblance to the Cobhams'.[127] Its overall conception is the same. There is an elaborate chest with effigies; the material used is again alabaster, and the suit of armour which Lord Bardolph wears is up-to-date Milanese. Exotic heraldic beasts are even included—the Phelips' eagle beneath the knight's feet and a wyvern beneath his wife's.[128] There can be little doubt that stylistically the tombs at Lingfield and Dennington are related. Since Bardolph died only five years before Cobham, it is natural to suppose that the Dennington tomb was commissioned first; and in all probability it was. However, a different hypothesis is possible. Bardolph's widow, Joan, died in March 1447, only a matter of months after Cobham. It cannot be ruled out that her daughter, Cobham's wife, ordered both. The Cobhams and their relations had co-operated on monuments before—in the 1360s and '70s. The same may have happened again.

For all the similarities between the tombs, however, there are differences. A number of these are quite minor. The head of Lord Bardolph, for example, is covered, whereas Cobham's is bare; and his wife, who survived him, is more fashionably attired than her widowed daughter. But these are of little consequence. More significant as regards the Cobhams' taste are the differences in the design and decoration of the chests. At Dennington the panelled sides are embellished with niches containing saints or weepers (now lost), whereas at Lingfield there are the standard quatrefoils containing shields of arms. In other words, at Lingfield the Cobham family's preference for heraldry triumphed again. There is a further difference—one that is perhaps small but none the less significant. On both tombs a little parapet runs round the top edge of the chest. At Dennington that parapet is simple and unadorned, whereas at Lingfield it is embattled. The choice of an embattled parapet at Lingfield is surely deliberate, for it picks up a feature of the tomb of the 1st Lord, hard by.[129] This was an important visual reference: it reinforced the message, constantly reiterated, of continuity in the family line. In other words, for all the influence of the Dennington tomb, the particular tastes

---

[127] Waller, 'Notes on the Monuments of the Cobham Family', 194.

[128] The wyvern, a Bardolph emblem, is shown beneath the feet of her daughter, Lady Cobham, at Lingfield.

[129] Embattled edges are not particularly common on late medieval tombs. Other examples are at Bottesford (Leics.), Swine (Yorks.), and Norbury (Derbys.): Crossley, *English Church Monuments*, 160, 216, 219.

of the Sterborough Cobhams showed through. Reginald's widow not only carried out her husband's testamentary wishes to the full; she also had regard for the long-standing commemorative preferences of his line.

Reginald's tomb brings to a fitting climax the series of Cobham monuments at Lingfield. There are a couple of later monuments to the family in the church, but by comparison with Reginald's these are modest affairs. The first, a brass in the north or Lady chapel, commemorates a member of a collateral line, Isabella (d. 1460), the wife of Reginald Cobham of Gatwick (M.S. X). Originally this consisted of a single female figure and inscription, but only the inscription remains.[130] The family of Cobham of Gatwick were a sub-branch of the Cobhams of Chafford, who in their turn were a sub-branch of the Cobhams of Randall.[131] The family lacked a regular burial-place of their own. In 1375 Sir William Cobham of Gatwick had requested burial at Charlwood, very close to Gatwick; but a few years later, in 1402 his brother, Ralph Cobham of Chafford, had been buried at Cobham itself.[132] Isabella's burial at newly rebuilt Lingfield affords evidence that some at least of the collateral Cobhams were drawn into the orbit of their Sterborough cousins. The other monument, in the north-eastern corner of the Lady chapel, is the tomb of the last of the Sterborough Cobhams, Sir Thomas, who died in 1471.[133] The monument consists of a marble chest, with shields on the panelled sides in the usual Cobham manner; but there is no effigy; and strangely the chamfered edge never seems to have held an epitaph.[134] The tomb was commissioned by Thomas's widow Anne, and in her will she asked to be buried in it herself.[135]

Although it is the Cobhams' monuments that dominate in Lingfield, there are monuments to other local gentry lying beside them. Lingfield was never the exclusive burial-place of one seigneurial family; other burials were accommodated. The reason for this was the sheer size of

---

[130] The figure had already gone by Aubrey's time. Waller provided a blank plate of brass to fill the indent. It is obvious from the outline that the brass was a standard product of London style 'D'. Isabella was shown with a horned head-dress.

[131] For the Cobhams of Gatwick, see below, 253.

[132] Lambeth Palace Library, Register of Archbishop Sudbury, fo. 80[r]; PRO, Reg. Marche: PROB 11/2A, fo. 21[r].

[133] Waller says that the tomb has been moved, but does not indicate its earlier location: Waller, 'Notes on the Monuments of the Cobham Family', 195.

[134] Waller noted that it never had an inscription: ibid. 195.   [135] Ibid.

Lingfield parish. Covering 9,000 acres, and stretching three and a half miles in each direction, it was one of the biggest in Surrey.[136] Within its bounds were many manors. Not all of these, admittedly, were held by resident lords. The principal manor was held by Hyde abbey, Winchester, and that of Sheffield by the Sussex family of Dallingridge.[137] But the others were held by resident, or partly resident, gentry. The manors of Blockfield and Ford were held by a junior branch of the Gaynesfords of neighbouring Crowhurst, while that of Puttenden was held by the Puttendens and, later, their successors, the Hadreshams.[138] From time to time, members of these gentry lines were buried in the church—as were others from outside the village whose lives were in some way associated with the Cobhams. Lingfield church was a popular—perhaps, indeed, a prestigious—place for burial.

One of the most attractive of the lesser brasses in the church is that of Katherine Stockett, a lady-in-waiting of the Cobhams (fig. 31). It is a tiny brass, no larger than many of those laid to children; the little demi-figure measures barely six inches. Katherine is shown in widow's attire with kirtle and veiled head-dress. The epitaph beneath the figure consists of one line: it merely invites prayers for her soul. No date of death is given, and none is known. On stylistic evidence, a date of engraving of c.1420 can be suggested.[139]

The modesty of the brass fittingly reflects Katherine's station in life. Katherine was sprung from a family of lesser proprietors in nearby Oxted. The site of the family's estate survives as Stocketts Farm between Oxted and Lingfield. Around 1300 her ancestor John atte Stockett was a tenant of John le Savage in the main manor in the village. Later members of the family added to their holdings, and in the fifteenth century 'Stocketts' itself was regarded as a manor.[140] The family's ambitions were

---

[136] In 1332 there were 89 taxpayers at Lingfield, making it one of the largest non-urban settlements in Surrey: *Surrey Taxation Returns, Fifteenths and Tenths: Part II: The 1332 Assessment*, ed. H. C. Johnson (Surrey Record Society, 33; 1932), 87–8.

[137] *VCH Surrey*, iv, 303–4, 308. After the extinction of the Dallingridges in the male line in 1469, Sheffield manor passed to their successors, the Lewknors.

[138] *VCH Surrey*, iv, 306–7.

[139] This was the date suggested by Stephenson, *List of Monumental Brasses in Surrey*, 346, and there seems no reason to dispute it. The brass is of style 'B'.

[140] *VCH Surrey*, iv, 318. In the tax of a fifteenth levied in 1332, John Stockett was assessed at 5s. and one Simon de Stockett at 2s. 2d. Only four other folk at Oxted were assesssed for more (*Surrey Taxation Returns, Part II*, 91). In the fourteenth century members of the Stockett family were witnesses to Gaynesford family charters: BL, MS Harley 392, fos. 15ᵛ, 29ʳ. In 1390 John Stockett of Oxted quitclaimed rights in Crowhurst to John Cobham of Hever: ibid. fos. 49ʳ⁻ᵛ.

FIG 31. Lingfield M.S. V: Katherine Stockett, engraved
c.1420

reflected in their appetite for education. In the 1340s Roger, son and
heir of a later John, was given a schooling at a cost to the bailiff of
10d. a week over thirty weeks.[141] The signs are that the family sought
advancement for themselves in Cobham service. In 1343 one John de
Stockett witnessed a deed on behalf of Reginald, Lord Cobham.[142] A
generation later, Katherine herself is found in the Cobham household.
Very likely, the Cobhams were the family around whom their world
revolved.

Katherine's position in the Cobhams' employment is attested in 1369.
In that year Joan, Lady Cobham, made a series of bequests to her in her
will. Katherine's status was evidently lowly; for Joan bequeathed to her
20 marks 'pro promotione sua' (for her advancement) or, in the event that
she had already been advanced, then only 10 marks. She also left her, as
she did her two other damsels, a furred mantle and a *coiffure* or head-
dress.[143] Katherine was evidently a respected and highly esteemed
servant. However, unfortunately, after 1369 nothing more is heard of her.
There is no evidence to indicate whether, or how far, she 'advanced'; or,
even, to suggest how long she remained in the Cobhams' service. That
she spent the whole, or virtually the whole, of her adult career with the
Cobhams seems a near-certainty: for if she had not, she would not have
been buried in the family chapel at Lingfield. Her adult career must have
been an exceptionally long one: for, if she was active in the 1360s and her
brass was not laid until, at the earliest, the 1410s, she must have been

---

[141] *VCH Surrey*, iv, 318.   [142] *CCR 1343–6*, 380.
[143] Flower, 'Notices of the Family of Cobham of Sterborough', 173–4, 181. She was described
as a 'domicella'.

almost eighty when she died.[144] In her early years, characteristically for a servant, she brought a number of her kinsfolk with her into the household. Another of Lady Joan's bequests was to a certain Eleanor Stockett, described as her servant, but occupying no particular position.[145] Eleanor may well have been a sister or niece of Katherine's.[146] It is tempting to see her as the person commemorated by a companion brass to Katherine's, formerly in the Lady chapel and now lost, but for which the indent survives. It consisted, like Katherine's, of a small female half-figure beneath which there was a short epitaph.[147] Possibly, in view of their similarity, the memorials were ordered together.

The Stocketts were a family typical of those lesser proprietors from whom the nobility recruited their household servants. Of yeoman rank and holding only a modest estate, they aspired to gentility through service. Service to a magnate or gentleman added to their dignity; something of their employer's lustre rubbed off onto them. The power of association meant a great deal to such folk. It was because of this that choice of burial-place was a matter of concern to them: perceptions of status were involved. When, around 1420, Katherine and perhaps too her sister were buried in the Lady chapel at Lingfield, indirectly the whole Stockett line was honoured. The modesty of the memorials was of little account. What was important was their presence amidst the memorials of the lords of Sterborough. The family were being honoured in the most prestigious burial-place locally.

Altogether higher in standing than the Stocketts was another local figure buried at Lingfield around the same time—the esquire, John Hadresham. Hadresham, who died in October 1417, was commemorated by a tomb with a brass in the north aisle (M.S. III). The tomb, which

[144] The absence of a date on the epitaph allows for the possibility that the brass was commissioned while the commemorated was living—and, accordingly, that she was even more aged when she died. On balance, however, the possibility has to be discounted. Far likelier is the opposite hypothesis: that she had died sometime before. Omission of the date of death is admittedly unusual on brasses of this date, but it is by no means unknown: the brass of John de Kingsfold and his wife (?c.1382) at Rusper (Sussex) has no date. Omission is most common on memorials to people of low status for whom economy was important. But an important exception is the brass of Nicolas Roland, sergeant-at-law, and his wife at Cople (Beds).

[145] She left 40s. to Eleanor 'if she is still with me': Flower, 'Notices of the Family of Cobham of Sterborough', 174 (incorrectly translated as 20s. on 181).

[146] An Eleanor, described as the daughter of John Stockett, figures as deforciant in a fine of 1372 (Pedes Finium; or, Fines Relating to the County of Surrey, ed. F. B. Lewis, SAC, extra vol., i; 1894, 142). However, since she appears alongside one John de Hampton, a skinner of London, and is presumably his wife, it is not clear whether she is to be identified with Eleanor, the servant.

[147] Noticed by Waller, 'Notes on the Monuments of the Cobham Family at Lingfield', 194, followed by Stephenson, List of Monumental Brasses in Surrey, 347.

abutted the wall, was destroyed in the eighteenth century and the slab is now relaid in the Lady chapel floor.[148] The brass is the work of London style 'B' (fig. 32). John is represented conventionally in plate armour, with his feet on a lion. Beneath the figure is a four-line epitaph and at the top and bottom of the slab are single shields with the Hadresham arms.

Hadresham had scarcely any connection with the Cobhams.[149] He sought burial at Lingfield simply because he held lands in the parish. He came from an old and well-endowed Surrey family.[150] His father had left him an extensive estate comprising the manors of Coombe Neville and Hadresham and other property in and around Lingfield and Limps-field.[151] From his uncle John, whose father had married a coheiress, he also inherited property in Wiltshire and Berkshire. His means were thus ample, and in 1412 he was said—modestly—to be worth at least £40 per annum. He added to his holdings in the Kent–Surrey borderlands: in 1408 he acquired from his cousin Joan properties and rents in Bletching-ley, Horne, and elsewhere. Through the working of ties of association he was brought into contact with other local gentry. On one occasion, he acted as a feoffee for his neighbour Reginald, Lord Cobham. But his principal associates were two Sussex knights, Sir Philip St Clair and Sir Andrew Sackville. He played only a minor role in local office-holding. He was a justice of the peace in Surrey from 1407 to 1411 and was several times a collector of taxes; but he was hardly one of the most active local gentry. Only once did he sit in parliament. He died in 1417 shortly after witnessing the return for the parliamentary election just held in Surrey. There was apparently no issue by his marriage, and his heirs were his two cousins, Alice Virly and Joan Silverton.

A knowledge of Hadresham's career sheds light on some otherwise puzzling aspects of his brass. For a man so relatively affluent, the brass is surprisingly modest. The figure is not large; there is no canopy or other mark of status; and instead of the usual four shields there are only two. The explanation for this must be that Hadresham was not one to seek the

---

[148] Waller, 'Notes on the Monuments of the Cobham Family at Lingfield', 198.

[149] He acted as a feoffee for Reginald Cobham on just one occasion: *CCR 1405–9*, 468–9. In 1375 his uncle and namesake had witnessed a charter alongside the same Reginald Cobham: BL, MS Harley 392, fo. 48ᵛ (Gaynesford cartulary).

[150] For his biography, see *House of Commons*, iii, 321–2.

[151] Coombe Neville lay a couple of miles east of Kingston-on-Thames, on the site of the present-day Coombe Hill. Hadresham is in Nutfield, between Lingfield and Redhill. Since the Hadreshams took their name from the latter manor, it may be assumed that this was their main seat.

FIG 32. Lingfield M.S. III: John Hadresham, d. 1417

limelight. He did not assume knighthood and he was not active in local affairs. To a remarkable degree, the brass seems to mirror his self-image. It is not known who commissioned the piece. The likeliest candidate is his widow Agnes, who was still alive in 1429. The fact that John is shown alone points to it being a widow's tribute to her husband. Agnes seems to have been scarcely less self-effacing than her husband. Her maiden name is not recorded and her familial connections are unknown. It is conceivable that she was of non-gentry descent.[152] Her role in family affairs appears to have been modest, and she only came into her own in widowhood.[153] Quite possibly, the brass accords with her own tastes as much as her husband's.

A number of other local layfolk are commemorated by memorials in the church. In the chancel is the small but beautifully engraved brass of a maiden lady (M.S. VIII). The young female is shown with the flowing hair usually associated with someone unmarried, and with an ornamented fillet around her head (fig. 33). The foot inscription is lost, but the stylistic evidence points to an engraving date of c.1450.[154] The identity of the commemorated is unknown. In the south chapel till the early eighteenth century was an inscription commemorating Joan, the widow of William Gaynesford, who died in 1453.[155] The Gaynesfords were a gentry family closely associated with the Cobhams. In the fourteenth and fifteenth centuries they frequently attested Cobham charters.[156] The senior branch of the family was established at Crowhurst, a few miles north of Lingfield, while a junior line was settled at Lingfield itself and was closely connected with its church.[157] In the 1430s, when Sir Reginald was rebuilding the nave, the Gaynesfords contributed to the cost of the glazing: in the north aisle windows there was a series of panels bearing the Gaynesford arms, which are now lost.[158]

---

[152] This is suggested by the shields on the brass. The Hadresham arms are not impaled as they would be for a husband and an armigerous wife.

[153] She failed in the essential wifely task of child-rearing; there was no issue by the marriage. When her husband died she was pregnant, but then either miscarried or lost the child in infancy.

[154] The brass is of London style 'D'.

[155] Aubrey, *Antiquities of the County of Surrey*, iii, 61. It is not apparent from Aubrey's note whether the inscription was accompanied by a figure.

[156] *CCR 1343–6*, 380; *1346–9*, 70; *1405–9*, 469.

[157] For the Gaynesfords, see G. R. French, 'A Brief Account of Crowhurst Church, Surrey, and its Monuments', *SAC*, 3 (1865), 39–62, esp. 61. The Gaynesfords of Lingfield held the manors of Blockfield and Ford. The founder of the line was William, son of the third John Gaynesford 'senior', who died in 1450 and is commemorated by a brass in Crowhurst church (illustrated in Stephenson, *Monumental Brasses of Surrey*, 156). William's wife Joan, the daughter of John Simons, was the person commemorated by the Lingfield brass.

[158] Aubrey, *Antiquities of the County of Surrey*, iii, 59; Peatling, *Ancient Stained and Painted Glass in Surrey*, 56–7.

FIG 33. Lingfield M.S. VIII: An unknown lady, *c.*1450

At one time on the floor, but now reset on the Lady chapel wall, are
two rather unusual monuments. These are a pair of effigial slabs made of
encaustic tiles but engraved in the manner of brasses. The better preserved of the two shows an elegantly dressed civilian wearing a bonnet,
under a low quadruple canopy, with a floriate pattern around the
edge.[159] The other, which is badly mutilated, again shows a civilian, but

[159] The tile memorials are noted in a report of the proceedings of the Archaeological Institute
in *Archaeological Journal*, 6 (1849), 176–7. The better-preserved figure is illustrated.

FIG 34. Lingfield M.S. VII: John Wyche, d. 1445

apparently without a canopy. Both can be dated *c.*1500–10, but the identity of the individuals commemorated is unknown.[160] In all probability they were members of one of the lesser gentry of the Lingfield area.

To one side of the gentry memorials is a group of smaller and less showy brasses commemorating the clergy of the college. Clerical brasses were laid in considerable number in collegiate foundations in the late Middle Ages. Large series can still be seen at Arundel, Eton, and Winchester. At Lingfield before the Reformation there were nearly a dozen such. Four still remain, and there were others which are now either lost or covered.[161] The two earliest—those of John Wyche (fig. 34) and James Veldon—are of a type much favoured by the fifteenth-century clergy:

[160] The attire and manner of execution of the figures are reminiscent of the mannerisms of London style 'D' brasses of *c.*1470–80. The measurements of the complete slab are 46 in. by 15 in., and of the broken one, 31 in. by 15 in. Each tile measures 15 in. square, three tiles being required to form an effigy.

[161] Under the choir stalls is apparently the full-length figure of a priest in mass vestments, *c.*1440: Stephenson, *List of Monumental Brasses in Surrey*, 348.

FIG 35. Lingfield M.S. XI: John Swetecock, d. 1469

small demi-figures in mass vestments with foot inscriptions. The two later brasses, to John Swetecock (fig. 35) and John Knoyll, have full-length figures. The presence of these brasses lends a distinctly clerical feel to the Lingfield chancel. A sense is conveyed of this being a collegiate enclave. The clergy, of course, had long claimed a historic right to burial in the chancel. However, by the fourteenth century, as the Cobham family's take-over at Cobham showed, they were confronted with intense competition from the laity. In the Cobham chancel the lay presence almost crowded out the clerical—although a few clerical brasses were still laid there.[162] At Lingfield a more even balance was struck between the two estates. Undeniably, the dominant feature of the chancel was Reginald Cobham's great tomb: and appropriately so, since he founded the college. But the Cobhams' other monuments did not greatly intrude; they were placed to one side or in the Lady chapel, and the chancel's integrity as a clerical burial place was largely preserved.

The families' contrasting treatment of the chancels points in the direction of a much larger truth. The churches of Lingfield and Cobham served as mausoleums for collateral branches of the same family—a family whose members regularly co-operated and interacted. Yet the differences between the two burial-places are as striking as the similarities. A number of the differences relate to matters of aesthetic and taste. The Cobhams of Sterborough, for example, never exhibited the consistent preference for brasses shown by their kinsfolk in Kent; they switched freely between brasses and tombs with relief effigies. Nor, when they chose their brasses, did they offer consistent patronage to any one workshop; they alternated between styles. Sometimes they chose 'B', and sometimes 'A' or 'D'—their choice at any time depending on the particular influences bearing on them.

But the biggest difference between the mausoleums relates to the messages which they convey. The two sets of monuments are witness to sharply different priorities. At Lingfield the emphasis is almost wholly on status and rank, while at Cobham it is on dynasticism and lineage. At Cobham the imagery of the brasses is designed to stress continuity of descent; at Lingfield, by contrast, the family's achievements and connections. At Lingfield the spectator is confronted with a dazzling array of the trappings of rank. Shields of arms line the sides of the tomb chests; the banneret's banner is shown on the brass of Eleanor Cobham; and

---

[162] Interestingly, many of the clerical brasses at Cobham were in fact laid in the nave. There are three brasses of priests in the nave floor today—those of Reginald Cobham (M.S. VIII), John Gery (M.S. XIV), and John Gladwyn (M.S. XV). Those of Gery and Gladwyn were noted as in the nave by Thorpe in the early eighteenth century: which, as suggested above (79), probably means that they were always there; Cobham's was noted as in the nave by Gough: 'the priest on a cross under a triple pediment between two shields gone' (Gough, *Sepulchral Monuments*, ii pt 2, 51). In addition to these brasses, there are a number of indents of clergy—one in the north aisle of a demi-figure in a cope, and two in the south aisle of priests in mass vestments (*Registrum Roffense*, 767–8; Lack, Saul, and Whittemore, *Monumental Brasses in St Mary Magdalene, Cobham*, 3, 74). Today, there are three brasses of clerks in the chancel—those of William Tanner, William Hobson (inscription only), and John Sprotte; but it should be remembered, as Gough pointed out, that the creation of Lord Darnley's burial vault in 1781 led to disturbance of the brasses on the south side.

Reginald II's nobility of lifestyle is praised on his epitaph.[163] The sheer size of the Sterborough line's tombs is proof of their aspirations to status. It would be altogether erroneous to imply the absence of these considerations at Cobham: many of the Cobhams' brasses are on the grandest scale, while the splendour of the family's funerals is attested by the tournament helms which hang in the chancel today.[164] None the less at Cobham the display of status is subordinated to, or is accompanied by, other concerns. The 3rd Lord's preoccupation with lineage is powerfully communicated by the retrospective brasses which he commissioned in the 1360s. The pain which his kinsfolk felt a generation later at the imminent extinction of the male line is indicated by the inclusion of the little boys' figures on the brasses of Braybrooke and Hawberk. The intense piety of the Cobhams is evidenced by the idiosyncratic epitaphs found on the earlier brasses and by the appearance of patron saints on the later.[165] These highly individualistic touches are absent at Lingfield. At Lingfield the commemorative imagery is almost entirely secular. It is not difficult to understand the reason for this. What preoccupied the Sterborough line was their loss of status. With every year that passed their lapse from blue-blooded nobility became clearer. They were desperate to regain and to reaffirm their former eminence. The commissioning of a series of grand funerary monuments was one highly visible way in which they did this.

---

[163] It reads (the parts now lost in brackets); 'De Steresburgh dominus de Cobham sic Reginaldus/Hic jacet his validus miles fuit ut leopardus/(Sagax in guerris satis audax omnibus) horis/In cunctis terris famam predavit honoris/Dapsilis in mensis formosus moregerosus/Largus in expensis imperteritus generosus/Et quando placuit messie quod moreretur/Expirans obijt in celis glorificetur/Mille quadringeno t(erno Julij numeres tres)/Migravit coelo sit sibi vero quies. Amen. Pater noster.' In other words, it is the noble attribute of hospitality that is stressed.

[164] C. Blair, 'The Funeral Helms at Cobham', 392–4; see above, 100 n. 71.

[165] See above, 97–100, 108.

⇥ 8 ⇤

Brasses Elsewhere to the Cobhams

THE Cobhams' appetite for commemorative display is amply attested by the two sets of monuments at Cobham and Lingfield. However, these are by no means the only memorials to members of the Cobham family. There are some half-dozen others—all of them brasses—in as many churches. For the most part, the people commemorated are Cobham spouses or collaterals. There are wide variations in the size and character of the memorials. The largest of the group, the brass at Chrishall (Essex), is a big triple-canopied composition, while the others are all in varying degrees smaller. To consider the brasses as a group risks imposing a somewhat artificial unity on them, for they are a scattered series, laid at different times in different places, and their shared characteristics are few. None the less, the risk is probably one worth taking. When considered as a group the brasses yield further insights into the Cobhams' commemorative tastes and self-image.

The brass most closely connected with the main series at Cobham is that at Chrishall (Essex), to Joan, daughter and heiress of John, 3rd Lord Cobham, and her husband Sir John de la Pole (d. 1380) (fig. 36). This is a magnificent memorial, as lavish as any at Cobham itself. The near life-size figures of Sir John and his wife are shown holding hands. John is depicted in armour with his left hand on his sword-belt and his right in the hand of his lady; his feet rest against a lion. Joan is attired in a framed, or nebulé, head-dress and a close-fitting kirtle with sleeve-lappets. Above the figures rises an elegant triple canopy—an unusual arrangement for a two-figure brass, but one paralleled on the contemporary alabaster monument to Godfrey Foljambe and his wife (c.1376) at Bakewell (Derbys.).[1] Between the heads of the figures is a shield with the

---

[1] Illus. in Crossley, *English Church Monuments*, 179; N. Pevsner, *Derbyshire*, 2nd edn. (Harmondsworth, 1978), pl. 34. The same arrangement is used as for the frame of the portraits of Sir John Eynsford and his wife in the St Albans Book of Benefactors, though here the two figures are both facing to the sinister: BL, MS Cotton Nero D. VII, fo. 112^v.

FIG 36. Chrishall M.S. I: Sir John de la Pole, d. 1380, and his wife, Joan

arms of de la Pole impaling Cobham, and these arms are repeated singly on shields above the canopy. Surrounding the whole was a marginal epitaph in French now largely lost. The brass is a superb example of the work of London style 'B'. On stylistic grounds, it can be dated to very shortly after John's death in 1380. Given that the brasses of the 1380s at Cobham are likewise from 'B', it is likely that the memorial was ordered by John, Lord Cobham, or, at least, by Lord Cobham in association with his daughter.[2]

A particularly attractive feature of the brass is the pose of the couple holding hands. Brasses showing the commemorated in this position enjoyed considerable popularity in the half-century or so from 1380.[3] The Chrishall brass comes near the beginning of the series. Roughly contemporary are the brasses of Sir John Harsick and his wife at Southacre (Norfolk) (style 'B') and Richard Torrington and his wife at Great Berkhamstead (Herts.) (style 'C').[4] From a few years later are some excellent style 'A' brasses—those of Sir Edward Cerne and his wife, 1393, at Draycot Cerne (Wilts.), John Hawley and his two wives, 1408, at Dartmouth (Devon), the two Freville couples, both c.1410 at Little Shelford (Cambs.), and Robert Hatfield and his wife, 1409 at Owston (Yorks.).[5] In the fifteenth century a few style 'D' brasses kept up the tradition: those of Thomas, Lord Camoys and his wife, 1421, at Trotton (Sussex) and Peter Halle and his wife, c.1430, at Herne (Kent). The pose also appears on sculptured monuments. Notable examples in alabaster include the

[2] The brass has been illustrated a number of times, most memorably in Boutell, *The Monumental Brasses of England*, frontispiece. Currently it lies on the floor of the south aisle, at the west end. It has been moved several times. In 1847, when Manning published the first scholarly note on it, it was in the nave, 'partly under the boards of a pew', and with only the middles of the figures visible (C. J. Manning, 'Notice of an Undescribed Sepulchral Brass', *Archaeological Journal*, 4, 1847, 338–40). A year or two later it was moved to the north side of the high altar, where Boutell found it (Boutell, *Monumental Brasses of England*). It was in this position in 1869 (according to a ground plan of the church hanging in the nave). Before 1900 it was removed to its present position in the so-called baptistery (excursion note, *Transactions of the Essex Archaeological Society*, new series, 7, 1900, 200–1). There is reason to believe that it may originally have been laid in the south aisle: see below, 203–4. The brass was restored by Waller; the blank strips of metal which fill the place of the original epitaph are his.

[3] An isolated, and altogether exceptional, example from the late thirteenth century is the semi-relief monument of a civilian and wife at Winterbourne Bassett (Wilts.): H. A. Tummers, *Early Secular Effigies in England: The Thirteenth Century* (Leiden, 1980), 147 and pl. 185.

[4] The Berkhamstead brass has long been thought to date from the 1350s, but in an unpublished paper Sally Badham makes a convincing case for identifying it as a style 'C' brass of the 1380s.

[5] The lost brass of Sir William Arundel and his wife, 1400, in Rochester Cathedral showed them holding hands. The indent survives: W. B. Rye, 'Tombs of Sir William Arundel and Others in Rochester Cathedral', *AC*, 13 (1880), 141.

effigies of Thomas Beauchamp, earl of Warwick, and his wife, 1369, at St Mary's, Warwick, Sir Sampson Strelley and his wife, 1391, at Strelley (Notts.), Ralph Greene and his wife, 1419, at Lowick (Northants.), and the duke and duchess of Somerset at Wimborne Minster (Dorset), 1444. A particularly fine example in copper-gilt is the tomb of Richard II and his queen in Westminster Abbey.

It is hard to know what, or how much, significance to read into the pose. As an artistic mannerism it enjoyed a relatively brief life-span. First appearing around 1370, it was already passing out of fashion by 1420.[6] One interpretation may be to see it as a response to the growing formality of late fourteenth-century effigial art. Figure design was becoming noticeably stiffer from around 1360. Hand-holding may have recommended itself as the essential counterpoint—the means by which the engravers could bring a degree of informality into an otherwise lifeless art. A strictly formalist explanation, however, while plausible and to a degree necessary, does not altogether convince. In particular, it does not account for the relative rarity of the pose: even in its heyday, hand-holding is found on only a minority of brasses or monuments. In consequence, a different explanation has recently been offered. Peter Coss has suggested that the pose may be taken to signify the deeply affective relationship which joined the couples commemorated.[7] As other scholars have noted, the period of its popularity coincided with the writing of some unusually expressive verse. Chaucer, Clanvow, and the 'courtly makers' were giving new and highly explicit voice to their inner feelings in poems written in the 1380s and 1390s. It may thus be the case, as Coss suggests, that the urge to self-expression which moved the poets moved some of the commemorated to seek similar self-expression on their tombs and brasses. This is a line of explanation with a definite appeal. Not only does it help to explain why the pose rose to popularity when it did; it also accounts for the selectivity with which it was used. However, a number of points may be raised in objection. Marriage in upper-class society in the Middle Ages was in many cases loveless, or near-loveless. Matches were contracted mainly for prudential reasons—for example, to forge an alliance or to acquire landed wealth. Spouses' first marriages were usually arranged by their parents. Joan Cobham was betrothed to John de la Pole when she was seven, and her father, the 3rd Lord, to his wife when he had been around twelve. Relations between husbands and

---

[6] The only extant late fifteenth-century example is that at Nether Heyford (Northants.) of 1487.

[7] P. Coss, *The Lady in Medieval England* (Stroud, 1998), 93–105.

wives were often distant and cold. It was not uncommon for husbands to take mistresses, and their wives paramours. Against this unpromising background, the notion that love in marriage could be celebrated on a memorial might appear improbable.

However, the picture of essentially loveless marriages needs to be strongly qualified. By the middle of the twelfth century it was the Church's view that love lay at the very heart of marriage. Human and divine love were considered inseparable: as St Bernard said, they formed part of the same ladder. Popes cited biblical authority in support of the view that husbands and wives should become one flesh in marriage; and much was made of St Paul's comment that marital union was like the union of Christ with his Church.[8] A host of preachers urged the importance of love in their sermons. Guibertus de Tornaco, a thirteenth-century mendicant, was particularly emphatic: husbands should love their wives; the love which unites a husband and wife should be founded on partnership because the two are equal and partners. Guibertus, like most preachers of the day, recognized that in practice matches might well be arranged by parents. But in that case, he argued, husbands and wives should grow together in marriage; by living an indivisible life they should develop a feeling of love which made mutual separation impossible.[9] In other words, affective love should flourish within the marital bond in those cases where it did not precede it.

In the light of this teaching, the notion that marital love could be celebrated on a memorial may appear less fanciful. Historians, indeed, are now generally agreed that not all upper-class marriages were loveless.[10] Richard II's marriage to Anne of Bohemia affords a good example. This was an alliance of convenience, sponsored by Pope Urban VI to nurture Anglo-Imperial relations, yet it quickly developed into one of the most companionate of all English royal marriages. In the same period, John of Gaunt's marriage to his first wife Blanche is thought to have been a fairly close one.[11] A century earlier, Henry III seems to have enjoyed quite affectionate ties with his wife Eleanor of Provence. It is natural, in the light of such evidence, to wonder if hand-holding could have

---

[8] C. Brooke, *The Medieval Idea of Marriage* (Oxford, 1989), 48–54, 267–8.

[9] N. Beriou and D. L. d'Avray, *Modern Questions about Medieval Sermons* (Spoleto, 1994), 128–31. I am very grateful to Prof. d'Avray for his advice on these matters.

[10] The view of medieval upper-class marriage as an essentially loveless institution presented in L. Stone, *The Family, Sex and Marriage in England, 1500–1800* (London, 1977), ch. 3, is now generally thought to be overstated. The comment of Beriou and d'Avray, *Modern Questions about Medieval Sermons*, 143 and n. 27, is apposite.

[11] Goodman, *John of Gaunt*, 360–1.

memorialized particularly intimate unions like these. Unfortunately, however, it is very difficult to say for certain. The dearth of evidence stands in the way. Disappointingly, all too little is known about the private lives of the couples shown in the pose. None the less, what evidence there is is suggestive. Richard II and his queen, a couple known to have been deeply devoted, are shown holding hands on their monument in Westminster Abbey; and the pose was employed at the king's request.[12] Equally illuminating is another case, that of the Lancastrian retainer Robert de Hatfield and his wife Ada. The Hatfields are commemorated by a style 'A' brass at Owston (Yorks.).[13] Robert is shown in civilian attire, and his wife alongside him. On the epitaph the two are described as being 'fully in right love'[14] and, above, they are shown holding hands. Robert commissioned the brass on his wife's death in 1409. There can be little doubt that he dictated the touching epitaph himself. This was a husband's tribute to a wife whom he sorely missed: a study in the strength of conjugal love.

The signs are, then, that hand-holding may well denote mutual affection. However, there remains a second problem—the possible significance of the variations in the positions of the hands. As Peter Coss has shown, the commemorateds' hands are shown in a number of different positions on brasses.[15] On some, the lady's hand is taken firmly in the grasp of her husband's, implying a relationship of male dominance. On one or two others the hands are merely pressed against one another, so as to imply a more equal tie; while on one more brass again, the de la Poles' at Chrishall, a third pose occurs—the lady grasping the man's hand: implying perhaps the dominance of the lady. As with the issue of hand-holding more generally, the difficulty arises of distinguishing the respective roles of artistic convention and client influence. The notion that clients might have wanted a particular hand pose to be shown on their brasses is not inconceivable: if they were keen enough to prescribe hand-holding in their contracts, they could have troubled to specify how the hands were to be shown. All the same, there is a dearth of evidence to support such an idea in the sources: on those occasions when hand-holding is specified in contracts it is usually without reference to

---

[12] Rymer, *Foedera*, vii, 797–8. It is also worth noting that the hand-holding pose on the Greene tomb at Lowick was employed at the client's (i.e. the widow's) request: Crossley, *English Church Monuments*, 30.

[13] For discussion, see C. R. Manning, 'Notes on a Brass of Robert de Haitfeld and Ada, his wife, Owston Church, Yorkshire', *Archaeological Journal*, 36 (1879), 172–3.

[14] 'En droiturel amour foies'.   [15] Coss, *Lady in Medieval England*, 100.

position.[16] On balance, then, the likelihood must be that artistic convention determined the pose. Two brasses in particular lend support to this suggestion. The two are the well-known examples at Trotton (1421) and Herne (c.1430). On both, the hands are pressed flat against one another. The two memorials came from the same workshop—the 'D' workshop in London; they date from within a few years of each other, and the second is simply a scaled-down version of the first. There is no individuality in the design; the same drawing-pattern was used for both. A similar conclusion can be drawn from study of the two 'B' brasses of the 1380s—those at Chrishall and Southacre. At first sight the Chrishall brass seems to differ from the others: it is the only one to show the lady grasping the man's hand. But the distinctiveness of the pose is more apparent than real. The position of the hands is merely a mirror image of that on the Southacre brass. In each case it is the figure on the right (the sinister) which engages the other's hand. But whereas at Chrishall it is the lady who is on the right, at Southacre it is the husband. There can be little doubt that the same pattern was used for both. On the Chrishall brass it is just conceivable that the figures were reversed to allow the showing of female dominance because Joan was an heiress. But on balance the idea is unlikely. Male armed figures were usually shown, as here, on the left, or dexter, side. To deduce the dominance of one or the other partner from the position of the hands would be unwise.

A further aspect of this splendid brass calls for discussion: its location. Why did it come to be laid in the church at Chrishall? Chrishall is a small village some 12 miles due south of Cambridge, high on the Essex downs. It was an outlying manor on the de la Poles' considerable, if scattered, estate. The family's main seat was at Castle Ashby (Northants.). Here there was a substantial manor-house, built around the beginning of the century by Walter Langton, bishop of Coventry and Lichfield.[17] The de la Poles' predecessors in the estate were mostly buried in Castle Ashby church. However, Sir John and his young widow were not; they were buried at the relatively remote spot of Chrishall.[18] How is their action to be explained?

---

[16] This was the case e.g. in the contract for the Greene tomb at Lowick, trans. printed in Crossley, *English Church Monuments*, 30.

[17] Bishop Langton had acquired the manor before 1306; in that year he received a grant of a licence to crenellate: *CPR 1301–7*, 462.

[18] McFarlane was puzzled by the location, too. Writing to Norman Scarfe, he said, 'I am not sure why Sir John and Lady de la Pole were buried at Crishall [sic]. Castle Ashby was their principal seat.' (K. B. McFarlane, *Letters to Friends, 1940–1966*, ed. G. L. Harriss, Oxford, 1997, 220).

The unconventional history of the de la Pole family sheds light on the problem. Sir John de la Pole was the grandson of the Hull wool merchant Richard de la Pole, the elder brother of the better-known Sir William de la Pole. The two de la Poles both made immense fortunes from trading. William was probably the more innovative of the two, reaping huge rewards from lending to Edward III. But Richard was also heavily involved with the crown, serving both Edward II and Edward III as butler.[19] Both brothers were anxious to establish themselves in the ranks of the gentry. In 1333 Richard acquired the manor of Milton (Northants.), which became his main residence. Towards the end of his life he arranged for his son and heir William to be married to a Northampton-shire lady. Through the influence of Ralph, Lord Basset, a courtier of local origin, a match was arranged with Margaret, the sister of John Peverel of Castle Ashby. The match offered the promise of respectability but little financial gain. Peverel might well sire a son and heir, and in that case the inheritance would pass down through the Peverel line. But in 1349 John unexpectedly died without issue, perhaps a victim of the plague.[20] Margaret was named as his heir. Contrary to their expectation, the de la Poles suddenly found themselves the possessors of a substantial inheritance. In addition to the main manor of Castle Ashby, the estate comprised the manors of Ashley and Chadstone (Northants.), Arlesey, Everton, and Potton (Beds.), Fulbrook and Westhall (Oxon.), Seething (Norfolk), Aspall, Debenham, and Grimston (Suffolk), and Chrishall (Essex). This far-flung string of manors had been assembled by dubious means by Bishop Walter Langton.[21] On his death in 1321 they had passed to his nephew Edmund Peverel and on the latter's death to his son, John, whose sister married William de la Pole.

The de la Poles' inheritance was an exceptionally scattered one. The manors were distributed across no fewer than six counties. From Seething in the east to the cluster of Thames valley manors was a dis-tance of some 200 miles. Scattered estates of this sort were always diffi-

---

[19] For the de la Poles, and Richard in particular, see R. Horrox, *The de la Poles of Hull* (East Yorkshire Local History Society; Hull, 1983). [20] *CIPM*, ix, no. 180.
[21] *VCH Northamptonshire*, iv (London, 1937), 233; *VCH Bedfordshire*, ii (London, 1906), 227, 238, 262; *Records of the Trial of Walter Langeton, Bishop of Coventry and Lichfield, 1307–1312*, ed. A. Beardwood (Camden Society, 4th series, 6; 1969), 88, 89, 95, 97, 206, 207, 256, 316, 340. Walter Langton, from 1296 bishop of Coventry and Lichfield, was Edward I's highly unpopular trea-surer. After Edward's death in 1307, he was arrested and put on trial for various misdemeanors including money-lending, but by 1311 he was back in favour. For his career, see *DNB*, xxxii, 129–32 (art. by Tout).

cult to manage. It was hard for the lord adequately to supervise his staff, and money tended to stick to the bailiffs' and reeves' fingers. There was little chance of welding the estate into a single economy. Moving live-stock, particularly sheep, backwards and forwards between manors was laborious and time-consuming. The sheer length of communications made decision-making slow. It was all but impossible to respond quickly and effectively to local market conditions.

Landowners responded to these difficulties in a variety of ways. One possibility was to sell off outlying manors to create a smaller and more compact estate. The de la Rivieres of Tormarton (Gloucs.) were one family who did this. Over a twenty-year period from the 1330s Sir John de la Riviere sold off most of his outlying Wiltshire and Bucking-hamshire manors to create a more coherent estate focused on south Gloucestershire.[22] A second possibility was to put some of the more distant manors out to lease. In the fifteenth century the Shirley family, whose main interests were in Leicestershire, leased a number of their manors in south Warwickshire.[23] Yet another possibility was totally to reorganize the estate: to tie it together more closely, an end that could be achieved by moving the family's seat from the periphery to the centre. One family which did this was the Russells, whose interests lay across southern England. In the early fourteenth century the Russells lived mainly on their manors in Dorset and the Isle of Wight; fifty years later they established themselves permanently at Dyrham, near Bristol.[24]

There is no evidence that the de la Poles had in mind fundamentally reorganizing their estate. In the years of their ownership, they preserved it largely in the shape in which they inherited it. Outlying manors were retained, and no obvious moves were taken to centralize the estate; if reforming measures were considered, they were firmly ruled out. It is admittedly hard to be certain on these matters in the absence of a family archive, but all the indications point to conservative management. A key indicator here is the retention of the traditional itinerant lifestyle. Other families at this time were gradually settling down on one or, at the most, two main manors and supervising the rest from these centres. The de la

---

[22] Saul, *Knights and Esquires*, 228–9; *VCH Buckinghamshire* (4 vols.; London, 1905–27), iv, 126.

[23] C. Carpenter, *Locality and Polity: A Study of Warwickshire Landed Society, 1401–1499* (Cambridge, 1992), 157.

[24] One factor in the Russells' decision to migrate may have been the vulnerability of their Isle of Wight properties to French attacks. In 1340 Sir Theobald Russell was mortally wounded while resisting the French: *VCH Hampshire* (5 vols.; London, 1900–12), v, 312. Clear evidence of the family's move to Dyrham is provided by the presence in Dyrham church of the brass of Sir Maurice Russell and his wife, commissioned on the latter's death in 1401.

Poles, however, still lived their lives on the move. Their itineraries took them in some years eastwards from Castle Ashby to Essex and in others south-west to the Thames valley. In the summer of 1355 William de la Pole travelled to Letcombe Basset (Berks.);[25] four years later he was at Chrishall, where he issued letters of enfeoffment,[26] and some seven years after that at Barnack (Northants.).[27] Between times he lived for the most part at Castle Ashby, which remained the family's main seat.[28] One attraction of these regular itineraries was that they facilitated proper supervision of the manorial staff. However, the de la Poles took other measures to reconcile geographical inconvenience with effective management. On occasion, they leased manors out. Sometime before 1361, Sir William granted the manor of Potton (Beds.) to his son and heir, Sir John.[29] But there is little evidence of conscious rationalization informing such grants. Potton was hardly an outlying manor; it was quite close to Castle Ashby. Overall, there is nothing to suggest that the de la Poles ever, as a matter of policy, forsook the periphery for the centre. They preferred moving around to selling-off. The old ways of life were kept up.

It is against this background that the family's growing interest in the manor of Chrishall from around 1360 needs to be judged. The evidence for this awakened interest is mainly physical. Over a twenty-year period, c.1360–80, Chrishall church was virtually rebuilt.[30] Only the responds of the tower arch and an arch in the north nave arcade were preserved from the earlier fabric. The new building was conceived in strikingly ambitious terms. Its scale and physical grandeur proclaimed seigneurial patronage. In style it was a fluent essay in early Perpendicular. Externally, it bore the characteristic Perpendicular profile (fig. 37). There was a tower at the west end, a four-bay nave with aisles and clerestory, both battlemented all round, north and south porches and a long chancel. The sources for the design were principally East Anglian. The lozenge-shaped arcade piers and the circular clerestory windows are of East Anglian origin. But there are a few hints of mendicant influence: the

---

[25] CCR 1354–60, 216.　　[26] BL, Cotton Ch. XII i.
[27] CCR 1354–60, 216; 1360–4, 412.
[28] Subject to his absences abroad (see below, 205).　　[29] CPR 1358–61, 584.
[30] The fullest account of the church, accompanied by a ground plan, is *Royal Commission on Historical Monuments (England): Essex*, i (London, 1916), 64–6, suggesting that the top storey of the tower and the nave clerestory both date from the fifteenth century. It is possible that the top of the tower with its distinctive chequer pattern is of this date, but there is no reason to suppose that the clerestory is. The church was twice restored in the nineteenth century: the nave in 1867 and the chancel in 1878; the chancel east window is of the latter date.

FIG 37. Chrishall church from the south west

high nave arcade and low clerestory elevation are characteristic of the friars' churches.[31] The interior gives a powerful impression of unity; it is built to a single design. However, there are signs of a break in the construction campaign. Particularly instructive are the variations in the window tracery. The tracery in the north aisle windows appears to be of a later date than that in the south; the south aisle tracery still retains Decorated forms. Moreover, there are variations in the moulding profiles. The mouldings of the nave arcade, with their continuous outer order, are of standard Perpendicular type, whereas in the south aisle there is a low arch over a tomb which uses ornate mouldings of Decorated form.[32] The conclusion to draw from this evidence is that the church was rebuilt in stages, the south aisle coming first, and the rest of the church later. The eastern part of the south aisle appears to have served as a family chapel. There are a number of features which suggest this. In the south-eastern corner is a piscina, which indicates the presence of an altar in the area;

[31] For mendicant influence on fourteenth-century ecclesiastical architecture, see R. K. Morris, 'Pembridge and Mature Decorated in Herefordshire', *Transactions of the Woolhope Naturalists' Field Club*, 42 (1977), 129–53, esp. 141–2. As Morris points out, circular windows are ultimately of mendicant origin: they were common in Italian Dominican churches of the late thirteenth century. At Chrishall, however, the immediate source must be East Anglian—albeit East Anglian mendicant.

[32] Illus. in F. Chancellor, *The Ancient Sepulchral Monuments of Essex* (London, 1890), pl. 154.

while immediately to the west is the tomb recess, mentioned above, containing the effigy of a lady.[33] The date of the recess can hardly be later than the mid-1370s: the mouldings prove as much. The natural assumption must be that the lady commemorated is a Peverel or a de la Pole. Indeed, there can be little doubt that she is Margaret, sister of John, the last of the Peverels, and wife of Sir William de la Pole. Evidence to support the hypothesis is provided by the two coats of arms flanking the door in the south porch: on the left is a fess for Peverel and on the right the wavy coat of de la Pole. Margaret presumably began rebuilding the church in the years of her widowhood, and the work was completed by her son.

The rebuilding of Chrishall church points to a major shift in the geographical focus of the de la Poles' interests and patronage. In the previous generation the family's presence had been most strongly felt at Castle Ashby. Castle Ashby was not only the family's main seat; it was the place with which they were most closely associated.[34] But in or around the 1370s their interests moved sharply to the east. Chrishall from now on claimed an increasing share of their favour. The fact that Margaret was buried at Chrishall suggests that the manor had been assigned to her as dower on her husband's death in the 1360s. Very likely, there were some substantial manorial buildings here. The large raised area, or 'ringwork', some 200 ft north-east of the church probably marks the site of the medieval manor-house and allied dwellings.[35] Whether Margaret added to the structures already existing is not known. The most visible sign of her presence in the village today is the rebuilt church. There can be little doubt that she considered this elegant new structure her mausoleum. She made her tomb there; and, almost certainly, she founded a chantry in the south aisle. Her example was to prove an inspiration to her successors. In the next generation her son and daughter-in-law were buried in the church close by her. The 'upgrading' of Chrishall gave it some of the characteristics of a lordship seat—there were a fine mausoleum church

[33] Ibid., 154.

[34] In his later years Sir William de la Pole was generally styled in royal letters patent and close 'of Castle Ashby': *CPR 1361–4*, 64; *CCR 1360–4*, 425–6. In the 1350s he had been known as 'the younger', to distinguish him from his uncle, the Hull merchant: *CCR 1354–60*, 71, 196.

[35] The site (scheduled ancient monument, Essex no. 20666) is in Park Wood: *Royal Commission on Historical Monuments: Essex*, i, 66. It consists of a raised area measuring 53 m east–west by 60 m north–south, surrounded by a ditch with a maximum width of 20 m. On the north side of the ditch is a large mound of spoil not considered part of the monument. There was a park at Chrishall by 1416: P. Reaney (ed.), *The Place-Names of Essex* (English Place-Name Society; 12; 1935), 523. I am grateful to Mrs N. R. Edwards for information on this site.

and a manorial dwelling close by: the marks of a significant lordly presence. In place of an estate centring solely on Castle Ashby was emerging
a polyfocal estate with two main centres.

Whether John actually spent more of his time at Chrishall than his
predecessors is hard to say. He may well have preferred to maintain the
itinerant lifestyle of his predecessors. What is clear is that he was never as
strongly identified with Castle Ashby as his father had been: unlike the
latter, he was not generally described as 'of Castle Ashby'. His decision
to seek burial in Chrishall church suggests a growing identity with the
eastern manors. Perhaps he had it in mind eventually to establish his
family's chief residence there. At the very least, he was loosening his
family's earlier and long-established ties with the west.

A factor which made possible the family's shift from one power base
to another was the relative shallowness of the geographical roots of their
power. By the later fourteenth century most of the gentry were establishing a much closer identity with their principal county of residence. Even
families with relatively scattered estates were tending to settle down in
one county. Typically, identity with a county found expression in
involvement in local office-holding and interaction with fellow gentry.[36]
The experience of the de la Poles, however, constituted something of an
exception to this pattern. Neither William nor John de la Pole ever struck
roots in a county of their choice in this way. The exceptionally wide
distribution of their manors was obviously a factor that prevented
them from so doing. But there was another problem—the nature of their
lifestyle. Both William and John were active soldiers: and they were often
away on service. William as a young man had fought with the Black
Prince at Crécy.[37] Later, in the winter of 1359–60 he had accompanied
the earl of March on Edward III's expedition to Rheims.[38] After the
coming of peace he was involved in crusading initiatives. In 1364 he and
a companion, Sir Thomas Ufford, sought Urban V's assistance in arranging a passage to the East, and it seems that they got as far as 'Romania'.[39]

---

[36] Saul, *Knights and Esquires*, 161–3, 257–8.
[37] *Crecy and Calais*, 135. [38] PRO, C76/38 m. 10.
[39] In Apr. 1364 Urban wrote on the knights' behalf to the queen of Sicily to arrange their
passage to Otranto, the port of embarkation for the east: Horrox, *The de la Poles of Hull*, 33. They
reached 'Romania' in the company of the exiled Archbishop Paulus of Thebes. 'Romania'—a
term which usually described the north-eastern Mediterranean—probably in this case means
Greece. In Jan. 1365 the two were seeking papal funds for an expedition to free Italy from a band
of English mercenaries: Luttrell, 'English Levantine Crusaders', 145. William de la Pole's endeavours evidently made an impact on the crusading class: his arms were included in the 26 coats on
the English tower of St Peter's castle at Bodrum: Tyerman, *England and the Crusades*, 314.

John de la Pole often saw service in the renewed warfare against the French. In 1369 he served with the earl of Pembroke in Cambridge's expedition to Aquitaine.[40] Shortly after Richard's accession he served with Thomas of Woodstock in a campaign to relieve the English expedition blockaded at Brest.[41] Finally, in spring 1378 he joined in John of Gaunt's much delayed, and ultimately unsuccessful, assault on St Malo.[42] Involvement in warfare was vital to the de la Poles' self-esteem, because it invested them with chivalric aura. But a consequence of the lengthy absences it involved was an unusual detachment from local affairs. William de la Pole held office only briefly in the 1360s: he served once as a justice of the peace in Essex and Bedfordshire, and his son did not hold office at all.[43] The family never established long-standing identification with a particular county. Their sense of territoriality was weak. It is against this highly fluid background that the burial of John and Joan de la Pole at Chrishall has to be seen. The de la Poles were newcomers to the ranks of gentle society. They did not have an established mausoleum. Their burial arrangements were improvised. John's mother provided them with a magnificent church at Chrishall. Following her interment there, they were happy to seek burial at her side.

A brass very close in date to the superb memorial at Chrishall is the more modest example at Clyffe Pypard (Wilts.). This is a simpler composition. It consists of the single figure of a knight with, at one time, a short foot inscription and a shield below and two more shields above (fig. 38). The brass, like that at Chrishall, is a product of London style 'B'. Because the epitaph is lost, there has been debate as to who it represents. Two authorities who have treated the matter have doubted whether it commemorates a Cobham at all. Aubrey, in the seventeenth century, attributed it to a knight of the de Quintin family, who held the manor of Bupton in Clyffe Pypard.[44] Boutell, in his *Manual* of 1849, disagreeing, maintained that it was likely to commemorate a Cobham, perhaps John, Lord

---

[40] PRO, C61/82 m. 12. One of John's attorneys was John, Lord Cobham, and another a certain Thomas de Craneford of Chrishall.

[41] PRO, E101/36/27: particulars of account. John was paid for service from 24 Oct. 1377 to 25 Jan. 1378. For the military activity of these years, see Saul, *Richard II*, ch. 3.

[42] PRO, E101/36/35: indentures and particulars of account. John was paid for service from 16 Mar. to 3 Sept.

[43] *CPR 1361–4*, 64. In the absence of rolls of justices of the peace for these counties, it is impossible to say whether he actually sat. In 1364 he anyway set off for the east.

[44] J. Aubrey, *Wiltshire: Topographical Collections, 1659–1670*, ed. J. E. Jackson (Wiltshire Archaeological and Natural History Society, Devizes, 1862), 165.

FIG 38. Clyffe Pypard M.S. I: an
unknown knight, probably Sir Henry
de Cobham, engraved c.1380

Cobham.[45] Kite, in his *Brasses of Wiltshire*, reverted to Aubrey's position, arguing that since the brass was sited in the south aisle, which had a long association with the Quintins, it was likely to commemorate a knight of the Quintin family.[46]

The weight of evidence suggests that on the matter of family identity Boutell was right: the brass commemorates a Cobham. The case for associating it with the Quintins is weak. The fact that in Kite's day the brass lay in the Quintin aisle is largely irrelevant: the brass is now on the other side of the church, in the north aisle; and it could have been moved any number of times. What Kite and Aubrey both overlooked is that the Quintin family were of little or no consequence locally in the Middle Ages; they only acquired the trappings of gentility in the sixteenth century. It is unlikely in the extreme that they were of armigerous rank in the Middle Ages; and yet the indents in the slab for three shields point to the commemoration of someone of armigerous descent.

The only family of armigerous standing to possess a manor in the village in the Middle Ages was that of Cobham. The Cobhams had acquired their holdings in Wiltshire in the thirteenth century. In the late 1270s the exchequer baron Sir John de Cobham 'the younger' acquired Clyffe Pypard and other manors in the county from the Somerset lord, Sir Michael de Columbers.[47] Around 1279 he took livery of seisin of his acquisitions.[48] Some ten years later, he settled some of the manors on his younger kin. Around 1290 he granted Clyffe Pypard to Roger, apparently his third son. Roger was described as lord of the manor in 1297 and in 1304 he had a grant of free warren there.[49] On his death without issue the manor reverted to John's son and heir, Henry, the 1st Lord. In 1306 Henry then granted it to his second son Sir Thomas, the first of the Cobhams of Beluncle (Kent).[50] Members of the Beluncle line appear to have been tenants of the manor for the rest of the century.[51]

There is every reason to suppose that the brass commemorates one of the Beluncle branch of the family. The candidate with the strongest claim

---

[45] Boutell, *Monumental Brasses of England*, 31.

[46] E. Kite, *The Monumental Brasses of Wiltshire* (London, 1860, repr. Bath, 1969), 20.

[47] See above, 17.

[48] BL, Harley Roll C 28: account of Sir John's expenses in taking seisin of his Wiltshire manors, 7 Edw. I.

[49] *VCH Wiltshire*, ix (London, 1970), 28.   [50] For the Cobhams of Beluncle, see above, 34.

[51] Thomas Cobham was the chief taxpayer at Clyffe Pypard in 1332: *Wiltshire Tax List of 1332*, 97. He and his wife, Agnes, made a settlement of the manor in 1342: *Abstracts of Feet of Fines Relating to Wiltshire for the Reign of Edward III*, ed. C. R. Elrington (Wiltshire Record Society, 29; 1974), no. 269.

is Henry, son and heir of Thomas the grantee.[52] Thomas himself appears
to have lived chiefly in Kent. Henry, however, lived at least part of the
time at Clyffe Pypard. His presence at the manor is attested in various
Cobham charters. In 1362, when Henry issued an acknowledgement of
a rent payment to himself, he did so by a deed place-dated at Clyffe
Pypard;[53] there is no evidence that he was ever resident at Beluncle.
Although a series of charters were issued by his kinsfolk at Beluncle in
the 1350s, his name never once appears among them.[54] The evidence of
Henry's tenure of Clyffe Pypard makes it likely, though not certain, that
he is the man commemorated by the brass. It is unclear when he died.
Thomas, his younger brother, who succeeded him in his manors, was to
die in 1367.[55] So Henry must have died sometime between 1362 and that
year. Unfortunately, since he did not hold in chief of the crown, there is
no inquisition post mortem.

Henry remains a shadowy figure. Next to nothing is known of him
beyond what is disclosed in the Cobham charters. From this material it
can be established that he had a wife Denise and that they had a son,
John, who predeceased him.[56] He had a remainderman's interest in the
Cobham manor of 'Stampete' in Sheppey.[57] He does not seem to have
held office or to have served on any commissions in either Wiltshire or
Kent. Possibly his lack of means counted against him. Yet the fact that he
is commemorated by a brass at Clyffe Pypard hints at a man of at least
some consequence. It is equally uncertain who could have commissioned
the brass. One possibility is that Henry commissioned it himself;
however, the absence of any documentation makes it difficult to prove
this. Another possibility is that his kinsfolk or executors were responsible. It is tempting to speculate on the involvement of the head of the
family, John, Lord Cobham—perhaps as an executor. Only a year or two
after Henry's death John commissioned the first of his many brasses for
Cobham. The Cobham brasses of this time, however, were all of London
style 'A', whereas Henry's is of 'B'. If John had been responsible for the
commission, Henry's brass too would surely have been 'A'. There are
stylistic grounds, however, for supposing that the brass is later than the

---

[52] The suggestion that the brass commemorates Henry was first made by N. E. Saul, 'Identifying the 14th Century Knight at Cliffe Pypard, Wilts.', *TMBS*, 12 pt 4 (1978), 314–18. Henry's
kinship to his father Thomas is given in a deed of 1362: Nichols, 'Memorials of the Family of
Cobham', 333.

[53] Nichols, 'Memorials of the Family of Cobham', 333.   [54] Ibid. 326, 333–4.

[55] This is the date given on his brass in Cobham church.

[56] BL, Cotton Ch. XXVII, 27; Society of Antiquaries, MS 728/3 fos. 17ᵛ–18ʳ.

[57] BL, Harley Ch. 52 I 29 (indenture place-dated Cooling, 1 Dec. 1348).

1360s. Its closest affinities are with brasses of c.1370–80, in particular with the examples at Chinnor (Oxon.) and Fletching (Sussex).[58] Thus it is possible that John could have ordered the brass retrospectively, after he had begun ordering brasses from 'B' for Cobham. It is evident from his work at Cobham that he was keenly interested in honouring the memory of his kin; and conceivably, his interest extended to his Wiltshire kinsman.

A later member of the Beluncle line is commemorated by a brass in Kent, right in the family heartland. This is Thomas Cobham of Beluncle (d. 1465), who is buried at Hoo St Werburgh. Thomas's brass is a good example of the work of London style 'B' (fig. 39). Thomas is shown in full armour. He is attired in a single breastplate, large pauldrons and couters, and a fauld fitted with tassets. His sword is slung in front of him, and he rests his feet on a dog. His wife Maud is shown in widow's attire. A foot inscription and four shields complete the composition.[59]

Thomas received livery of his estates in 1435.[60] He does not appear to have been active in local government, and he never assumed knighthood. However, he played a minor role in affairs in the Rochester area. In 1453 he attested a charter relating to lands in Rochester, and six years later he served as a warden of Rochester bridge.[61] His wife's maiden name is not recorded. On his death on 8 June 1465 he was succeeded by his son John.

The Cobhams of Beluncle were among the least conspicuous of the Cobham cadet branches. The reason for this was their relative lack of means. In the fifteenth century their only manor was that of Beluncle in Hoo. They had a few other lands in Kent, but it seems that they lost possession of Clyffe Pypard. For most of the fourteenth century they had lived under the shadow of their grander neighbours, the lords of Cobham. After the extinction of the Cobhams in the male line in 1408 they emerged more clearly in their own right. Later members of the

[58] Illus. respectively in Macklin, *The Brasses of England*, 51, and Clayton (ed.), *Catalogue of Rubbings of Brasses and Incised Slabs*, pl. 8.

[59] The inscription and shields are replacements by Waller: Lack, Saul, and Whittemore, *Monumental Brasses in St Mary Magdalene, Cobham*, 24.

[60] Nichols, 'Memorials of the Family of Cobham', 325–6. His father's estates were enfeoffed. The feoffees were members of the substantial knightly family of Cheyne of Shurland in Sheppey—Sir William Cheyne and his younger brother Simon, founder of the Sussex branch of the family. The Cheynes' associates overlapped with the Cobhams': e.g. they both knew the Pympes of Nettlestead. For William Cheyne, see *House of Commons*, ii, 557–8.

[61] Medway Archives Office, Drc/T308; Nichols, 'Memorials of the Family of Cobham', 334.

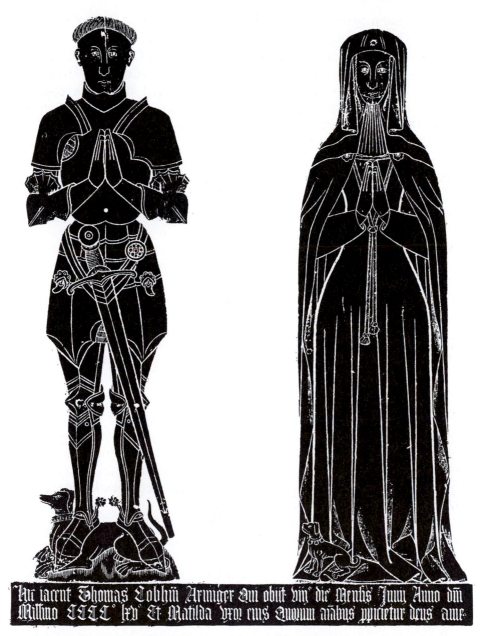

FIG 39. Hoo St Werburgh M.S. V: Thomas Cobham, d. 1465, and his wife, Maud

family figured from time to time in local government. In the 1470s a second Thomas Cobham served as a justice of the peace and a commissioner of array in Kent, and a century later one John Cobham as a justice of the peace and commissioner of sewers.[62] But theirs was a world of limited horizons. They were never to be numbered among the county élite; nor did they mix with the greater gentry. The scarcity of their memorials reflects this. In death, as in life, they kept a low profile. The grandest of their memorials, that to the second Sir Thomas (d. 1367), was paid for by his cousin.[63] Their other memorials were humbler. Their main achievement was to cling onto their gentle status. Thomas's brass is witness to that: he is attired in armour. But socially their place was in the lesser gentry.

Another member of a Cobham cadet branch is commemorated by a brass at Hever (Kent). This was John Cobham 'of Devonshire' (d. 1399), whose chief residence was at Hever. The brass is a surprisingly modest one. There is no figure: only a set of four coats of arms (of which three are lost) and an inscription (fig. 40).[64] The inscription reads:

Johan de Cobham de Devenshire Esquier qe murust le xii jour del mois de / Novembr' lan de grace MCCCLXXXXIX Et Dame Johane dame de Leukenore / sa femme et Renaud lour fitz gisont icy Dieux de lour almes eyt mercy Amen.

The brass formerly lay on a tomb chest under the tower which is still extant. At some stage—very likely when the tower was turned into a vestry—it was relaid on the floor adjacent. In 1871, as a modern inscription records, the inscription and 'one remaining escutcheon' were transferred to the wall.[65] The Purbeck slab, in which metal blanks substitute for the missing parts, remains on the floor.

John Cobham was a scion of the family of Cobham of Randall.[66] His elder brother was Sir Thomas Cobham of Randall, who died in 1394. By an agreement made between the brothers in 1362, John was awarded the manor of Hever and lands in the hundred of Hoo, presumably in return for surrendering to his sibling his rights to Randall.[67] It is unclear how he came to acquire an interest in Devon. The Cobhams of Randall were

---

[62] *CPR 1467–77*, 353, 618; *1560–3*, 438; *1563–6*, 23; *1569–72*, 225.
[63] MS. IV at Cobham; for which, see above, 91.   [64] The brass is of London style 'B'.
[65] Griffin and Stephenson, *Monumental Brasses in Kent*, 121. John Cobham's brass is illustrated, without commentary, in Belcher, *Kentish Brasses*, ii, 68.
[66] For his career, see *House of Commons*, ii, 607–8.
[67] Nichols, 'Memorials of the Family of Cobham', 335.

FIG 40. Hever M.S. I: Inscription to John Cobham, d. 1399, his wife, Joan, and their son, Reynold

only distantly related to the Devon branch of the Cobham family, which was seated at Blackborough, near Cullompton. A possible explanation may be the Cobhams' connections with the Courtenay earls of Devon. John's senior kinsman John, Lord Cobham, was married to Margaret, daughter of Hugh, earl of Devon, and it was her brother, the distinguished soldier Sir Peter Courtenay, who in 1383 interceded on John's behalf for a royal licence for the crenellation of his manor-house at Hever.[68]

John was a very active gentleman. In the course of a twenty-year career he held office not only in Kent but in Surrey and Sussex. He acquired the income qualifications for holding office through his marriage to the wealthy widow, Joan de Lewknor. Joan brought with her manors in Sussex and Kent and the east midlands. John began his office-holding career as a tax collector in Sussex in 1380. Four years later he served in a similar capacity in Surrey. Intermittently in the 1380s he also served as a commissioner of array in Sussex and a justice of the peace in Surrey. In 1392 he was appointed a deputy to Thomas of Woodstock, duke of Gloucester, as constable in the Court of Chivalry. On eight occasions he was elected a knight of the shire in parliament—twice for Sussex, and three times each for Surrey and Kent. A factor which probably assisted him in election to parliament was his connection with the royal household. In or shortly before 1388 he had entered the king's

[68] *CPR 1381–5*, 326; in the letters he is referred to, as on the brass, as 'John Cobham of Devonshire'. Cobham should probably be regarded as the builder of the original Hever castle. Its modest dimensions have survived the modern overlay. The rectangular gatehouse is the most notable survivor from the medieval period.

service as an esquire of the household, probably as a result of Courtenay influence, and he remained in the king's pay until his death.[69] In the winter of 1394–5 he accompanied Richard II on his expedition to Ireland. In the summer of 1399 he accompanied Richard to Ireland again, but this expedition was interrupted by Bolingbroke's return. Shortly after coming back to England, on 12 November he died.

For a man so active and well connected John's brass is surprisingly modest. There is no figure, and there are no accessories of the kind found on the Cobhams' other memorials at Cobham or Lingfield. How far the brass's modesty is a reflection of John's own wishes is unclear. John gave no instructions for the brass in his will: he simply asked to be buried under the bell-tower of St Peter's church, Hever, next to his wife Joan and their son Reynold.[70] Such impressions as we have of him suggest someone who would have preferred something grander. He appears to have been a man of flamboyant style. In his will he insisted that he be given a lavish send-off. He set aside the considerable sum of £30 for the costs of his funeral, and he enjoined his executors to find twenty poor men to stand vigil over his tomb for forty days. His piety appears to have tended towards the showy and the self-indulgent. He displayed immoderate concern for his soul: he asked for a chantry to be provided for his benefit at Hever to be served by two chaplains, and he assigned £20 to be spent on 10,000 masses and 30 trentals of St Gregory. There is no evidence that he had any leaning to commemorative austerity. In view of this, it is the more surprising that his brass is so simple and unassuming. It is tempting to ask why. One obvious possibility is that he was let down by his executors. In 1399 the people who had been closest to him when he had drawn up his will—his second wife and his son—were gone; and, as a result, the task of honouring his memory fell to other, less committed folk.[71] Yet against this has to be set the overall size of the monument of which the brass forms a part. The tomb and its architectural surrounds are grandiose in conception, filling virtually the whole of the

[69] CPR 1385–9, 506.

[70] Lambeth Palace Library, Register of Archbishop Arundel, i, fo. 165ʳ.

[71] The executors were Guy Mone, bishop of St David's, Ralph Cobham of Chafford, Ralph Cobham of Devon, who was the testator's brother, and one William Smyth of Hever: ibid. Guy Mone was a Kentishman: he made his will at Charlton (Kent) and requested burial at Leeds priory (Lambeth Palace Library, Register of Archbishop Arundel, i, fos. 246ᵛ–247ʳ). He went to Ireland with Richard in 1399: *The Episcopal Registers of St David's, 1397–1518*, ed. R. F. Isaacson (Cymmrodorion Record Series, 6; 2 vols.; 1917), i, 118–21. He was a courtier who served Richard as keeper of the privy seal and treasurer. For his career, see Tout, *Chapters in the Administrative History of Medieval England*, iv, 8, 49; v, 53. Ralph Cobham of Chafford (d. 1402), John's cousin, was the esquire to be commemorated by the half-effigy and inscription at Cobham: above fig. 16.

south wall of the tower.[72] Over the chest, its lid originally inlaid with brasses, rises a lofty stone canopy, elaborately cusped underneath and with a trefoil in the head. In the spandrels are two shields bearing Cobham's arms, and crowning the central finial is a boldly carved head, possibly John Cobham's.[73] While the brasses themselves are modest, the monument as a whole emphatically is not; it is highly impressive. Clearly John's executors did not let him down.

The nature of John's commemorative intent is best explained in the context of his choice of burial place. John asked to be buried 'under the bell-tower' at Hever, and his request was respected. The bell-tower was an unusual choice for burial. John ruled out a more prestigious location—for example, on the north side of the chancel, where Sir Thomas Boleyn, Anne's father, was later to be buried. Evidently, the tower meant something to him. The reason for this is very likely that he built it. Unfortunately, dating the tower is difficult, for there are few architectural details which afford clues. The plinth moulding at the base, however, is suggestive of a date in the later fourteenth and the fifteenth centuries.[74] In the late Middle Ages, it was by no means unusual for country gentry to undertake the rebuilding of towers as a way of perpetuating their memory: Ralph and Goditha Stathum and their son rebuilt the tower at Morley (Derbys.), and the Catesby family did so at Ladbroke (Warks.).[75] The loftiness of the west tower at Hever certainly carries with it a hint of a lord's preoccupation with prestige. Quite possibly, John rebuilt the structure in its entirety; alternatively, it is possible that he simply strengthened it and then added the shingle spire, which is today its most notable feature. In either event, the tower has a claim to be John's real monument. The tomb with its brass is best considered a monument within a monument.

John Cobham's brass is very different in character from those commissioned by other members of the Cobham family at this time. It is not only smaller and simpler; it is much less self-conscious. Yet in one highly significant respect it bears witness to broadly the same concerns. Like the brasses of Braybrooke and Hawberk, Joan, Lady Cobham's, husbands, at

---

[72] This is not noticed in the description of Hever in Newman, *West Kent*, 309.

[73] The head is very likely reset but its original position is unclear. The carving is distinctive. The man is shown wearing a close-fitting cap with long sides, which comes down over his ears. The vigour and distinctiveness suggest that a likeness was intended.

[74] There are also lancet openings near the top which are probably re-set.

[75] W. Lack, H. M. Stuchfield, and P. Whittemore, *The Monumental Brasses of Derbyshire* (London, 1999), 146; C. Carpenter, 'The Religion of the Gentry of Fifteenth-Century England', in D. Williams (ed.), *England in the Fifteenth Century* (Woodbridge, 1987), 65–6.

Cobham, it shows an unusual interest in children. The epitaph mentions not only John and his wife; it also mentions their son. The boy is identified by name—Reynold. This is a highly unusual touch for a brass of this date, and it must be a reflection of John's influence. The boy mattered to him. Young Reynold was his only son and heir, the embodiment of his hopes for the future. With his premature death—when exactly is unknown—his aspirations to establish a dynasty at Hever were dashed; his line was ended. He had a daughter for whom he intended a good marriage: in his will he stipulated that she was to wed only with the consent of his executors.[76] However, it seems that she let him down and married beneath her.[77] The brass epitaph is thus witness to the disappointment of this busy and ambitious man's hopes—just as the brasses at Cobham are witness to the disappointment of Joan's. The future held out little or no promise to John. He felt the pain deeply; and so too do we.

One other member of the Cobham family has a brass perpetuating his memory, and that is Sir John Harpedon, the fifth and last husband of Joan, Lady Cobham, who died in 1438. Harpedon's brass is in Westminster Abbey (fig. 41). It originally lay on a tomb in the chapel of St John the Evangelist, but is now in the north ambulatory.[78] Precisely why Harpedon was accorded the honour of burial in Westminster Abbey is not clear. His family background is obscure. His name suggests that he was descended from Sir John Harpedon, the Poitevin knight who was seneschal of Saintonge in the 1370s.[79] This John Harpedon's son, another John, acquired the lordship of Belleville and entered French allegiance, rising to the office of chamberlain to Charles VI.[80] Although it cannot be proved, there is a fair likelihood that John Harpedon, Joan's husband, was this second John's son.[81] It is conceivable that burial in the abbey was his reward for entering English allegiance.

[76] Lambeth Palace Library, Register of Archbishop Arundel, i, fo. 165ʳ.

[77] She married one John Bierden, an obscure figure of whom nothing is known: Manning and Bray, *History of Surrey*, ii, 363. Could she have eloped?

[78] The brasses of Harpedon and Abbot Estney were moved to the ambulatory to make way for the monument to General Wolfe: Wright, *Brasses of Westminster Abbey*, 22.

[79] For his career, on which the Anonimalle chronicler was well informed, see *The Anonimalle Chronicle 1333 to 1381*, ed. V. H. Galbraith (Manchester, 1927), 115, 116, 188.

[80] The younger John's French allegiance was noted in his father's inquisition in 1396: *CIPM*, xvii, no. 289. For the role of the younger John in French politics, see J. B. Henneman, *Olivier de Clisson and Political Society in France under Charles V and Charles VI* (Philadelphia, 1996), 139, 203, 312 n. 49. He acquired the lordship of Belleville by his father's marriage to Jeanne, Olivier de Clisson's sister; for the Clisson genealogy, see ibid. 205.

[81] In his inquisition post mortem of 1438, his father was said to have been called 'John': PRO, C139/86/28 m. 10.

FIG 41. Westminster Abbey M.S. VIII: Sir John Harpedon, d. 1438

Like Joan's earlier husbands, Harpedon was primarily a soldier. He took an active part in Henry V's wars in France. In 1415 he fought at Agincourt under the banner of Sir John Cornwall, and from 1417 he served in Normandy under the same commander.[82] As a result of his exploits in Normandy, he received the grant of a lordship and manors in the duchy.[83] In or before 1419 he switched to service in Aquitaine. In the summer of 1419 Henry empowered him to negotiate a truce for the castles of Mirembel, Cosnac, and Montendre.[84] Harpedon appears to have been abroad for most of the 1420s: at least, he makes no appearance in English records.[85] However, by the 1430s he had largely retired.[86] In his final years he lived in England. For the duration of his marriage to Joan he had control of the Cobham and de la Pole inheritances *iure uxoris*.[87] But after Joan's death, he had to live largely on his patrimonial estates, which were less ample.[88] Although a relative newcomer to English landed society, Harpedon was by no means an outsider. He appears to have been a widely connected man. One of his earliest associates was his retinue commander, Sir John Cornwall, later Lord Fanhope, whose wife was Henry IV's sister, while later he gained the favour of Humphrey of Gloucester, whom he named as a feoffee.[89] If the heraldry

---

[82] Nicolas, *History of the Battle of Agincourt*, 380; PRO, E101/51/2.

[83] Harpedon received grants of the lordship of Chanteloup and the manors of Cerences and 'Appely' in the Cotentin (*Catalogue des Rolles Gascons, Normans et François*, ed. T. Carte, 2 vols.; London, 1743, i, 257). [84] *Catalogue des Rolles Gascons*, i, 258.

[85] Harpedon held the stewardship of Queen Katherine's manor of Watlington (Oxon.) from 1422 to his death: *VCH Oxfordshire*, viii, ed. M. D. Lobel (London, 1964), 218. There is no evidence that he discharged the duties of the office in person, however.

[86] In 1435 he was acting as arbitrator in a dispute involving Sir Lewis Robsart, another captain: *CCR 1429–35*, 355.

[87] It is not known when he married Joan. A *terminus ante quem* of June 1428 is provided by a reference in Glover's notes to an indenture which he possessed containing evidences relating to the descent of the Cobham estates: Nichols, 'Memorials of the Family of Cobham', 341.

[88] He was lord of Harpsden (Oxon.): *Feudal Aids*, iv, 200. According to his inquisition, he also held Swinbrook in the same county (PRO, C139/86/28). In an exchequer court case of 1434 he was described as 'of Berkshire' (BL, Harley Roll C 30); so presumably he held lands there too. Again according to his inquisition, in Huntingdonshire he held the former de la Pole manors of Everton and Offord by life grant from his wife's daughter and her husband Sir Thomas Brooke. There were no children by his marriage to Joan; his heir was said to be Isabella, wife of Robert Olyver, esquire, the daughter of Elizabeth, daughter of Gilbert, brother of Harpedon's father John (PRO, C139/86/28).

[89] He served under Cornwall in both the 1415 and 1417 expeditions: see above, n. 82. Cornwall, an active soldier and a KG, married Elizabeth, Henry IV's sister, and widow of John Holand, earl of Huntingdon, who was executed for treason in 1400. For Cornwall, see *Complete Peerage*, v, 253–4. For his connection with Humphrey of Gloucester, see PRO, C139/86/28 m. 10.

on his tomb is correct, he may also have been connected with the Mortimer earls of March.[90]

Harpedon's brass, which is a product of London style 'B', is one of the most accomplished of its period. It is a sizeable composition, and beautifully engraved. John is depicted in armour with characteristic rectangular besagews over the armpits and a long fauld of lames. There are four shields, two on each side, and surrounding the whole was a marginal epitaph, now lost.[91] Harpedon's Cobham connection is attested by the heraldry—the Cobham chevrons appearing on the upper sinister and lower dexter shields. By Cobham standards, however, the brass is a rather impersonal composition. It displays none of the individuality that is a feature of the family's other brasses. And the reason for this is clear: Harpedon died a widower. His wife, Joan, Lady Cobham, had died four years before: and his connection with the family—or, rather, with this last member of the family—was gone. Only in a very loose sense can this be considered 'a Cobham brass'. Very likely, the commission was arranged by executors who had little or no knowledge of the Cobhams at all.

The brasses of John Harpedon and Thomas Cobham of Beluncle very nearly draw the series of brasses and monuments to the Cobham family to a close. Only one monument was to come later. This was the tomb chest at Lingfield of Sir Thomas Cobham (d. 1471), which lacks an effigy or epitaph.[92] In all, some two dozen memorials survive to members of the family. However, a number of other brasses were commissioned which are no longer extant. These, in their different ways, can add to our understanding of the Cobhams and their commemorative tastes.

The earliest of the lost brasses was one formerly at Nettlestead (Kent). According to a manuscript history of Nettlestead manor-house, which drew on notes by Philpot, there was 'a Brass Plate formerly prefixed to one of the flat stones, now lying in the lower Chancel of Nettlestead church, whereon' there was a Latin inscription. The inscription read:

---

[90] The top dexter shield shows a pierced molet charged with a martlet, for Harpedon, impaling Mortimer quartered with de Burgh. In what degree Harpedon was related to the Mortimers is not clear, but it is possible that the connection came through the female line.
[91] Except for the words 'mensis maii', the inscription had been lost by 1723 when Dart compiled his inventory of monuments in the abbey: J. Dart, *Westmonasterium: or, The History and Antiquities of the Abbey Church of St Peter's Westminster* (2 vols.; London n.d.), ii, 1. Harpedon died in May 1438: PRO, C139/86/28.   [92] See above, 180.

Hic jacet Domina Margareta de Cobham quondam uxor Willelmi Pimpe Militis quae obiit 4 Sept' 1337.[93]

There can be little doubt that the lady commemorated by the brass was Margaret, the daughter or sister of Henry, Lord Cobham, and wife of the distinguished Kent knight, Sir William Pympe. The Pympes were a family who had close relations with the Cobhams. They were active in local affairs, and both William and his son frequently attested Cobham charters.[94] Margaret predeceased her husband by over thirty years: William was to survive until the 1370s. What the brass looked like is unclear. The fact that only an inscription is mentioned does not necessarily rule out the possibility of a figure. It was usual for the heralds in the seventeenth century to record only epitaphs and coats of arms, because their main preoccupation was with lineage. Given the early preference of the Cobham family for figure brasses, it may well be that there was a figure here. Indeed, quite possibly the Cobhams were involved in arranging the commission. It is interesting that Margaret should have been identified by her maiden name—'de Cobham'—which is unusual for a married lady. At the very least, the inspiration for commemoration by a brass may well have come from Cobham.

Another Cobham brass which is no longer extant is that of Joan, the widow of Reginald, 1st Lord Cobham of Sterborough (d. 1369), formerly at St Mary Overy, Southwark (now Southwark cathedral). There is little difficulty in visualizing the character of this memorial, because Joan gave precise instructions for it in her will. She asked for a plain marble slab to be laid over her body, inlaid with a metal cross ('una crux de metallo in medio lapidis'), and with the following epitaph around the edge:

> Vous qe par ici passietz
> Pur lalme Johane de Cobham prietz.[95]

What Joan had in mind was a simple cross brass with a marginal epitaph. The slightly later examples of such brasses at Cassington (Oxon.) and Beddington (Surrey) provide extant parallels.[96] Joan's tastes were austere in the extreme. She settled for one of the simplest of all forms

---

[93] Ball, 'Stained Glass Windows of Nettlestead Church', 278. Ball cited a quarto MS of 20 pages, the cover of which was endorsed 'Writing by Miss Morland 1812'. It is clear from his earlier discussion (249), however, that the MS drew on notes by Philpot.

[94] See above, 94–5.

[95] Flower, 'Notices of the Family of Cobham', 169. The will is dated 12 Aug. 1369.

[96] For cross brasses, see Norris, *Monumental Brasses: The Memorials*, 196–7. The brasses at Cassington and Beddington are illustrated in Boutell, *Monumental Brasses*, pls. 26, 28 respectively.

of funerary monument. No hint of worldliness was to appear: religious imagery was to dominate. Moreover, she insisted on burial outside—by the entrance door with the image of the Virgin Mary over it. Joan's was one of the few medieval brasses known to have been laid in an external position.[97]

The fortunate survival of Joan's will affords a convenient opportunity to judge a patron's commemorative taste alongside the evidence of her piety. Joan took a quite exceptional interest in her memorial. In most cases, testators simply set aside a sum to pay for a 'stone' and left it at that. But Joan's attitude was different. She gave detailed instructions for her brass. She wanted it to convey a particular religious message. This is suggestive of a lady of more than conventional piety. How far do the terms of her will bear this impression out?

Joan's will was a lengthy document, and evidently the product of reflection. As so often, there were many bequests to kinsfolk, servants, and friends. Joan showed herself particularly generous to her staff: we have seen that she made careful provision for Katherine Stocket.[98] But her greatest concern was to ensure the well-being of her soul. She specified precisely the form of her funeral. She ordered that twelve poor men clothed in black cloaks and hoods were to carry twelve wax torches in procession to St Mary's church; and immediately after celebration of the Mass, six of the torches were to be offered at the altar of the Virgin Mary, and the other six at the altar of St Mary Magdalene. She allowed 40 marks to cover the costs of her funeral. She also specified a long series of bequests to the convent of St Mary in Southwark. She set aside £20 for the fabric fund, 40s. for the prior, 20s. for each canon in priest's orders, and 10s. for each canon who was not; and, additionally, she left 3s. 4d. for the bell-ringers. Joan also remembered her local parish church in Southwark, St Mary Magdalene: she left 100s. to the church's fabric fund, 20s. to the incumbent, and 6s. 8d. to each of the chaplains. In addition, she left 10 marks for the purchase of ornaments for the choir of St Peter's, Lingfield. These were bequests which amply attest the conventional sincerity of Joan's piety. Yet they afford little or no indication of any deeper sensibilities. That self-conscious, rather affected, humility which led

---

[97] Sir Thomas Brooke of Thorncombe, whose son, another Thomas, married the daughter of Joan, the Cobham heiress, requested burial outside the church under a plain slab (*House of Commons*, ii, 379). Whether or not his wish was respected is not clear; but when his wife died in 1437, the two of them were commemorated under a very fine slab—inside the church and with brasses: see below, 230–2.

[98] See above, 182.

her to seek burial outside is absent. There are occasional hints in the document of her more other-worldly concerns. There is a puzzling bequest of 20s. and a ring with a sapphire to one Alice, a senior nun of Barking; Alice's relation to Joan is unstated.[99] Furthermore, there is evidence of her tastes in devotional reading: 'a book of the Apocalypse' and a Book of Hours are mentioned. Much the clearest link with the religiosity of the brass, however, is provided by the evidence of her fear of purgatory. Joan was terrified of the trials to come. Almost the first instruction given in the will is for the immediate performance of soul masses. 'Before everything else after my decease', she says, '7,000 masses are to be celebrated, and these on no account to be delayed: the masses are to be celebrated by the canons of Tonbridge and Tandridge and by the friars of the four mendicant orders in London, and they shall have for their pains £29. 3s. 4d.'. The same eager appetite for intercession informs her epitaph. Its two brief lines take the form of a blunt request: 'passers-by, pray for the soul of Joan de Cobham'. This directness suggests that, as death approached, nothing else greatly mattered to her. Both testament and brass are informed by a sense of urgency. This was a lady terrified of the sufferings that lay ahead.

Obvious similarities are to be observed between Joan's deeply felt piety and the austere penitential piety of several other members of the Cobham family, notably John, the 3rd Lord. A notable characteristic of Joan's piety was a highly self-conscious, almost anguished, humility: a humility which led her to seek burial outside. A similar humility characterized Lord Cobham's piety: it found expression in the opening words of his epitaph—'from earth I was made, to earth shall I return'. A generation earlier, another Cobham lady is known to have cultivated a self-consciously pious lifestyle. In a funeral sermon of 1344 Bishop Sheppey of Rochester had commended this 'Lady Cobham' for the singular rigour of her devotions.[100] One way of interpreting Joan Cobham's piety is to

---

[99] Could Alice have been someone whose manner of life she admired?

[100] W. A. Pantin, *The English Church in the Fourteenth Century* (Cambridge, 1957), 255–6, 276. Sheppey commended 'Lady Cobham' ('domine de Cobham') in a sermon prepared for her funeral in 1344. In the event, the sermon was never given, for the archbishop of Canterbury preached in his stead; but the text of Sheppey's remarks survives as New College, Oxford MS 92. It is likely that the 'Lady Cobham' was Joan (*née* Beauchamp), first wife of John, 2nd Lord Cobham. She was alive in 1343, and yet dead by 1348, by which time her husband was remarried: *Complete Peerage*, iii, 344; Nichols, 'Memorials of the Family of Cobham', 346. It is not known where this Lady Cobham was buried. Conceivably it was in Sheppey's own cathedral of Rochester seeing that he was the preacher.

suppose that she had embraced the life of a vowess. In the late Middle Ages it became highly fashionable for upper-class widows to create a kind of 'holy household' in their establishments.[101] Examples of such widows are Marie de St Pol, countess of Pembroke, from the fourteenth century and Cecily, duchess of York, from the fifteenth. Duchess Cecily, in C. A. J. Armstrong's words, sought consciously to achieve 'a type of individual sanctity'.[102] The character of these ladies' piety was strongly meditative. They reflected in their private chambers or chapels on the insights of devotional literature: Duchess Cecily owned copies of the Golden Legend and various mystical works. Moreover, they found inner peace by contemplating images and representations of saints. There are indications that Lady Joan's devotional life could well have been of this sort. She had a chapel in her house at Southwark, and it is evident from her will that this was a chamber well furnished and equipped with images.[103] She also had a confessor in her service—her chaplain William de Wrotham, to whom she left 10 marks.[104] She was deeply committed in her devotions. Like other widows, she read works of piety and contemplation. She refers to a number of such works in her will—a book of 'the Apocalypse', which she left to her son, and a Book of Hours, which she left to one Katherine de Layton. Images were important to her. She had a crucifix with an Agnus Dei, which she bequeathed to her granddaughter Joan; and she had a paxbrede with an image of the Crucifixion.[105] It is possible that meditative reflection on the Crucifixion played a major role in her piety. Indeed, it is tempting to regard her preoccupation with the crucifix as being an important influence on her choice of memorial.

---

[101] J. C. Ward, *English Noblewomen in the Later Middle Ages* (London, 1992), 144–5. The earlier Lady Cobham had also sought to incorporate due religious observance into her life. According to Bishop Sheppey, it was her normal practice to say Matins, the hours of Our Lady, and the seven Psalms before leaving her chamber in the morning or speaking to a stranger; and during Mass, when the priest was silent, she would say her Paternosters and Hail Marys or some private prayers: Pantin, *English Church in the Fourteenth Century*, 256.

[102] C. A. J. Armstrong, *England, France and Burgundy in the Fifteenth Century* (London, 1983), 141.

[103] She refers to the 'clerk of her chapel' (who may or may not have been the same as her chaplain): Flower, 'Notices of the family of Cobham of Sterborough', 181. She bequeathed a fine set of vestments to Lingfield church: an altar frontal with the arms of Berkeley and Cobham, a dalmatic, a green tunicle worked with gold thread, and a green cope: ibid. 178.   [104] Ibid. 181.

[105] A paxbrede was a small plate of ivory, metal, or wood with a representation of a holy subject (often but not necessarily the Crucifixion), which at Mass was passed round among the congregation to receive the kiss of peace. For an example, see R. E. M. Wheeler, 'A Pax at Abergavenny', *Antiquaries Journal*, 10 (1930), 356–8.

The lost brasses of Joan, Lady Cobham, and Margaret Pympe are ones which we know about from contemporary or later sources. But quite possibly there were other Cobham brasses of which we know nothing. There is evidence in their wills that some of the Cobhams of Randall were commemorated by monuments, perhaps by brasses. The later Cobhams of Randall were buried at Boxley priory, near Maidstone. In his will of 1405 Sir Reginald Cobham of Randall asked to be buried in Boxley priory church 'next to the burial-place' of his father.[106] The fact that his father's burial-place was remembered suggests that it was marked by a monument. Yet if that was the case, the monument has not survived, and there is no record of its appearance.[107]

In just one instance, however, we can posit a possible connection between a despoiled slab and an attested Cobham burial. In the chapel on the north side of the chancel at Charlwood (Surrey), largely obscured by the organ, is a despoiled Purbeck slab probably of late fourteenth-century date with indents near the bottom of two shields. In his will of 1375 Sir William Cobham of Gatwick asked to be buried at Charlwood.[108] Quite possibly this was the slab which contained his brass. The man commemorated, as the shields indicate, was someone armigerous, and the slab is of appropriate size for a single figure. However, without an inspection of the slab as a whole, it would be rash to suggest an identification with William as anything more than a possibility.

When examining the Cobhams' tombs and brasses, it is easy to be dazzled by the splendour of the memorials at Cobham itself and Lingfield. But the monuments at these churches represent only a portion of the whole. The Cobhams were a widely ramified clan. They spawned many cadet branches; and several Cobham cadets were buried and commemorated in other churches. Discussion of these other Cobham memorials confirms the family's preference for brasses. Other than at Lingfield, after 1320 they commissioned no stone or alabaster monuments. The

---

[106] Lambeth Palace Library, Register of Archbishop Arundel, i, fo. 226ᵛ. Reginald's father was Sir Thomas (d. 1394); the latter's will has not survived: *House of Commons*, ii, 609 (where 'Boxley' of the will is misread as 'Birling').

[107] Boxley was largely swept away at the Dissolution, although the guest-house and parts of the church remain.

[108] Lambeth Palace Library, Register of Archbishop Sudbury, fo. 80ʳ. The will is summarized in *Testamenta Vetusta*, i, 96. William Cobham of Gatwick was a member of the Chafford sub-branch of the Cobhams of Randall. His younger brother was Ralph Cobham of Chafford, who was buried at Cobham: Society of Antiquaries, MS 728/3, fos. 18ʳ–19ᵛ; see below, Appendix. He was an MP for Surrey in 1371 and 1372: *CCR 1370–4*, 289, 476. For the descent of the manor of Charlwood, see *VCH Surrey*, iii, 184.

brasses of the Cobham offspring or cadets varied in character and size, reflecting variations in the means of those commemorated. The striking homogeneity which characterizes the series at Cobham itself is absent. One characteristic, however, is common to them all, and that is the concern of the commemorated for prayers. While it may be coincidental, it is none the less appropriate that one of the three surviving words on the Chrishall brass should be 'priez'.

⇥ 9 ⇤

Conclusion: Lineage and Commemoration

IF monuments can be said to bring us closer to the commemorated, then the monuments at Cobham, Lingfield, and elsewhere bring us very close to the Cobhams. The surviving tombs and brasses to the family—totalling some two dozen in all—are notable as much for their distinctiveness as for their near-uniformly high quality. The assumption underlying this study is that by attending closely to their witness we can learn something of the hopes and anxieties of those they commemorate.

Tombs and brasses, however, are a highly problematic source for the historian. They need to be interpreted with care, just like any corpus of documentary material. A number of the problems to which they give rise are unique to funerary sculpture as such. Among the most important of these is the highly stylized nature of the medium. Medieval monumental effigies were not portraits; and they drew on the engraver's assumptions as much as the client's. The question accordingly needs to be asked: how are the respective roles of engraver and client to be separated and identified? A second, and connected, difficulty centres on the relationship of the client to the commemorated. The great majority of medieval monuments were not commissioned by those whom they commemorate; they were commissioned by their executors or kin. So a second question arises: whose aspirations are chiefly reflected in the memorial—those of the deceased or his agents? Overarching these questions is a broader issue, which can be said to inform them both—how far can the monuments be used as a guide to self-image at all?

The most serious of these methodological difficulties is the highly stylized nature of the memorials. From no later than the thirteenth century, tombs and brasses in England were effectively being mass-produced: large numbers—many hundreds or more—were turned out each year.[1] Differentiation in the product range was necessarily limited. Each of the main workshops carried its stock effigial types. These types were differentiated principally by costume—figures in armour for gentlemen, civilian-attired figures for the burgess or franklin class, and figures in vestments for priests. There were admittedly wide variations of size: effigies could come large or small, to suit the client's pocket; and accessories like canopies could be included or omitted, as appropriate. But the ability of the client to exert significant influence on the design of the effigies was limited. There is no evidence that customers were greatly, if at all, concerned about this. What chiefly preoccupied them was the representation of status. And in this area they could see that their expectations were amply satisfied by the engravers. A wide range of emblematic devices was on offer—shields of arms to attest lineage and connections, collars and bastard feudal devices to indicate magnate affiliation, merchants' marks and distinctive foot-rests to show the trades of the merchant class. This concern for the representation of status was a by-product of the growing appreciation of selfhood in this period. The same quality of selfhood was reflected in a taste for lengthier inscriptions. On a number of late-medieval epitaphs rich genealogical detail was included, sometimes, as at Launde (Leics.), stretching generations back. On the epitaphs of knights it became increasingly common to record battles fought or victories won. Equally indicative of enhanced selfhood was the growing popularity of patron saints on memorials. St George and the Virgin, for example, were shown on the brass of Sir Nicholas Hawberk at Cobham, and St Christopher on that of William Complyn at Weeke (Hants.). It was to the saintly intercessors who adorned their memorials that the commemorated looked for mediatory assistance in the afterlife.

Thus a case can be argued that, despite the limitation placed on customer influence by serial production, a client could purchase a memorial reasonably suited to his taste. And, granted that that was the case, it is surely legitimate to interpret brasses as a source for self-image. However, another difficulty needs to be considered. Only a smallish proportion of the brasses produced were actually commissioned by those they represent: John, 3rd Lord Cobham's, brass at Cobham is a familiar example; and John Hampton's brass at Minchinhampton (Gloucs.), from a century later, is another. Generally, memorials were ordered after the subject's death by his executors or relatives. There is thus potentially the danger

---

[1] Non-effigial Purbeck marble slabs were being mass-produced before this date.

that when analysing a memorial we discover more about the aspirations of the commemorated's agents than about the commemorated himself. The problem is undoubtedly a serious one. A number of fairly familiar medieval monuments were executed many years after their subjects' deaths. Edward III's monument in Westminster Abbey, for example, was not executed until 1386, some nine years after the king's death, while the admittedly de luxe monument at St Mary's, Warwick, of Richard Beauchamp, earl of Warwick, was executed in stages well over a decade after the earl's death in 1439.[2] However, there are grounds for thinking that these celebrated examples were exceptional. Roger Greenwood's analysis of fifteenth-century Norwich wills has shown that testators usually expected their memorials to be in place within a year or two of the date of death.[3] A significant number of testators, indeed, specifically asked for their 'stones' to be ready for the first anniversary of their death, which suggests that a year was the usual time allowed for the task; and just a few even insisted that their stone be laid more quickly still—in three months or six. Exactly how fast a commission could be executed depended on a variety of factors—chief among them being the size of the memorial and its location. The making of a large and elaborate memorial would obviously take longer than a small one; and carriage to a distant church could produce delay. But, making allowance for these exceptions, it is probably fair to say that most brasses were laid within a year or so of the subject's death. If that were the case, then it is not unreasonable to take them as a guide to the latter's self-image and aspirations.

A further point needs to be made in this connection. The distinction between the client and the commemorated can be exaggerated. Generally, clients were people who had been very close to the commemorated. In most cases, indeed, they were executors or immediate kin. Husbands, for example, commissioned brasses to their wives, widows to their husbands, children to their parents, and, increasingly, even parents to their children. Sometimes clients were acting on detailed instructions given in a will. Sir Thomas Stathum (d. 1470) laid down in very precise terms the form that his brass at Morley (Derbys.) was to take. His executors were to lay

a stone of marble with iii ymages of laton oon image maade aftir me and th othir ii aftir both my wifis we all knelyng with eche on of us a rolle in our

[2] CPR 1385–9, 127; Crossley, *English Church Monuments*, 30–1; Lindley, *Gothic to Renaissance: Essays on Sculpture in England*, 62–8.

[3] R. Greenwood, 'Wills and Brasses: Some Conclusions from a Norfolk Study', in J. Bertram (ed.), *Monumental Brasses as Art and History* (Stroud, 1996), 92.

handis unto our Lady saint Marye and to saint Christophore over our heedis with iiii scochons of myn armes and both my wifis armes quarterly to gedir.[4]

Thomas Stathum's brass still survives on its tomb at Morley. It is true that the figures are shown recumbent and not kneeling, but in every other respect his instructions were followed. The majority of testators, however, left much briefer instructions for their executors. Ralph Cobham of Chafford, for example, requested a 'marble stone carved with his arms and an inscription';[5] at no point did he mention an effigy, though in the event he got one. Forty years later, Sir Reginald Cobham of Sterborough asked simply for a tomb of alabaster.[6] There is no reason to suppose that the lack of detail about memorials in wills implies a lack of interest in them. Monuments could constitute significant displays of family power. They were thus highly important to a family's reputation and self-image. More likely, the existence of a body of assumptions about monuments rendered elaborate detail unnecessary. In most cases, patron and testator knew perfectly well what was expected of them. They implicitly accepted that if space (and means) allowed, there should be a figure of the deceased; that the character of that figure should be determined by his or her rank—an armoured effigy for a knight, a civilian one for a burgess, and so on; that for a person of armigerous rank there should be a coat of arms, and for a woolman or clothier a merchant's mark; and that in the epitaph there should be a request for prayers. These were generally understood—and generally recognized—conventions.

Yet it is always possible to identify a handful of exceptions. One of the most striking relates to a brass of a Cobham kinsman—Sir Thomas Brooke, who was buried at Thorncombe (Dorset). Thomas Brooke was a belted knight; thus he might be expected to have been shown in armour. In fact, he is shown as a civilian (fig. 42). It is possible that his unconventional attire is connected with a second oddity: the fact that his instructions for his memorial were substantially overridden. In his will of May 1415 Brooke had asked for simple and unobtrusive burial. He requested that his body be placed where people 'goth over into the church at the south side ryghte as they mowe stappe on me, and a flat playne stone save my name ygraved tharin'.[7] Brooke was a Lollard sympathizer, and his

---

[4] Norris, *Monumental Brasses: The Craft*, 90.
[5] PRO, Reg. Marche: PROB 11/2A, fo. 21[r].
[6] Lambeth Palace, Register of Archbishop Stafford, fo. 142[r].
[7] *Fifty Earliest English Wills*, ed. F. J. Furnivall (Early English Text Society, original series, 78; 1882), 26–7.

FIG 42. Thorncombe M.S. I: Sir Thomas Brooke, d. 1418, and his wife, Joan, engraved *c*.1437

will is strongly Lollard in character.[8] But his wife's opinions were very different: her piety was orthodox.[9] Accordingly, some twenty years later, when she commissioned a brass to cover the graves of them both, she chose one on highly conventional lines with near life-size figures; and she pointedly had it placed inside the church and not outside. None the less, the memorial was not entirely a standard production-line job; it incorporated some unusual features. In the first place, as we have seen, Thomas's figure was represented in civilian attire, not armour; and, secondly, the language of the marginal epitaph was English and not, as was more usually the case, Latin.[10] If either of these features had appeared alone, it would hardly be cause for comment. But when both are found together, it is tempting to suspect the involvement of the client. The most likely explanation is that Joan was making token concession to her late husband's wishes. The use of the vernacular directly recalls the vernacular of Thomas's will, while the insistence that he be shown as a civilian may originate in the Lollards' contempt for warfare, which would have made an armoured figure inappropriate.[11] On matters of detail Joan was prepared to defer to her husband. But on the fundamentals she stood firm. Her appetite for commemorative splendour triumphed.

Other examples can be cited of monuments with a background in family disagreement and tension. Philip Morgan has recently highlighted the case of the Fitzherbert monuments at Norbury (Derbyshire).[12] In Norbury church there is a set of three very fine alabaster monuments to the Fitzherberts dating from the late fifteenth and early sixteenth centuries. Two of the series—those of Nicholas (d. 1473) and Ralph (d. 1483) and their wives—were retrospective commissions of the 1490s. It seems likely that they were commissioned by Ralph's son, John (d. 1531), a querulous man, who was on bad terms with his brother, and who sired no son; their origins lay in John's sense of the

---

[8] Brooke was an associate of Oldcastle, and his son married Oldcastle's step-daughter, Joan: see above, 31. For his career, see *House of Commons*, ii, 379.

[9] Joan was the daughter and coheiress of Simon Hanham, a Gloucestershire gentleman, and widow of Robert Cheddar of Bristol.

[10] The content of the inscription is fairly routine (chiefly concerned with dates of death), except at the end where there is this flourish: '. . . on who soules God have mercy and pite that for us dyed on the rode tree Amen.' This closing phrase is unusual and distinctive, and very non-Lollard. Presumably Joan requested it.

[11] Lollard criticism of war is hinted at in Clanvow's treatise 'The Two Ways': K. B. McFarlane, *Lancastrian Kings and Lollard Knights* (Oxford, 1972), 203. The Lollards were particularly critical of crusading: *Knighton's Chronicle*, 289.

[12] Unpublished paper given at the Monumental Brass Society annual conference, University of Sheffield, 5 Sept. 1999.

vulnerability of his lineage. Towards the end of his life, John ordered a third tomb, this one for himself. Here, tensions of a different sort are evident. John's epitaph conspicuously omits mention of his wife, Benedicta.[13] Before 1517, John had driven her from his house, accusing her of lewdness. The two were buried separately. He provided for his own tomb and she for hers.[14]

The Fitzherberts' antagonisms remind us of how intra-family discord could be reflected in monuments. But generally, when faced with death, families closed ranks. Commemorated and executors—whether husband and wife or father and son—spoke with one voice. And the reason for this is clear. A memorial honoured a family as much as it did an individual. When Joan Brooke commissioned the fine memorial at Thorncombe, she did so partly to redeem the family name. She believed that the honour and worship of the Brooke line were at stake. There is evidence that the reverse was the case: that the absence of a memorial could bring shame to a family. In 1471 Margaret Paston rebuked her son for his failure to commission a memorial to his father. She noted that five years had passed since the latter's death, and 'it is a shame and a thing much spoken of in this country that your father's grave stone is not made'.[15] In the lineage-centred world of late medieval England it was usual for the individual's identity to be subsumed to some degree in that of the kin group. In consequence, the aspirations of a family could be reflected in a memorial as much as those of the individual commemorated. There can be little doubt that this was the case with the Cobhams' memorials. In the monuments at both 'Cobham churches'—Cobham and Lingfield—individual and family identities are subtly mixed. Because of the survival alongside the memorials of part of the Cobham archive, it is possible to distinguish and separate the two. In cases where no archive is extant to shed light on a monument, separation is admittedly less easy to achieve. None the less, the attempt should not be abandoned. Monuments have a context in time and place. If these witnesses to the past are to be properly understood, that context needs to be explored. Every monument, however modest, can tell a story—about those whom it commemorates and those responsible for it being there. The recovery and understanding of that story hold the key to its character.

[13] Lack, Stuchfield, and Whittemore, *Monumental Brasses of Derbyshire*, 160.
[14] Benedicta was commemorated by an incised slab, her husband by a tomb.
[15] *Paston Letters and Papers of the Fifteenth Century*, ed. N. Davis (2 vols.; Oxford, 1971–6), i, no. 212.

Of all medieval brasses, those of the Cobham family must be numbered among the most rewarding to study. Not only do they include some of the largest and finest examples from the Middle Ages to have come down to us; the happy survival, alongside them, of the Cobham archive allows us to say something of the context in which they were conceived and executed.

The creation of the Cobham mausoleum stemmed largely from the initiative of the 'founder', John, 3rd Lord Cobham. It was Lord Cobham's vision that turned Cobham church into a village Westminster Abbey. The background to his commemorative scheme was provided by the establishment of Cobham college. The college, a kind of chantry foundation, was a community of priests charged with praying in perpetuity for the souls of the Cobham dead. Lord Cobham's college was conceived on the grand scale. Originally, provision was made for five priests, but later the number rose to eleven. Lord Cobham was at least partly concerned to enhance the honour and dignity of his line. Establishing a family mausoleum was a self-consciously magnificent act; it drew attention to the patron's generosity and the lavishness of his means. At the same time, it bore visible witness to his lordship; it was an expression of the ties binding family and place. To this background, the brasses could be seen as ensigns of lineage. They were substitutes for the subjects themselves: a kind of link between the living and the dead. However, these worldly considerations were by no means the only influence on Cobham. He was no less concerned with preparations for the afterlife. A deeply pious man, he lived in terror of the sufferings to come. The mere thought of the trials and the torments of purgatory appalled him. Central to his vision for his foundation at Cobham was the need to secure the safe passage of his soul. Cobham college was to be a mighty storehouse of prayer. However, in acting as he did, he was not thinking only of his own soul; he wanted his Cobham kinsfolk to benefit too. And this was where the brasses fitted in. The rows of latten figures were to be *aides-mémoires* to prayer, a reminder to the chaplains of the souls committed to their care. In a sense, the figures were akin to a bede roll in a monastery: a store of memory, a roll-call of those to be regularly remembered.

Cobham's patronage of brasses needs to be seen in the context of his religious and architectural patronage more generally. Cobham was a very active patron—one of the most enthusiastic of his age. He left his mark on other churches besides Cobham. In London he enlarged St Dunstan-in-the-East, the church near his house in Lower Thames Street. According to the contract with Nicholas Typerton, he was responsible for paying for a new porch and south aisle.[16] There are indications that he also completed the work initiated by his de la Pole kin on the fabric at Chrishall. An important local project in which he was involved was the rebuilding of Rochester bridge. In 1381 the old bridge over the Medway had been swept away by massive ice floes.[17] In March 1383 Cobham was appointed to a commission with Henry Yevele to carry out essential repairs.[18] After completion of initial underpinning, it became clear that the bridge was damaged beyond repair. Accordingly, in July 1387 a new arrangement was made whereby Cobham and the Cheshire knight, Robert Knolles, undertook to provide a completely new bridge, finding the greater part of the money themselves. Work on the new fabric proceeded quickly, and by late 1391 it was substantially complete. In a move utterly characteristic of him, Cobham provided for a chantry chapel to be included in the design. According to his letters of instruction, transcribed in the Rochester register, prayers were to be said for the souls of his wife, his daughter and son-in-law, Robert Knolles, and others.[19] Just as at Cobham, Cobham combined piety with the pursuit of honour.

Lord Cobham's most ambitious project, however, was a secular one—the building (or perhaps the rebuilding) of Cooling castle, by the Thames estuary. Cobham was granted a licence to crenellate the castle on 10 February 1381.[20] It is possible that work on the site had already begun by that date; and certainly it was to go on for another five years. The castle was conceived on the grandest scale.[21] It consisted of two large rectangular enclosures with circular angle towers. The outer enclosure measured some 440 by 290 ft, and the inner one to its west 196 by 170 ft. The total area enclosed by the walls was over 8 acres—in other words, roughly twice the area of the equivalent area at contemporary Bodiam. On the south side of the outer courtyard was a massive gateway flanked by two semi-circular towers 40 ft high. Over the main archway of the gate Cobham placed an inscription which boasted of the castle's contribution to the cause of national defence:

---

[16] BL, Harley Ch. 48 E 43.   [17] *Westminster Chronicle*, 2.

[18] *CPR 1381–5*, 262. For a full discussion of the rebuilding of Rochester bridge, see Britnell, 'The New Bridge', 43–59.

[19] *CPR 1391–6*, 550; BL, MS Faustina C V, fos. 91ʳ–92ʳ (Rochester priory letter book).

[20] *CPR 1377–81*, 596.

[21] There is no proper survey of Cooling castle. However, there are brief descriptions in Jessup, *Kent*, 132–3; Newman, *West Kent and the Weald*, 231–2; W. N. Nichols, *Cooling, Kent, and its Castle* (Redhill, n.d.), 13. The important documentation for its building is calendared, and in the case of some documents printed, in D. Knoop, G. P. Jones, and N. B. Lewis, 'Some Building Activities of John, Lord Cobham', *Transactions Quattuor Coronati Lodge*, 45 (1935), 48–53; (without discussion) L. B. Larking, 'Cowling Castle', *AC*, 2 (1859), 95–102. Yevele was employed as consultant architect for the project: Harvey, *English Medieval Architects*, 361–2.

> Knouwyth that beth and schul be
> That I am mad in help of the cuntre
> In knowyng of whyche thyng
> Thys is chartre and wytnessyng.

Despite the claims of this doggerel, the castle in reality contributed nothing to national defence. The structure showed few, if any, of the characteristics of a coastal fort; the machicolations were decorative not functional; and on the southern side the site was overlooked by rising ground. It is doubtful if the castle could ever have withstood a siege. Cooling is best seen as a status symbol, a witness to the Cobhams' power in north Kent. It was a plaything, a 'castle of chivalry': the embodiment in stone of the knightly values that Lord Cobham lived by.

The projects which Lord Cobham initiated identify him as one of the most active and generous patrons of his day. No earlier member of the Cobham family had shown himself so energetic in commissioning works. Nor did any of his collateral kin initiate anything comparable. Reginald, 1st Lord Cobham, his kinsman, had built a splendid new castle for himself at Sterborough; but he appears to have built little else.[22] The impression left by the evidence is that the 3rd Lord was deliberately projecting himself: deliberately seeking to leave a mark on the world.

John's energy and drive are the more remarkable given the unhappy dynastic prospect which faced him. John was fated to be the last in his family's male line. He sired no son; or, at least, if he did, none survived. Until her death in the mid-1380s his heiress was his daughter, Joan, Lady de la Pole; after that, his granddaughter, another Joan. Thus at the time when he was most actively engaged in building, he would have known that he had no son to succeed him: the Cobham name would die out. There is no indication that he thought of settling the inheritance on any collateral males. By Cobham's lifetime it was becoming common for the nobility to settle their estates on their heirs male.[23] Yet Cobham never did so. When he levied a fine on his estates in 1396, he settled them in fee tail.[24] Implicitly he accepted his granddaughter's succession. Like a few others of his rank, he preferred an heir general to a distant heir male.[25]

The question thus arises: what could have been the reason for

---

[22] The tower of Lingfield church may possibly have been an exception. For the rebuilding of Sterborough, see above, 135.

[23] McFarlane, *Nobility of Later Medieval England*, 268–78.

[24] Nichols, 'Memorials of the Family of Cobham', 350–1.

[25] McFarlane, *Nobility of Later Medieval England*, 72–3.

Cobham's activity? Why was he willing to spend so freely when the future of his family looked so uncertain? There was little immediate gain to him; it was his granddaughter's husband who would be the ultimate beneficiary. But Cobham was not the only proprietor without a male heir to act in this way. Numerous others, of both rural and urban background, did the same. Richard Whittington in London, Geoffrey Massy in Cheshire, and John Fastolf in Norfolk are good examples.[26] All these men spent extravagantly on chantries, hospitals, and fine dwellings; Fastolf, as McFarlane showed, spent a whole fortune.[27] Ironically, it seems to have been childlessness itself which was the spur to activity. The reason was that it removed all the usual brakes on expenditure. Where there was a son and heir to inherit, the family capital had to be preserved intact. But where there was no son waiting to take over, the family paterfamilias could spend as he liked; he was unfettered. Lord Cobham found himself in just this position. He had no obligations to an adult son. He could spend to his heart's content; and he did. Indeed, there are signs that he spent excessively. The building of Cooling alone would have taxed his resources. Expenditure of at least £500 on the castle is recorded, and the total cost of the project could probably have been more than £1,000.[28] The annual value of the Cobham estates at the time was probably in the order of £300–400.[29] At the same time, he was paying for work on Cobham church, Rochester bridge, and St Dunstan-in-the-East, London. The signs are that he met the bills by drawing on some of his granddaughter's income.[30] Even so, there is evidence that he was overspending. In 1389 he made arrangements for the discharge of a debt of £400 to the Essex knight, Sir William Coggeshall;[31] and six years later he was paying off a debt of £500 to two Londoners, Hugh Sprot and Thomas Newington.[32] It is hardly surprising in the circumstances that the refurbishment of Cobham church was left unfinished at his death.[33]

None the less, it would be misleading to suggest that Cobham was acting in flagrant disregard of his granddaughter's interests. This was emphatically not the case. Cobham's attitude towards her seems to have been watchful and protective. His principal concern was to ensure that the memory of the Cobhams lived on. If the Cobham line were to die

[26] R. Davies, 'Religious Sensibility', in C. Given-Wilson (ed.), *An Illustrated History of Late Medieval England* (Manchester, 1996), 111.
[27] K. B. McFarlane, 'The Investment of Sir John Fastolf's Profits of War', *Transactions of the Royal Historical Society*, 5th series, 7 (1957).
[28] Knoop, Jones, and Lewis, 'Some Building Activities of John, Lord Cobham'.
[29] See below, Appendix.   [30] Ibid.   [31] BL, Harley Ch. 48 E 51.
[32] BL, Harley Ch. 48 F 5.   [33] See above, 54.

out, then at least there would be some physical witness to their fame. The family's greatness and wealth, their local power and influence, would be attested by an array of monuments—the machicolated gateway at Cooling, the brasses in Cobham church, the new aisle and south porch at St Dunstan's, and, most publicly of all, the bridge chapel at Rochester. These were buildings or monuments that would be a substitute for the family themselves. Cobham's instincts were ones which were very common among the wealthy childless of medieval England. From the next century there is the familiar example of Henry VI's treasurer, Ralph, Lord Cromwell. Lord Cromwell had no issue of his body at all. His coheiresses were distant collaterals who spent years fighting over his inheritance after his death. Yet he was a manic builder. He constructed the celebrated tower keep at Tattershall (Lincs.). He rebuilt the parish church at Tattershall. He spent huge sums on manor-houses at South Wingfield, Collyweston, and Lambley.[34] In essence, his outlook was the same as Cobham's: he used stonework to perpetuate his memory. While the name of Cromwell might vanish, the great buildings raised by the last of the name would ensure that it was never forgotten.

It is a truism of cultural history that the commissioning of prestige works can be indicative of anxiety.[35] At one level, the raising of great monuments can attest confidence, pride, and ambition; at another, it can betray insecurity and fear. In Cobham's case, the spur to activity was looming dynastic extinction. After two centuries the main line of the family was coming to an end. So the question arose: how were the family's name and identity to be preserved? Cobham's answer was through the witness of stone, latten, and glass: in other words, by building and refurbishing churches and commissioning monuments. If there was a touch of the Ozymandias in his strategy, then at least, unlike Shelley's king of Egypt, he had no reason to despair: it was a strategy that worked. Lord Cobham is remembered to this day.

But there was a second, and complementary, strand to Lord Cobham's schemes for his family. This was the 'reinvention' of the Cobham lineage. Cobham, while he was reconciled to the ending of his line, was anxious that his lineage's identity should live on in that of his successors; he

[34] M. W. Thompson, 'The Construction of the Manor at South Wingfield, Derbyshire', in G. de G. Sieveking *et al.* (eds.), *Problems in Economic and Social Archaeology* (London, 1976), 417–38; idem, *The Decline of the Castle* (Cambridge, 1987), 64–6, 87–91.

[35] In a medieval context M. Camille, *Mirror in Parchment: The Luttrell Psalter and the Making of Medieval England* (London, 1998) is particularly suggestive; ch. 2 interprets the famous feasting scene in the context of the economic hardship of the early fourteenth century.

wanted the new family to become, in a sense, like Cobhams themselves. The person through whom he intended to achieve this strategy was his granddaughter Joan; Joan was envisaged as a sort of bridge between the old world and the new. By the end of the 1380s, after the deaths first of her parents and then of her first husband, her grandfather had taken her under his wing. He brought her to live at Cobham. In 1391 he arranged for her to be remarried to the courtier knight, Sir Reginald Braybrooke. A few years afterwards, when he had retired to Maiden Bradley, he granted her and her husband residence at Cooling. In every way, he clothed the young lady in a Cobham identity; the de la Pole identity into which she had been born was replaced by a Cobham identity by adoption. When the old man died in 1408, she became the bearer and transmitter of the traditions of the Cobham lineage. In formal documents she invariably styled herself: 'Joan, Lady of Cobham' ('Johanna domina de Cobham').[36] It was this style which she employed on the brasses that she commissioned for her two husbands in c. 1408. And in 1434, after her death, it was this style which her daughter and son-in-law employed on the brass which they laid to her memory.[37]

Joan's later career was thus largely spent acting in a role chosen for her by her grandfather. The position in which she found herself was akin to that of many an aristocratic heiress before her—she was the bearer of a patrilineal discourse. Her own identity as a woman was virtually suppressed, while instead she was assigned that of a representative of the male lineage.[38] Among earlier heiresses who had found themselves in this role was Roesia de Verdun, heiress of the honor of Brandon (War.). In the early 1220s Roesia was married to a wealthy Shropshire magnate, Sir Theobald le Boteler. In normal circumstances, she would have assumed the title 'Lady Boteler'. Yet in defiance of custom, like Joan, she kept her earlier identity; she styled herself 'Roesia de Verdun'. Similarly in the 1190s Millicent, the sister of Sir Robert de Stafford III, became

[36] Nichols, 'Memorials of the Family of Cobham', 344.

[37] It could be added that Joan also accepted her grandfather's conception of himself. On the brasses which she commissioned to her two husbands, Braybrooke and Hawberk, she described herself as 'heir of Sir John de Cobham, founder of this college'. It was as 'founder of the college' that John was most anxious to present himself: see above, 98.

[38] Other Cobham women appear to have acted, whether consciously or unconsciously, as representatives of the male lineage. An obvious example is Joan, the widow of Reginald, 1st Lord Cobham of Sterborough. Joan and her Berkeley kin were almost certainly responsible for commissioning Reginald's tomb at Lingfield: see above, 151. In that capacity they must have had some influence on the choice of heraldry. Yet that heraldry affords a perfect image of Reginald's own world. It is virtually impossible to establish where Reginald's influence on the tomb ended and his widow's began.

bearer of the Stafford name after her brother's death without issue. When she married the local knight Sir Hervey Bagot, the latter adopted his wife's Stafford name and it was as Staffords that his descendants were known.[39] Cases of this sort were not uncommon. Generally when a man married an heiress from a more distinguished family, it was the latter's identity which triumphed and the latter's surname which passed to succeeding generations. Thus, in Joan, Lady Cobham's, case it was the Cobham identity which triumphed over the de la Pole because the Cobhams were the more distinguished dynasty. But in the next generation, interestingly, the honours were evenly balanced. The Brookes, into whom Joan's daughter married, had never received parliamentary summonses, as the Cobhams had; none the less, their estates more than matched those of the Cobhams in size. So on this occasion it was the Brooke surname which was adopted—while, to balance it, the Cobham name was used for the peerage title. The younger Joan's son, the first of the new line, called himself Edward Brooke, Lord Cobham—an elegant compromise between the claims of the two dynasties.

The Cobhams' brasses at Cobham bear vivid witness to the family's dynastic crisis in the fifteenth century. In the centre of the front row lies the brass of Joan the family heiress, with its dazzling array of Cobham, de la Pole, and Braybrooke heraldry celebrating the descent and connections of the Cobham family. To right and left of it lie the brasses, which Joan herself commissioned, of two of her husbands, with the diminutive figures of the three boys who died young but who, had they survived, would have carried forward the Cobham identity. In this magnificent set of brasses we feel something of the pain caused by dynastic failure. But what is interesting is that in all sorts of ways the severity of the disruption is glossed over. On the husbands' epitaphs Joan's Cobham identity is stressed: she is styled 'Joan, Lady of Cobham'. On her own brass the series of arms draws attention to her place in the family's line of descent; the present and the past are linked as in a seamless web. Most remarkably of all, the little groups of children at her feet depict her as the fecund matriarch, the bridge between the present and the future. This carefully selected group of images was intended to convey the continuing strength

---

[39] For these examples see Coss, *Lady in Medieval England*, 12. Cf. the case of the Bodrugans, a Cornish family. The main line of the Bodrugans ended in the mid-fourteenth century in the person of Joan, the family heiress. Joan married twice. On the death of her second husband, Ralph Trenoweth, *c*.1376, Joan resumed the Bodrugan surname and transmitted it to her children. Thus the Bodrugan line was reborn (J. Whetter, *Cornish People in the Fifteenth Century*, Gorran, 1999, 20–1).

of the lineage: to imply the onward march of the Cobhams across the generations. The message of Joan's brass was powerfully reinforced by the earlier monuments in the church. In the side aisles, and stretching across the chancel, were the memorials of Joan's forebears. The presence of these monuments was witness to the hundreds of years that the Cobhams had lived at Cobham. It bore witness to the almost mystical union of family and place that was the essence of the medieval idea of lineage. There was a sense in which every monument at Cobham made a claim of sorts about lineage. Easily the most brazen in its claims was Joan's. On this memorial, every possible device was used to emphasize continuity and gloss over the transition from the old world to the new. Even so, there was no concealing the seriousness of the break that had occurred. Joan's death in 1434 marked the end of an era. With ironic appropriateness, that break was marked by a long gap in the laying of brasses. No memorials to the Brookes were to be laid at Cobham for some seventy years. More than anything else, it is this hiatus that gives the lie to the carefully managed fictions of continuity.

If a crisis of lineage is the main theme which emerges from a study of the brasses at Cobham, a very different one emerges from a study of the contemporary tombs and brasses at Lingfield. The brasses and monuments at Lingfield again form a superb series. They dominate the chancel and side chapels. The tomb of Reginald III in the chancel is particularly showy; it virtually blocks the view to the altar. But the monuments at Lingfield exhibit little of the homogeneity of those at Cobham. At Cobham a consistent commemorative style was espoused. Every member of the family was commemorated by a brass;[40] and the brasses were all of the same design. But this was not the case at Lingfield. The Cobhams of Sterborough showed far greater variety of taste. Some of them commissioned stone or alabaster effigies, and some brasses; some chose tomb chests, while others did not. There is a sense that a broader range of influences was brought to bear than at Cobham.

Yet for all their obvious variety, the monuments at Lingfield convey a very clear message. The Cobhams of Sterborough were worried about status. Unlike their collateral kin, they did not bother themselves greatly about continuity; they kept going in the male line for nearly a century longer. But they were deeply perturbed about their social standing.

---

[40] Or at least every member of the family after 1300 was—allowing for the possibility that the cross slabs commemorate early Cobhams: see above, 81.

Reginald, Lord Cobham, Edward III's counsellor and friend, had done particularly well for himself. He had been summoned to parliament as a peer. His son, early on in his career, had likewise received summonses. But from 1372, the parliamentary summonses stopped. No later member of the family was to be honoured in this way. The family had lost its claim to nobility. Henceforth, they were to be counted gentry and not lords—very grand gentry certainly, but gentry none the less.

The Cobhams' preoccupation with status can be observed in the character of their monuments. The more rapidly the pace of decline accelerated, the grander the family's monuments became. The first tomb in the series—that of Reginald, the 1st Lord—was a relatively straightforward job, notable chiefly for its heraldry. The tomb of the 2nd Lord was a product of similar design—a mainstream London monument with a fine effigy and heraldry; but this time the epitaph made play of the subject's noble attributes. In the later monuments the level of elaboration increased. Eleanor, the first wife of Reginald III, was commemorated by a brass of exceptional delicacy and splendour. Not only is heraldry again prominent; for the first time a canopy was included. An appropriate climax was reached with Reginald's own monument of 1446—a bombastic commission, centre-stage in the chancel, which dominates its surroundings. These later monuments—and Reginald III's in particular—were conceived essentially as status symbols. They were affirmations of hierarchy in the face of the realities of decline.

The family's preoccupation with status shows in the monuments in other ways. It is interesting, for example, that on Eleanor's brass a banner was included in the composition. Banners are relatively rare on brasses. The banner—the rectangular banner—was a mark of military status: it denoted the higher of the two ranks of knighthood—banneret rank as opposed to that of bachelor. Technically, the Cobhams of Sterborough were knights banneret. The distinction was important to them—for while they may have lost their place in the peerage, at least they had the consolation of this lesser honour to cherish. In general, it is noticeable how prominently heraldry figures on the monuments at Lingfield. The tomb chests of both the first and the third Reginalds have rich armorials on their sides. Such dazzling displays served to convey an image of Cobham power—for, in a sense, the family's importance could be measured in the importance of those with whom they were associated. It is noticeable, too, how descent from the 'founder', the 1st Lord, is emphasized in the later tombs. Features of the 'founder's' tomb are picked up on the later ones—the use of heraldry on the side panels, for example, and the placing of an embattled edge round the top. Selective quotation from the 'founder's' tomb could help both to associate his descendants with his greatness and to gloss over the grim reality of their decline.

A study of the monuments at Cobham and Lingfield is thus indicative of the anxieties and concerns of the two lineages commemorated. In the case of the senior line at Cobham the biggest source of concern was the prospect of dynastic extinction. In the case of their kinsfolk at Sterborough it was the ignominy of social decline. For each family the evidence of anxieties is to be found in the design and detailing of the monuments. Visual display was used as a means to smooth over or to conceal the pains of transition.

Unfortunately, it is hard to go into such detail about the concerns and preoccupations of the other branches of the family. There are simply too few monuments to analyse. The tombs of the most senior collateral line, the Cobhams of Randall, with one exception have been lost, while those of the Cobhams of Beluncle and Chafford number a mere handful each. The indications, however, are that these other lineages had a less distinct commemorative identity than their kinsfolk. Probably only the Cobhams of Randall established a mausoleum of their own—at Boxley priory near Maidstone. Members of other branches tended to seek burial at Cobham. Sir Thomas Cobham of Beluncle, Maud, Lady Cobham of Randall, and Ralph Cobham of Chafford were all buried at Cobham in the lifetime of the 3rd Lord. Only after the extinction of the senior line did new burial patterns in the family emerge. The presence of so many Cobham brasses at Cobham affords a powerful witness to the clannishness which was the Cobhams' hallmark.

When focusing so strongly on the secular aspects of commemoration it is easy to form the impression that secular concerns provided the main spur to funerary commemoration. Sometimes this was the case, but not always. An equal or stronger motivation is likely to have been the deceased's fear of the terrors to come. The growing popularity of monuments in the late Middle Ages was closely linked to official recognition of the doctrine of purgatory. By 1215 it was recognized by the Church that the sufferings of the soul could be eased by the prayers of the living. In consequence, it became common for people to think of commissioning monuments as stimuli to prayer. Commonly, chantries, monuments, and bede rolls were deployed together in a holistic strategy for the afterlife. The need to elicit prayer exerted a major influence on the design of monuments. On tomb effigies the deceased was generally shown with his or her hands at prayer, while on epitaphs the words 'pray for the soul of . . .' or 'on whose soul may God have mercy' were rarely, if ever, absent. We have seen that on the grander monuments of the period the emphasis on prayer was heavily overlain with secular imagery; but rarely was it lost sight of altogether. In Western Christendom the dying were never forgetful of their dependence on the prayers of the living.

On few series of medieval monuments is the theme of the afterlife more evident than on those of the Cobhams. On the earliest surviving brass at Cobham, that of Joan de Cobham, a pardon is offered as a reward for prayer.[41] On many of the later brasses, which flank Joan's, appeals for prayer figure prominently in the epitaphs. On the brasses ordered by the 'founder' there are anguished appeals for prayer, while strikingly on the brass of Reginald, the clerical member of the family, the words 'Orate pro anima . . .' are engraved on the cross shaft in which his effigy is shown. The same preoccupation with prayer is found on brasses to members of the family elsewhere. At Chrishall one of the three remaining words of the epitaph is appropriately 'priez', while at St Mary Overy, Southwark, the epitaph on Joan Cobham's brass consisted simply of a stark appeal for prayers—with above it, in the place usually occupied by a figure, the cross—the symbol of redemption.

The other-worldly preoccupation of these epitaphs directly mirrors the preoccupations of the Cobhams' wills. In almost every will from the family we find the same overriding concern with intercession. Joan Cobham of Sterborough was probably more emphatic than most when she directed her executors: 'Before everything else after my decease, 7,000 masses are to be celebrated for my soul, and these on no account to be delayed.'[42] None the less, her prodigious appetite for masses was one shared by the majority of her kinfolk. Sir William Cobham of Gatwick, by no means the wealthiest of the clan, provided for as many as 5,000 masses in his will of 1375.[43] Thirty years later, his kinsman Ralph Cobham of Chafford provided for an unspecified number of masses to be celebrated in no fewer than three churches—Higham priory, Cobham college, and a church in London.[44] In 1400 his wealthier and more distinguished relative Reginald, Lord Cobham of Sterborough, made the

---

[41] Offers of pardon are not uncommon on brasses and monuments of the early fourteenth century. Other examples are found at Edvin Ralph (Herefs.), St Buryan (Cornwall), Winchester Cathedral, and elsewhere: Marshall, 'The Church of Edvin Ralph and Some Notes on Pardon Monuments', 40–55. Later they became rarer, but enjoyed renewed popularity on the eve of the Reformation.

[42] Flower, 'Notices of the Family of Cobham of Sterborough', 169.

[43] Lambeth Palace Library, Register of Archbishop Arundel, i, fo. 226ʳ.

[44] PRO, Reg. Marche: PROB 11/2A, fo. 21ʳ.

grandest provision of all: he set aside 100 marks for his funeral and the celebration of his anniversary day, and then another £30 for the singing of 10,000 masses for his soul as soon as possible after his death.[45] His contemporary, the affluent esquire John Cobham of Hever, was equally lavish in his planning. John's will provided for £30 to be spent on his funeral and another £20 on 10,000 masses and 30 trentals of St Gregory.[46] The evidence of these wills illustrates very clearly the role which brasses played in strategies for the afterlife. The commissioning of brasses and the endowment of masses and chantries went together. The brass was a reminder to the living of their obligations to the dead: it was an *aide-mémoire* to prayer. The original meaning of 'commemoration' had been regular remembrance in prayer; only later did it come to describe the laying of a memorial. The extension of meaning was one which arose directly from the overlap of function.

A final question that needs to be considered is: how far can the Cobhams' interest in memorials be fitted into the history of gentry culture more generally? Were the members of the Cobham clan broadly representative of their class in the manner and scale of their commemoration?

There can be little doubt that much in the Cobhams' experience was by and large typical. By the late fourteenth century, many gentry families were creating mausoleums in their local churches. The Astleys were doing so at Astley (Warks.), the de la Beches at Aldworth (Berks.), the Etchinghams at Etchingham (Sussex), the Malyns at Chinnor (Oxon.), the Bovilles and Wingfields at Letheringham (Suffolk), and many other families elsewhere. However, it seems likely that the Cobhams stood in the forefront of this movement. For most of the fourteenth century the burial of high-status laity in parochial chancels was uncommon. The place where such people were usually buried was a side aisle or transept. However, in the later decades of the century attitudes began to change. The Cobhams' dramatic take-over of the chancel at Cobham hints at the more proprietorial attitude that was to come.

Creation of these family mausoleums points to the gentry's greatly increased self-awareness. In the century or two after the Norman Conquest, these knightly folk had lived in the shadow of their feudal overlords. The social and political world in which they moved was

---

[45] Flower, 'Notices of the Family of Cobham of Sterborough', 184.
[46] *House of Commons*, ii, 608.

principally that of the feudal honor. Many of them chose burial along-side their overlords in the honorial monastery. By the beginning of the thirteenth century, however, with the decline of the honor and the weak-ening of feudal ties, these people started to develop an outlook and an identity of their own. Increasingly the manor, their principal place of residence, became the focus of their attentions; and in many cases they assumed its name. At the same time, with the narrowing of the definition of kin, their consciousness of their lineage increased; and lineage was closely identified with the uninterrupted possession of a landed estate. In this strongly manor-centred world, the parish church came to occupy for them the role which the monasteries had long performed for the nobility. The parish church was simultaneously an extension and an expression of family power: it was a symbol of lordship; and the tombs and brasses which lined its side aisles and chapels affirmed the historicity of the family's lineage. The attitude of proprietorship which the gentry evinced had its origins in the late Anglo-Saxon period. In the tenth and eleventh centuries thegns and ealdormen, acting in similarly proprietorial way, had built what were to be the first parish churches; and they had built them very largely for their own use. After the Conquest, in the age of monastic expansion, there was a shift of resources into the building and endowment of monasteries. By the second or third quarter of the thir-teenth century, however, this latter era was passing. Monastic founda-tions were becoming fewer, and the flow of land to monasteries was in decline. The attentions of the knightly class gradually returned to the parish churches. For a 'newish' family like the Cobhams identification with a parish church came naturally.[47]

But if in a number of respects the experience of the Cobhams was typical, in others it was much less so. What seems without parallel is the sheer number of memorials which the Cobhams commissioned. Some-thing over two dozen memorials to members of the family have come down to us—a dozen at Cobham itself and the rest elsewhere. A number of other families commissioned large numbers of memorials scattered across several churches—the examples of the Bedingfields and the Berneys in East Anglia come to mind; but none did so on quite the scale

---

[47] For discussion of these themes, see Saul, *Scenes From Provincial Life*, ch. 5; P. Morgan, 'Making the English Gentry', in P. R. Coss and S. D. Lloyd (eds.), *Thirteenth Century England, V* (Woodbridge, 1995), 21–8. R. H. Bloch, *Etymologies and Genealogies: A Literary Anthropology of the French Middle Ages* (Chicago, 1983), ch. 2; R. Morris, *Churches in the Landscape* (London, 1989), 248–9. It is possible that church and manor-house originally stood together at Cobham; for this suggestion, see above, 38.

of the Cobhams. Moreover, the sheer concentration of memorials in one church—Cobham itself—stands out. It is true that other parish or collegiate churches can show fine series of tombs. For example, there are the magnificent series to the FitzAlans at Arundel, and to the Gascoignes and the Redmans at Harewood. But the FitzAlans were a family of baronial, and later comital, rank; and the number of monuments at Harewood is considerably inferior to that at Cobham. Among gentry mausoleums Cobham is unique.

This aspect of the Cobhams' experience obviously calls for explanation. The reason is essentially to be found in one of the Cobhams' strongest characteristics—their clannishness. Until the early fifteenth century the Cobhams were a highly prolific brood. In each generation they produced a number of cadets—sometimes three or four or more. Normally, under the rules of primogeniture the heir would have succeeded to everything and the cadets would have fallen in status. But under the system of gavelkind that operated in Kent it was usual for the lands to be shared. Moreover, a number of the Cobham cadets married well: John 'the younger's' brother and half-brother, for example, both married heiresses; and by the end of the fourteenth century junior branches of the family were established all over west Kent and east Surrey—indeed, further afield too, for example in Devon.[48] Several of these people were buried and commemorated in churches near their seats. Yet a number of them were interred in the 'mother' church at Cobham. The family's sense both of a common ancestry and a shared identity was strong. Kin solidarity showed in a number of ways. One such was their readiness to assist each other in business matters. But another, hardly less striking, was their acceptance of a uniform commemorative style at Cobham. When the 3rd Lord set the fashion for laying brasses at Cobham, they all went along with it. There is none of the stylistic individualism which we encounter at Lingfield.

If the sheer number of the Cobham brasses is striking, so too is the richness of their textual and figurative repertory. Generally in the half-century or so after the Black Death there was a trend to simplicity—even austerity—in brass design. Effigial brasses were drawn with almost cheese-paring economy, and much less interest than before was shown in elaborate canopied surrounds. But the richer of the Cobham brasses constitute something of an exception to this trend. On a number of the brasses the repertory is extended. Three or four of them, for

---

[48] There was a branch of the family at Blackborough, near Cullompton.

example, draw on religious imagery. The Virgin and Child are shown on the brasses of the 3rd Lord and his wife; the Trinity is shown on Braybrooke's, and the Trinity, the Virgin and Child, and St George on Hawberk's. Several of the marginal epitaphs are sharply divergent from the contemporary norms. Those on the brasses commissioned by the 3rd Lord are particularly distinctive. But most remarkable of all is the interest shown in children. The depiction of offspring on monuments was still fairly rare in the early 1400s. However, on Braybrooke's brass there are the two little figures for his sons, and on Hawberk's the one for his own son, while on Joan Cobham's brass of 1434 there is a group each of boys and girls. How is the inclusion of these features to be explained?

In general terms, the character of memorials underwent a change in the late Middle Ages. As Binski has argued, there was a gradual recovery of a sense of the person commemorated.[49] In the early medieval period the narrative of the person, which had been central to Roman commemoration, had been erased, and instead the emphasis was placed increasingly on the theme of salvation. In the wake of the twelfth-century renaissance, however, there was something of a shift back. By the later twelfth century sculptors were showing a new interest in effigial art, and through the medium of the effigy the dead were given a voice. In the thirteenth century this interest in effigies grew stronger, becoming more complex as it did so. To some extent, what was involved was a growing 'individualism'; none the less, it was an individualism with clear limits. The deceased was never seen as a unique human being, but much more as a socially and culturally constructed entity. Image and text were geared to positioning his person within a system: and that system was the set of strategies for the afterlife which implicated both the living and the dead in a relationship of mutual obligation.

This shift in the character of the memorial forms the background to the expansion in the emblematic range which is so noticeable on memorials of the later Middle Ages. Narrative epitaphs, votive scrolls, representations of saints, and the whole repertory of heraldic and bastard feudal insignia were deployed in the twin tasks of locating the deceased in this world and involving the spectator in assisting him in the afterlife. The visual enrichment found on the brasses at Cobham may be seen in the context of these developments. In particular, the inclusion of saints and the growing length of epitaphs reflect the positioning of the brass at the centre of a complex and wide-ranging religious discourse.

[49] P. Binski, *Medieval Death: Ritual and Representation* (London, 1996), 92–111.

The changing character of the brass and the enlargement of the range of motifs allowed clients a new opportunity to shape memorials in their image, and to make them a witness to their concerns and preoccupations. Evidence of this phenomenon is found in the increasing tendency for memorials to be used to convey secular as well as religious messages. The series of monuments to the Cobhams illustrates the point clearly. On the brasses and monuments at Lingfield the emphasis is placed on marks of status—shields of arms, banners, and crests or emblems like the Moor's head: anything, indeed, that could associate the family with the greatness won for it by the 1st Lord. At Cobham itself, on the other hand, the emphasis was placed on symbols of continuity—hence the decidedly avant-garde interest in the depiction of children. In the longer term, the depiction of children on memorials was to herald a fundamental shift in their character. Instead of being, as they had been, largely retrospective, they became prospective: anticipatory; future generations were to be honoured as well as generations past. But the reason for their inclusion on the brasses at Cobham was less general than particular. The Cobhams were facing the ultimate disappointment for a gentry family—extinction in the male line. John, the 3rd Lord, so successful in many other respects, failed as a dynast; he had no son to succeed him. The solution which he and his granddaughter conceived was to make the latter the bearer of the family's identity. Accordingly, on the early fifteenth-century memorials she is shown as the symbol of continuity. On her husbands' epitaphs she is referred to as 'the lady of Cobham', while on her own brass she is shown with a bevy of boys and girls at her feet—attesting the triumph of hope over reality.

On first inspection, the splendid memorials to the Cobhams at Cobham and Lingfield appear witnesses to the confidence and the well-being of the two families. These are memorials on the very grandest scale; and many of them are superb examples of the engraver's art. Yet beneath the surface there lurks a story of failure—in the case of the one family, genetic failure; and in the case of the other, reaction to the loss of status. If evidence is sought for the view that display can be a reaction to failure, it can be found here. These mighty memorials capture in their imagery not only—as would be expected—the Cobhams' strategy for the salvation of their souls but also their fears and anxieties concerning the all-too-transient glories of this world.

APPENDIX

The Estates of the Cobhams

THE evidence relating to the Cobhams' estates is disappointingly thin. There are no continuous runs of manorial accounts. The most valuable material is to be found in the Harleian collection in the British Library. Here there are accounts for the manors of Cobham for 1290–1 and Hinton (Wilts.) for 1310–11, and some views of account for the de la Pole estates.[1] This material apart, we have to rely chiefly on Botevile's history of the family, the feet of fines, and that indispensable resource of the medievalist, the inquisitions post mortem.

The most useful source for the early landholdings of the family is Francis Botevile's history, written in the 1580s. According to Botevile, the founder of the family, Henry de Cobham, bought the manor of Cobham, with lands in Shorne, from Sir William Quatremere, a knight of Henry II's. A decade or two later, his son and heir John acquired the neighbouring manor of Cooling.[2] These two manors were to constitute the core of the family's inheritance. From other sources we learn of further acquisitions made by the family at this time. According to Hasted, Henry acquired the manor of Aldington (or Addington), in Thurnham, across the River Medway near Maidstone.[3] Again according to Hasted, John 'the elder', Henry's son, acquired the manor of West Chalk near Gravesend by his marriage to his second wife, Joan Neville.[4] John's brothers Reginald and William both appear to have been very active in the land market. In 1246, according to a fine, Reginald acquired the manor of Beluncle, in Hoo St Werburgh, while at roughly the same time his younger brother William acquired that of East Shelve, in Lenham, near Maidstone.[5]

---

[1] BL, Harley Rolls D 1; G 34.

[2] Holinshed, *Chronicles*, iv, 778–9. Henry de Cobham held Cobham as Quatremere's tenant; in 1222 it was Quatremere's heir, another William, who paid relief on the fee to the king: *The Great Roll of the Pipe for the Sixth Year of the Reign of King Henry III, Michaelmas 1222*, ed. G. A. Knight (Pipe Roll Society, new series, 51; 1999), 63.

[3] Hasted, *History of Kent*, v, 525. The family's connection with this place is recalled by Cobham Manor, between Thurnham and Hollingbourne.

[4] Hasted, *History of Kent*, iii, 459–60.

[5] Ibid. iv, 8–9; v, 435. Reginald and William both died without surviving issue. The lands of both brothers therefore reverted to the main line of the family. East Shelve was later to pass to the Cobhams of Sterborough, and Beluncle to the junior line which had its seat there.

A generation later the family acquired its first block of lands outside the south-east. Around 1278 John 'the younger', the Exchequer baron, purchased a block of manors in north Wiltshire from Sir Michael de Columbers. These were the manors of Bincknoll, Broad Hinton, Beckhampton, and Clyffe Pypard.[6] Around the same time, a marriage was arranged between John's son and heir, Henry, and Maud de Columbers, as a result of which Chisbury, also in Wiltshire, came to the family.[7] It is likely that John simultaneously acquired the manor of Sidling in Dorset, although no mention of it is made in the conveyancing. Sidling was another Columbers manor and it is later found descending with the Cobham manors.[8]

In John's lifetime the pace of expansion was kept up in Kent and the south-east. A major factor in the family's advance was a series of good marriages. The first of these was Henry de Cobham of Randall's marriage to Joan, one of the Penchester coheiresses. The Penchesters were a major landowning family in west Kent and had wide estates in the Weald around Penshurst. On the death of Joan's father, Sir Stephen de Penchester, in 1298 Henry inherited half of his estates—principally, the manors of Allington, Tunstall, Hever, and Elmley.[9] It was this block of lands which formed the core of the inheritance of the Cobhams of Randall. Three generations later, another good marriage brought further additions to this line's inheritance. Sir Thomas Cobham of Randall won the hand of Maud, the daughter of Thomas Morice, a wealthy pleader of London and the common serjeant. Maud brought with her property at Wrotham, Trottiscliffe, and elsewhere in Kent and rents and messuages in Middlesex.[10] In 1394 her son, Reginatd, exchanged the Middlesex lands for the manor of Milton, near Gravesend.[11]

A sub-branch of the Cobhams of Randall was the family of Cobham of Chafford. Thomas, the founder of this branch, was the youngest of the four sons of Sir Henry de Cobham of Randall.[12] His original estate was at Chafford, near Penshurst,[13] but like his father he quickly added to his lands by marriage.

---

[6] *CPR 1281–92*, 178; and see above, 17.   [7] *CPR 1281–92.*

[8] *CCR 1279–88*, 161; J. Hutchins, *The History and Antiquities of the County of Dorset* (4 vols.; London, 1861–70), iv, 502. John, 2nd Lord Cobham, was to settle the property on his son: Nichols, 'Memorials of the Family of Cobham', 323.

[9] Moor, *Knights of Edward I*, iv, 32–5; Bellewes, 'The Cobhams and Moresbys of Rundale and Allington', 154–5. The manor of Hever, near Chiddingstone, is not mentioned in the division but is likely to have come to the family at this time. By the 1330s the family also held the manor of Mayton in Sturry. It is unclear, however, from whom the manor was acquired: Hasted, *History of Kent*, ix, 80. Henry, founder of the line, is commemorated by a tomb in Shorne church, near Cobham. Randall was a manor in Shorne.

[10] *House of Commons*, ii, 609. It is this Maud who is commemorated by M.S. VI at Cobham.

[11] Bellewes, 'Cobhams of Rundale', 157.

[12] Society of Antiquaries MS 728/3, fos. 18ʳ–19ᵛ.

[13] Chafford is at the southern end of the parish of Penshurst. It probably came to the Cobhams of Randall as part of the Penchester inheritance, but it does not figure in the list of manors in Sir Stephen's inquisition post mortem. Hasted does not give a descent of the property (Hasted, *History of Kent*, iii, 250–1).

His wife, Elizabeth, was the daughter and heiress of John de Gatwick, and through her he acquired the manors of Gatwick in Charlwood (Surrey) and—apparently—of Wickham, near Steyning (Sussex).[14] These properties were divided in the next generation between Thomas's sons William and Ralph—the latter occupying Chafford.[15] But on Ralph's death without issue they were brought together again and passed down through the Gatwick line of the family.

Shortly after Henry de Cobham of Randall snapped up the Penchester heiress, another junior member of the family secured for himself a good marriage. On the Kent–Surrey border the Cobhams had a well-to-do tenant, William de Hever of Prinkham.[16] William's heirs were his two daughters. John claimed one of the daughters for his half-brother, William, and the other for his younger half-brother, Reginald.[17] William was to die childless in 1321, with the result that his younger brother inherited both shares.[18] The inheritance was a considerable one. There were five manors: East Shelve and Broadfield in Lenham, Aston Lodge in Eynsford, and Chiddingstone, all in Kent, and Prinkham, later renamed Sterborough (Surrey).[19] This group of manors formed the core endowment of the family of Cobham of Sterborough.

In the early fourteenth century a third junior member of the family assembled a sizeable—though in his case an impermanent—estate for himself. This was Ralph de Cobham, the youngest of the six sons of Sir John 'the younger'. Ralph enjoyed a highly successful career in magnate service. Around 1310 he came to the notice of a lord with wide estates locally, John de Warenne, earl of Surrey, and he became one of the earl's leading intimates.[20] According to the inquisition taken on his death, Ralph held the manors of Tyburn (Middlesex), Langney (Sussex), Medmenham (Bucks.), Ardington (Berks.), Thetford (Norfolk), and various other lands.[21] However, he transmitted very few of these properties to his son, for he held most of them as a life tenant of the earl. The son was to die in 1378 without issue.[22] For all the superficial brilliance of his career, Ralph brought no permanent gains to his family.

In the mid- to late fourteenth century the Cobhams' estates expanded more slowly. Only one branch of the family substantially added to their lands, and that was the Cobhams of Sterborough. The original lands of the Sterborough branch were already extensive. However, Reginald, in his mid-century heyday,

---

[14] *VCH Surrey*, iii, 184; *VCH Sussex*, vi, i, 230; Nichols, 'Memorials of the Family of Cobham', 347.

[15] Ralph Cobham of Chafford (d. 1402) is commemorated by M.S. IX at Cobham.

[16] William took his name from the manor of Hever in Kingsdown, not from the better-known Hever near Edenbridge: Hasted, *History of Kent*, ii, 481.

[17] See above, 123.   [18] *CIPM*, vi, no. 260.   [19] Ibid.; *VCH Surrey*, iv, 304.

[20] The Warennes held the lordship of Reigate (Surrey), which on the earl's death passed to the Fitzalan earls of Arundel.   [21] *CIPM*, vi, no. 703.

[22] This was John, 'son of the Countess Marshal', who died in 1378, so called because his mother took as her second husband Thomas of Brotherton, earl of Norfolk, the earl marshal: *Complete Peerage*, ix, 598. For his place of burial, see above, 24 n. 79.

greatly added to them. Marriage again played a role. Reginald's well-born wife Joan, daughter of Thomas, Lord Berkeley, brought him the reversion of the manor of Langley Burrell (Wilts.). Additionally, his years of service to the crown brought him the odd manor or two in lieu of fees: West Cliff, near Dover, came to him this way.[23] But, more than anything else, the profits of war gave him the means to buy land: Oxted (Surrey) was probably the most valuable of his purchases. By the time of his death in 1361 Reginald's inheritance had doubled in size. It consisted of the manors of Oxted and Sterborough (Surrey), Hever in Hoo, East Shelve, Bowzell, Aldington, Hiltesbury and Austin in Eynsford (Kent), Northeye (Sussex), and Leigh Delamare and Langley Burrell (Wilts.).[24] Reginald's son and successor, Reginald II, made further, albeit temporary, additions to the inheritance. By his second marriage to Eleanor, daughter and coheiress of John, Lord Maltravers, and widow of Sir John Arundel, he acquired a life interest in a string of manors in the south and west of England—Sherrington, Codford, Boyton, Corton, Winterbourne Stoke, Coate, Elston, Stapleford, Hill Deverill, and Great Somerford (Wilts.), Morden, Witchampton, Philipston, Wimborne St Giles, Loders, Worth Maltravers, Lytchett Maltravers, and Langton Maltravers (Dorset), Stonehouse (Gloucs.) and Cucklington and Stoke Trister (Som.), all from the Maltravers inheritance, and thirds of Aynho (Northants.) and Old Shoreham, Cudlow, and Chancton (Sussex) from the Arundel estates.[25] These properties, however, were all lost to the family on Eleanor's death, for she had a son by her first marriage (to John Arundel). Even so, in the fifteenth century the Cobhams of Sterborough were much the richest of the collateral lines. The inquisition on Thomas, the last of his line, listed him as holding in Kent alone manors at Austin in Eynsford, Chiddingstone, West Cliff, East Shelve and Broadfield, Hiltesbury, Sharnden and Hoo; and to these should be added his properties in other counties.[26]

The holdings of the parent branch of the family at Cobham, by contrast, underwent very little change in the fourteenth century. The family picked up no more than one or two properties. Shortly before 1300 John Cobham 'the younger' acquired the manor of Beckley in north Kent: this appears in his inquisition post mortem of 1300.[27] A little later, either he or his son Henry acquired that of Bekesbourne, near Canterbury.[28] Some time after that, either Henry or John, the 2nd Lord, picked up the small manor of Stanpit in Sheppey.[29] But there were losses to be set against these gains. In 1363, for

---

[23] See above, 134.   [24] *CIPM*, xi, no. 59.   [25] Ibid. xviii, no. 760.

[26] *Calendarium Inquisitionum Post Mortem sive Escaetarum*, iv (London, 1828).

[27] *CIPM*, iii, no. 602.

[28] The earliest reference to the family's possession of Bekesbourne comes in an enfeoffment of 1331: Nichols, 'Memorials of the Family of Cobham', 342.

[29] BL, Harley Ch. 48 E 36: an enfeoffment of the manors of Cobham and Stanpit (or Stonepit?). It is possible that the manor came to the family by the marriage of John, 2nd Lord, to Agnes, daughter of Richard Stone of Dartford: BL, Harley Ch. 52 I 29.

example, the 3rd Lord handed over the manor of West Chalk to his newly founded college at Cobham; and by 1372 the manor of Broad Hinton (Wilts.) appears to have been sold.[30]

At its greatest extent the Cobham estate stretched to roughly a dozen manors and other properties—the manors of Cobham itself, Cooling, Beckley, West Chalk, Beluncle, Stone, and Bekesbourne, all in Kent, Sidling in Dorset, Broad Hinton, Bincknoll, Chisbury, Clyffe Pypard, and Beckhampton all in Wiltshire, various other lands in Kent, some tenements in London, the lordship of Shamel hundred in Kent, and the advowson of Worplesdon (Surrey). For a family aspiring to baronial rank this estate hardly constituted an ample endowment. Most late-medieval baronial estates were much larger.[31] Even at its greatest extent it represented the bare minimum needed to sustain a lord in his dignity. However, at intervals it shrank as manors were hived off onto younger sons. In the 1290s, for example, John Cobham 'the younger' granted Clyffe Pypard to his third son, Roger. On Roger's death the manor reverted to John's son and heir, Henry, but was then quickly granted out again to another younger son, Thomas, the founder of the Cobhams of Beluncle; and members of the Beluncle line appear to have been tenants of the manor for most of the century.[32] In 1315 Henry demised another of his Wiltshire properties—Broad Hinton—for life to his son and heir, John, although twenty years later the property rejoined the rest of the estate when John succeeded his father.[33] West Chalk (Kent) was also demised for a time. In 1333 Henry granted the manor to one of his younger sons, Thomas;[34] at some stage it was reunited with the main family lands; and then in 1363 it was alienated to the college.

In view both of their limited means and their obvious desire to provide for their younger kin, it is scarcely surprising to find the Cobhams periodically slipping into debt. There is evidence of this in the early fourteenth century. In 1344 John, the 2nd Lord, was obliged to demise his manor of West Chalk to the Londoner, Andrew Aubrey, for sixteen years to pay off a debt of £300.[35] Later in the century, when the 3rd Lord embarked on his building campaign, pledging and borrowing became more common. In 1384 Lord Cobham made an arrangement to pay off half of a debt of £200 to Sir Robert Knolles.[36] Twelve years later he negotiated an agreement with two London merchants for the repayment of a debt of £500.[37] It is tempting to wonder how, or how far, the family's problems of indebtedness affected their standing in the peerage. It may be that the 2nd Lord's uncertain finances contributed to the irregularity of his summons to parliament. Yet the 3rd Lord, whose finances were more uncertain still, was regularly summoned for some forty years. There is little evidence that

---

[30] *VCH Wiltshire*, xii, 110.
[31] Cf. e.g. the estates of the Maltravers and the Badlesmeres: above, 140, 161, 254.
[32] *VCH Wiltshire*, ix, 27–8.   [33] Nichols, 'Memorials of the Family of Cobham', 322.
[34] Ibid. 344.   [35] BL, Harley Ch. 48 E 10.
[36] BL, Harley Ch. 48 E 49.   [37] BL, Harley Ch. 48 F 5; see above, 54.

the 3rd Lord was strapped for cash:[38] at Cobham he employed the best talent of the day; and in the end, albeit with some effort, he was able to satisfy his creditors.[39] How did he remain solvent?

The answer to this question is very likely that he drew on the income of his granddaughter's extensive estates. By the late 1380s his granddaughter, Joan, was heiress to both the Cobham and the de la Pole inheritances. She was heiress to the Cobham inheritance by descent from her mother, the 3rd Lord's daughter Joan, while she took over the de la Pole estates following the death in quick succession of her father and her 'idiot' brother. By the time of her death in 1434 she was a wealthy lady. She had had possession of the de la Pole estates since 1388. These consisted of the manors of Arlesey, Everton, and Potton (Beds.), Castle Ashby, Ashley, Chadstone, and Cotton (Northants.), Chesterton (Hunts.), Chrishall and Radwinter (Essex), Seething (Norfolk), Aspall, Debenham and Grimston (Suffolk), and Fulbrook and Westhall (Oxon.).[40] In 1391 she married Sir Reginald Braybrooke and settled with her husband in Kent. Her grandfather granted the couple a lease of the manors of Cobham and Cooling.[41] A view of account for the year 1402–3 shows that a substantial payment was made to Lord Cobham from Braybrooke's receiver.[42] The signs are that it was the de la Pole fortune that enabled him to keep up his lavish building schemes.

Estimating the Cobhams' disposable income in the fourteenth century is a hazardous exercise. The only source to give us continuous runs of figures for manors is the inquisitions post mortem, and this information is misleading. The figures are estimates of leasehold value, and not statements of income. In default, we have to make the best use we can of the manorial material in the cartulary at Hatfield and in the Dering collection in the British Library. There is some useful documentation for the manor of Cobham itself in both these sources—an account roll for the year 1290–1 in the British Library and a rental of the manor in the cartulary. In the Dering collection there is also an account roll for the manor of Broad Hinton (Wilts.) for a few years later and, helpfully, from the beginning of the fifteenth century some accounts for the de la Pole manors.

The sources for the manor of Cobham itself show it to have been a valuable property. Admittedly the rent roll was not long: according to the rental in the cartulary, total receipts only came to £10. 15s. 11d.[43] But the demesne was a big

---

[38] Except that he may have intended rebuilding the nave but then had to hold back. See above, 54.

[39] A series of receipts of the 3rd Lord in the Capper Brooke collection indicates that in the end he paid his bills: CKS, U601 E4–17, E21, E22, E29.

[40] These were all manors either acquired by Richard de la Pole or inherited from the Peverels. The one exception is Radwinter, which came to Joan as dower from her first marriage to Sir Robert Hemenhale. [41] Hatfield House, Deed 78/9.

[42] BL, Harley Roll A 36. The sum handed over was £45. 6s. 8d. Could this have been part of the rent for Cooling? The document does not say so. Conceivably it was part of some separate arrangement between Braybrooke and the 3rd Lord.

[43] Hatfield House, MS 306, fos. 44ʳ–54ᵛ.

one—unusually so for a gentry manor. In 1290–1 some 550 acres were under plough. The main crops grown were wheat, which accounted for some 37 per cent of the total yield, and barley, which accounted for 45 per cent; legumes took up only a tiny acreage.[44] Most of the produce was consumed by the household—naturally enough for a manor on which the lord was resident. Income from sales was fairly modest—£28. 10s. 3d. from sales of corn, mainly wheat, and £17. 15s. 6d. from 'issues of the manor'—sales of wood and pasturage. An important sideline was the rearing of sheep for their wool. Some £15 were realized from the sale of 520 fleeces that year.[45]

By the mid-fifteenth century the manor of Cobham had been put out to farm. A view of the account for the period 1449–56 shows it in the hands of a consortium of three lessees.[46] Cobham was now treated as a cash manor: the lord was resident at either Cooling or in the west country. Receipts for the period of the account were agreed at the audit as totalling £107; originally the figure of £138 had been entered, but this was struck out. How much significance we can read into either or both figures is hard to say, but there seems little doubt that the manor was worth less to its lord in the 1450s than it had been a century before.

The only other Cobham manor for which estate material survives is Broad Hinton (Wilts.). Among the documentation in the British Library is a view of account for Hinton for the year 1310–11.[47] The property was again quite a valuable one. Total receipts for the year came to £59. 9s. 11d. An untitled paragraph—it appears to refer to rents and corn sales together—accounted for the greater part of the sum—£50. 8s. 8d. At the year's end a cash surplus of £30 was handed over to the lord (Henry de Cobham).

From around the same time we have a stray account for Shamel hundred—the hundred around Cobham and Shorne, which the Cobhams held.[48] This gives us our sole insight into the Cobhams' income from jurisdiction. In theory, the profits were considerable. The bailiff was held liable for £32. 15s. 0d. However, of this sum £10 was accounted for by arrears. Of the remainder, £19. 6s. 5d. came from rents of assize and only £3. 8s. 7d. from profits of the court. In other words, the proportion accounted for by the exercise of hundredal jurisdiction was very small.

From the beginning of the fifteenth century we have a handful of accounts relating to the former estates of the de la Poles. Among the most informative of these documents are a couple of receiver generals' accounts—one in the name of William Audymer and the other in the name of John Clerk, and both covering the year 1402–3.[49] The manors by now were all leased. Thus what the

---

[44] T. May, 'Estates of the Cobham Family in the Later Thirteenth Century', *AC*, 84 (1970), 211–30.
[45] BL, Harley Roll D 1.   [46] BL, Harley Roll D 4.   [47] BL, Harley Roll G 34.
[48] BL, Harley Roll D 2. The document is dated the ninth regnal year of King Edward. It is not clear whether this is Edward I or Edward II.
[49] BL, Harley Rolls A 36; A 37.

accounts list is the sums due from the farmers. Audymer's account lists the following sums payable: £56. 11s. 9d. from Westhall and Fulbrook (Oxon.), £7. 6s. 8d. from Ashley (Northants.), £4 from Cotton (Northants.), £13. 14s. 8d. from Potton (Beds.), and £15. 5s. 4d. due in rents from Arlesey (Beds.). Clerk's account—it seems that he covered a different area—lists the sums of £26. 6s. 8d. due from 'Brunham', £13. 17s. 5d. from Chrishall, £31. 4s. 8d. from Radwinter (Essex), £5. 3s. 10d. from Seething (Norfolk), and £20 from Aspall (Suffolk). In all, Audymer accounted for receipts (excluding arrears) of £97 and Clerk for receipts of about £100. On the basis of this evidence, it is reasonable to suppose that receipts from the de la Pole estates as a whole came to some £250 per annum or more. The manors of Castle Ashby and Chadstone are not mentioned, and these must have been worth at least £50 between them. How much the Cobham manors were worth in this period is hard to say in the absence of parallel accounts. But bearing in mind that the number of manors was about the same, and that some of them were quite valuable, an estimate of £300–400 may not be too far from the truth.

Genealogies

The Cobhams of Cobham

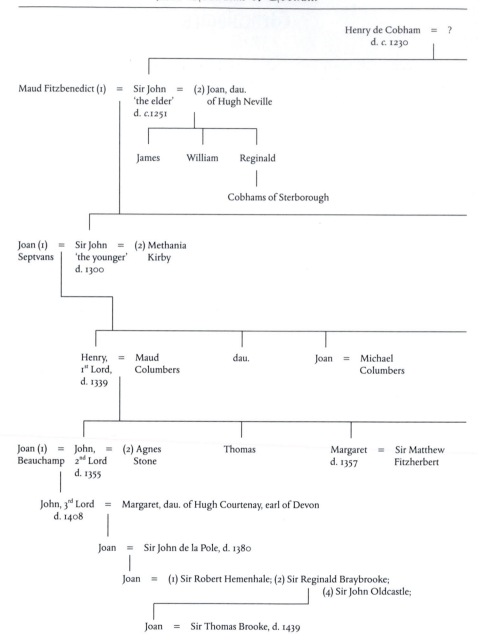

Henry de Cobham = ?
d. c. 1230

Maud Fitzbenedict (1) = Sir John = (2) Joan, dau.
'the elder' of Hugh Neville
d. c.1251

James   William   Reginald

Cobhams of Sterborough

Joan (1) = Sir John = (2) Methania
Septvans 'the younger' Kirby
d. 1300

Henry, = Maud   dau.   Joan = Michael
1st Lord, Columbers   Columbers
d. 1339

Joan (1) = John, = (2) Agnes   Thomas   Margaret = Sir Matthew
Beauchamp 2nd Lord Stone   d. 1357   Fitzherbert
         d. 1355

John, 3rd Lord = Margaret, dau. of Hugh Courtenay, earl of Devon
d. 1408

Joan = Sir John de la Pole, d. 1380

Joan = (1) Sir Robert Hemenhale; (2) Sir Reginald Braybrooke;
       (4) Sir John Oldcastle;

Joan = Sir Thomas Brooke, d. 1439

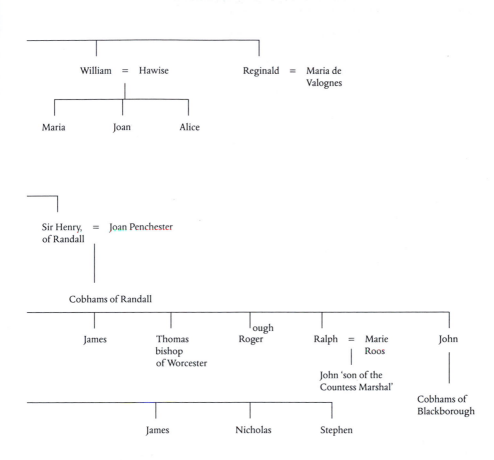

William = Hawise

Reginald = Maria de
Valognes

Maria   Joan   Alice

Sir Henry, = Joan Penchester
of Randall

Cobhams of Randall

James   Thomas   Roger   Ralph = Marie   John
bishop   Roos
of Worcester

John 'son of the
Countess Marshal'

Cobhams of
Blackborough

James   Nicholas   Stephen

(3) Sir Nicholas Hawberk;

(5) Sir John Harpedon

The Cobhams of Sterborough

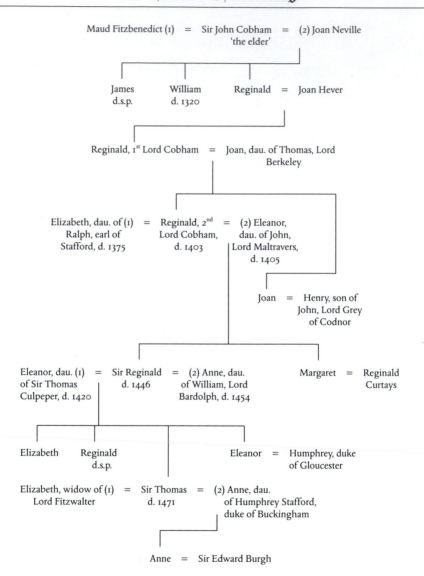

Maud Fitzbenedict (1) = Sir John Cobham = (2) Joan Neville
'the elder'

James   William   Reginald   =   Joan Hever
d.s.p.   d. 1320

Reginald, 1st Lord Cobham = Joan, dau. of Thomas, Lord
Berkeley

Elizabeth, dau. of (1) = Reginald, 2nd = (2) Eleanor,
Ralph, earl of   Lord Cobham,   dau. of John,
Stafford, d. 1375   d. 1403   Lord Maltravers,
d. 1405

Joan = Henry, son of
John, Lord Grey
of Codnor

Eleanor, dau. (1) = Sir Reginald = (2) Anne, dau.   Margaret = Reginald
of Sir Thomas   d. 1446   of William, Lord   Curtays
Culpeper, d. 1420   Bardolph, d. 1454

Elizabeth   Reginald   Eleanor = Humphrey, duke
d.s.p.   of Gloucester

Elizabeth, widow of (1) = Sir Thomas = (2) Anne, dau.
Lord Fitzwalter   d. 1471   of Humphrey Stafford,
duke of Buckingham

Anne = Sir Edward Burgh

The Cobhams of Randall

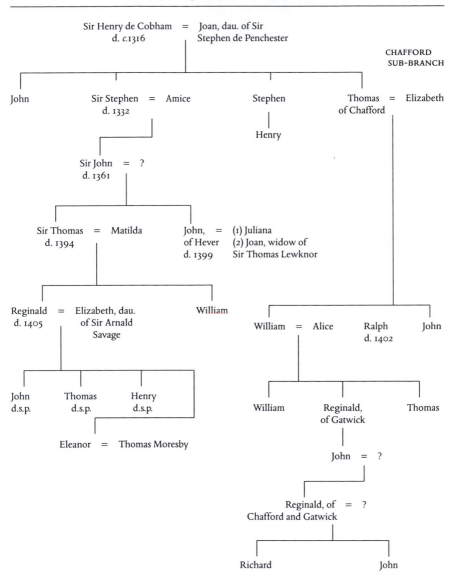

The Cobhams of Beluncle

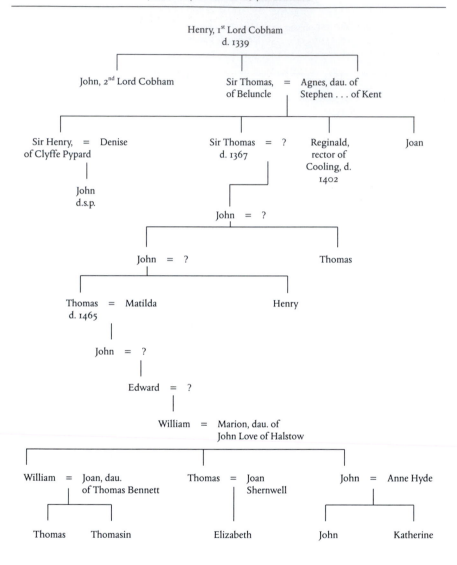

Maps and Diagram

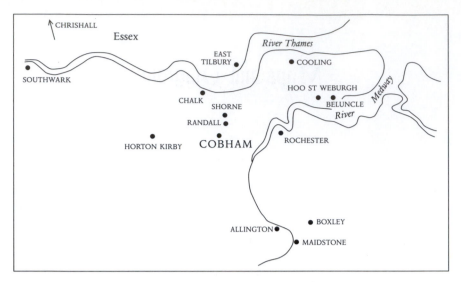

MAP 1. North Kent: The Cobham heartland

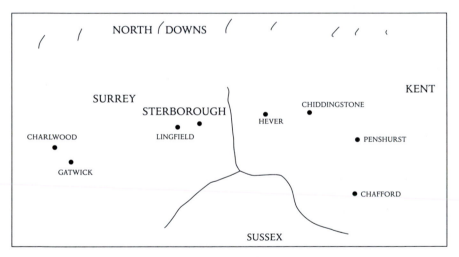

MAP 2. East Surrey and West Kent

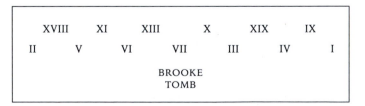

LAYOUT OF THE COBHAM FAMILY BRASSES ON THE CHANCEL FLOOR AT COBHAM

Numbers refer to brasses in Mill Stephenson,
List of Monumental Brasses in the British Isles

Bibliography

A. UNPRINTED SOURCES

London, British Library

Additional Charters
Additional Manuscripts
Arundel MS 68   Confraternity Register of Christ Church, Canterbury
Cotton Charters
Cotton MS Faustina C V   Rochester priory letter book
Cotton MS Nero C VIII   Wardrobe book, 1334–7
Cotton MS Nero D VII   St Albans Book of Benefactors
Harley Charters and Rolls
MS Harley 392   Gaynesford family cartulary
Lansdowne MS 874   Notes and drawings by William Smith

London, Historical Manuscripts Commission

Report 20714   Archives of Rochester Bridge Trust

London, Lambeth Palace Library

Register of Archbishop Arundel
Register of Archbishop Langham
Register of Archbishop Stafford
Register of Archbishop Sudbury

London, Public Record Office

C1   Early chancery proceedings
C61   Gascon rolls
C71   Scottish rolls
C76   Treaty rolls
C81   Chancery warrants
C131   Proceedings for debt
C139   Inquisitions post mortem
E101   Exchequer, Accounts Various
E404   Warrants for issue
PROB 11/2A   Prerogative Court of Canterbury wills

London, Society of Antiquaries

MS 423   Waller's church notes
MS 728/3   Book of pedigrees collected by William Smith

Hatfield House

MS 306   Cobham family cartulary

Maidstone, Centre for Kentish Studies

U601   Capper Brooke Collection

Medway Archives Office, Strood

Drc/T308   An enfeoffment

Minet Library, Camberwell

MS 1/713 O.S.   Notes of David Powell

Surrey History Centre, Woking

2399/7/3   Lingfield Vestry Minute Book
2399/9/1   Lingfield PCC, finance committee minutes
2399/9/4   Lingfield PCC, finance committee minutes

B. PRINTED SOURCES

Abstracts of Feet of Fines Relating to Wiltshire for the Reign of Edward III, ed. C. R. Elrington (Wiltshire Record Society, 29; 1974).
Anglo-Norman Letters and Petitions, ed. M. D. Legge (Anglo-Norman Text Society, 3; 1941).
The Anonimalle Chronicle, 1333–1381, ed. V. H. Galbraith (Manchester, 1927).
Bede's Ecclesiastical History of the English People, ed. B. Colgrave and R. A. B. Mynors (Oxford, 1969).
Book of Bartholomew Bolney, ed. M. Clough (Sussex Record Society, 63; 1964).
Calendar of Charter Rolls.
Calendar of Close Rolls.
Calendar of Fine Rolls.
Calendar of Inquisitions Post Mortem.
Calendar of Memoranda Rolls (Exchequer) Michaelmas 1326–Michaelmas 1327 (London, 1968).
Calendar of Papal Registers, III, 1342–62.
Calendar of Patent Rolls.
Catalogue des Rolles Gascons, Normans et François, ed. T. Carte (2 vols.; London, 1743).
Chronica Adae Murimuth et Roberti de Avesbury, ed. E. M. Thompson (Rolls series; 1889).
Chronica Johannis de Reading et Anonymi Cantuariensis, 1346–1367, ed. J. Tait (Manchester, 1914).
The Chronicle of Adam Usk, 1377–1421, ed. C. Given-Wilson (Oxford, 1997).
Chronicles of the Revolution, 1397–1400, ed. C. Given-Wilson (Manchester, 1993).
Chronicon de Lanercost, ed. J. Stevenson (Maitland Club; Edinburgh, 1839).
Chronicon Galfridi le Baker de Swynebroke, ed. E. M. Thompson (Oxford, 1889).
Collection of the Wills of the Kings of England, ed. J. Nichols (London, 1780).
The Complete Works of John Gower, ed. G. C. Macaulay (4 vols.; Oxford, 1899–1902).
Crecy and Calais, ed. G. Wrottesley (London, 1898).

Curia Regis Rolls, vii, 1213–15 (London, 1935).

Curia Regis Rolls, xi, 1223–24 (London, 1955).

Documents Illustrating the Crisis of 1297–98 in England, ed. M. Prestwich (Camden Society, 4th series, 24; 1980).

Documents of the Baronial Movement of Reform and Rebellion, 1258–67, ed. R. F. Treharne and I. J. Sanders (Oxford, 1973).

English Medieval Rolls of Arms, I, 1244–1334, ed. R. W. Mitchell (Heraldry Society of Scotland; 1983).

The Episcopal Registers of St David's, 1397–1518, ed. R. F. Isaacson (Cymmrodorion Record series, 6; 2 vols.; 1917).

Feet of Fines Relating to Wiltshire for the Reigns of Edward I and Edward II, ed. R. B. Pugh (Wiltshire Record Society, 1; 1939).

Feudal Aids (6 vols.; London, 1899–1920).

Fifty Earliest English Wills, ed. F. J. Furnivall (Early English Text Society, original series 78; 1882).

FROISSART, J., *Chronicles*, ed. T. Johnes (2 vols.; London, 1862).

The Great Roll of the Pipe for the Sixth Year of the Reign of King Henry III, Michaelmas 1222, ed. G. A. Knight (Pipe Roll Society, new series, 51; 1999).

The Itinerary of John Leland, ed. L. Toulmin Smith (5 vols.; London, 1907–10).

Knighton's Chronicle, 1337–1396, ed. G. Martin (Oxford, 1995).

The Life of the Black Prince by the Herald of Sir John Chandos, ed. M. K. Pope and E. C. Lodge (Oxford, 1910).

List of Sheriffs for England and Wales (PRO, Lists and Indexes, 9; 1898).

Literae Cantuarienses, ed. J. B. Sheppard (Rolls series; 3 vols.; 1887–9).

Memoranda Roll for the Tenth Year of the Reign of King John (1207–8), ed. R. A. Brown (Pipe Roll Society, new series, 31; 1957).

Nicholai Uptoni de Studio Militari Libri Quatuor, ed. E. Bysshe (London, 1654).

NICHOLS, J. G., 'Memorials of the Family of Cobham', *Collectanea Topographica et Genealogica*, 7 (1841).

Paston Letters and Papers of the Fifteenth Century, ed. N. Davis (2 vols.; Oxford; 1971–6).

Patent Rolls of the Reign of Henry III (London, 1901–3).

Pedes Finium: or, Fines Relating to the County of Surrey, ed. F. B. Lewis (*SAC*, extra vol., i; 1894).

Records of Gravesend, i, ed. W. H. Hart (Gravesend, 1878).

Records of the Trial of Walter Langeton, Bishop of Coventry and Lichfield, 1307–12, ed. A. Beardwood (Camden Society, 4th series, 6; 1969).

Register of Edward, the Black Prince (4 vols.; London, 1930–43).

The Register of Henry Chichele, Archbishop of Canterbury, 1414–1443, ed. E. F. Jacob (4 vols.; Oxford, 1943–7).

Registrum Hamonis de Hethe Diocesis Roffensis A.D. 1319–1352, ed. C. Johnson (Canterbury and York Society; 2 vols.; 1948).

Registrum Roberti Winchelsey Cantuariensis Archiepiscopi A.D. 1294–1313, ed. R. Graham (2 vols.; Oxford, 1952).

Registrum Roffense, ed. J. Thorpe (London, 1769).

Report of Manuscripts in Various Collections, vii (Historical Manuscripts Commission, 55; London, 1914).

Rotuli Parliamentorum (6 vols.; London, 1767–77).

Rotuli Scotiae, ed. D. Macpherson *et al.* (London, 1814).

RYMER, T., *Foedera, Conventiones, Litterae, etc.*, ed. G. Holmes (20 vols.; London, 1704–35).

Scotland in 1298, ed. H. Gough (London, 1888).

Select Cases in the Court of King's Bench under Edward I, i, ed. G. O. Sayles (Selden Society, 55; 1936).

SMYTH, J., *The Berkeley MSS. I and II, The Lives of the Berkeleys; III, The Hundred of Berkeley*, ed. J. Maclean (Gloucester, 1883–5).

Surrey Taxation Returns, Fifteenths and Tenths: Part II: The 1332 Assessment, ed. H. C. Johnson (Surrey Record Society, 33; 1932).

Testamenta Cantiana: A Series of Extracts from Fifteenth and Sixteenth Century Wills. West Kent, ed. L. L. Duncan (London, 1906).

Testamenta Eboracensia: Selection of the Wills from the Registry at York, iii, ed. J. Raine (Surtees Society, 45; 1864).

Testamenta Vetusta, ed. N. H. Nicolas (2 vols.; London, 1826).

Treaty Rolls, II: 1337–1339, ed. J. Ferguson (London, 1972).

The Tropenell Cartulary, ed. J. S. Davies (Wiltshire Archaeological Society; Devizes, 1908).

WALSINGHAM, T., *Chronicon Anglie, 1328–1388*, ed. E. M. Thompson (Rolls series; 1874).

—— *Ypodigma Neustriae*, ed. H. T. Riley (Rolls series; 1876).

The Wardrobe Book of William de Norwell, 12 July 1338 to 27 May 1340, ed. M. Lyon, B. Lyon, and H. S. Lucas (Brussels, 1983).

The Westminster Chronicle, 1381–1394, ed. L. C. Hector and B. F. Harvey (Oxford, 1982).

Wiltshire Inquisitions Post Mortem from the Reign of King Edward III, ed. E. Stokes (Index Library, 48; 1914).

The Wiltshire Tax List of 1332, ed. D. A. Crowley (Wiltshire Record Society, 45; 1989).

Wykeham's Register, ed. T. F. Kirby (Hampshire Record Society; 2 vols.; 1896–9).

C. SECONDARY SOURCES

ALEXANDER, J. and BINSKI, P. (eds.), *The Age of Chivalry: Art in Plantagenet England, 1200–1400* (London, 1987).

ARMSTRONG, C. A. J., *England, France and Burgundy in the Fifteenth Century* (London, 1983).

ARNOLD, A. A., 'Cobham College', *AC*, 27 (1905).

ASHMOLE, E., *The Institutions, Law and Ceremonies of the Order of the Garter* (London, 1672).

ASTON, M., 'Segregation in Church', in W. J. Sheils and D. Wood (eds.), *Women in the Church* (Studies in Church History, 27; 1990).

AUBREY, J., *Natural History and Antiquities of the County of Surrey* (5 vols.; London, 1718–19, repr. 1975).

—— *Wiltshire: Topographical Collections, 1659–70*, ed. J. E. Jackson (Wiltshire Archaeological and Natural History Society; Devizes, 1862).

AYTON, A., 'Edward III and the English Aristocracy at the Beginning of the Hundred Years War', in M. Strickland (ed.), *Armies, Chivalry and Warfare in Medieval Britain and France* (Stamford, 1998).

—— *Knights and Warhorses: Military Service and the English Aristocracy under Edward III* (Woodbridge, 1994).

BADHAM, S., *Brasses from the North East: A Study of the Brasses Made in Yorkshire, Lincolnshire, Durham and Northumberland in the Pre-Reformation Period* (London, 1979).

—— 'The Suffolk School of Brasses', *TMBS*, 13 pt 1 (1980).

—— 'Status and Salvation', *TMBS*, 15 pt 5 (1996).

—— 'Techniques for Incising Inscriptions', *MBS Bulletin*, 78 (May, 1998).

—— 'Monumental Brasses and the Black Death: A Reappraisal', *Antiquaries Journal*, 80 (forthcoming).

—— and NORRIS, M., *Early Incised Slabs and Brasses from the London Marblers* (London, 1999).

BALDWIN, J. L., *The King's Council in England during the Middle Ages* (Oxford, 1913).

BALL, W. E., 'The Stained Glass Windows of Nettlestead Church', *AC*, 28 (1909).

BARBER, R., *Edward, Prince of Wales and Aquitaine* (London, 1978).

BATTEN, J., 'The Barony of Beauchamp of Somerset', *Proceedings of the Somerset Archaeological and Natural History Society*, 36 (1890).

BELCHER, W. D., *Kentish Brasses* (2 vols.; London, 1888–1905).

BELLEWES, G. O., 'The Cobhams and Moresbys of Rundale and Allington', *AC*, 29 (1911).

BERIOU, N. and D'AVRAY, D. L., *Modern Questions about Medieval Sermons* (Spoleto, 1994).

BERTRAM, J., *Brasses in Germany: Some Reflections upon Recent Discoveries* (privately published, Oxford, 1997).

—— 'Past Writers on Brasses', in J. Bertram (ed.), *Monumental Brasses as Art and History* (Stroud, 1996).

BINSKI, P., 'Chartham, Kent, and the Court', *TMBS*, 13 pt 1 (1980).

—— 'Monumental Brasses', in J. Alexander and P. Binski (eds.), *Age of Chivalry: Art in Plantagenet England* (London, 1987).

—— *Medieval Death: Ritual and Representation* (London, 1996).

—— 'The Stylistic Sequence of London Figure Brasses', in J. Coales (ed.), *The Earliest English Brasses: Patronage, Style and Workshops, 1270–1350* (London, 1987).

—— *Westminster Abbey and the Plantagenets: Kingship and the Representation of Power, 1200–1400* (New Haven and London, 1995).

BLAIR, C., 'The Funeral Helms at Cobham', *Monumental Brass Society Bulletin*, 79 (Sept. 1998).

BLAIR, W. J., 'English Monumental Brasses before 1350. Types, Patterns and Workshops', in J. Coales (ed.), *The Earliest English Brasses: Patronage, Style and Workshops, 1270–1350* (London, 1987).

—— 'Henry Lakenham, Marbler of London, and a Tomb Contract of 1376', *Antiquaries Journal*, 60 (1980).

—— 'John Smith of Brightwell Baldwin', *MBS Bulletin*, 81 (May 1999).

BLATCHLY, J. M., 'Further Notes on the Monumental Brasses of Surrey and the Collection of Rubbings at Castle Arch', *SAC*, 68 (1972).

—— 'The Lost and Mutilated Memorials of the Bovile and Wingfield Families at Letheringham', *Proceedings of the Suffolk Institute of Archaeology*, 33 (1974).

BLOCH, R. H., *Etymologies and Genealogies: A Literary Anthropology of the French Middle Ages* (Chicago, 1983).

BOND, F., *The Chancel of English Churches* (London, 1916).

BOUTELL, C., *Monumental Brasses and Slabs* (London, 1847).

—— *The Monumental Brasses of England: A Series of Engravings on Wood* (London, 1849).

BRITNELL, R., 'The New Bridge', in N. Yates and J. M. Gibson (eds.), *Traffic and Politics: The Construction and Management of Rochester Bridge, AD 43–1993* (Woodbridge, 1994).

BROOKE, C., *The Medieval Idea of Marriage* (Oxford, 1989).

BROWN, R. A., COLVIN, H. M., and TAYLOR, A. J., *The History of the King's Works: The Middle Ages* (2 vols.; London, 1963).

BURGESS, C. R., '"A Fond Thing Vainly Imagined"', in S. Wright (ed.), *Parish, Church and People* (Leicester, 1988).

—— '"For the Increase of Divine Service". Chantries in the Parish in Late Medieval Bristol', *JEH*, 36 (1985).

BURROWS, M., *The Family of Brocas of Beaurepaire* (London, 1886).

CAMILLE, M., *Mirror in Parchment: The Luttrell Psalter and the Making of Medieval England* (London, 1998).

CARPENTER, C., *Locality and Polity: A Study of Warwickshire Landed Society, 1401–1499* (Cambridge, 1992).

—— 'The Religion of the Gentry of Fifteenth-Century England', in D. Williams (ed.), *England in the Fifteenth Century* (Woodbridge, 1987).

CARPENTER, D. A., *The Battles of Lewes and Evesham* (Keele, 1987).

—— *The Reign of Henry III* (London, 1996).

CATTO, J. I., 'Sir William Beauchamp between Chivalry and Lollardy', in C. Harper-Bill and R. Harvey (eds.), *The Ideals and Practice of Medieval Knighthood, III* (Woodbridge, 1990).

CHANCELLOR, F., *The Ancient Sepulchral Monuments of Essex* (London, 1890).

Church Monuments Society Newsletter.

CLAYTON, M. (ed.), *Catalogue of Rubbings of Brasses and Incised Slabs*, 2nd edn. (London, 1968).

COALES, J. (ed.), *The Earliest English Brasses: Patronage, Style and Workshops, 1270–1350* (London, 1987).

The Complete Peerage, ed. G. E. Cokayne *et al.* (12 vols. in 13, London, 1910–57).

COOK, G. H., *Medieval Chantries and Chantry Chapels*, 2nd edn. (London, 1963).

COOPER, H. J., 'Some Surrey Wills in the Prerogative Court of Canterbury, I', *SAC*, 51 (1950).

COSS, P., *The Lady in Medieval England* (Stroud, 1998).

CROSSLEY, F. H., *English Church Monuments A.D. 1150–1500* (London, 1921).

DART, J., *Westmonasterium: or, the History and Antiquities of the Abbey Church of St Peter's Westminster* (2 vols.; London, n.d.).

DAVIDSON-HOUSTON, C. E. D., 'Sussex Monumental Brasses, Part II', *Sussex Archaeological Collections*, 77 (1936).

DAVIES, R., 'Religious Sensibility', in C. Given-Wilson (ed.), *An Illustrated History of Late Medieval England* (Manchester, 1996).

Dictionary of National Biography (63 vols.; London, 1885–1900).

DINN, R., '"Monuments Answerable to Mens Worth". Burial Patterns, Social Status and Gender in Late Medieval Bury St Edmunds', *JEH*, 46 (1995).

DRUITT, H., *A Manual of Costume as Illustrated by Monumental Brasses* (London, 1906, repr. 1970).

DU BOULAY, F. R. H., 'Gavelkind and Knight's Fee in Medieval Kent', *EHR*, 77 (1962).

DUGDALE, W., *The Antiquities of Warwickshire*, 2nd edn. (2 vols.; London, 1730).

The Ecclesiologist, 24 (1863).

EMDEN, A. B., *A Biographical Register of the University of Cambridge to 1500* (Cambridge, 1963).

—— *A Biographical Register of the University of Oxford to A.D. 1500* (3 vols.; Oxford, 1957–9).

EMMERSON, R., 'Monumental Brasses. London Design, c.1420–1485', *Journal of the British Archaeological Association*, 131 (1978).

—— 'William Browne's Taste in Brasses', *TMBS*, 12 pt 4 (1978).

FERNIE, E. C., 'Contrasts in Methodology and Interpretation of Medieval Ecclesiastical Architecture', *Archaeological Journal*, 145 (1988).

FISHER, J. H., *John Gower: Moral Philosopher and Friend of Chaucer* (London, 1965).

FLEMING, P. W., 'Charity, Faith, and the Gentry of Kent, 1422–1529', in T. Pollard (ed.), *Property and Politics: Essays in Later Medieval English History* (Gloucester, 1984).

FLOWER, J. W., 'Notices of the Family of Cobham of Sterborough Castle, Lingfield, Surrey', *SAC*, 2 (1864).

FOSS, E., *The Judges of England* (9 vols.; London, 1848–64).

FOWLER, K., *The King's Lieutenant: Henry of Grosmont, First Duke of Lancaster, 1310–1361* (London, 1969).

FRENCH, G. R., 'A Brief Account of Crowhurst Church, Surrey, and its Monuments', *SAC*, 3 (1865).

FRESHFIELD, E., *Wills, Leases and Memoranda in the Book of Records of the Parish of St Christopher Le Stock* (London, 1895).

FRYDE, E. B., *William de la Pole: Merchant and King's Banker* (London, 1988).

FRYDE, N., *The Tyranny and Fall of Edward II* (Cambridge, 1979).

GARDNER, A., *Alabaster Tombs of the Pre-Reformation Period in England* (Cambridge, 1940).

GIVEN-WILSON, C., *The English Nobility in the Late Middle Ages* (London, 1987).

—— 'Richard II and the English Nobility', in A. Goodman and J. L. Gillespie (eds.), *Richard II: The Art of Kingship* (Oxford, 1999).

GOODMAN, A., *John of Gaunt: The Exercise of Princely Power in Fourteenth-Century Europe* (London, 1992).

GOUGH, R., *The Sepulchral Monuments of Great Britain* (3 vols. in 5; London, 1786–99).

GOVER, J. E. B., MAWER, A., and F. M. STENTON (eds.), *The Place-Names of Surrey* (English Place-Name Society, 11; 1982).

GREEN, C. and WHITTINGHAM, A. B., 'Excavations at Walsingham Priory, Norfolk, 1961', *Archaeological Journal*, 125 (1968).

GREENHILL, F. A., 'On the Ghosts of Some Brasses Formerly in Canterbury Cathedral', *AC*, 65 (1952).

GREENWOOD, R., 'Haines's Cambridge School of Brasses', *TMBS*, 11 pt 1 (1971).

—— 'Wills and Brasses: Some Conclusions from a Norfolk Study', in J. Bertram (ed.), *Monumental Brasses as Art and History* (Stroud, 1996).

GRIFFIN, R., 'The Heraldry in the Cloisters of the Cathedral Church of Christ at Canterbury', *Archaeologia*, 66 (1915–16).

—— and STEPHENSON, M., *A List of Monumental Brasses Remaining in the County of Kent in 1922* (Ashford and London, 1922).

GRIFFITHS, R. A., *The Reign of Henry VI* (London, 1981).

—— 'The Trial of Eleanor Cobham. An Episode in the Fall of Duke Humphrey of Gloucester', *Bulletin of the John Rylands Library*, 51 (1968–9).

HAINES, H., *A Manual of Monumental Brasses* (London, 1861, repr. Bath, 1970).

HARDCASTLE, E. D., 'Chiddingstone', *Aspects of Edenbridge*, 5 (1983), 20–46.

HARVEY, B., *Westminster Abbey and its Estates in the Middle Ages* (Oxford, 1977).

HARVEY, J. H., *English Medieval Architects: A Biographical Dictionary down to 1550*, 2nd edn. (1984).

—— *Henry Yevele, c.1320 to 1400: The Life of an English Architect* (London, 1944).

—— *Medieval Craftsmen* (London, 1975).

—— *The Perpendicular Style, 1330–1485* (London, 1978).

HASTED, E., *The History and Topographical Survey of the County of Kent*, 2nd edn. (12 vols.; Canterbury, 1797–1801).

HENNEMAN, J. B., *Olivier de Clisson and Political Society in France under Charles V and Charles VI* (Philadelphia, 1996).

HEWITT, H. J., *The Black Prince's Expedition of 1355–1357* (Manchester, 1958).

HIGHFIELD, J. R. L., 'The Promotion of William of Wickham to the See of Winchester', *JEH*, 4 (1953).

HOEY, L. R., 'Style, Patronage and Artistic Creativity in Kent Parish Church Architecture: c.1180–c.1260', *AC*, 115 (1995).

HOLINSHED, R., *Chronicles of England, Scotland and Ireland* (6 vols.; 1807–8).

HOLMES, G., *The Estates of the Higher Nobility in Fourteenth-Century England* (Cambridge, 1957).

—— *The Good Parliament* (Oxford, 1975).

HORROX, R., *The de la Poles of Hull* (East Yorkshire Local History Society; Hull, 1983).

HUGHES, J., *Pastors and Visionaries: Religion and Secular Life in Late Medieval Yorkshire* (Woodbridge, 1988).

HULL, F. and KEEN, R. A., 'English Politics and the Sheriff of Kent, 1378', *AC*, 71 (1957).

HUSSEY, C., 'Cobham, Kent-III: A Medieval Parish', *Country Life*, 4 Feb., 1944.

—— 'Cobham, Kent-IV: Cobham College', *Country Life*, 11 Feb., 1944.

HUTCHINS, J., *The History and Antiquities of the County of Dorset* (4 vols.; London, 1861–70).

JESSUP, R. F., *Kent*, 7th edn. (London, 1950).

JONES, M., 'The Fortunes of War: The Military Career of John, second Lord Bourchier (d. 1400)', *Essex Archaeology and History*, 26 (1995).

KENT, J. P. C., 'Monumental Brasses: A New Classification of Military Effigies, c.1360–c.1485', *Journal of the British Archaeological Association*, 3rd ser., 12 (1949).

KITE, E., *The Monumental Brasses of Wiltshire* (London, 1860, repr. Bath, 1969).

KNOOP, D., JONES, G. P., and LEWIS, N. B., 'Some Building Activities of John, Lord Cobham', *Transactions Quattuor Coronati Lodge*, 45 (1935).

KNOWLES, D., *The Religious Orders in England*, i (Cambridge, 1962).

LACK, W., SAUL, N. E., and WHITTEMORE, P. J., *The Monumental Brasses in St Mary Magdalene, Cobham, Kent* (London, 1998).

—— STUCHFIELD, H. M., and WHITTEMORE, P., *The Monumental Brasses of Cambridgeshire* (London, 1995).

—— *The Monumental Brasses of Derbyshire* (London, 1999).

L'ANSON, E., 'Mural Paintings Formerly Existing in Lingfield Church', *SAC*, 1 (1858).

LARKING, L. B., 'Cowling Castle', *AC*, 2 (1859).

LEROY, B., *Le royaume de Navarre à la fin du Moyen Age. Gouvernement et société* (Aldershot, 1990).

LE STRANGE, H., *Le Strange Records: A Chronicle of the Early Le Stranges* (London, 1916).

LEVESON GOWER, G., 'Inventories of the College of Lingfield', *SAC*, 7 (1880).

LEWIS, N. B., 'The "Continual Council" in the Early Years of Richard II', *EHR*, 41 (1926).

LINDLEY, P., *Gothic to Renaissance: Essays on Sculpture in England* (Stamford, 1995).

LLEWELLYN, N., 'Honour in Life, Death and the Memory. Funeral Monuments in Early Modern England', *Transactions of the Royal Historical Society*, 6th ser., 6 (1996).

—— *The Art of Death: Visual Culture in the English Death Ritual c.1500–c.1800* (London, 1991).

LONDON, H. S., 'John Philipot, M. P., Somerset Herald, 1624–1645', *AC*, 60 (1947).

LUNT, W. E., *Financial Relations of the Papacy with England, 1327–1534* (Cambridge, Mass., 1962).

LUTTRELL, A., 'English Levantine Crusaders, 1363–1367', *Renaissance Studies*, 2 (1988).

MacCULLOCH, D., *Thomas Cranmer: A Life* (New Haven and London, 1996).

McFARLANE, K. B., *John Wycliffe and the Beginnings of English Nonconformity* (London, 1952).

—— 'The Investment of Sir John Fastolf's Profits of War', *Transactions of the Royal Historical Society*, 5th series, 7 (1957).

—— *Lancastrian Kings and Lollard Knights* (Oxford, 1972).

—— *The Nobility of Later Medieval England* (Oxford, 1973).

—— *Letters to Friends, 1940–1966*, ed. G. L. Harriss (Oxford, 1997).

MACKLIN, H. W., *Monumental Brasses*, 1st edn. (London, 1890).

—— *The Brasses of England* (London, 1907).

MacMICHAEL, N. H., 'Kentish Items: Cobham and Goudhurst', *TMBS*, 9 pt 9 (1962).

MADDICOTT, J. R., *Law and Lordship: Royal Justices as Retainers in Thirteenth- and Fourteenth-Century England* (*Past and Present Supplement*, 4; 1978).

—— *Simon de Montfort* (Cambridge, 1994).

—— *Thomas of Lancaster, 1307–1322* (Oxford, 1970).

MANNING, C. R., *A List of the Monumental Brasses Remaining in England* (London, 1846).

—— 'Notes on a Brass of Robert de Haitfeld and Ada, his Wife, Owston Church, Yorkshire', *Archaeological Journal*, 36 (1879).

—— 'Notice of an Undescribed Sepulchral Brass', *Archaeological Journal*, 4 (1847).

MANNING, O. and BRAY, W., *The History and Antiquities of the County of Surrey* (3 vols.; London, 1804–14).

MARKS, R., *Stained Glass in England during the Middle Ages* (London, 1993).

MARSHALL, G., 'The Church of Edvin Ralph and Some Notes on Pardon Monuments', *Transactions of the Woolhope Naturalists' Field Club* (1924–6).

MARTINDALE, A., 'Patrons and Minders: The Intrusion of the Secular into Sacred Spaces in the Late Middle Ages', in D. Wood (ed.), *The Church and the Arts* (Studies in Church History, 28; 1992).

MAXWELL LYTE, H. C., 'An Account Relating to Sir John Cobham', *Antiquaries Journal*, 2 (1922).

MAY, T., 'The Cobham Family in the Administration of England, 1200–1400', *AC*, 82 (1968).

—— 'Estates of the Cobham Family in the Later Thirteenth Century', *AC*, 84 (1970).

MOBERLY, G. H., *Life of William of Wykeham* (Winchester, 1887).

MOOR, C., *Knights of Edward I* (Harleian Society, 80–4; 1929–32).

MORGAN, P., 'Making the English Gentry', in P. R. Coss and S. D. Lloyd (eds.), *Thirteenth Century England, V* (Woodbridge, 1995).

MORRIS, R., *Churches in the Landscape* (London, 1989).

MORRIS, R. K., 'Pembridge and Mature Decorated in Herefordshire', *Transactions of the Woolhope Naturalists' Field Club*, 42 (1977).

NAIRN, I. and PEVSNER, N., *Surrey*, 2nd edn. (Harmondsworth, 1971).

NEWMAN, J., *West Kent and the Weald* (Harmondsworth, 1969).

NICHOLS, J., *The History and Antiquities of Leicestershire* (4 vols.; London, 1795–1811).

NICHOLS, J. G., 'Register of the Sepulchral Inscriptions in the Church of the Grey Friars', *Collectanea Topographica et Genealogica*, 5 (1838).

NICHOLS, W. N., *Cooling, Kent, and its Castle* (Redhill, n.d.).

NICHOLSON, R., *Edward III and the Scots* (Oxford, 1965).

NICOLAS, N. H., *History of the Battle of Agincourt* (London, 1833, repr. 1971).

—— 'Observations on the Institution of the Most Noble Order of the Garter', *Archaeologia*, 31 (1846).

NORMAN, A. V. B., 'Two Early Fourteenth Century Military Effigies', *Church Monuments*, 1 pt 1 (1985).

NORRIS, M. W., *Monumental Brasses: The Memorials* (2 vols.; London, 1977).

—— *Monumental Brasses: The Craft* (London, 1978).

—— 'Views on the Early Knights, 1786–1970', in J. Coales (ed.), *The Earliest English Brasses: Patronage, Style and Workshops, 1270–1350* (London, 1987).

NORRIS, M. (ed.), *Monumental Brasses: The Portfolio Plates of the Monumental Brass Society* (Woodbridge, 1988).

O'GRADY, HON. MRS, 'Bishop Cobham, 1317–1327: His Monument and Work in Worcester Cathedral', *Reports and Papers of the Associated Architectural Societies*, 26 (1902).

ORME, N. I., *English Schools in the Middle Ages* (London, 1973).

OWEN EVANS, H. F., 'Tormarton, Glos.', *TMBS*, 11 pt 4 (1972).

PAGE-PHILLIPS, J., *Children on Brasses* (London, 1970).

—— *Palimpsests: The Backs of Monumental Brasses* (London, 1980).

PALMER, J. J. N., *England, France and Christendom, 1377–99* (London, 1972).

PANOFSKY, E., *Tomb Sculpture: Its Changing Aspects from Ancient Egypt to Bernini* (London and New York, 1964).

PANTIN, W. A., *The English Church in the Fourteenth Century* (Cambridge, 1957).

PAXTON, F., *Christianizing Death: The Creation of a Ritual Process in Early Medieval Europe* (Ithaca, N.Y., 1990).

PEARCE, E. H., *Thomas de Cobham, Bishop of Worcester, 1317–1327* (London, 1923).

PEATLING, A. V., *Ancient Stained and Painted Glass in the Churches of Surrey*, ed. F. C. Eeles (Surrey Archaeological Society; 1930).

PERCEVAL, C. S., 'Notes to the Pedigree of Cobham of Sterborough', *SAC*, 2 (1862).

PERROY, E., *The Hundred Years War* (London, 1965).

PEVSNER, N., *Cambridgeshire*, 2nd edn. (Harmondsworth, 1970).

—— *Derbyshire*, 2nd edn. (Harmondsworth, 1978).

—— *Herefordshire* (Harmondsworth, 1963).

PHILLIPS, J. R. S., *Aymer de Valence, Earl of Pembroke, 1307–1324* (Oxford, 1972).

POLLOCK, F. and MAITLAND, F. W., *History of English Law before the time of Edward I* (2 vols.; Cambridge, 1898).

POWELL, J. E. and WALLIS, K., *The House of Lords in the Middle Ages* (London, 1968).

PRESTWICH, M., *Edward I* (London, 1988).

PRIOR, E. S. and GARDNER, A., *An Account of Medieval Figure Sculpture in England* (Cambridge, 1912).

PROBERT, G., 'The Riddles of Bures Unravelled', *Essex Archaeology and History*, 16 (1984–5).

RAMSAY, J. H., *The Genesis of Lancaster, 1307–1399* (2 vols.; Oxford, 1913).

RAMSAY, N. L., 'Introduction', in R. Glover and T. Milles, *The Kings of England Ever Since It Was So Called*, ed. D. Parker (London, 1995).

REANCY, P., *The Place-Names of Essex* (English Place-Name Society, 12; 1935).

RICHMOND, C., 'The Nobility and the Wars of the Roses. The Parliamentary Session of January 1461', *Parliamentary History*, 18 (1999).

ROBERTS, A. K. B., *St George's Chapel, Windsor Castle, 1348–1416. A Study in Early Collegiate Administration* (Windsor, 1947).

RODWELL, W., 'The Buildings of Vicars' Close', in L. S. Colchester (ed.), *Wells Cathedral: A History* (Shepton Mallet, 1982).

ROGERS, N., 'Brasses in their Art-Historical Context', in J. Bertram (ed.), *Monumental Brasses as Art and History* (Stroud, 1996).

—— 'English Episcopal Monuments, 1270–1350', in J. Coales (ed.), *The Earliest English Brasses: Patronage, Style and Workshops, 1270–1350* (London, 1987).

ROSKELL, J. S., CLARK, L., and RAWCLIFFE, C., *The History of Parliament: The House of Commons* (4 vols.; Stroud, 1992).

Royal Commission on Historical Monuments (England). Essex, i (London, 1916).

RYE, W. B., 'Tombs of Sir William Arundel and Others in Rochester Cathedral', *AC*, 13 (1880).

SADLER, A. G., *The Indents of Lost Monumental Brasses in Kent: Part I* (privately published, 1975).

—— *The Indents of Lost Monumental Brasses in Kent: Part II* (privately published, 1976).

SALZMAN, L. F., *Building in England down to 1540* (Oxford, 1952, repr. 1992).

SANDFORD, F., *Genealogical History of the Kings and Queens of England* (London, 1677).

SANDLER, L. F., *Gothic Manuscripts, 1285–1385* (2 vols.; London, 1986).

SAUL, N. E., 'Identifying the 14th Century Knight at Cliffe Pypard, Wilts.', *TMBS*, 12 pt 4 (1978).

—— 'The Religious Sympathies of the Gentry in Gloucestershire, 1200–1500', *Transactions of the Bristol and Gloucestershire Archaeological Society*, 98 (1980).

—— *Knights and Esquires: The Gloucestershire Gentry in the Fourteenth Century* (Oxford, 1981).

—— 'The Despensers and the Downfall of Edward II', *EHR*, 99 (1984).

—— *Scenes From Provincial Life: Knightly Families in Sussex, 1280–1400* (Oxford, 1986).

—— 'The Fragments of the Golafre Brass in Westminster Abbey', *TMBS*, 15 pt 1 (1992).

—— *Richard II* (New Haven and London, 1997).

—— 'Shottesbrooke Church: A Study in Knightly Patronage', *Medieval Art and Architecture in the Windsor and Reading Region* (British Archaeological Association; Leeds, forthcoming).

SHAW, W. A., *The Knights of England* (2 vols.; London, 1906).

SHERBORNE, J., *War, Politics and Culture in Fourteenth-Century England*, ed. A. Tuck (London, 1994).

SOUTHWICK, L., 'The Armoured Effigy of Prince John of Eltham in Westminster Abbey and Some Closely Related Military Monuments', *Church Monuments*, 2 (1987).

SQUIBB, G. D., *The High Court of Chivalry* (Oxford, 1959).

STATHAM, S. P. H., *History of the Castle, Town and Port of Dover* (London, 1899).

STEPHENSON, M., *A List of Monumental Brasses in the British Isles* (London, 1926, repr. 1964).

—— *A List of Monumental Brasses in Surrey* (Bath, 1970).

STONE, L., *The Family, Sex and Marriage in England, 1500–1800* (London, 1977).

—— *Sculpture in Britain: The Middle Ages*, 2nd edn. (Harmondsworth, 1972).

STOREY, R. L., *The End of the House of Lancaster* (London, 1966).

SUFFLING, E. R., *English Church Brasses from the 13th to the 17th Century* (London, 1910, repr. 1970).

SUMPTION, J., *The Hundred Years War: Trial by Battle* (London, 1990).

TESTER, P., 'Notes on the Medieval Chantry College at Cobham', *AC*, 79 (1964).

THOMPSON, M. W., 'The Construction of the Manor at South Wingfield, Derbyshire', in G. de G. Sieveking *et al.* (eds.), *Problems in Economic and Social Archaeology* (London, 1976).

—— *The Decline of the Castle* (Cambridge, 1987).

THOMSON, J. A. F., 'Knightly Piety and the Margins of Lollardy', in M. Aston and C. Richmond (eds.), *Lollardy and the Gentry in the Later Middle Ages* (Stroud, 1997).

THRUPP, S. L., *The Merchant Class of Medieval London (1300–1500)* (Chicago, 1948).

TORR, V., 'The Sedilia and Altar Drains', *AC*, 43 (1931).

TOUT, T. F., *Chapters in the Administrative History of Medieval England* (6 vols.; Manchester, 1920–33).

—— 'The Tactics of the Battles of Boroughbridge and Morlaix', *Collected Papers of Thomas Frederick Tout* (3 vols.; Manchester, 1932–4).

TOWER, R., 'The Family of Septvans', *AC*, 40 (1928).

TUCK, A., *Richard II and the English Nobility* (London, 1973).

TUMMERS, H. A., *Early Secular Effigies in England: The Thirteenth Century* (Leiden, 1980).

TYERMAN, C., *England and the Crusades, 1095–1588* (Chicago, 1988).

TYSON, D. B., 'The Epitaph of Edward, the Black Prince', *Medium Aevum*, 46 (1977).

VALE, J., *Edward III and Chivalry: Chivalric Society and its Context, 1270–1350* (Woodbridge, 1982).

VALE, M. G. A., *Piety, Charity and Literacy among the Yorkshire Gentry, 1370–1480* (Borthwick Papers, 50; York, 1976).

——and VALE, J., 'Knightly Codes and Piety', in N. E. Saul (ed.), *Age of Chivalry: Art and Society in Late Medieval England* (London, 1992).

VALLANCE, A., 'Cobham Collegiate Church', *AC*, 43 (1931).

Victoria County History of Bedfordshire, ii (London, 1906).

Victoria County History of Buckinghamshire, iv (London, 1927).

Victoria County History of Hampshire (5 vols.; London, 1900–12).

Victoria County History of Kent (3 vols.; London, 1908–32).

Victoria County History of Northamptonshire, iv (London, 1937).

Victoria County History of Oxfordshire, viii (London, 1964).

Victoria County History of Surrey (4 vols.; London, 1902–12).

Victoria County History of Wiltshire (15 vols. and continuing; London, 1957–).

WALLER, J. G., 'The Lords of Cobham, their Monuments and the Church', *AC*, 11 (1877).

——'Notes on the Monuments of the Cobham Family at Lingfield', *SAC*, 5 (1871).

——and WALLER, L. A. B., *A Series of Monumental Brasses from the 13th to the 16th Century* (London, 1864, repr. 1975).

WARD, J. C., *English Noblewomen in the Later Middle Ages* (London, 1992).

WEDGWOOD, J. C., *History of Parliament, 1439–1509: Biographies* (London, 1936).

WAUGH, W. T., 'Sir John Oldcastle', *EHR*, 20 (1905).

WEEVER, J., *Ancient Funerall Monuments* (London, 1631).

WHEELER, R. E. M., 'A Pax at Abergavenny', *Antiquaries Journal*, 10 (1930).

WHETTER, J., *Cornish People in the Fifteenth Century* (Gorran, 1999).

WILSON, C., 'The Medieval Monuments', in P. Collinson, N. Ramsay, and M. Sparks (eds.), *A History of Canterbury Cathedral* (Oxford 1995).

WINSTON, C., 'An Account of the Painted Glass in the East Window of Gloucester Cathedral', *Archaeological Journal*, 20 (1863).

WOOD-LEGH, K. L., *Perpetual Chantries in Britain* (Cambridge, 1965).

WRIGHT, J. S. N., *The Brasses of Westminster Abbey* (London, 1969).

YATES, N. and GIBSON, J. M. (eds.), *Traffic and Politics. The Construction and Management of Rochester Bridge, AD 43–1993* (Woodbridge, 1994).

YOUNG, C. R., *The Making of the Neville Family 1166–1400* (Woodbridge, 1996).

C. Theses

BUTLER, L. H., 'Robert Braybrooke, Bishop of London (1381–1404), and his Kinsmen' (University of Oxford D.Phil. thesis, 1952).

FAULKNER, K. H., 'Knights and Knighthood in Early Thirteenth-Century England' (University of London Ph.D. thesis, 1998).

OOSTERWIJK, S., '"Litel Enfaunt that Were but Late Borne": The Image of the *Infans* in Medieval Culture in North-Western Europe' (University of Leicester Ph.D. thesis, 1999).

PRATT, S., 'The Collegiate Church of St Peter, Lingfield, Surrey' (University College, London, MA thesis, 1993).

QUICK, J. A., 'Government and Society in Kent, 1232–1280' (University of Oxford D.Phil. thesis, 1986).

SHENTON, C., 'The English Court and the Restoration of Royal Prestige, 1327–1345' (University of Oxford D.Phil. thesis, 1995).

List of Sources for Illustrations

The publishers wish to thank the following who have kindly given permission to reproduce the illustrations indicated. Figs. 1–2 the author; 3 Kent Archaeological Society; 5–22 William Lack; 23 British Library Board; 24 Executors of the estate of Ken Gravett; 25 the author; 26 National Monuments Record; 27–35 the author; 36 Monumental Brass Society; 37–40 the author; 41 Monumental Brass Society; 42 the author.

Index